BY THE LIGHT OF THE GLOW-WORM LAMP

Three Centuries of Reflections on Nature

BY THE LIGHT OF THE GLOW-WORM LAMP

Three Centuries of Reflections on Nature

Edited by

Alberto Manguel

Plenum Trade • New York and London

Library of Congress Cataloging-in-Publication Data

Manguel, Alberto.
    By the light of the glow-worm lamp : three centuries of
reflections on nature / edited by Alberto Manguel.
        p.   cm.
    Includes bibliographical references and index.
    ISBN 0-306-45991-4 (hardbound). -- ISBN 0-306-45992-2 (pbk. : alk.
paper)
    1. Natural history. 2. Nature.   I. Title.
QH81.M254   1998
508--dc21
                                                            98-26198
                                                                CIP

The author gratefully acknowledges the use of the following materials:

Annie Dillard, "Nightwatch" from *Pilgrim at Tinker Creek*, Copyright © 1974 by Annie Dillard. Reprinted by permission of HarperCollins, Inc.

Diane Ackerman, "King Penguins" from *The Moon by Whale Light*, Copyright © 1991 by Diane Ackerman. Reprinted by permission of Random House, Inc.

Rachel Carson, "The Marginal World" from *The Edge of the Sea*, Copyright © 1955 by Rachel Carson. Reprinted by permission of Granada Publishing.

Vladimir Nabokov, "Butterflies" from *Speak, Memory*, Copyright © 1975 by Vladimir Nabokov. Reprinted by permission of Weidenfeld & Nicolson.

Barry Lopez, "The Narwahl" from *Arctic Dreams: Desire and Imagination in a Northern Landscape*, Copyright © 1986 by Barry Lopez. Reprinted by permission of Charles Scribners's Sons.

ISBN 0-306-45991-4 (Hardbound)
ISBN 0-306-45992-2 (Paperback)

© 1998 Alberto Manguel
Plenum Press is a Division of Plenum Publishing Corporation
233 Spring Street, New York, N.Y. 10013

http://www.plenum.com

10 9 8 7 6 5 4 3 2 1

Printed in the United States of America

To Douglas LePan

There is the song of white-throats through the land;
I sing within. The overarching bright
Blue sky, horizoned as the robin's egg,
Describes my hope. To make you understand,
Those tones of borrowed eloquence I beg,
Wood full of birds, bending of morning light.

—From "Sonnet" in *The Wounded Prince,* by Douglas LePan

CONTENTS

INTRODUCTION

". . . and listening to the soothing sounds outside my tent,
I set out to write my days' observations
by the light of the glow-worm lamp."

—FLORENTINO AMEGHINO IN EL CHACO, 1902

Sometime in the third century B.C., when the cities were small and familiar and the countryside vast and mysterious, the Syracusean poet Theocritus decided that the tale of lovers' sorrows would best be served by placing it in an idealized country setting of poetic perfection. Even though a few inquisitive souls, notably Aristotle, had observed nature on its own terms and reported more or less accurately their observations, the literary reality proposed by Theocritus in his *Idylls* found more favor among readers than the *reportage* of other earnest-minded Greek writers such as Hesiod, who in the eighth century B.C. had outlined the farmer's tasks in *The Works and the Days.*

Certain poets chose to keep a foot in either field. Three centuries later, Virgil made his the landscape of Theocritus's *Idylls*, but since Virgil was someone who knew first-hand the quality of real country life, he also followed Hesiod's model. If his *Eclogues* described golden imaginary sites, then his *Georgics* dealt instead with practical farming advice on crops, weather, forestry, cattle, and bee-keeping. Sometimes Virgil showed a preference for the more earthbound vision: his second *Georgic* seems to favor the beauties not of the ideal but of the tangible Roman countryside, more precious to him than the marvelous lands seen or imagined by travellers—a case of the grass being greener on *this* side of the fence:

But neither the forests of wealthy Media nor the lovely Ganges,
Nor gold-rich Hermus
Compares with our land (. . .)

1

It is a land full of heavy corn
And Campanian wine, olive-trees and fertile herds.
Here the stallion gallops proudly over the plains,
Here the sheep and the bulls
—the sacrificial victims bathed in the holy waters of Clitumnus—
Lead our Roman victories to the temples of the gods.
Here spring and summer are eternal.

From Virgil onward throughout the Middle Ages and well into the Renaissance, Nature retained in the literary eye both its golden and its earthy qualities. The uncultivated stretches of land that lay outside the cities were dangerous places haunted by robbers, murderers, wild beasts, and witches—all creatures against which society defined itself—and the social imagination liked to conjure up another wilderness in which not the worst but the best elements of life were found. Those who ventured even further into the world were seen as courageous daredevils, emissaries of civilization who (if they returned alive) brought back to the cities accounts of the places they had visited and the wonders they had seen. This *Wanderlust*, however, was not considered the proper pursuit of the scholar, rather the result of the mad restlessness of youth.

Writing to the Doge of Venice from the Vaucluse, in 1352, the Italian poet Petrarch confessed that, in his early years, it had been his purpose not only "to follow Homer's advice to inspect the manners of men and their high cities," but also "to gaze upon new lands, mountain peaks, famous seas, lauded lakes, secluded founts, mighty rivers, and all the world's varied sites. I thought that thus I might become learned, more expeditiously and briefly, and not only at expense of trouble but with great pleasure." He travelled much and then, from his study, chronicled what he observed, as in his famous description of his ascent of Mount Ventoux. For Petrarch, as for most of his contemporaries, the real world was a book in which God had written cautionary lessons for the soul, and what youth had seen, old age was meant to reflect upon.

Against such landscapes, the lost eden of Theocritus's fiction became a literary commonplace and those who wished to revile the ills of urban civilization, could do so by singing the praises of cozy country life.

Fair quiet, have I found thee here,
And Innocence my Sister dear!

Mistaken long, I sought you then
In busie Companies of Men.
You sacred Plants, if here below,
Only among the Plants you grow.
Society is all but rude,
To this delicious Solitude.

So wrote Andrew Marvell around 1650. More than a hundred years later, Jean-Jacques Rousseau, in his *Confessions*, began to look at Nature under the guiding light of Goddess Reason. "Madmen, you who constantly complain about Nature, learn that all your sufferings come from yourselves alone." Nature could teach her own lessons to those who were willing to pay attention, and Rousseau began to collect and catalogue Marvell's plants and flowers not as poetical allegories or cautions against human corruption, but as fascinating creations in themselves.

Rousseau was not alone: a passion for collecting specimens started to spread through Europe. And eventually the collector, the assembler of a hodge-podge of specimens and rarities, *bric-à-brac* and *objets trouvés*, became an explorer, turning his cabinet of curiosities into a scholarly museum, teaching himself to see.

In England, at about the same time, writers began to break with the ranks of neoclassicism, leaving their studies to write about nature as first-hand observers. James Thompson in *The Seasons* and John Gray in his country poems led the way for Robbie Burns, Samuel Taylor Coleridge, and especially William Wordsworth who had this to say:

For nature then . . .
To me was all in all.

To those who would not go out into the countryside and see the world, the wandering poet admonished:

The world is too much with us; late and soon,
Getting and spending, we lay waste our powers:
Little we see in Nature that is ours.

For Wordsworth, as for the other Romantic poets, it was not a question of choice: the study of nature as its own subject did not detract from the study of humankind, *au contraire*. Lord Byron agreed.

There is a pleasure in the pathless woods,
There is a rapture on the lonely shore,
There is society, where none intrudes,
By the deep Sea, and music in its roar:
I love not Man the less, but Nature more.

Gradually, the tone shifted from lyrical to clinical. With the Industrial Revolution, scientific writing acquired a firmer grip on the popular imagination. Travellers who had brought news of the wonders of the world in earlier centuries, now were required to report on those wonders in a scientifically elegant manner, describing as precisely as possible the spectacle unfolding outside the human realm, in order to discover its secret mechanics and mysterious laws. And even those who stayed at home were expected to look into their gardens, ponds, and orchards, reporting on what they saw. But what they saw was often disquieting.

Throughout Europe, North and South America, scientific journals flourished to offer a podium for many observers of the natural world. The periodical *Nature*, founded in London in 1869, set out to provide lay readers with information on scientific matters, news of recent discoveries, chronicles of travel, and essays of related subjects. Among its early contributors was Charles Darwin who, as a young man, more than thirty years earlier, had established the scientific ground rules for his time. Margaret Atwood, in *Survival*, notes that toward the middle of the nineteenth century "Nature's personality underwent a change; she remained a female deity, but became redder in tooth and claw as Darwinism infiltrated literature."

It is extraordinarily moving to follow the observant twenty-two year old Darwin on his voyage around the world on *H.M.S. Beagle*. He records, wide-eyed and marvelously serious, the world that has been slowly going on its business since it inconceivably began and which, almost by miracle, no other man had seen before in the same unencumbered way. What surprises today's reader of Darwin's accounts is not necessarily the brilliance or clarity of his observations, though these qualities are indeed much in evidence, but the simple fact that no one else had seen fit to record them. In a sense, he is like the first man who pointed a finger to the heavens and made a note of the existence of the sun.

The nineteenth century was, without doubt, the golden age of nature writing, inventing itself in the process of its writing. The range and scope of its themes and styles is overwhelming, and seems to follow in the wake of the advance of the imperialist European powers. Throughout the continent, notably in France, Germany, and the Scandinavian countries, nature writing came into its own, taking as its subject not only the home landscapes but those of South America, Asia, and Africa. It was however in England, under Darwin's challenging and challenged guidance, that nature and travel writing excelled.

And yet, even in England, the genre was far from homogeneous. At the same time as Darwin was soberly going about his natural business, other Englishmen were going about theirs in more eccentric ways. The pious zoologist Philip Henry Gosse, concerned with reconciling the biblical story of Creation with the ever-increasing discovery of fossils and the theories of the impious Darwin, proposed a first instant in time that contained a vast, perhaps infinite, past. God—said Gosse—created the world with its fossil remains, but the creatures to whom these remains belonged were not required to exist. The fossils were real and the biblical story was true; only the actual unfolding of time before Creation had not taken place. Ridiculing Gosse's theory, the novelist Charles Kingsley objected to the idea of a prankster god who would have planted a vast and superfluous lie in the rocks.

Another marvelous eccentric was the great explorer of South America, Charles Waterton, for whom no creature in the whole of creation was anything less than admirable. Waterton indulged his curiosity and that of his friends to rather unorthodox extremes. "He had no idea that he was doing anything out of the general course of things," noted his biographer, Father J. Wood, "if he asked a visitor to accompany him to the top of a lofty tree to look at a hawk's nest, or if he built his stables so that the horses might converse with each other, or his kennel so that his hounds should be able to see what was going on." To instruct a friend on the nature of dogs, he hid under the table on his terrace; when his friend sat down, the old gentleman, who was close to eighty at the time, growled savagely and bit his friend's leg "in such a practically canine manner that I really had no idea at the time but that some fierce dog was attacking my lower extremities." Another time, suffering from a sprained ankle during a North American expedition and being told by his doctor that he might alleviate the discomfort by holding his ankle under a pump, Waterton decided to seek the largest pump available and eventually held his foot under Niagara Falls. "As I held my leg under the Falls," he wrote, "I tried to meditate on the immense difference there was betwixt a house pump and this tremendous cascade of nature, and what effect it might have upon the sprain;

but the magnitude of the subject was too overwhelming, and I was obliged to drop it."

Not all Waterton's experiments in observation were successful. In order to confirm the popular notion that the vampire bat lived on blood, during his wanderings in the Brazilian jungle he decided to sleep with his big toe outside his hammock with the purpose of tempting the creature. Unfortunately, the bat spurned him and attacked instead the toe of a native servant which, Waterton remarked ruefully, "seemed to have all the attractions."

Throughout the nineteenth century and up to World War I, seemingly everyone in England—scientists, layfolk, men, and women whose main occupation was not that of science or letters, devotees and dilettantes alike—indulged in nature writing as something between a social obligation and a spiritual exercise. "The only lasting peacefulness is Nature," wrote the water-colourist Beatrix Potter. Clergymen such as Charles A. Hall, philosophers such as Grant Allen, poets such as John Clare, gold-mining experts such as Thomas Belt, novelists such as W. H. Hudson, military men such as D. D. Cunningham, all agreed and wrote wonderful passages of observation and reflection.

During and between the World Wars, such becalmed views were obviously shattered. Emblematic of this bleakness and despair was a story by 'Saki,' pen-name of the English writer H. H. Munro, who described an ornithologist going about his business in the aftermath of a battle. In "Birds on the Western Front" no mention is made of the slaughter, nothing except the faithful recording of natural observations, and yet in the sober facts lie all the despair and the sorrow.

Finally, in the 1950s and 1960s, a different form of nature writing emerged, what the writer Diane Ackerman calls "a crossroads where physical and literary adventure converged." Addressed to a readership more or less aware of its ecological responsibility and more or less familiar, at least through the electronic media, with the furthest corners of the planet, nature writing in the second half of the twentieth century has something of the philosophical concerns of its earliest precursors and not much of the imperialistic heroics of its immediate predecessors. Many of its representatives come from America. Pioneers such as Rachel Carson and eloquent observers such as Annie Dillard or Barry Lopez have revived the genre, paying attention to native wisdom and allowing a new tone and a new meaning to pervade their stories.

In February of 1998, in response to a protest group opposing the building of yet another major highway through the British countryside, the Archbishop of Canterbury, Dr. George Carey, accused the protesters of "worshipping the natural world above God." "Creation," said the Archbishop, is "for God and for humanity only under God. We are the pinnacle of God's creation." From the height of his pulpit, the Archbishop was expressing the viewpoint of most logging firms, developers, oil companies, mining enterprises, and all manner of multinationals for whom immediate human profit overrides every other concern. Nature—these entities tell us—is a vast supermarket set up by God for the benefit of the human race. Against such arrogant nonsense nature writers set up their proofs. They recount their experiences, file their reports, offer their observations, lend an eye and ear to our planet, and give tongue to its music, as it turns gracefully to the light of the distant glow-worm stars.

LANDSCAPE

The seeming significance of nature's appearances, their un-changing strangeness to the senses, and the thrilling response which they awaken in the mind of man . . . . If we could only write near enough to the facts, and yet with no pedestrian calm, but ardently, we might transfer the glamour of reality direct upon our pages.

—ROBERT LOUIS STEVENSON
Henry David Thoreau, May 1880

THE FALKLAND ISLANDS

CHARLES DARWIN

On *March 1st*, 1833, and again on *March 16th*, 1834, the *Beagle* anchored in Berkeley Sound, in East Falkland Island. This archipelago is situated in nearly the same latitude with the mouth of the Strait of Magellan; it covers a space of one hundred and twenty by sixty geographical miles, and is little more than half the size of Ireland. After the possession of these miserable islands had been contested by France, Spain, and England, they were left uninhabited. The Government of Buenos Ayres then sold them to a private individual, but likewise used them, as old Spain had done before, for a penal settlement. England claimed her right, and seized them. The Englishman who was left in charge of the flag was consequently murdered. A British officer was next sent, unsupported by any power: and when we arrived, we found him in charge of a population, of which rather more than half were runaway rebels and murderers.

The theatre is worthy of the scenes acted on it. An undulating land, with a desolate and wretched aspect, is everywhere covered by a peaty soil and wiry grass, of one monotonous brown colour. Here and there a peak or ridge of gray quartz rock breaks through the smooth surface. Every one has heard of the climate of these regions; it may be compared to that which is experienced at the height of between one and two thousand feet on the mountains of North Wales; having, however, less sunshine and less frost, but more wind and rain.*

---

*From accounts published since our voyage, and more especially from several interesting

MAY 16TH   I will now describe a short excursion which I made round a part of this island. In the morning I started with six horses and two Gauchos: the latter were capital men for the purpose, and well accustomed to living on their own resources. The weather was very boisterous and cold, with heavy hailstorms. We got on, however, pretty well, but, except the geology, nothing could be less interesting than our day's ride. The country is uniformly the same undulating moorland; the surface being covered by light brown withered grass and a few very small shrubs, all springing out of an elastic peaty soil. In the valleys here and there might be seen a small flock of wild geese, and everywhere the ground was so soft that the snipe were able to feed. Besides these two birds there were few others. There is one main range of hills, nearly two thousand feet in height, and composed of quartz rock, the rugged and barren crests of which gave us some trouble to cross. On the south side we came to the best country for wild cattle; we met, however, no great number, for they had been lately much harassed.

In the evening we came across a small herd. One of my companions, St. Jago by name, soon separated a fat cow; he threw the bolas, and it struck her legs, but failed in becoming entangled. Then dropping his hat to mark the spot where the balls were left, while at full gallop, he uncoiled his lazo, and after a most severe chase, again came up to the cow, and caught her round the horns. The other Gaucho had gone on ahead with the spare horses, so that St. Jago had some difficulty in killing the furious beast. He managed to get her on a level piece of ground, by taking advantage of her as often as she rushed at him; and when she would not move, my horse, from having been trained, would canter up, and with his chest give her a violent push. But when on level ground it does not appear an easy job for one man to kill a beast mad with terror. Nor would it be so, if the horse, when left to itself without its rider, did not soon learn, for its own safety, to keep the lazo tight; so that, if the cow or ox moves forward, the horse moves just as quickly forward; otherwise, it stands motionless leaning on one side. This horse, however, was a young one, and would not stand still, but gave into the cow as she struggled. It was admirable to see with what

---

letters from Captain Sulivan, R.N., employed on the survey, it appears that we took an exaggerated view of the badness of the climate of these islands. But when I reflect on the almost universal covering of peat, and on the fact of wheat seldom ripening here, I can hardly believe that the climate in summer is so fine and dry as it has lately been represented.

dexterity St. Jago dodged behind the beast, till at least he contrived to give the fatal touch to the main tendon of the hind leg; after which, without much difficulty, he drove his knife into the head of the spinal marrow, and the cow dropped as if struck by lightning. He cut off pieces of flesh with the skin to it, but without any bones, sufficient for our expedition. We then rode on to our sleeping place, and had for supper "carne con cuero," or meat roasted with the skin on it. This is as superior to common beef as venison is to mutton. A large circular piece taken from the back is roasted on the embers with the hide downwards and in the form of a saucer, so that none of the gravy is lost. If any worthy alderman had supped with us that evening, "carne con cuero," without doubt, would soon have been celebrated in London.

During the night it rained, and the next day (17TH) was very stormy, with much hail and snow. We rode across the island to the neck of land which joins the Rincon del Toro (the great peninsula at the S.W. extremity) to the rest of the island. From the great number of cows which have been killed, there is a large proportion of bulls. These wander about single, or two and three together, and are very savage. I never saw such magnificent beasts; they equalled in the size of their huge heads and necks the Grecian marble sculptures. Captain Sulivan informs me that the hide of an average-sized bull weighs forty-seven pounds, whereas a hide of this weight, less thoroughly dried, is considered as a very heavy one at Monte Video. The young bulls generally run away for a short distance; but the old ones do not stir a step, except to rush at man and horse; and many horses have been thus killed. An old bull crossed a boggy stream, and took his stand on the opposite side to us; we in vain tried to drive him away, and failing, were obliged to make a large circuit. The Gauchos in revenge determined to emasculate him and render him for the future harmless. It was very interesting to see how art completely mastered force. One lazo was thrown over his horns as he rushed at the horse, and another round his hind legs; in a minute the monster was stretched powerless on the ground. After the lazo has once been drawn tightly around the horns of a furious animal, it does not at first appear an easy thing to disengage it again without killing the beast; nor, I apprehend, would it be so if the man was by himself. By the aid, however, of a second person throwing his lazo so as to catch both hind legs, it is quickly managed; for the animal, as long as its hind legs are kept outstretched, is quite helpless, and the first man can with his hands loosen his lazo from the horns, and then quietly mount his horse; but the moment the second man, by backing ever so little, relaxes the strain, the lazo slips off the legs of the struggling beast, which then rises free, shakes himself, and vainly rushes at his antagonist.

During our whole ride we saw only one troop of wild horses. These animals, as well as the cattle, were introduced by the French in 1764, since which time both have greatly increased. It is a curious fact, that the horses have never left the eastern end of the island, although there is no natural boundary to prevent them from roaming, and that part of the island is not more tempting than the rest. The Gauchos whom I asked, though asserting this to be the case, were unable to account for it, except from the strong attachment which horses have to any locality to which they are accustomed. Considering that the island does not appear fully stocked, and that there are no beasts of prey, I was particularly curious to know what has checked their originally rapid increase. That in a limited island some check would sooner or later supervene, is inevitable; but why has the increase of the horse been checked sooner than that of the cattle? Captain Sulivan has taken much pains for me in this inquiry. The Gauchos employed here attribute it chiefly to the stallions constantly roaming from place to place, and compelling the mares to accompany them, whether or not the young foals are able to follow. One Gaucho told Captain Sulivan that he had watched a stallion for a whole hour, violently kicking and biting a mare till he forced her to leave her foal to its fate. Captain Sulivan can so far corroborate this curious account, that he has several times found young foals dead, whereas he has never found a dead calf. Moreover, the dead bodies of full-grown horses are more frequently found, as if more subject to disease or accidents than those of the cattle. From the softness of the ground their hoofs often grow irregularly to a great length, and this causes lameness. The predominant colours are roan and iron-grey. All the horses bred here, both tame and wild, are rather small sized, though generally in good condition; and they have lost so much strength, that they are unfit to be used in taking wild cattle with the lazo: in consequence, it is necessary to go to the great expense of importing fresh horses from the Plata. At some future period the southern hemisphere probably will have its breed of Falkland ponies, as the northern has its Shetland breed.

The cattle, instead of having degenerated like the horses, seem, as before remarked, to have increased in size, and they are much more numerous than the horses. Captain Sulivan informs me that they vary much less in the general form of their bodies and in the shape of their horns than English cattle. In colour they differ much; and it is a remarkable circumstance, that in different parts of this one small island, different colours predominate. Round Mount Usborne, at a height of from 1,000 to 1,500 feet above the sea, about half of some of the herds are mouse or lead-coloured, a tint which is not common in other parts of the island. Near Port Pleasant dark brown prevails, whereas south of Choiseul Sound (which almost divides the island into two parts), white beasts with black heads and feet are the most common: in all parts black, and some spotted animals may be observed. Captain Sulivan remarks, that the difference in the prevailing colours was so obvious, that in looking for the herds near Port Pleasant, they appeared for a long distance like black spots, while south of Choiseul Sound they appeared like white spots on the hill-sides. Captain Sulivan thinks that the herds do not mingle; and it is a singular fact, that the mouse-coloured cattle, though living on the high land, calve about a month earlier in the season than the other coloured beasts on the lower land. It is interesting thus to find the once domesticated cattle breaking into three colours, of which some one colour would in all probability ultimately prevail over the others, if the herds were left undisturbed for the next several centuries.

The rabbit is another animal which has been introduced, and has succeeded very well; so that they abound over large parts of the island. Yet, like the horses, they are confined within certain limits; for they have not crossed the central chain of hills, nor would they have extended even so far as its base, if, as the Gauchos informed me, small colonies had not been carried there. I should not have supposed that these animals, natives of northern Africa, could have existed in a climate so humid as this, and which enjoys so little sunshine that even wheat ripens only occasionally. It is asserted that in Sweden, which any one would have thought a more favourable climate, the rabbit cannot live out of doors. The first few pair, moreover, had here to contend against preexisting enemies, in the fox and some large hawks. The French naturalists have considered the black variety a distinct species, and called it Lepus Magellanicus.* They imagined that Magellan, when talking of an animal under the name of "conejos" in the Strait of Magellan, referred to this species; but he was alluding to a

*Lesson's "Zoology of the Voyage of the *Coquille*," tom. i., p. 168. All the early voyagers, and especially Bougainville, distinctly state that the wolf-like fox was the only native animal on the island. The distinction of the rabbit as a species, is taken from peculiarities in the fur, from the shape of the head, and from the shortness of the ears. I may here observe that the difference between the Irish and English hare rests upon nearly similar characters, only more strongly marked.

small cavy, which to this day is thus called by the Spaniards. The Gauchos laughed at the idea of the black kind being different from the grey, and they said that at all events it had not extended its range any further than the grey kind; that the two were never found separate; and that they readily bred together, and produced piebald offspring. Of the latter I now possess a specimen, and it is marked about the head differently from the French specific description. This circumstance shows how cautious naturalists should be in making species; for even Cuvier, on looking at the skull of one of these rabbits, thought it was probably distinct!

The only quadruped native to the island* is a large wolf-like fox (Canis antarcticus), which is common to both East and West Falkland. I have no doubt it is a peculiar species, and confined to this archipelago; because many sealers, Gauchos, and Indians, who have visited these islands, all maintain that no such animal is found in any part of South America. Molina, from a similarity in habits, thought that this was the same with his "culpeu;"† but I have seen both, and they are quite distinct. These wolves are well known, from Byron's account of their tameness and curiosity, which the sailors, who ran into the water to avoid them, mistook for fierceness. To this day their manners remain the same. They have been observed to enter a tent, and actually pull some meat from beneath the head of a sleeping seaman. The Gauchos also have frequently in the evening killed them, by holding out a piece of meat in one hand, and in the other a knife ready to stick them. As far as I am aware, there is no other instance in any part of the world, of so small a mass of broken land, distant from a continent, possessing so large an aboriginal quadruped peculiar to itself. Their numbers have rapidly decreased; they are already banished from that half of the island which lies to the eastward of the neck of land between St. Salvador Bay and Berkeley Sound. Within a very few years after these islands shall have become regularly settled, in all probability this fox will be classed with the dodo, as an animal which has perished from the face of the earth.

At night (17TH) we slept on the neck of land at the head of Choiseul Sound, which forms the south-west peninsula. The valley was pretty well sheltered from the cold wind; but there was very little brushwood for

---

*I have reason, however, to suspect that there is a field-mouse. The common European rat and mouse have roamed far from the habitations of the settlers. The common hog has also run wild on one islet: all are of a black colour: the boars are very fierce, and have great tusks.

†The "culpeu" is the Canis Magellanicus brought home by Captain King from the Strait of Magellan. It is common in Chile.

fuel. The Gauchos, however, soon found what, to my great surprise, made nearly as hot a fire as coals; this was the skeleton of a bullock lately killed, from which the flesh had been picked by the carrion-hawks. They told me that in winter they often killed a beast, cleaned the flesh from the bones with their knives, and then with these same bones roasted the meat for their suppers.

MAY 18TH   It rained during nearly the whole day. At night we managed, however, with our saddle-cloths to keep ourselves pretty well dry and warm; but the ground on which we slept was on each occasion nearly in the state of a bog, and there was not a dry spot to sit down on after our day's ride. I have in another part stated how singular it is that there should be absolutely no trees on these islands, although Tierra del Fuego is covered by one large forest. The largest bush in the island (belonging to the family of Compositae) is scarcely so tall as our gorse. The best fuel is afforded by a green little bush about the size of common heath, which has the useful property of burning while fresh and green. It was very surprising to see the Gauchos, in the midst of rain and everything soaking wet, with nothing more than a tinder-box and piece of rag, immediately make a fire. They sought beneath the tufts of grass and bushes for a few dry twigs, and these they rubbed into fibres; then surrounding them with coarser twigs, something like a bird's nest, they put the rag with its spark of fire in the middle and covered it up. The nest being then held up to the wind, by degrees it smoked more and more, and at last burst out in flames. I do not think any other method would have had a chance of succeeding with such damp materials.

MAY 19TH   Each morning, from not having ridden for some time previously, I was very stiff. I was surprised to hear the Gauchos, who have from infancy almost lived on horseback, say that, under similar circumstances, they always suffer. St. Jago told me, that having been confined for three months by illness, he went out hunting wild cattle, and in consequence, for the next two days, his thighs were so stiff that he was obliged to lie in bed. This shows that the Gauchos, although they do not appear to do so, yet really must exert much muscular effort in riding. The hunting wild cattle, in a country so difficult to pass as this is on account of the swampy ground, must be very hard work. The Gauchos say they often pass at full speed over ground which would be impassable at a slower pace; in the same manner as a man is able to skate over thin ice. When hunting, the party endeavours to get as close as possible to the herd without being discovered. Each man carries four or five pair of the bolas; these he throws one after the other at as many cattle, which, when once entangled, are left for some days, till they become a little exhausted by hunger and struggling. They are then let free, and driven towards a small herd of tame animals, which have been brought to the spot on purpose. From their previous treatment, being too much terrified to leave the herd, they are easily driven, if their strength last out, to the settlement.

The weather continued so very bad that we determined to make a push, and try to reach the vessel before night. From the quantity of rain which had fallen, the surface of the whole country was swampy. I suppose my horse fell at least a dozen times, and sometimes the whole six horses were floundering in the mud together. All the little streams are bordered by soft peat, which makes it very difficult for the horses to leap them without falling. To complete our discomforts we were obliged to cross the head of a creek of the sea, in which the water was as high as our horses' backs; and the little waves, owing to the violence of the wind, broke over us, and made us very wet and cold. Even the iron-framed Gauchos professed themselves glad when they reached the settlement, after our little excursion.

✳   ✳   ✳

The geological structure of these islands is in most respects simple. The lower country consists of clay-slate and sandstone, containing fossils, very closely related to, but not identical with, those found in the Silurian formations of Europe; the hills are formed of white granular quartz rock. The strata of the latter are frequently arched with perfect symmetry, and the appearance of some of the masses is in consequence most singular. Pernety* has devoted several pages to the description of a Hill of Ruins, the successive strata of which he has justly compared to the seats of an amphitheatre. The quartz rock must have been quite pasty when it underwent such remarkable flexures without being shattered into fragments. As the quartz insensibly passes into the sandstone, it seems probable that the former owes its origin to the sandstone having been heated to such a degree that it became viscid, and upon cooling crystallized. While in the soft state it must have been pushed up through the overlying beds.

In many parts of the island the bottoms of the valleys are covered in an extraordinary manner by myriads of great loose angular fragments of

---

*Pernety, "Voyage aux Isles Malouines," p. 526.

the quartz rock, forming "streams of stones." These have been mentioned with surprise by every voyager since the time of Pernety. The blocks are not waterworn, their angles being only a little blunted; they vary in size from one or two feet in diameter to ten, or even more than twenty times as much. They are not thrown together into irregular piles, but are spread out into level sheets or great streams. It is not possible to ascertain their thickness, but the water of small streamlets can be heard trickling through the stones many feet below the surface. The actual depth is probably great, because the crevices between the lower fragments must long ago have been filled up with sand. The width of these sheets of stones varies from a few hundred feet to a mile; but the peaty soil daily encroaches on the borders, and even forms islets wherever a few fragments happen to lie close together. In a valley south of Berkeley Sound, which some of our party called the "great valley of fragments," it was necessary to cross an uninterrupted band half a mile wide, by jumping from one pointed stone to another. So large were the fragments, that being overtaken by a shower of rain, I readily found shelter beneath one of them.

Their little inclination is the most remarkable circumstance in these "streams of stones." On the hill-sides I have seen them sloping at an angle of ten degrees with the horizon; but in some of the level, broad-bottomed valleys, the inclination is only just sufficient to be clearly perceived. On so rugged a surface there was no means of measuring the angle; but to give a common illustration, I may say that the slope would not have checked the speed of an English mail-coach. In some places, a continuous stream of these fragments followed up the course of a valley, and even extended to the very crest of the hill. On these crests huge masses, exceeding in dimensions any small building, seemed to stand arrested in their headlong course; there, also, the curved strata of the archways lay piled on each other, like the ruins of some vast and ancient cathedral. In endeavouring to describe these scenes of violence one is tempted to pass from one simile to another. We may imagine that streams of white lava had flowed from many parts of the mountains into the lower country, and that when solidified they had been rent by some enormous convulsion into myriads of fragments. The expression "streams of stones," which immediately occurred to every one, conveys the same idea. These scenes are on the spot rendered more striking by the contrast of the low, rounded forms of the neighbouring hills.

I was interested by finding on the highest peak of one range (about seven hundred feet above the sea) a great arched fragment, lying on its convex side, or back downwards. Must we believe that it was fairly pitched up in the air, and thus turned? Or, with more probability, that there existed formerly a part of the same range more elevated than the point on which this monument of a great convulsion of nature now lies. As the fragments in the valleys are neither rounded nor the crevices filled up with sand, we must infer that the period of violence was subsequent to the land having been raised above the waters of the sea. In a transverse section within these valleys, the bottom is nearly level, or rises but very little towards either side. Hence the fragments appear to have travelled from the head of the valley; but in reality it seems more probable that they have been hurled down from the nearest slopes; and that since, by a vibratory movement of overwhelming force,* the fragments have been levelled into one continuous sheet. If during the earthquake† which in 1835 overthrew Concepcion, in Chile, it was thought wonderful that small bodies should have been pitched a few inches from the ground, what must we say to a movement which has caused fragments many tons in weight, to move onwards like so much sand on a vibrating board, and find their level? I have seen, in the Cordillera of the Andes, the evident marks where stupendous mountains have been broken into pieces like so much thin crust, and the strata thrown on their vertical edges; but never did any scene, like these "streams of stones," so forcibly convey to my mind the idea of a convulsion, of which in historical records we might in vain seek for any counterpart; yet the progress of knowledge will probably some day give a simple explanation of this phenomenon, as it already has of the so long-thought inexplicable transportal of the erratic boulders, which are strewed over the plains of Europe.

❋　❋　❋

I have little to remark on the zoology of these islands. I have before described the carrion-vulture or Polyborus. There are some other hawks, owls, and a few small land-birds. The water-fowl are particularly numerous, and they must formerly, from the accounts of the old navigators,

---

*"Nous n'avons pas été moites saisis d'etonnement à la vûe de l'innombrable quantité de pierres de toutes grandeurs, bouleversées les unes sur les autres, et cependant rangées, comme si elles avoient été amoncelées négligemment pour remplir des ravins. On ne se lassoit pars d'admirer les effets prodigieux de la nature."—*Pernety*, p. 526.

†An inhabitant of Mendoza, and hence well capable of judging, assured me that, during the several years he had resided on these islands, he had never felt the slightest shock of an earthquake.

have been much more so. One day I observed a cormorant playing with a fish which it had caught. Eight times successively the bird let its prey go, then dived after it, and although in deep water, brought it each time to the surface. In the Zoological Gardens I have seen the otter treat a fish in the same manner, much as a cat does a mouse: I do not know of any other instance where dame Nature appears so wilfully cruel. Another day, having placed myself between a penguin (Aptenodytes demersa) and the water, I was much amused by watching its habits. It was a brave bird; and till reaching the sea, it regularly fought and drove me backwards. Nothing less than heavy blows would have stopped him; every inch he gained he firmly kept, standing close before me erect and determined. When thus opposed he continually rolled his head from side to side, in a very odd manner, as if the power of distinct vision lay only in the anterior and basal part of each eye. This bird is commonly called the jackass penguin, from its habit, while on shore, of throwing its head backwards, and making a loud strange noise, very like the braying of an ass; but while at sea, and undisturbed, its note is very deep and solemn, and is often heard in the night-time. In diving, its little wings are used as fins; but on the land, as front legs. When crawling, it may be said on four legs, through the tussocks or on the side of a grassy cliff, it moves so very quickly that it might easily be mistaken for a quadruped. When at sea and fishing, it comes to the surface for the purpose of breathing with such a spring, and dives again so instantaneously, that I defy any one at first sight to be sure that it was not a fish leaping for sport.

Two kinds of geese frequent the Falklands. The upland species (Anas Magellanica) is common, in pairs and in small flocks, throughout the island. They do not migrate, but build on the small outlying islets. This is supposed to be from fear of the foxes: and it is perhaps from the same cause that these birds, though very tame by day, are shy and wild in the dusk of the evening. They live entirely on vegetable matter. The rock-goose, so called from living exclusively on the sea-beach (Anas antarctica), is common both here and on the west coast of America, as far north as Chile. In the deep and retired channels of Tierra del Fuego, the snow-white gander, invariably accompanied by his darker consort, and standing close by each other on some distant rocky point, is a common feature in the landscape.

In these islands a great logger-headed duck or goose (Anas brachyptera), which sometimes weighs twenty-two pounds, is very abundant. These birds were in former days called, from their extraordinary manner of paddling and splashing upon the water, race-horses; but now they are named, much more appropriately, steamers. Their wings are too small and weak to allow of flight, but by their aid, partly swimming and partly flapping the surface of the water, they move very quickly. The manner is something like that by which the common house-duck escapes when pursued by a dog; but I am nearly sure that the steamer moves its wings alternately, instead of both together, as in other birds. These clumsy, logger-headed ducks make such a noise and splashing, that the effect is exceedingly curious.

Thus we find in South America three birds which use their wings for other purposes besides flight; the penguin as fins, the steamer as paddles, and the ostrich as sails: and the Apteryx of New Zealand, as well as its gigantic extinct prototype the Dinornis, possess only rudimentary representatives of wings. The steamer is able to dive only to a very short distance. It feeds entirely on shell-fish from the kelp and tidal rocks; hence the beak and head, for the purpose of breaking them, are surprisingly heavy and strong: the head is so strong that I have scarcely been able to fracture it with my geological hammer; and all our sportsmen soon discovered how tenacious these birds were of life. When in the evening pluming themselves in a flock, they make the same odd mixture of sounds which bullfrogs do within the tropics.

In Tierra del Fuego, as well as at the Falkland Islands, I made many observations on the lower marine animals,* but they are of little general interest. I will mention only one class of facts, relating to certain zoophytes in the more highly-organized division of that class. Several genera (Flustra, Eschara, Cellaria, Crisia, and others) agree in having singular movable

---

*I was surprised to find, on counting the eggs of a large white Doris (this sea-slug was three and a half inches long), how extraordinarily numerous they were. From two to five eggs (each three-thousandths of an inch in diameter) were contained in a spherical little case. These were arranged two deep in transverse rows forming a ribbon. The ribbon adhered by its edge to the rock in an oval spire. One which I found, measured nearly twenty inches in length and half in breadth. By counting how many balls were contained in a tenth of an inch in the row, and how many rows in an equal length of the ribbon, on the most moderate computation there were six hundred thousand eggs. Yet this Doris was certainly not very common: although I was often searching under the stones, I saw only seven individuals. *No fallacy is more common with naturalists, than that the numbers of an individual species depend on its powers of propagation.*

organs (like those of Flustra avicularia, found in the European seas) attached to their cells. The organ, in the greater number of cases, very closely resembles the head of a vulture; but the lower mandible can be opened much wider than in a real bird's beak. The head itself possesses considerable powers of movement, by means of a short neck. In one zoophyte the head itself was fixed, but the lower jaw free; in another it was replaced by a triangular hood, with a beautifully fitted trap-door, which evidently answered to the lower mandible. In the greater number of species, each cell was provided with one head, but in others each cell had two.

The young cells at the end of the branches of these corallines contain quite immature polypi, yet the vulture-heads attached to them, though small, are in every respect perfect. When the polypus was removed by a needle from any of the cells, these organs did not appear in the least affected. When one of the vulture-like heads was cut off from a cell, the lower mandible retained its power of opening and closing. Perhaps the most singular part of their structure is, that when there were more than two rows of cells on a branch, the central cells were furnished with these appendages, of only one-fourth the size of the outside ones. Their movements varied according to the species; but in some I never saw the least motion; while others, with the lower mandible generally wide open, oscillated backwards and forwards at the rate of about five seconds each turn; others moved rapidly and by starts. When touched with a needle, the beak generally seized the point so firmly, that the whole branch might be shaken.

These bodies have no relation whatever with the production of the eggs or gemmules, as they are formed before the young polypi appear in the cells at the end of the growing branches; as they move independently of the polypi, and do not appear to be in any way connected with them; and as they differ in size on the outer and inner rows of cells, I have little doubt, that in their functions, they are related rather to the horny axis of the branches than to the polypi in the cells. The fleshy appendage at the lower extremity of the sea-pen (described at Bahia Blanca) also forms part of the zoophyte, as a whole, in the same manner as the roots of a tree form part of the whole tree, and not of the individual leaf or flower-buds.

In another elegant little coralline (Crisia?), each cell was furnished with a long-toothed bristle, which had the power of moving quickly. Each of these bristles and each of the vulture-like heads generally moved quite independently of the others, but sometimes all on both sides of a branch, sometimes only those on one side, moved together coinstantaneously;

sometimes each moved in regular order one after another. In these actions we apparently behold as perfect a transmission of will in the zoophyte, though composed of thousands of distinct polypi, as in any single animal. The case, indeed, is not different from that of the sea-pens, which, when touched, drew themselves into the sand on the coast of Bahia Blanca. I will state one other instance of uniform action, though of a very different nature, in a zoophyte closely allied to Clytia, and therefore very simply organized. Having kept a large tuft of it in a basin of salt-water, when it was dark I found that as often as I rubbed any part of a branch, the whole became strongly phosphorescent with a green light: I do not think I ever saw any object more beautifully so. But the remarkable circumstance was, that the flashes of light always proceeded up the branches, from the base towards the extremities.

The examination of these compound animals was always very interesting to me. What can be more remarkable than to see a plant-like body producing an egg, capable of swimming about and of choosing a proper place to adhere to, which then sprouts into branches, each crowded with innumerable distinct animals, often of complicated organizations? The branches, moreover, as we have just seen, sometimes possess organs capable of movement and independent of the polypi. Surprising as this union of separate individuals in a common stock must always appear, every tree displays the same fact, for buds must be considered as individual plants. It is, however, natural to consider a polypus, furnished with a mouth, intestines, and other organs, as a distinct individual, whereas the individuality of a leafbud is not easily realized; so that the union of separate individuals in a common body is more striking in a coralline than in a tree. Our conception of a compound animal, where in some respects the individuality of each is not completed, may be aided, by reflecting on the production of two distinct creatures by bisecting a single one with a knife, or where Nature herself performs the task of bisection. We may consider the polypi in a zoophyte, or the buds in a tree, as cases where the division of the individual has not been completely effected. Certainly in the case of trees, and judging from analogy in that of corallines, the individuals propagated by buds seem more intimately related to each other, than eggs or seeds are to their parents. It seems now pretty well established that plants propagated by buds all partake of a common duration of life; and it is familiar to every one, what singular and numerous peculiarities are transmitted with certainty, by buds, layers, and grafts, which by seminal propagation never or only casually reappear.

LA PAMPA

R. B. CUNNINGHAME GRAHAM

All grass and sky, and sky and grass, and still more sky and grass, the pampa stretched from the *pajonales* on the western bank of the Paraná right to the stony plain of Uspallata, a thousand miles away.

It stretched from San Luis de la Punta down to Bahia Blanca, and again crossing the Uruguay, comprised the whole republic of that name and a good half of Rio Grande, then with a loop took in the *misiones* both of the Paraná and Paraguay.

Through all this ocean of tall grass, green in the spring, then yellow, and in the autumn brown as an old boot, the general characteristics were the same.

A ceaseless wind ruffled it all and stirred its waves of grass. Innumerable flocks and herds enamelled it, and bands of ostriches ("Mirth of the Desert," as the gauchos called them) and herds of palish-yellow deer stood on the tops of the *cuchillas* and watched you as you galloped past.

Down in the south, the Patagonian hare, mataco, and the quirquincho scudded away or burrowed in the earth. Towards the middle region of this great galloping ground, the greatest that God made—perhaps He could not possibly have made a better, even had He tried—great armadillos and iguanas showed themselves, and in the north, around the deep metallic-toned *isletas* of hard-wood *montes*, flocks of macaws—red, yellow, and bright blue—floated like butterflies. Up in the north, anteaters (the tamandúa of the Guaranís) and tapirs wandered, looking as if they had escaped from out the Ark.

Over the whole extent the teru-tero hovered, screamed, whistled, and circled just above your horse's head. From every *monte* and from every maize field flew chattering flocks of parakeets.

Tigers and pumas inhabited the woods, right from the Estero Ñembuco, which I have crossed so often with the mud and water to my horse's cinch, down to the Antarctic beech forests of Sandy Point.

In all the rivers *nutrias* and *lobos* and the carpincho, with its great red teeth, swam with their heads awash, laid flat upon the stream, just like a seal at sea.

Vizcachas burrowed, and wise, solemn little owls sat at the entrance of their burrows making pretence to guard them, as does a sentinel before a palace door.

Locusts occasionally visited the pampa, blackening the sun, devouring all the crops, and disappearing just as they had come.

"Where is the *manga*?" was a familiar question on the plains, and grave and bearded men reined in their horses, their ponchos suddenly clinging to their sides, just as a boat's sail clings around the mast when it has lost the wind, and pointing with a lean, brown finger stained with tobacco juice, replied, "Por allacito, en los Porongos," and then departed, just as ships speak to each other on the sea. The north wind filled the air with cottony filaments, and the *pampero*, roaring like a whole rodeo that had taken fright, levelled the houses and the grass. The air was full in summer of a perpetual twittering of insects that hung invisible, whilst in the winter the white hoarfrost in early morning silvered the grass, and hung congealed upon the tops of stakes, just as it did in the old world in which the poet-king penned the *Cantar de los cantares* two thousand years ago.

All that, was what the pampa had inherited from nature. When I first knew it, it looked just as it must have looked on the morning of the seventh day in far-off Nabothea, that old-world Entre Ríos, when the Creator rested and, looking earthwards, saw that it was good.

Man had but little altered it, but for a peach grove here and here, a white estancia house or a straw-coloured rancheria or *pulpería*, built either at the pass of some great river or on a hill, as that at the Cuchilla de Peralta, by which the mule-trail, used since the Conquest, led, winding upon its way towards Brazil.

Men passed each other seated upright on their *recaos*, driving their horses in a bunch in front of them, swinging their whips around their heads.

They passed, shouting a salutation, or if too far off to be heard, waving a hand, and sank into the plain just as a vessel sinks into the sea, the body of the horse first disappearing, then the man, poncho, and, last of all, his hat. The waves of grass appeared to swallow him, and as men rode they kept their eyes fixed on the horizon, or, if at night, upon a star. When the night caught them on the plains, after first hobbling the mare, they tied a horse to a long *soga*, making, if neither stick nor bone were to be found, a knot in the rope's end, stamping it in, and lying down upon it.

They smoked a cigarette or two, looked at the stars a little, and took good care to place their heads in the direction towards which they had to journey, for in the midst of sunrise nothing was easier than to mistake the point you aimed at, and wander back upon the trail.

In that green ocean, as the proverb said, "He who wanders from the trail is lost"; and it was true enough, as many a heap of bones, to which a shred of tattered cloth still clung, most amply testified, as you came on them on a gallop, looking perhaps for horses stolen or strayed. Your companion might or might not rein up his horse, but certainly would point in passing, and remark: "See where the grass grows rank around the bones; there has a Christian died."

"Christian" was used more as a racial than a religious term, the Indians usually being called *los bravos, los infieles, los tapes*, the latter usually applied either to the descendants of the Charruas in the Banda Oriental, or to the Indian Mansos of the Missions of the north. How much the aforesaid *infieles* and the *tapes* had left their impress on the speech and the life of the gauchos, might be seen by the national costume of the poncho and the *chiripá*. These, as the early writers tell us, were adapted from the "infidel we found dwelling in all these plains, when first Don Pedro de Mendoza came with his following to conquer for his lord, and to proclaim the glory of the name of Him who, though born in a stable, is higher than all kings." In the current pampa speech the words *bagual, ñandú, ombú* and *vincha, tatú, tacuará*, and *bacaray*, with almost all the names of plants, of shrubs and trees, recalled the influence of the Indians, the Quichuas, and Guaranís, the Pampas and Pehuelches, Charruas, and the rest of those who once inhabited the land.

Las boleadoras, known to the gauchos as *las tres Marías*, was the distinctive weapon of the southern plains. With them the Indians slew many of Don Pedro de Mendoza's men at the first christianising of the River Plate, and with them also did the fierce gaucho troops who rose under Elio and Liniers crash in the skulls of various English, *luteranos*—for so the good

Dean Funes styles them in his history—who under Whitelock had attacked the town. Only upon the pampa, in the whole world, was this
tremendous weapon ever known. None of the pampa tribes used bows
and arrows, for with them the *bolas*, and in especial the single stone, fixed
to a plaited thong of hide and called *la bola perdida*, quite supplied their
place.

In fact, for no land but the pampa, that is, in the Americas (for it could
well be used in Africa and Asia), are *las tres Marías* fit. In North America
the plains are bushy or the grass is long as hay, conditions which would
militate against the throwing of a weapon which, often thrown a yard or
two behind the quarry's legs, sprang from the ground and then entangled
them.

Nothing could be more typical of the wild life of forty years ago upon
the plains than was the figure of a gaucho dressed in his poncho and his
chiripá, his naked toes clutching the stirrups, his long iron spurs kept in
position by a thong of hide dangling below his heels, his hair bound back
by a red silk handkerchief, his eyes ablaze, his silver knife passed through
his sash and *tirador*, and sticking out just under his right elbow, his *pingo*
with its mane cut into castles and its long tail floating out in the breeze as,
twisting *las tres Marías* round his head, he flew like lightning down a slope,
which the mere European horseman would have looked on as certain
death, intent to "ball" one of a band of fleet *ñandús* all sailing down the
wind.

Letting the *bolas* go, so easily, it seemed as if his will and not his hand
directed them, they hurtled through the air, revolving on their own axis
sixty or seventy yards, and, when the *sogas* met the ostriches' neck, the
centrifugal force being averted, the balls fell down and, wrapping tightly
round the legs, soon threw the giant bird upon its side. Ten or twelve
bounds brought up the hunter, who, springing from his saddle, his huge
iron spurts clanking like fetters on the ground, either put hobbles on his
horse, or if he felt quite sure of him, threw the long reins upon the ground,
confident that it, trained by experience to know a step upon the reins
involved a pull upon the mouth, would stand obediently.

Then, drawing his *facón*, the gaucho either stuck it deeply into the
bird, low down upon the breast, or if occasion served, drawing a spare set
of *boleadoras* from around his waist, or taking them from underneath the
cojinillo of the *recao*, crashed in his victim's skull. Sometimes, indeed,
with a *revés* of the *facón* they used to cut the ostrich's head off at a blow;

but this wanted a sharp and heavy knife, and an arm with which to wield it, strong beyond ordinary.

I have seen a gaucho, hunting wild colts or ostriches, in the very action of swinging the *bolas* round his head, have his horse fall with him, alight upon his feet, and without losing the command of the direction of his swing, catch his own horse as it, springing to its feet, was just about to leave him helpless afoot upon the plains.

Afoot upon the plains—that was indeed a phrase of fear upon the pampas of the south. No mariner afloat upon the waves, his mainstay but a little boat, was in a worse condition than the man who, from some cause or other, found himself horseless in the vast sea of grass.

From having been as free as a bird, he instantly became as helpless as the same bird with a wing broken by a shot.

If cattle saw him, they not infrequently attacked him, when his one chance of safety (on the open plains) was to lie down and, simulating death, to let them smell him, which when they had done, if he lay still enough, they turned and went away. When the pedestrian approached a house, the troop of dogs that every gaucho kept surrounded him like wolves, barking and snapping at his legs if it were daytime, or falling on him literally like wolves if it should happen to be dark. Small streams, which generally had muddy bottoms, and through which his horse had plunged, sinking down to the cinch, but always getting through, to the man afoot became impassable, making him wander up and down their banks, perhaps for miles, till he could find a "pass."

If by an evil chance he lost his way, his fate was sealed, especially upon that portion where distances were great between estancias, and where marauding Indians on a *malón* would kill him if they saw him, just as a boy kills a young bird when it runs fluttering across his path. To lose one's horse and saddle was worse than bankruptcy; in fact, was so considered, as in the story of a Frenchman who seeing a gaucho standing idly about, inquired why he did not go out and work.

"Work, *madre mía*," said the man, "how can I work when I am bankrupt?"

"What then," the Frenchman said, "you have been in commerce, and fallen upon a bad affair; poor man, I pity you." The gaucho stared at him, and answered, "In commerce—never in my life, but at a *pulpería* some infidel or other stole my horse and saddle, with *lazo*, *bolas*, and a *cojinillo* that I bought up in Rioja, and left me without shade."

Poor man, how could he work, afoot and saddleless? No doubt before the Conquest men crossed the plains afoot; but painfully, taking perhaps long years to go from the Atlantic to the Andes, groping along from stream to stream, as the first navigators felt their way from cape to cape, coasting along the bays.

The coming of the horse gave a new life to the vast plains; for nature seemed to welcome horses once again, from the long interval between the times in which the Tertian eight-footed horse roamed on the pampas, which now are populated by the descendants of the thirteen mares and the three stallions that Pedro de Mendoza left behind when he sailed back to Spain, after his first attempt to colonise.

This is the way I recollect it. First came short grasses, eaten close down by sheep, then thistles that grew as high as a man's head, a wilderness, through which the cattle had made a labyrinth of paths; then coarser grasses, and by degrees wiry, brown bents, until at length almost all sign of grass was lost, where the pampas joined the stony plains of Patagonia in the south.

Northwards, the waving grasses also grew sparser, till in the Jesuit Missions, clumps of yatays encroached upon the plains, which ended finally in the dense woods of Paraguay.

Silence and solitude were equally the note of north and south, with a horizon bounded by what a man could see when sitting on his horse.

There were few landmarks, but in the southern and the middle districts a dark ombú, standing beside some lone *tapera* and whose shade fell on some rancho or estancia, although the proverb said, "The house shall never prosper upon whose roof is thrown the shade of the ombú."

Well did the ancient Quichuas name the plains, with the word signifying "space," for all was spacious—earth, sky, the waving continent of grass, the enormous herds of cattle and of horses, the strange effects of light, the fierce and blinding storms and, above all, the feeling in men's minds of freedom, and of being face to face with nature, under those southern skies.

THE ATLANTIC FOREST

THOMAS BELT

We were so tired, that notwithstanding our miserable and crowded quarters, we slept soundly, but were up at daylight, and soon ready for our journey again, after Rito had made a little coffee, and I had compensated our host for our lodging. The scenery around was very fine, and the place might have been made an earthly paradise. To the north-east a spur of the forest came down to within a mile of the house; in front were grassy hills and clumps of brushwood and trees, with a clear gurgling stream in the bottom; and beyond, in the distance, forest-clad mountains. As usual, the family had a pet animal. Before we left, a pretty fawn came in from the forest to be fed, and eyed us suspiciously, laying its head back over its shoulders, and gazing at us with its large, dreamy-looking eyes. The woman told us it had a wild mate in the woods, but came in daily to visit them, the dogs recognising and not molesting it. Our road still lay within a few miles of the dark Atlantic forest, the clouds lying all along the first range, concealing more than they exposed. There was a sort of gloomy grandeur about the view; so much was hidden, that the mind was left at liberty to imagine that behind these clouds lay towering mountains and awful cliffs. The road passed within a short distance of the rock of Cuapo, and, leaving my horse with Rito, I climbed up towards it. A ridge on the eastern side runs up to within about 200 feet of the summit, and so far it is accessible. Up this I climbed to the base of the brown rock, the perpendicular cliff towering up above me; here and there were patches of grey, where lichens clung to the rock, and orchids, ferns, and small shrubs grew in the clefts and on ledges. There were two fine orchids in flower, which grew not only on the rock, but on some stunted trees at its base; and beneath some fallen rocks grew a pretty club-moss, and two curious little ferns (*Aneimea oblongifolia* and *hirsuta*), with the masses of spores on stalks rising from the pinnules. The rock was the same as that of Peña Blanca, but the vegetation was entirely distinct. To the south-west there was a fine view down the Juigalpa valley to the lake, with Ometepec in the distance, and some sugar-loaf hills nearer at hand. The weather had cleared up, white cumuli only sailed across the blue aerial ocean. The scene had no feature in it of a purely tropical character, excepting that three gaudy macaws were wheeling round and round in playful flight, now showing all red on the under surface, then turning all together, as if they were one body, and showing the gorgeous blue, yellow, and red of the upper side gleaming in the sunshine; scream-ing meanwhile as they flew with harsh, discordant cries. This gaudy-coloured and noisy bird seems to proclaim aloud that it fears no foe. Its formidable beak protects it from every danger, for no hawk or predatory mammal dares attack a bird so strongly armed. Here the necessity for concealment does not exist, and sexual selection has had no check in developing the brightest and most conspicuous colours. If such a bird was not able to defend itself from all foes, its loud cries would attract them; its bright colours direct them to its own destruction. The white cockatoo of Australia is a similar instance. It is equally conspicuous amongst the dark-green foliage by its pure white colour, and equally its loud screams pro-claim from afar its resting-place, whilst its powerful beak protects it from all enemies excepting man. In the smaller species of parrots the beak is not sufficiently strong to protect them from their enemies, and most of them are coloured green, which makes them very difficult to distinguish amongst the leaves. I have been looking for several minutes at a tree, in which were scores of small green parrots, making an incessant noise, without being able to distinguish one; and I recollect once in Australia firing at what I thought was a solitary "green leek" parrot amongst a bunch of leaves, and to my astonishment five "green leeks" fell to the ground, the whole bunch of apparent leaves having been composed of them. The bills of even the smallest parrots must, however, be very useful to them to guard the entrances to their nests in the holes of trees, in which they breed.

I believe that the principal use of the long sharp bill of the Toucan is also that of a weapon with which to defend itself against all its enemies, especially when nesting in the hole of a tree. Any predatory animal must face this formidable beak if seeking to force an entrance to the nest; and I know by experience that the toucan can use it with great quickness and effect. I kept a young one of the largest Nicaraguan species (*Ramphastus tocard*) for some time, until it one day came within reach of and was killed by my monkey. It was a most comical-looking bird when hopping about, and though evidently partial to fruit, was eager after cockroaches and other insects; its long bill being useful in picking them out of crevices and corners. It used its bill so dexterously that it was impossible to put one's hand near it without being struck, and the blow would always draw blood. That in the tropics birds should have some special development for the protection of their breeding-places is not to be wondered at when we reflect upon the great number of predatory mammals, monkeys, raccoons, opossums, etc., that are constantly searching about for nests and devouring the eggs and young ones. I have already mentioned the great danger they run from the attacks of the immense armies of foraging ants, and the importance of having some means of picking off the pioneers, that they may not return and scent the trail for the advance of the main body, whose numbers would overcome all resistance.

After examining round the rock without finding any place by which it could be ascended, I rejoined Rito in the valley below, and we continued our journey. We passed over some ranges and wide valleys, where there was much grass and a few scattered huts, but very little cattle; the country being thinly populated. On the top of a rocky range we stayed at a small house for breakfast, and they made us ready some tortillas. As usual, there seemed to be three or four families all living together, and there were a great number of children. The men were two miles away at a clearing on the edge of the forest, looking after their "milpas," or maize patches. The house, though small, was cleaner and tidier than the others we had seen, and in furniture could boast of a table and a few chairs, which showed we had chanced to fall on the habitation of one of the well-to-do class. The ceiling of the room we were in was made of bamboo-rods, above which maize was stored. The women were good-looking, and appeared to be of nearly pure Spanish descent; which perhaps accounted for the chairs and table, and also for the absence of any attempt at gardening around the house—for the Indian eschews furniture, but is nearly always a gardener.

We finished our homely breakfast and set off again, crossing some more rocky ranges, and passing several Indian huts with orange trees growing around them, and at two o'clock in the afternoon reached the small town of Comoapa, where I determined to wait for Velasquez. Looking about for a house to stay at, we found one kept by a woman who formerly lived at Santo Domingo, and who was very glad to receive us;

though we found afterwards she had already more travellers staying with her than she could very well accommodate.

I had shot a pretty mot-mot on the road, and proceeded to skin it, to the amusement and delight of about a dozen spectators, who wondered what I could want with the "hide" of a bird, the only skinning that they had every seen being that of deer and cattle. A native doctor, who was staying at the house, insisted on helping me, and as the mot-mot's skin is very tough, he did not do much harm. The bird had been shot in the morning, and some one remarking that no blood flowed when it was cut, the doctor said, with a wise air, that that class of birds had no blood, and that he knew of another class that also had none, to which his auditors gave a satisfied, "Como no" ("Why not?"). He also gave us to understand that he had himself at one time skinned birds, and being evidently looked up to as an authority on all subjects by the simple country people, he was unwilling that his reputation should suffer by it being supposed that a stranger had come to Comoapa who knew something that he did not. Having skinned my bird and put it out in the sun to dry, I took a stroll through the small town, and found it composed mostly of huts inhabited by Mestizos, with a tumble-down church and a weed-covered plaza. Around some of the houses were planted mango and orange trees, but there was a general air of dilapidation and decay, and not a single sign of industry or progress visible.

Velasquez arrived at dusk, having ridden from Libertad that day. About a dozen of us slung our hammocks in the small travellers' room, where, when we had all got to rest, we looked like a cluster of great bats hanging from the rafters. No one could get along the room without disturbing everyone else, and the next morning all were early astir; we got our animals saddled as soon as possible, and set off on our journey. It was a clear and beautiful morning, and a cool breeze from the north-east fanned us as we rode blithely over grassy savannahs and hills. High up in the air soared a couple of large black vultures, floating on the wind, and describing large circles without apparent movement or exertion, scanning from their airy height the country for miles around, on the look out for their carrion food. Like all birds that soar, both over sea and land, when it is calm the vultures are obliged to flap their wings when they fly; but when a breeze is blowing they are able to use their specific gravity as a fulcrum, by means of which they present their bodies and outstretched wings and tails at various angles to the wind, and literally sail. How often, when becalmed on southern seas, when not a breath of air was stirring and the sails idly flapped against the mast, have I seen the albatross, the petrel, and the Cape-pigeon resting on the water, or rising with difficulty, and only by the constant motion of their long wings able to fly at all. But when a breeze sprang up they were all life and motion, wheeling in graceful circles, now presenting one side, now the other, to view, descending rapidly with the wind, and so gaining velocity to turn and rise up again against it. Then, as the breeze freshened to a gale, the petrels darted about, playing round and round the scudding ship, at home on the wings of the storm, poising themselves upon the wind as instinctively and with as little effort as a man balances himself on his feet. How the old times came up again as I rode over the savannah, and the soaring vultures brought back to my mind the wheeling stormy petrels that darted about whilst under close-reefed top-soils we scudded before the gale, rounding the stormy southern cape; when great blue seas, "green glimmering towards the summit," towered on every side, or struck our gallant ship like a sledge, making it shiver with the blow, and sending a driving cloud of spray from stem to stern. Then the petrels were in their element; then they darted about, now on one side, now on the other—above, below, now here, now there—all life and motion; as if their greatest pleasure was, like Ariel, "to ride on the curled cloud" and "point the tempest."

We were travelling nearly parallel with the edge of the great forest which was two or three miles away on our right; in all other directions the river was bounded by ranges, some grassed to their tops, others with forests climbing up their steep sides, excepting where white cliffs gave no foothold for the trees. We passed several grass-thatched huts inhabited by half-clad Indians or Mestizos, who generally possess a few cows and, away on the edge of the forest, small clearings of maize. These people, with unlimited fertile land at their disposal, were all sunk in what looked like squalid poverty; but they had a roof over their heads, and sufficient, though coarse, food; and they cared for nothing more. Our road lay a couple of miles to the north of the village of Huaco, where much of the maize of the province is grown; the road then led over many swampy valleys, and our beasts had hard work plunging through the mud. We passed through La Puerta, a scattered collection of Indian huts; then over a river called the Aguasco, running to the east, and probably emptying into the Rio Grande. There were a few orange trees about some of the huts, but most of the people were Mestizos, or half-breeds, and nothing but weeds grew around their habituations. Their plantations of maize were always some miles distant, and they never seem to think of moving their houses nearer to their clearings on the edge of the forest. Nearly always when I asked the question, I found that the grown-up people had been born on the spot where they lived, and they are evidently greatly attached to the localities where they have been brought up. Probably when the settlements were first made, forest land lay near, in which they made their clearings and raised their crops of corn. Since then the edge of the forest has been beaten back some miles to the north-east; but the people cling to the old spots, where, generation after generation, their ancestors have lived and died. A new house could be built in a few days, closer to the forest; but they prefer travelling several miles every day to and from their clearings, rather than desert their old homes.

Beyond the Aguasco, we had to travel over a swampy plain for about a mile, our animals plunging all the time through about three feet of mud. This plain was covered with thousands of guayava trees, laden with sufficient fruit to make guava jelly for all the world. After floundering through the swamp, we reached more savannahs, and then entered a beautiful valley, well grassed, and with herds of fine cattle, horses, and mules grazing on it. The grass was well cropped, and looked like pasture-land at home. The ground was now firmer, and we got more rapidly across it. A block of wild Muscovy ducks flew heavily across the plain, looking very like the tame variety; and I do not wonder at sportsmen sometimes being unwilling to fire at them, thinking that they might be domestic ducks. The tame variety is very prolific, and sits better on its eggs than the common duck. I have seen twenty ducklings brought out at a single hatching. They are very good eating, and a large one has nearly as much flesh upon it as an average-sized goose.

About dusk on these plains, which extended around for several miles, we reached the cattle hacienda of Olama, where was a large tile-roofed house, near a river of the same name. The natives of Nicaragua seldom give distinctive names to their rivers, but call them after the towns or villages on their banks. Thus, at Olama, the river was called the Olama river; higher up, at Matagalpa, the same stream is called the Matagalpa river; and at Jinotego the Jinotego river. The Caribs, however, who live on the rivers, and use them as highways, have names for them all; but to the agricultural Indians and Mestizos of the interior, they are but reservoirs of water, crossed at distant points by their roads, and everywhere amongst them I found the greatest ignorance to prevail as to the connection of the different streams, and of their outflow to the ocean. All the streams about Olama flow eastward, and join together to form the Rio

Grande, that reaches the Atlantic about midway between Blewfields and the river Wanks; it is very incorrectly marked on all the maps of Nicaragua that I have seen.

The Caribs from the lower parts of the river occasionally come up in their canoes to Olama, and bring with them common guns and iron pots that they have obtained from the mahogany cutters at the mouth of the river. These they barter for dogs. I could not ascertain what they wanted with the dogs, but both at this place and at Matagalpa I was told of the great value the Caribs put on them. Although the people of Olama expressed great surprise that the "Caritos," as they call the river Indians, should take so much trouble to obtain dogs, they had not had the curiosity to ask them what they wanted them for. Some people near the river have even commenced to rear dogs, to supply the demand. The Caribs had a special liking for black ones, and did not value those of any other colour so much. They would barter a gun or a large iron pot for a single dog, if it was of the right colour.

The common dogs of Central America are a mongrel breed—not differing, I believe, from those of Europe. There are usually a number of curs about the Indian houses that run out barking at a stranger, but seldom bite.

The hairless dogs, mentioned by Humboldt, as being abundant in Peru,* are not common in Central America, but there are a few to be met with. At Colon I saw several. They are of a shining dark colour, and are quite without hair, excepting a little on the face and on the top of the tail. Both in Peru and Mexico this variety was found by the Spanish conquerors. It would be interesting to have these dogs compared with the hairless dogs of China, which Humboldt says have certainly been extremely common since very early times. Perhaps another link might be added to the broken chain of evidence that connects the peoples of the two countries.

A large naked dog-like animal is figured by Clavigero as one of the indigenous animals of Mexico. It was called *Xoloitzcuintli* by the Mexicans; and Humboldt considers it was distinct from the hairless dog, and was a large dog-like wolf. Its name does not support this view; *Xoloitzcuintli* literally means "a servant dog," from "*Xolotl*," a slave or servant, and *itzcuintli*, a dog; and we find the word *Xolotl* in *Huexlotl*, the Aztec name of the common turkey, which was domesticated by them, and largely used as

---

*"Aspects of Nature," vol. i. p. 109.

food. I am led to believe from this, that *Xolotl* was applied to any animal that lived in the house or was domesticated, and that the *Xoloitzcuintli* was merely a large variety of the hairless dog. Clavigero's description of it would fit the hairless dog of the present day very well, excepting the size; he says, it was four feet long, totally naked, excepting a few stiff hairs on its snout, and ash coloured, spotted with black and tawny.

Tschudi makes two races of indigenous dogs in tropical America. 1. The *Canis caraibicus* (Lesson), without hair, and which does not bark. 2. The *Canis inga* (Tschudi), the common hairy dog, which has pointed nose and ears, and barks.* The small eatable dog of the Mexicans was called by them *Techichi*; and Humboldt derives the name from *Tetl*, a stone, and says that it means "a dumb dog," but this appears rather a forced derivation. *Chichi* is Aztec for "to suck;" and it seems to me more probable that the little dogs they eat, and which are spoken of by the Spaniards as making very tender and delicate food, were the puppies of the *Xoloitzcuintli*, and that *Techichi* meant "a sucker."

Whether the hairless dog was or was not the *Techichi* of which the Mexicans made such savoury dishes is an open question, but there can be no doubt that the former was found in tropical America by the Spanish conquerors, and that it has survived to the present time, with little or no change. That it should not have intermixed with the common haired variety, and lost its distinctive characters, is very remarkable. It has not been artificially preserved, for instead of being looked on with favour by the Indians, Humboldt states that in Peru, where it is abundant, it is despised and ill-treated. Under such circumstances, the variety can only have been preserved through not interbreeding with the common form, either from a dislike to such unions, or by some amount of sterility when they are formed. This is, I think, in favour of the inference that the variety has been produced by natural and not by artificial selection, for diminished fertility is seldom or never acquired between artificial varieties.

Man isolates varieties, and breeds from them, and continuing to separate those that vary in the direction he wishes to follow, a very great difference is, in a comparatively short time, produced. But these artificial varieties, though often more different from each other than some natural species, readily interbreed, and if left to themselves, rapidly revert to a common type. In natural selection there is a great and fundamental difference. The varieties that arise can seldom be separated from the parent

---

*J. J. von Tschudi, quoted by Humboldt, "Aspects of Nature," English edition, vol. i. p. 111.

form and from other varieties, until they vary also in the elements of reproduction. Thousands of varieties probably revert to the parent type, but if at last one is produced that breeds only with its own form, we can easily see how a new species might be segregated. As long as varieties interbreed together and with the parent form, it does not seem possible that a new species could be formed by natural selection, excepting in cases of geographical isolation. All the individuals might vary in some one direction, but they could not split up into distinct species whilst they occupied the same area and interbred without difficulty. Before a variety can become permanent, it must be either separated from the others, or have acquired some disinclination or inability to interbreed with them. As long as they interbreed together, the possible divergence is kept within narrow limits, but whenever a variety is produced, the individuals of which have a partiality for interbreeding, and some amount of sterility when crossed with another form, the tie that bound it to the central stock is loosened, and the foundation is laid for the formation of a new species. Further divergence would be unchecked, or only slightly checked, and the elements of reproduction having begun to vary, would probably continue to diverge from the parent form, for Darwin has shown that any organ in which a species has begun to vary, is liable to further change in the same direction.* Thus one of the best tests of the specific difference of two allied forms living together, is their sterility when crossed, and nearly allied species separated by geographical barriers are more likely to interbreed than those inhabiting the same area. Artificial selection is more rapid in its results, but less stable than that of nature, because the barriers that man raises to prevent intermingling of varieties are temporary and partial, whilst that which nature fixes when sterility arises is permanent and complete.

For these reasons I think that the fact that the hairless dog of tropical America has not interbred with the common form, and regained its hairy coat, is in favour of the inference that the variety has been produced by natural and not by artificial selection. By this I do not mean that it has arisen as a wild variety, for it is probable that its domestication was an important element amongst the causes that led to its formation, but that it has not been produced by man selecting the individuals to breed from that had the least covering of hairs. I cannot agree with some eminent naturalists that the loss of a hairy covering would always be disadvantageous.

---

*See "Animals and Plants under Domestication," vol. ii. p. 241.

My experience in tropical countries has led me to the conclusion that in such parts at least there is one serious drawback to the advantages of having the skin covered with hair. It affords cover for parasitical insects, which, if the skin were naked, might more easily be got rid of.

No one who has not lived and moved about amongst the bush of the tropics can appreciate what a torment the different parasitical species of *acarus* or ticks are. On my first journey in northern Brazil, I had my legs inflamed and ulcerated from the ankles to the knees, from the irritation produced by a minute red tick that is brushed off the low shrubs, and attaches itself to the passer-by. This little insect is called the "Mocoim" by the Brazilians, and is a great torment. It is so minute that except by careful searching it cannot be perceived, and it causes an intolerable itching. If the skin were thickly covered with hair, it would be next to impossible to get rid of it. Through all tropical America, during the dry season, a brown tick (*Ixodes bovis*), varying in size from a pin's head to a pea, is very abundant. In Nicaragua, in April, they are very small, and swarm upon the plains, so that the traveller often gets covered with them. They get up on the tips of the leaves and shoots of low shrubs, and stand with their hind legs stretched out. Each foot has two hooks or claws, and with these it lays hold of any animal brushing past. All large land animals seem subject to their attacks. I have seen them on snakes and iguanas, on many of the large birds, especially on the curassows, and they abound on all the larger mammals, together with some of the small ones. Sick and weak animals are particularly infested with them, probably because they have not the strength to rub and pick them off, and they must often hasten, if they do not cause their death. The herdsmen, or "vacqueros," keep a ball of soft wax at their houses, which they rub over their skin when they come in from the plains, the small "garrapatos" sticking to it, whilst the larger ones are picked off. How the small ones would be got rid of if the skin had a hairy coat I know not, but the torment of the ticks would certainly be greatly increased.

There are other insect parasites, for the increase and protection of which a hairy coating is even more favourable than it is for the ticks. The *Pediculi* are specially adapted to live amongst hair, their limbs being constructed for clinging to it. They deposit their nits or eggs amongst it, fastening them securely to the bases of the hairs. Although the *pediculi* are almost unknown to the middle and upper classes of civilized communities, in consequence of the cleanliness of their persons, clothing, and houses, they abound amongst savage and half-civilized people. A slight immunity from the attacks of *acari* and *pediculi* might in a tropical country more than compensate an animal for the loss of its hairy coat, especially in the case of the domesticated dog, which shelters with its master, has not to seek for its food at night, and is protected by being domiciled with man from the attacks of stronger animals. In the huts of savages dogs are greatly exposed to the attacks of parasitical insects, for vermin generally abound in such localities. Man is the only species amongst the higher primates that lives for months and years, often from generation to generation, on the same spot. Monkeys change their sleeping places almost daily. The ourang-outang, that makes a nest of the boughs of trees, is said to construct a fresh one every night. The dwelling-places of savages, often made of, or lined with, the skins of animals, with the dusty earth for a flour, harbour all kinds of insect vermin, and produce and perpetuate skin disease, due to the attacks of minute *sarcopti*; and if the dog by losing its hair should obtain any protection from these and other insect pests, instead of wondering that a hairless breed of dogs has been produced in a tropical country, I am more surprised that haired ones should abound. That they do so must, I think, be owing to man having preferred the haired breeds for their superior beauty and greater variety, and encouraged their multiplication.

THE FALLS OF NIAGARA

TWO BROTHERS (ANONYMOUS)

This, of all places the great attraction of the Continent of America, is known to everyone, everywhere. Who has not heard of the Falls, who has not read of them? But the question, who has seen them? is one which not a large number on this side of the Atlantic can answer in the affirmative. All those who can spare the time and the money should go and see for themselves, and with the probable benefit derived from the sea voyage, and the many objects of interest to visit in America they would not be dissatisfied with their trip. The idea, that the huge volume of water is continually in motion, that at any time of the day or night that one looks, at all seasons, it is always moving, is very grand. The icy coldness of winter has no power to impede the force of this mighty cataract, but huge icicles are formed in the less turbulent parts, while the great volume of water still continues to pour over the rocks with its deep rumbling noise.

The Falls of Niagara are on a river of the same name, which forms a connecting link between lakes Erie and Ontario, and divides a portion of the State of New York on its western boundary from Canada. Goat Island is an island which divides the river into two portions, thereby causing two cataracts, one of which is known as the American, the other as the Canadian Fall. The Canadian, for volume of water is very superior to the American; it also goes by the name of the Horse Shoe Fall, and is the one which commands the greater amount of attention.

To reach Niagara from New York is a journey of a little more than 400 miles, but which can be easily accomplished by rail in a short space of time. From Quebec also one may easily find one's way to the Falls, either by the

Grand Trunk Railway as far as Toronto, and then by boat across the Lake, or the entire distance may be most pleasantly traversed in one of the excellent steamboats which ply on the St. Lawrence river.

The Falls of Niagara are about fourteen miles from the village of Niagara, which is situated on Lake Ontario, and as the traveller approaches the shore in the steamboat, he may plainly see the spray from the Falls at this distance.

Like all other places of world-wide renown and of public resort the charges made for everything are very high. The hotels are conducted on the American plan of two and a half dollars a day, so that not much increase in expense is found in this item, but the price asked for drives in open carriages and flys is very large, and the immense quantity of turnpikes one has to pass through is almost fabulous, so that in making a bargain the payment of the driver is not the only charge to be taken into account.

As the visitor approaches the Falls, and more particularly the English visitor, strange feelings come over him at the idea of realizing by ocular demonstration the fact which he has heard of and known for so long; he fancies within himself what the first glance will disclose, and conjures up in his mind whether he will be disappointed as many people are at first appearance of the water, some exclaiming "Why, is that all?" But although numbers after travelling long distances are prone to make this remark, there are few who will not retract on a closer acquaintance. It is necessary that the Falls should be seen from various points of view before an opinion is given, and it is often observed that they ought to be visited two or three times before one can sufficiently realize the full grandeur of this mighty torrent, of ninety millions of tons of water pouring over, each consecutive hour.

The Falls may be seen either from the American or the Canadian side; the Americans would very likely say they could be seen to better advantage on their side, and the Canadians would make the same remark with regard to theirs, but there is little doubt that the Canadian is of the two, preferable. On the American side are two first-rate hotels, namely, the International Hotel, and the Cataract House; the Canadian side is represented by the Clifton House, which is in every way also first-rate. The best places from which to view the Falls are from boats on the Niagara River, from Goat Island, or from Table Rock. At Table Rock one has perhaps as fine a view as any. Up to the summer of the present year there has been a little steamer of the name of The Maid of the Mist, from which visitors might obtain a beautiful view, but the proprietors finding they could sell her to advantage, took her through the Whirlpool (a place a little way down the river) at considerable risk (in fact no vessel has been known to do it before), and so this feature has accordingly been done away with.

To go underneath the huge volume of water is a feat which many people think they must do, but to a sensible person the feat is a very poor one. The idea is that the sun can be seen so beautifully reflected through the fall, but when one is dressed from head to foot in waterproof supplied for the occasion, and is conscious of water to the extent of about three or four ordinary shower baths being poured down on to one's head, and into one's eyes, the appreciation of this little adventure is rather speculative than real. As there is supposed to be a little danger, there are plenty of people anxious to do it, and in return they receive if they wish a ticket to certify the same.

The extreme beauty of the Niagara Falls as seen from every point of view is something impossible to imagine until the realization is placed before one's eyes, and the magnitude of the stupendous cataract is one which only becomes fully known on close acquaintance. But Niagara has never been in a want of praises, and those who extol her, number legion. The wonders of the place and the novelty of the scene, are well calculated to inspire one with new feelings, and to increase the number of enthusiastic admirers of this wonderful revelation of nature. This mighty effort of nature has been visited by celebrities from all parts of the globe, the most recent being the Prince of Wales, Prince Alfred, Prince Napoleon, and the inimitable Blondin. On the occasion of the visit of the Prince of Wales, the Falls were illuminated, an experiment never before tried; it is said that it answered beyond expectation. It was across the Niagara river that Blondin placed his rope, and it was here that this extraordinary man came into such notoriety. The height of the American Fall is 166 feet, and the Canadian 160 feet, thus it may well be imagined that had he fallen he would have suffered for his temerity. Occasionally such accidents have occurred as that of men being carried over the cataract, and on such occasions they have never been saved from destruction. Almost immediately after the water has descended, comparative stillness seems to supervene, but this is only on the surface, there being a very powerful under current, so that had Blondin fallen , the probability is that he would have been carried away by this. Three miles down the river is the Whirlpool, and beyond that, the water being more quiet, any vestiges of those who have been precipitated over have sometimes been found.

A mile and a half below the Falls is a beautiful Suspension Bridge which is well known to engineers, its proportions being very elegant. It connects American soil with Canadian, and is constantly traversed by railway trains. Although in England people have heard so much of the Falls of Niagara, and have such a desire to see them, it is a curious fact that there are many persons living within a very few miles who have never visited them; this is remarkable when one thinks of the wonder of the sight, but it is only another example, certainly a very remarkable one, that those who are in the vicinity of anything very wonderful do not sufficiently appreciate its beauties.

At a distance of two miles from the Clifton House Hotel is the Burning Spring, so called from the presence of a large quantity of gas which ignites on the application of a light. The water is very unpleasant to the taste, but many people drink it on account of its medicinal qualities. Above the spring is fixed a large pipe through which the gas ascends and the flame burns to a great height. The fee for exhibition is a few cents, and this being one of the sights in the locality, like everything else, must be "done."

In 1814, when Great Britain was at war with the United States, this part of the country was the theatre of a great deal of fighting, and the Canadians have many treasured traditions of daring exploits in defence of their soil. At Queenstown, a few miles from the Falls, a battle was fought, in which the British were victors, but at the cost of the death of the general commanding, Isaac Brock. A monument has been erected on the spot in his memory, but it was left for posterity to do that which was the duty of contemporaries.

FAUNA AND FLORA
OF NEVADA

MARK TWAIN

About an hour and a half before daylight we were bowling along smoothly over the road—so smoothly that our cradle only rocked in a gentle, lulling way, that was gradually soothing us to sleep and dulling our consciousness—when something gave away under us! We were dimly aware of it, but indifferent to it. The coach stopped. We heard the driver and conductor talking together outside, and rummaging for a lantern, and swearing because they could not find it; but we had no interest in whatever had happened, and it only added to our comfort to think of those people out there at work in the murky night, and we snug in our nest with the curtains drawn. But presently, by the sounds, there seemed to be an examination going on, and then the driver's voice said:

"By George, the thoroughbrace is broke!"

This startled me broad awake—as an undefined sense of calamity is always apt to do. I said to myself: "Now, a thoroughbrace is probably part of a horse, and doubtless a vital part, too, from the dismay in the driver's voice. Leg, maybe—and yet how could he break his leg waltzing along such a road as this? No it can't be his leg. This is impossible, unless he was reaching for the driver. Now, what can be the thoroughbrace of a horse, I wonder? Well, whatever comes, I shall not air my ignorance in this crowd, anyway."

Just then the conductor's face appeared at a lifted curtain, and his lantern glared in on us and our wall of mail matter. He said:

"Gents, you'll have to turn out a spell. Thoroughbrace is broke."

We climbed out into a chill drizzle, and felt ever so homeless and dreary. When I found that the thing they called a "thoroughbrace" was the massive combination of belts and springs which the coach rocks itself in, I said to the driver, "I never saw a thoroughbrace used up like that before, that I can remember. How did it happen?"

"Why, it happened by trying to make one coach carry three days' mail—that's how it happened," said he. "And right here is the very direction which is wrote on all the newspaper-bags which was to be put out for the Injuns for to keep 'em quiet. It's most uncommon lucky, becuz it's so nation dark I should 'a' gone by unbeknowns if that air thoroughbrace hadn't broke."

I knew that he was in labour with another of those winks of his, though I could not see his face, because he was bent down at work; and wishing him a safe delivery, I turned to and helped the rest get out the mail-sacks. It made a great pyramid by the roadside when it was all out. When they had mended the thoroughbrace we filled the two boots again, but put no mail on top, and only half as much inside as there was before. The conductor bent all the seat-backs down, and then filled the coach just half full of mail-bags from end to end. We objected loudly to this, for it left us no seats. But the conductor was wiser than we, and said a bed was better than seats, and, moreover, this plan would protect his thoroughbraces. We never wanted any seats after that; the lazy bed was infinitely preferable. I had many an exciting day, subsequently, lying on it reading the statutes and the dictionary, and wondering how the characters would turn out.

The conductor said he would send back a guard from the next station to take charge of the abandoned mail-bags, and we drove on.

It was now just dawn; and as we stretched our cramped legs full length on the mail-sacks, and gazed out through the windows across the wide wastes of greensward clad in cool powdery mists, to where there was an expectant look in the eastern horizon, our perfect enjoyment took the form of a tranquil and contented ecstasy. The stage whirled along at a spanking gait, the breeze flapping curtains and suspended coats in a most exhilarating way; the cradle swayed and swung luxuriously, the pattering of the horses' hoofs, the cracking of the driver's whip, and his "Hi-yi! g'lang!" were music; the spinning ground and the waltzing trees appeared to give us a mute hurrah as we went by, and then slack up and look after us with interest, or envy, or something; and as we lay and smoked the pipe of peace and compared all this luxury with the years of tiresome city life that had gone before it, we felt that there was only one complete and satisfying happiness in the world, and we had found it.

After breakfast, at some station whose name I have forgotten, we three climbed up on the seat behind the driver, and let the conductor have our bed for a nap. And by-and-bye, when the sun made me drowsy, I lay down on my face on top of the coach, grasping the slender iron railing, and slept for an hour or more. That will give one an appreciable idea of those matchless roads. Instinct will make a sleeping man grip a fast hold of the railing when the stage jolts, but when it only swings and sways, no grip is necessary. Overland drivers and conductors used to sit in their places and sleep thirty or forty minutes at a time, on good roads, while spinning along at the rate of eight or ten miles an hour. I saw them do it, often. There was no danger about it: a sleeping man *will* seize the irons in time when the coach jolts. These men were hard worked, and it was not possible for them to stay awake all the time.

By-and-bye we passed through Marysville, and over the Big Blue and Little Sandy; thence about a mile, and entered Nebraska. About a mile farther on, we came to the Big Sandy—one hundred and eighty miles from St. Joseph.

As the sun was going down, we saw the first specimen of an animal known familiarly over two thousand miles of mountain and desert—from Kansas clear to the Pacific Ocean—as the "jackass rabbit." He is well named. He is just like any other rabbit, except that he is from one-third to twice as large, has longer legs in proportion to his size, and has the most preposterous ears that ever were mounted on any creature *but* a jackass. When he is sitting quiet, thinking about his sins, or is absent-minded or unapprehensive of danger, his majestic ears project above him conspicuously; but the breaking of a twig will scare him nearly to death, and then he tilts his ears back gently and starts for home. All you can see, then, for the next minute, is his long grey form stretched out straight, and "streaking it" through the low sage-brush, head erect, eyes right, and ears just canted a little to the rear, but showing you where the animal is all the time, the same as if he carried a jib. Now and then he makes a marvelous spring with his long legs, high over the stunted sage-brush, and scores a leap that would make a horse envious. Presently he comes down to a long graceful "lope," and shortly he mysteriously disappears. He has crouched behind a sage-bush, and will sit there and listen and tremble until you get within six feet of him, when he will get under way again. But one must shoot at this creature once, if he wishes to see him throw his heart into his heels, and do the best he knows how. He is frightened clear through now, and he lays his long ears down on his back, straightens himself out like a yard-stick every spring he makes, and scatters miles behind him with an easy indifference that is enchanting.

Our party made this specimen "hump himself," as the conductor said. The Secretary started him with a shot from the Colt; I commenced spitting at him with my weapon; and all in the same instant the old "Allen's" whole broadside let go with a rattling crash, and it is not putting it too strong to say that the rabbit was frantic. He dropped his ears, set up his tail, and left for San Francisco at a speed which can only be described as a flash and a vanish! Long after he was out of sight we could hear him whiz.

I do not remember where we first came across "sage-brush," but as I have been speaking of it I may as well describe it. This is easily done, for if the reader can imagine a gnarled and venerable live oak-tree reduced to a little shrub two feet high, with its rough bark, its foliage, its twisted boughs, all complete, he can picture the "sage-brush" exactly. Often, on lazy afternoons in the mountains, I have lain on the ground with my face under a sage-bush, and entertained myself with fancying that the gnats among its foliage were Liliputian birds, and that the ants marching and countermarching about its base were Liliputian flocks and herds, and myself some vast loafer from Brobdingnag waiting to catch a little citizen and eat him.

It is an imposing monarch of the forest in exquisite miniature, is the "sage-brush." Its foliage is a greyish green, and gives that tint to desert and mountain. It smells like our domestic sage, and "sage-tea" made from it tastes like the sage-tea which all boys are so well acquainted with. The sage-brush is a singularly hardy plant, and grows right in the midst of deep sand, and among barren rocks, where nothing else in the vegetable world would try to grow, except "bunch-grass."* The sage-bushes grow from three to six or seven feet apart, all over the mountains and deserts of the Far West, clear to the borders of California. There is not a tree of any kind in the deserts, for hundreds of miles—there is no vegetation at all in a regular desert, except the sage-brush and its cousin the "greasewood," which is so much like the sage-brush that the difference amounts to little.

---

*"Bunch-grass" grows on the bleak mountain-sides of Nevada and neighbouring terri-tories, and offers excellent feed for stock, even in the dead of winter, wherever the snow is blown aside and exposes it; notwithstanding its unpromising home, bunch-grass is a better and more nutritious diet for cattle and horses than almost any other hay or grass that is known—so stock-men say.

Camp-fires and hot suppers in the deserts would be impossible but for the friendly sage-brush. Its trunk is as large as a boy's wrist (and from that up to a man's arm), and its crooked branches are half as large as its trunk—all good, sound, hard wood, very like oak.

When a party camps, the first thing to be done is to cut sage-brush, and in a few minutes there is an opulent pile of it ready for use. A hole a foot wide, two feet deep, and two feet long, is dug, and sage-brush chopped up and burned in it till it is full to the brim with glowing coals. Then the cooking begins, and there is no smoke, and consequently no swearing. Such a fire will keep all night, with very little replenishing; and it makes a very sociable camp-fire, and one around which the most impossible reminiscences sound plausible, instructive, and profoundly entertaining.

Sage-brush is very fair fuel, but as a vegetable it is a distinguished failure. Nothing can abide the taste of it but the jackass and his illegitimate child, the mule. But their testimony to its nutritiousness is worth nothing, for they will eat pine-knots, or anthracite coal, or brass fillings, or lead pipe, or old bottles, or anything that comes handy, and then go off looking as grateful as if they had had oysters for dinner. Mules and donkeys and camels have appetites that anything will relieve temporarily, but nothing satisfy. In Syria, once, at the head-waters of the Jordan, a camel took charge of my overcoat while the tents were being pitched, and examined it with a critical eye, all over, with as much interest as if he had an idea of getting one made like it; and then, after he was done figuring on it as an article of apparel, he began to contemplate it as an article of diet. He put his foot on it, and lifted one of the sleeves out with his teeth, and chewed and chewed at it, gradually taking it in, and all the while opening and closing his eyes in a kind of religious ecstasy, as if he had never tasted anything as good as an overcoat before in his life. Then he smacked his lips once or twice, and reached after the other sleeve. Next he tried the velvet collar, and smiled a smile of such contentment that it was plain to see that he regarded that as the daintiest thing about an overcoat. The tails went next, along with some percussion-caps and cough candy, and some fig-paste from Constantinople. And then my newspaper correspondence dropped out, and he took a chance in that—manuscript letters written for the home papers. But he was treading on dangerous ground now. He began to come across solid wisdom in those documents that was rather weighty on his stomach; and occasionally he would take a joke that would shake him up till it loosened his teeth: it was getting to be perilous times with him, but he held his grip with good courage and hopefully, till at last he began to stumble on statements that not even a camel could swallow with impunity. He began to gag and gasp, and his eyes to stand out, and his forelegs to spread, and in about a quarter of a minute he fell over as stiff as a carpenter's workbench, and died a death of indescribable agony. I went and pulled the manuscript out of his mouth, and found that the sensitive creature had choked to death on one of the mildest and gentlest statements of fact that I ever laid before a trusting public.

I was about to say, when diverted from my subject, that occasionally one finds sage-bushes five or six feet high, and with a spread of branch and foliage in proportion, but two or two and a half feet is the usual height.

Shooting the Rapids
in a Batteau

Henry David Thoreau

It was with regret that we turned our backs on Chesuncook, which Mc-Causlin had formerly logged on, and the Allegash lakes. There were still longer rapids and portages above; among the last the Ripogenus Portage, which he described as the most difficult on the river, and three miles long. The whole length of the Penobscot is two hundred and seventy-five miles, and we are still nearly one hundred miles from its source. Hodge, the assistant State Geologist, passed up this river in 1837, and by a portage of only one mile and three quarters crossed over into the Allegash, and so went down that into the St. John, and up the Madawaska to the Grand Portage across to the St. Lawrence. His is the only account that I know of an expedition through to Canada in this direction.

He thus describes his first sight of the latter river, which, to compare small things with great, is like Balboa's first sight of the Pacific from the mountains of the Isthmus of Darien. "When we first came in sight of the St. Lawrence," he says, "from the top of a high hill, the view was most striking, and much more interesting to me from having been shut up in the woods for the two previous months. Directly before us lay the broad river, extending across nine or ten miles, its surface broken by a few islands and reefs, and two ships riding at anchor near the shore. Beyond, extended ranges of uncultivated hills, parallel with the river. The sun was just going down behind them, and gilding the whole scene with its parting rays."

About four o'clock, the same afternoon, we commenced our return voyage, which would require but little if any poling. In shooting rapids the boatmen use large and broad paddles, instead of poles, to guide the boat with. Though we glided so swiftly, and often smoothly, down, where it had cost us no slight effort to get up, our present voyage was attended with far more danger; for if we once fairly struck one of the thousand rocks by which we were surrounded the boat would be swamped in an instant. When a boat is swamped under these circumstances, the boatmen commonly find no difficulty in keeping afloat at first, for the current keeps both them and their cargo up for a long way down the stream; and if they can swim, they have only to work their way gradually to the shore.

The greatest danger is of being caught in an eddy behind some larger rock, where the water rushes up stream faster than elsewhere it does down, and being carried round and round under the surface till they are drowned. McCauslin pointed out some rocks which had been the scene of a fatal accident of this kind. Sometimes the body is not thrown out for several hours. He himself had performed such a circuit once, only his legs being visible to his companions; but he was fortunately thrown out in season to recover his breath.*

In shooting the rapids, the boatman had this problem to solve: to choose a circuitous and safe course amid a thousand sunken rocks, scattered over a quarter or half a mile, at the same time that he is moving steadily on at the rate of fifteen miles an hour. Stop he cannot; the only question is, where will he go? The bowman chooses the course with all his eyes about him, striking broad off with his paddle, and drawing the boat by main force into her course. The sternman faithfully follows the bow.

We were soon at the Aboljacarmegus Falls. Anxious to avoid the delay, as well as the labor, of the portage here, our boatmen went forward first to reconnoitre, and concluded to let the batteau down the falls, carrying the baggage only over the portage. Jumping from rock to rock until nearly in the middle of the stream, we were ready to receive the boat and let her down over the first fall, some six or seven feet perpendicular. The boatmen stand upon the edge of a shelf of rock, where the fall is perhaps nine or ten feet perpendicular, in from one to two feet of rapid water, one on each

---

*I cut this from a newspaper. "On the 11th (instant?) [May, '49], on Rappogenes Falls, Mr. John Delantee, of Orono, Me., was drowned while running logs. He was a citizen of Orono, and was twenty-six years of age. His companions found his body, enclosed it in bark, and buried it in the solemn woods." [Thoreau]

Thoreau's guide in 1853, Joe Aitteon, was later drowned on a West Branch drive. In keeping with the tradition on the Penobscot, his mates identified the place where he was last seen alive on the river. There they hung his caulked boots from a branch of a tall pine.

side of the boat, and let it slide gently over, till the bow is run out ten or twelve feet in the air; then, letting it drop squarely, while one holds the painter, the other leaps in, and his companion following, they are whirled down the rapids to a new fall, or to smooth water.

In a very few minutes they had accomplished a passage in safety, which would be as foolhardy for the unskillful to attempt as the descent of Niagara itself. It seemed as if it needed only a little familiarity, and a little more skill, to navigate down such falls as Niagara itself with safety. At any rate, I should not despair of such men in the rapids above Table-Rock, until I saw them actually go over the falls, so cool, so collected, so fertile in resources are they. One might have thought that these were falls, and that falls were not to be waded through with impunity, like a mud-puddle. There was really danger of their losing their sublimity in losing their power to harm us. Familiarity breeds contempt. The boatman pauses, perchance, on some shelf beneath a table-rock under the fall, standing in some cove of backwater two feet deep, and you hear his rough voice come up through the spray, coolly giving directions how to launch the boat this time.

Having carried round Pockwockomus Falls, our oars soon brought us to the Katepskonegan, or Oak Hall carry, where we decided to camp half-way over, leaving our batteau to be carried over in the morning on fresh shoulders. One shoulder of each of the boatmen showed a red spot as large as one's hand, worn by the batteau on this expedition; and this shoulder, as it did all the work, was perceptibly lower than its fellow, from long service. Such toil soon wears out the strongest constitution. The drivers are accustomed to work in the cold water in the spring, rarely ever dry; and if one falls in all over he rarely changes his clothes till night, if then, even. One who takes this precaution is called by a particular nickname, or is turned off. None can lead this life who are not almost amphibious.

McCauslin said soberly, what is at any rate a good story to tell, that he had seen where six men were wholly under water at once, at a jam, with their shoulders to handspikes. If the log did not start, then they had to put out their heads to breathe. The driver works as long as he can see, from dark to dark, and at night has not time to eat his supper and dry his clothes fairly, before he is asleep on his cedar bed. We lay that night on the very bed made by such a party, stretching our tent over the poles which were still standing, but reshingling the damp and faded bed with fresh leaves.

❋   ❋   ❋

In the morning we carried our boat over and launched it, making haste lest the wind should rise. The boatmen ran down Passamagamet, and soon after Ambejijis Falls, while we walked round with the baggage. We made a hasty breakfast at the head of Ambejijis Lake on the remainder of our pork, and were soon rowing across its smooth surface again, under a pleasant sky, the mountains being now clear of clouds in the northeast. Taking turns at the oars, we shot rapidly across Deep Cove, the foot of Pamadumcook, and the North Twin, at the rate of six miles an hour, the wind not being high enough to disturb us, and reached the Dam at noon. The boatmen went through one of the log sluices in the batteau, where the fall was ten feet at the bottom, and took us in below.

Here was the longest rapid in our voyage, and perhaps the running this was as dangerous and arduous a task as any. Shooting down sometimes at the rate, as we judged, of fifteen miles an hour, if we struck a rock we were split from end to end in an instant. Now like a bait bobbing for some river monster, amid the eddies, now darting to this side of the stream now to that, gliding swift and smooth near to our destruction, or striking broad off with the paddle and drawing the boat to right or left with all our might, in order to avoid a rock. I suppose that it was like running the rapids of the Sault Sainte Marie, at the outlet of Lake Superior, and our boatmen probably displayed no less dexterity than the Indians there do. We soon ran through this mile, and floated in Quakish Lake.

After such a voyage, the troubled and angry waters, which once had seemed terrible and not to be trifled with, appeared tamed and subdued; they had been bearded and worried in their channels, pricked and whipped into submission with the spike-pole and paddle, gone through and through with impunity, and all their spirit and their danger taken out of them, and the most swollen and impetuous rivers seemed but playthings henceforth. I began, at length, to understand the boatman's familiarity with, and contempt for, the rapids.

"Those Fowler boys," said Mrs. McCauslin, "are perfect ducks for the water." They had run down to Lincoln, according to her, thirty or forty miles, in a batteau, in the night, for a doctor, when it was so dark that they could not see a rod before them, and the river was swollen so as to be almost a continuous rapid, so that the doctor *cried*, when they brought him up at daylight, "Why, Tom, how did you see to steer?" "We didn't steer much,—only kept her straight." And yet they met with no accident. It is true, the more difficult rapids are higher up than this.

When we reached the Millinocket opposite to Tom's house, and were waiting for his folks to set us over, for we had left our batteau above the

Grand Falls, we discovered two canoes, with two men in each, turning up this stream from Shad Pond, one keeping the opposite side of a small island before us, while the other approached the side where we were standing, examining the banks carefully for muskrats as they came along. The last proved to be Louis Neptune and his companion, now, at last, on their way up to Chesuncook after moose; but they were so disguised that we hardly knew them. At a little distance they might have been taken for Quakers, with their broad-brimmed hats and overcoats with broad capes, the spoils of Bangor, seeking a settlement in this Sylvania,—or, nearer at hand, for fashionable gentlemen the morning after a spree.

Met face to face, these Indians in their native woods looked like the sinister and slouching fellows whom you meet picking up strings and paper in the streets of a city. There is, in fact, a remarkable and unexpected resemblance between the degraded savage and the lowest classes in a great city. The one is no more a child of nature than the other. In the progress of degradation the distinction of races is soon lost. Neptune at first was only anxious to know what we "kill," seeing some partridges in the hands of one of the party, but we had assumed too much anger to permit of a reply. We thought Indians had some honor before. But—"Me been sick. Oh, me unwell now. You make bargain, then me go." They had in fact been delayed so long by a drunken frolic at the Five Islands, and they had not yet recovered from its effects. They had some young mus-quash in their canoes, which they dug out of the banks with a hoe, for food, not for their skins, for musquash are their principal food on these expeditions. So they went on up the Millinocket, and we kept down the bank of the Penobscot, after recruiting ourselves with a draught of Tom's beer, leaving Tom at his home.*

Thus a man shall lead his life away here on the edge of the wilderness, on Indian Millinocket stream, in a new world, far in the dark of a continent, and have a flute to play at evening here, while his strains echo to the stars, amid the howling of wolves; shall live, as it were, in the primitive

---

*As Thoreau predicted, "the tide of fashionable travel" has finally "set that way" and the settlements have encroached on the Maine woods. Just above "old Fowler's" carry from Millinocket Stream to Quakish Lake, is the paper mill town of Millinocket. Above there the Bangor and Aroostook Railroad cuts from the village of Norcross on North Twin Lake across to the settlement of Grindstone on the East Branch, at the mouth of which is the small town of Medway. From there a road follows the course of the West Branch through East Millinocket and Dolby—where "Uncle George" McCauslin's setter camp at the mouth of the Little Schoodic River has been flowed out—then through Millinocket, on past the foot of Ktaadn, ultimately reaching Greenville by way of Ripogenus Dam at the foot of Chesuncook Lake.

age of the world, a primitive man. Yet he shall spend a sunny day, and in
this century be my contemporary; perchance he shall read some scattered
leaves of literature, and sometimes talk with me. Why read history, then, if
the ages and the generations are now? He lives three thousand years deep
into time, an age not yet described by poets. Can you well go further back
in history than this? Ay! ay!—for there turns up but now into the mouth of
Millinocket stream a still more ancient and primitive man, whose history is
not brought down even to the former.

In a bark vessel sewn with the roots of the spruce, with horn-beam
paddles, he dips his way along. He is but dim and misty to me, obscured
by the aeons that lie between the bark canoe and the batteau. He builds no
house of logs, but a wigwam of skins. He eats no hot bread and sweet cake,
but musquash and moose meat and the fat of bears. He glides up the
Millinocket and is lost to my sight, as a more distant and misty cloud is
seen flitting by behind a nearer, and is lost in space. So he goes about his
destiny, the red face of man.

After having passed the night, and buttered our boots for the last time,
at Uncle George's, whose dogs almost devoured him for joy at his return,
we kept on down the river the next day, about eight miles on foot, and then
took a batteau, with a man to pole it, to Mattawamkeag, ten more. At the
middle of that very night, to make a swift conclusion to a long story, we
dropped our buggy over the half-finished bridge at Oldtown, where we
heard the confused din and clink of a hundred saws, which never rest, and
at six o'clock the next morning one of the party was steaming his way to
Massachusetts.

What is most striking in the Maine wilderness is the continuousness
of the forest, with fewer open intervals or glades than you had imagined.
Except the few burnt lands, the narrow intervals on the rivers, the bare
tops of the high mountains, and the lakes and streams, the forest is uninterrupted. It is even more grim and wild than you had anticipated, a damp
and intricate wilderness, in the spring everywhere wet and miry. The
aspect of the country, indeed, is universally stern and savage, excepting
the distant views of the forest from hills, and the lake prospects, which are
mild and civilizing in a degree.

The lakes are something which you are unprepared for; they lie up so
high, exposed to the light, and the forest is diminished to a fine fringe on
their edges, with here and there a blue mountain, like amethyst jewels set
around some jewel of the first water,—so anterior, so superior, to all the
changes that are to take place on their shores, even now civil and refined,

and fair as they can ever be. These are not the artificial forests of an English king,—a royal preserve merely. Here prevail no forest laws but those of nature. The aborigines have never been dispossessed, nor nature disforested.

It is a country full of evergreen trees, of mossy silver birches and watery maples, the ground dotted with insipid, small, red berries, and strewn with damp and moss-grown rocks,—a country diversified with innumerable lakes and rapid streams, peopled with trout and various species of *leucisci*, with salmon, shad, and pickerel, and other fishes; the forest resounding at rare intervals with the note of the chickadee, the blue-jay, and the woodpecker, the scream of the fish-hawk and the eagle, the laugh of the loon, and the whistle of ducks along the solitary streams; at night, with the hooting of owls and howling of wolves; in summer, swarming with myriads of black flies and mosquitoes, more formidable than wolves to the white man.

Such is the home of the moose, the bear, the caribou, the wolf, the beaver, and the Indian. Who shall describe the inexpressible tenderness and immortal life of the grim forest, where Nature, though it be midwinter, is ever in her spring, where the moss-grown and decaying trees are not odd, but seem to enjoy a perpetual youth; and blissful, innocent Nature, like a serene infant, is too happy to make a noise, except by a few tinkling, lisping birds and trickling rills?

What a place to live, what a place to die and be buried in! There certainly men would live forever, and laugh at death and the grave. There they could have no such thoughts as are associated with the village graveyard,—that make a grave out of one of those moist evergreen hummocks!

> Die and be buried who will,
> I mean to live here still;
> My nature grows ever more young
> The primitive pines among.

I am reminded by my journey how exceedingly new this country still is. You have only to travel for a few days into the interior and back parts even of many of the old States, to come to that very America which the Northmen, and Cabot, and Gosnold, and Smith, and Raleigh visited. If Columbus was the first to discover the islands, Americus Vespucius and Cabot, and the Puritans, and we their descendants, have discovered only the shores of America. While the republic has already acquired a history world-wide, America is still unsettled and unexplored. Like the English in New Holland, we live only on the shores of a continent even yet, and hardly know where the rivers come from which float our navy. The very timber and boards and shingles of which our houses are made grew but yesterday in a wilderness where the Indian still hunts and the moose runs wild. New York has her wilderness within her own borders; and though the sailors of Europe are familiar with the soundings of her Hudson, and Fulton long since invented the steamboat on its waters, an Indian is still necessary to guide her scientific men to its headwaters in the Adirondack country.

Have we even so much as discovered and settled the shores? Let a man travel on foot along the coast, from the Passamaquoddy to the Sabine, or to the Rio Bravo, or to wherever the end is now, if he is swift enough to overtake it, faithfully following the windings of every inlet and of every cape, and stepping to the music of the surf,—with a desolate fishing-town once a week, and a city's port once a month to cheer him, and putting up at the light-houses, when there are any,—and tell me if it looks like a discovered and settled country, and not rather, for the most part, like a desolate island, and No-Man's Land.

We have advanced by leaps to the Pacific, and left many a lesser Oregon and California unexplored behind us. Though the railroad and the telegraph have been established on the shores of Maine, the Indian still looks out from her interior mountains over all these to the sea. There stands the city of Bangor, fifty miles up the Penobscot, at the head of navigation for vessels of the largest class, the principal lumber depot on this continent, with a population of twelve thousand, like a star on the edge of night, still hewing at the forests of which it is built, already overflowing with the luxuries and refinement of Europe, and sending its vessels to Spain, to England, and to the West Indies for its groceries,—and yet only a few axemen have gone "up river," into the howling wilderness which feeds it.

The bear and deer are still found within its limits; and the moose, as he swims the Penobscot, is entangled amid its shipping, and taken by foreign sailors in its harbor. Twelve miles in the rear, twelve miles of railroad, are Orono and the Indian Island, the home of the Penobscot tribe, and then commence the batteau and the canoe, and the military road; and sixty miles above, the country is virtually unmapped and unexplored, and there still waves the virgin forest of the New World.

HEAVENLY PLACE

PRISCILLA WAKEFIELD

MY DEAR BROTHER,

You must partake of the pleasures and difficulties of our journey, through the almost uncultivated parts of the country on the shores of St. John's river. We have penetrated as far as St. Juan's, and wandered into the interior parts, whenever curiosity or inclination pointed the way. If we have seen neither stately palaces, nor populous cities, nor other works of men; we have beheld with admiration the works of God, displayed in the wild majestic scenery of the sublime forests, that have stood uninterrupted for ages, and have afforded shelter to innumerable tribes of animals of all kinds; quadrupeds, birds, insects, and reptiles, whose different forms, habits, and peculiarities in seeking their prey, avoiding their enemies, and rearing their young, afford a continual fund of amusement, that raises new wonder by their variety, and the ingenuity of their contrivances to obtain their ends, which has been implanted in them by their wise Creator.

Never have my thoughts been more devoutly raised to Heaven, than in some of our rambles through these magnificent forests; especially of an evening, when we have prepared our bed of dried leaves, under the canopy of a branching oak, or a lofty pine; the moon's silver rays casting a modest light through the trees, and the whip-poor-will lulling us with his melancholy note to sleep; assisted by the lowing of distant herds of cattle, or the shrill whooping of the crane. Of a morning we have been awakened by the beams of the new-risen sun, and the cheerful crowing of the wild turkey-cocks, calling to each other from the tops of the highest trees. In spring they begin at break of day, and crow till sun-rise, saluting their fellows on the return of light. I cannot give you an idea of what I felt at the first view of these forests, composed of such a variety of trees, superior in beauty and grandeur to any I had ever beheld before; but I will try to give a faint description of a few of the most striking.

The laurel magnolia reaches to the height of an hundred feet: the trunk is perfectly upright, rising in the form of a stately column; the milk-white flowers, resembling full-blown roses, are surrounded by a circle of dark-green shining leaves, that set them off to great advantage; in the centre stands the young cone, which is of a flesh-colour, and towards autumn grows very large and changes to a crimson, and as it opens, shows multitudes of coral-red berries, which hang from the cones by a white silky thread. The wood of this tree, when seasoned, is of a straw colour, and harder than that of the poplar.

The palmetto royal, or Adam's needle, is a singular tree: they grow so thick together, that a bird can scarcely penetrate between them. The stiff leaves of the sword-plant, standing straight out from the trunk, form a barrier that neither man nor beast can pass: it rises with an erect stem, about ten or twelve feet high, crowned with a chaplet of dagger-like green leaves, with a stiff sharp spur at the end: this thorny crown is tipped with a pyramid of white flowers, shaped like a tulip or a lily. To these flowers succeed a large fruit, much like a cucumber in form, but when ripe, of a deep purple colour. Garlands and festoons of creeping shrubs hang upon the branches of the forest trees, and seem to bind them together. Amongst others, grape-vines of uncommon size, climb round the trunks, and twine to the very top, but the fruit is small and ill-tasted.

The long moss fixes itself, and takes root on the arms of the trees; and hangs pendant, like long streamers of many feet in length, waving in that wind in a fantastical manner. In order to prepare it for use, it is thrown into shallow water and exposed to the sun, where it soon rots, and the furry outside is dissolved; when taken out, beaten, and cleaned, nothing re-mains but the inside fibres, which are black and like horse-hair, and are equally proper for stuffing mattresses, chair-bottoms, saddles, etc. The Spaniards in South America, we are told, work them into cables. Cattle and deer are glad, in the winter season, to feed upon this moss, whilst it is fresh.

One species of the cypress, from its prodigious height and size, strikes the beholder with awe: it generally grows in the water, or on low, moist situations, near the banks of great rivers and lakes, that are covered several months in the year with water. The lower part of the trunk spreads out into many divisions, like buttresses, that seem designed to support the vast body of the tree, and form large, strong, serpentine roots, that strike off in every direction. The main trunk rises from these, like a straight pillar, to a prodigious height, and then divides into a wide, spreading top, like a canopy, where eagles securely fix their nests: cranes, storks, and paroquets, venture to approach the royal bird, and often perch on these inaccessible branches. The paroquets are allured by the seeds, which are their favourite repast. The trunk of this tree, hollowed out, forms an excellent canoe, and is frequently used for that purpose. Many trees, shrubs, and plants, of a more diminutive size, deserve a stranger's admiration. One species of hibiscus is extremely elegant: it is a very tall shrub, growing like a pyramid, adorned with large, expanded, crimson flowers. Besides these, and hundreds more, equally remarkable for their beauty, the shrubs are overrun by a pale pink convolvolus, with a deep crimson eye, which forms a delicate contrast with its dark green leaves.

In this excursion we have sometimes taken up our abode for the night near the banks of a river, or on the borders of a lake, where I have often amused myself in watching the pelicans catch fish. Sancho, who is a good marksman, shot one of them; it is larger than a tame goose, with very short legs and webbed feet: its bill is of a great length, and bent like a scythe; but the large pouch beneath it is the most extraordinary part of the bird, and seems calculated to carry water, or hide the prey that it has caught. The colour is much like that of a gull. Sancho's gun has generally procured us a good supper: we were sure of either curlews, willets, snipes, sand-birds, or some kind of water-fowl; to which we frequently added oysters, that were to be found in abundance in the water close to the shores. Mr. Franklin and I performed the office of cooks: we kindled a fire, by rubbing two pieces of dry wood together, and then contrived to roast our fowl with a spit of Sancho's making. Our concert at going to rest was not so harmonious as in the woods, where the birds chaunted our lullaby. The buzzing of mosquitoes, (a huge species of gnat,) the noise and restlessness of sea-fowl, thousands of toons, herons, pelicans, curlews, and others roosting around us, but above all the roaring of crocodiles, for a long time prevented me from closing an eye, till, worn out by the exercise of the day, I lost myself in spite of their discordant cries. One evening I had strayed from my companions to a promontory covered with orange-trees, taking with me my fishing-tackle, intending to catch some fish for our supper. The sky, richly illuminated with the tints of the setting sun, and the shores and islets embellished with flowering shrubs and plants, presented a charming scene: multitudes of water-fowl were seeking their food, before they retired to rest; amongst others, I remarked the coots, with half-spread wings, tripping over the little coves, and hiding themselves in the tufts of long grass: young broods of the summer teal skimmed the still surface of the water, following the old ones, unconscious of danger, till overtaken by the greedy trout, who, in his turn, became the prey of the subtle alligator. In a shallow part, flowing over a bed of gravel, beneath the rock where I had chosen my seat, rose a number of little pyramidal hills, formed of gravel-stones, by a species of small cray-fish, as a secure place of refuge for their young, from the attacks of their natural enemy, the goldfish. Small companies of the boldest of the old cray-fish ventured out, and defied the gold fish, who continually returned to the charge. The sight of this battle was new, and interested my attention so much, that I never perceived a huge alligator, that lay concealed under the edge of the projecting rock on which I sat: he was at least eighteen feet long, and covered with an impenetrable coat of mail. In one dreadful moment he darted out of the water, opened his terrific jaw, and spouted both wind and water out of his nostrils. Resistance was vain: flight was my only refuge. His unwieldy size made it difficult for him to climb over the edge of the promontory, which gave me an instant to take to my heels, and endeavour to ascend a tree. I had not reached the first branches, when an Indian hearing my cries, rushed out of the thickets, and, with heroic courage, came to my deliverance. Happily, he was armed with a club as well as a tomahawk. Being prepared for the attack, and extremely active, he struck the alligator a violent blow across the head with a club, which stunned him a little: before he could recover himself, a second stroke fell with still greater violence, and deprived him of the power of moving his jaw. He attempted to get away, but my Indian friend was too nimble for him, and dispatched him with his tomahawk.

I descended the tree, and expressed my gratitude, as well as I could, by signs: by this time, the rest of our party came up, and heard with horror the particulars of my escape.

Mr. Franklin presented the Indian with several trinkets, and a bottle of rum, of which they are immoderately fond; and accepted his invitation to his village, which was only two miles off. There were about eight or ten habitations, in a row or street, facing a fresh-water stream, covered with yellow lilies. Some of the young men were naked up to their hips, in the water, fishing with rods and lines; whilst many of the boys were diverting themselves in shooting frogs with bows and arrows.

Our kind conductor led us to his hut, where his wife roasted acorns for our supper, and prepared a dish of rice, mixed with oil made from the acorns of a live oak. I retired to rest, but could not forget the alligator: his image pursued me in my sleep, I even fancied that he had drawn me under water. The return of day rejoiced me, and presenting a variety of different objects, diverted me from the frightful idea that had taken possession of my mind.

Remember me tenderly to Catherine and Louisa, and tell them I have collected a number of beautiful butterflies and insects for their cabinet, which I shall send to England by the first opportunity.

Your affectionate,
Arthur Middleton

THREE NATURAL
DISASTERS

JOHN JAMES AUDUBON

THE EARTHQUAKE

Travelling through the Barrens of Kentucky (of which I shall give you an account elsewhere) in the month of November, I was jogging on one afternoon, when I remarked a sudden and strange darkness rising from the western horizon. Accustomed to our heavy storms of thunder and rain, I took no more notice of it, as I thought the speed of my horse might enable me to get under shelter of the roof of an acquaintance, who lived not far distant, before it should come up. I had proceeded about a mile, when I heard what I imagined to be the distant rumbling of a violent tornado, on which I spurred my steed, with a wish to gallop as fast as possible to the place of shelter; but it would not do, the animal knew better than I what was forthcoming, and, instead of going faster, so nearly stopped, that I remarked he placed one foot after another on the ground with as much precaution as if walking on a smooth sheet of ice. I thought he had suddenly foundered, and, speaking to him, was on the point of dismounting and leading him, when he all of a sudden fell a-groaning piteously, hung his head, spread out his four legs, as if to save himself from falling, and stood stock still, continuing to groan. I thought my horse was about to die, and would have sprung from his back had a minute more elapsed, but at that instant all the shrubs and trees began to move from their very roots, the ground rose and fell in successive furrows, like the ruffled waters of a lake, and I became bewildered in my ideas, as I too plainly discovered that all this awful commotion in nature was the result of an earthquake.

I had never witnessed any thing of the kind before, although, like every other person, I knew of earthquakes by description. But what is description compared with the reality? Who can tell of the sensations which I experienced when I found myself rocking as it were on my horse, and with him moved to and fro like a child in a cradle, with the most imminent danger around, and expecting the ground every moment to open, and present to my eye such an abyss as might engulf myself and all around me? The fearful convulsion, however, lasted only a few minutes, and the heavens again brightened as quickly as they had become ob-scured; my horse brought his feet to the natural position, raised his head and galloped off as if loose and frolicking without a rider.

I was not, however, without great apprehension respecting my family, from which I was yet many miles distant, fearful that where they were the shock might have caused greater havock than I had witnessed. I gave the bridle to my steed, and was glad to see him appear as anxious to get home as myself. The pace at which he galloped accomplished this sooner than I had expected, and I found, with much pleasure, that hardly any greater harm had taken place than the apprehension excited for my own safety.

Shock succeeded shock almost every day or night for several weeks, diminishing, however, so gradually as to dwindle away into mere vibra-tions of the earth. Strange to say, I for one became so accustomed to the feeling as rather to enjoy the fears manifested by others. I never can forget the effects of one of the slighter shocks which took place when I was at a friend's house, where I had gone to enjoy the merriment that, in our western country, attends a wedding. The ceremony being performed, sup-per over, and the fiddles tuned, dancing became the order of the moment. This was merrily followed up to a late hour, when the party retired to rest. We were in what is called, with great propriety, a *Log-house*, one of large dimensions, and solidly constructed. The owner was a physician, and in one corner were not only his lancets, tourniquets, amputating-knives, and other sanguinary apparatus, but all the drugs which he employed for the relief of his patients, arranged in jars and phials of different sizes. These had some days before made a narrow escape from destruction, but had been fortunately preserved by closing the doors of the cases in which they were contained.

As I have said, we had all retired to rest, some to dream of sighs and smiles, and others to sink into oblivion. Morning was fast approaching, when the rumbling noise that precedes the earthquake began so loudly, as to waken and alarm the whole party, and drive them out of bed in the greatest consternation. The scene which ensued it is impossible for me to describe, and it would require the humorous pencil of CRUICKSHANK to do justice to it. Fear knows no restraints. Every person, old and young, filled with alarm at the creaking of the log-house, and apprehending instant destruction, rushed wildly out to the grass enclosure fronting the building. The full moon was slowly descending from her throne, covered at times by clouds that rolled heavily along, as if to conceal from her view the scenes of terror which prevailed on the earth below. On the grass-plat we all met, in such condition as rendered it next to impossible to discriminate any of the party, all huddled together in a state of almost perfect nudity. The earth waved like a field of corn before the breeze: the birds left their perches, and flew about now knowing whither; and the Doctor, recollecting the danger of his gallipots, ran to his shop-room, to prevent their dancing off the shelves to the floor. Never for a moment did he think of closing the doors, but, spreading his arms, jumped about the front of the cases, pushing back here and there the falling jars; with so little success, however, that before the shock was over, he had lost nearly all he possessed.

The shock at length ceased, and the frightened females, now sensible of their dishabille, fled to their several apartments. The earthquakes produced more serious consequences in other places. Near New Madrid, and for some distance on the Mississippi, the earth was rent asunder in several places, one or two islands sunk for ever, and the inhabitants fled in dismay towards the eastern shores.

A FLOOD

Many of our larger streams, such as the Mississippi, the Ohio, the Illinois, the Arkansas and the Red River, exhibit at certain seasons the most extensive overflowings of their waters, to which the name of *floods* is more appropriate than the term *freshets*, usually applied to the sudden rising of smaller streams. If we consider the vast extent of country through which an inland navigation is afforded by the never-failing supply of water furnished by these wonderful rivers, we cannot suppose them exceeded in magnitude by any other in the known world. It will easily be imagined what a wonderful spectacle must present itself to the eye of the traveller, who for the first time views the enormous mass of waters, collected from the vast central regions of our continent, booming along, turbid and swollen to overflowing, in the broad channels of the Mississippi and Ohio, the latter of which has a course of more than a thousand miles, and the former of several thousands.

To give you some idea of a *Booming Flood* of these gigantic streams, it is necessary to state the causes which give rise to it. These are, the sudden melting of the snows on the mountains, and heavy rains continued for several weeks. When it happens that, during a severe winter, the Allegheny Mountains have been covered with snow to the depth of several feet, and the accumulated mass has remained unmelted for a length of time, the materials of a flood are thus prepared. It now and then happens that the winter is hurried off by a sudden increase of temperature, when the accumulated snows melt away simultaneously over the whole country, and the south-easterly wind which then usually blows, brings along with it a continued fall of heavy rain, which, mingling with the dissolving snow, deluges the alluvial portions of the western country, filling up the rivulets, ravines, creeks and small rivers. These delivering their waters to the great streams, cause the latter not merely to rise to a surprising height, but to overflow their banks, wherever the land is low. On such occasions, the Ohio itself presents a splendid, and at the same time an appalling spectacle; but when its waters mingle with those of the Mississippi, then, kind reader, is the time to view an American flood in all its astonishing magnificence. At the foot of the Falls of the Ohio, the water has been known to rise upwards of sixty feet above its lowest level. The river, at this point, has already run a course of nearly seven hundred miles, from its origin at Pittsburg, in Pennsylvania, during which it has received the waters of its numberless tributaries, and overflowing all the bottom lands or valleys, has swept along the fences and dwellings which have been unable to resist its violence. I could relate hundreds of incidents which might prove to you the dreadful effects of such an inundation, and which have been witnessed by thousands besides myself. I have known, for example, of a cow swimming through a window, elevated at least seven feet from the ground, and sixty-two feet above low-water mark. The house was then surrounded by water from the Ohio, which runs in front of it, while the neighbouring country was overflowed; yet the family did not remove from it, but remained in its upper portion, having previously taken off the sashes of the lower windows, and opened the doors. But let us return to the Mississippi.

There the overflow is astonishing; for no sooner has the water reached the upper part of the banks, than it rushes out and overspreads the whole of the neighbouring swamps, presenting an ocean overgrown with stupendous forest-trees. So sudden is the calamity, that every individual, whether man or beast, has to exert his utmost ingenuity to enable him to escape from the dreaded element. The Indian quickly removes to the hills of the interior, the cattle and game swim to the different stripes of land that remain uncovered in the midst of the flood, or attempt to force their way through the waters until they perish from fatigue. Along the banks of the river, the inhabitants have rafts ready made, on which they remove themselves, their cattle and their provisions, and which they then fasten with ropes or grape-vines to the larger trees, while they contemplate the melancholy spectacle presented by the current, as it carries off their houses and wood-yards piece by piece. Some who have nothing to lose, and are usually known by the name of *Squatters*, take this opportunity of traversing the woods in canoes, for the purpose of procuring game, and particularly the skins of animals, such as the deer and bear, which may be converted into money. They resort to the low ridges surrounded by the waters, and destroy thousands of deer, merely for their skins, leaving the flesh to putrefy.

The river itself, rolling its swollen waters along, presents a spectacle of the most imposing nature. Although no large vessel, unless propelled by boats, laden with produce, which running out from all the smaller streams, float silently towards the City of New Orleans, their owners meanwhile not very well assured of finding a landing-place even there. The water is covered with yellow foam and pumice, the latter having floated from the Rocky Mountains of the north-west. The eddies are larger and more powerful than ever. Here and there tracts of forest are observed undermined, the trees gradually giving way, and falling into the stream. Cattle, horses, bears and deer are seen at times attempting to swim across the impetuous mass of foaming and boiling water; whilst here and there a Vulture or an Eagle is observed perched on a bloated carcass, tearing it up in pieces, as regardless of the flood, as on former occasions it would have been of the numerous *sawyers* and *planters*, with which the surface of the river is covered, when the water is low. Even the steamer is frequently distressed. The numberless trees and logs that float along break its paddles and retard its progress. Besides, it is on such occasions difficult to procure fuel to maintain its fires; and it is only at very distant intervals that a wood-yard can be found which the water has not carried off.

Following the river in your canoe, you reach those parts of the shores that are protected against the overflowing of the waters, and are called *Levees*. There you find the whole population of the district at work repairing and augmenting those artificial barriers, which are several feet above the level of the fields. Every person appears to dread the opening of a *crevasse*, by which the waters may rush into his fields. In spite of all exertions, however, the crevasse opens, the water bursts impetuously over the plantations, and lays waste the crops which so lately were blooming in all the luxuriance of spring. It opens up a new channel, which, for aught I know to the contrary, may carry its waters even to the Mexican Gulf.

I have floated on the Mississippi and Ohio when thus swollen, and have in different places visited the submersed lands of the interior, propelling a light canoe by the aid of a paddle. In this manner I have traversed immense portions of the country overflowed by the waters of these rivers, and, particularly whilst floating over the Mississippi bottom-lands, I have been struck with awe at the sight. Little or no current is met with, unless when the canoe passes over the bed of a bayou. All is silent and melancholy, unless when the mournful bleeting of the hem-Raven is heard, as the foul bird rises, disturbed by your approach, from the carcass on which it was allaying its craving appetite. Bears, Cougars, Lynxes, and all other quadrupeds that can ascend the trees, are observed crouched among their top branches. Hungry in the midst of abundance, although they see floating around them the animals on which they usually prey, they dare not venture to swim to them. Fatigued by the exertions which they have made in reaching the dry land, they will there stand the hunter's fire, as if to die by a ball were better than to perish amid the waste of waters. On occasions like this, all these animals are shot by hundreds.

Opposite the City of Natchez, which stands on a bluff bank of considerable elevation, the extent of inundated land is immense, the greater portion of the tract lying between the Mississippi and the Red River, which is more than thirty miles in breadth, being under water. The mail-bag has often been carried through the immersed forests, in a canoe, for even a greater distance, in order to be forwarded to Natchitochez.

But now, kind reader, observe this great flood gradually subsiding, and again see the mighty changes which it has effected. The waters have now been carried into the distant ocean. The earth is everywhere covered by a deep deposit of muddy loam, which in drying splits into deep and narrow chasms, presenting a reticulated appearance, and from which, as the weather becomes warmer, disagreeable, and at times noxious, exhalations arise, and fill the lower stratum of the atmosphere as with a dense fog. The banks of the river have almost everywhere been broken down in a greater or less degree. Large streams are now found to exist, where none were formerly to be seen, having forced their way in direct lines from the upper parts of the bends. These are by the navigator called *short-cuts*. Some of them have proved large enough to produce a change in the navigation of the Mississippi. If I mistake not, one of these, known by the name of the *Grand Cut-off*, and only a few miles in length, has diverted the river from its natural course, and has shortened it by fifty miles. The upper parts of the islands present a bulwark consisting of an enormous mass of floated trees of all kinds, which have lodged there. Large sand-banks have been completely removed by the impetuous whirls of the waters, and have been deposited in other places. Some appear quite new to the eye of the navigator, who has to mark their situation and bearings in his log-book. The trees on the margins of the banks have in many parts given way. They are seen bending over the stream, like the grounded arms of an overwhelmed army of giants. Everywhere are heard the lamentations of the farmer and planter, whilst their servants and themselves are busily employed in repairing the damages occasioned by the floods. At one crevasse an old ship or two, dismantled for the purpose, are sunk, to obstruct the passage opened by the still rushing waters, while new earth is brought to fill up the chasms. The squatter is seen shouldering his rifle, and making his way through the morass, in search of his lost stock, to drive the survivors home, and save the skins of the drowned. New fences have everywhere to be formed; even new houses must be erected, to save which from a like disaster, the settler places them on an elevated platform supported by pillars made of the trunks of trees. The lands must be ploughed anew, and if the season is not too far advanced, a crop of corn and potatoes may yet be raised. But the rich prospects of the planter are blasted. The traveller is impeded in his journey, the creeks and smaller streams having broken up their banks in a degree proportionate to their size. A bank of sand, which seems firm and secure, suddenly gives way beneath the traveller's horse, and the next moment the animal has sunk in the quick-sand, either to the chest in front, or over the crupper behind, leaving its master in a situation not to be envied.

Unlike the mountain-torrents and small rivers of other parts of the world, the Mississippi rises but slowly during these floods, continuing for several weeks to increase at the rate of about an inch in the day. When at its height, it undergoes little fluctuation for some days, and after this subsides as slowly as it rose. The usual duration of a flood is from four to six weeks, although, on some occasions, it is protracted to two months.

Every one knows how largely the idea of floods and cataclysms enters into the speculations of the geologist. If the streamlets of the European Continent afford illustrations of the formation of strata, how much more must the Mississippi, with its ever-shifting sand-banks, its crumbling shores, its enormous masses of drift timber, the source of future beds of coal, its extensive and varied alluvial deposits, and its mighty mass of waters rolling sullenly along, like the flood of eternity!

THE HURRICANE

Various portions of our country have at different periods suffered severely from the influence of violent storms of wind, some of which have been known to traverse nearly the whole extent of the United States, and to leave such deep impressions in their wake as will not easily be forgotten. Having witnessed one of these awful phenomena, in all its grandeur, I shall attempt to describe it for your sake, kind reader, and for your sake only, the recollection of that astonishing revolution of the etherial element even now bringing with it so disagreeable a sensation, that I feel as if about to be affected by a sudden stoppage of the circulation of my blood.

I had left the village of Shawaney, situated on the banks of the Ohio, on my return from Henderson, which is also situated on the banks of the same beautiful stream. The weather was pleasant, and I thought not warmer than usual at that season. My horse was jogging quietly along, and my thoughts were, for once at least in the course of my life, entirely engaged in commercial speculations. I had forded Highland Creek, and was on the eve of entering a tract of bottom land or valley that lay between it and Canoe Creek, when on a sudden I remarked a great difference in the aspect of the heavens. A hazy thickness had overspread the country, and I for some time expected an earthquake, but my horse exhibited no propensity to stop and prepare for such an occurrence. I had nearly arrived at the verge of the valley, when I thought fit to stop near a brook, and dismounted to quench the thirst which had come upon me.

I was leaning on my knees, with my lips about to touch the water, when, from my proximity to the earth, I heard a distant murmuring sound of an extraordinary nature. I drank, however, and as I rose on my feet, looked toward the south-west, where I observed a yellowish oval spot, the appearance of which was quite new to me. Little time was left me for consideration, as the next moment a smart breeze began to agitate the taller trees. It increased to an unexpected height, and already the smaller branches and twigs were seen falling in a slanting direction towards the ground. Two minutes had scarcely elapsed, when the whole forest before me was in fearful motion. Here and there, where one tree pressed against another, a creaking noise was produced, similar to that occasioned by the violent gusts which sometimes sweep over the country. Turning instinctively toward the direction from which the wind blew, I saw, to my great astonishment, that the noblest trees of the forest bent their lofty heads for a while, and unable to stand against the blast, were falling into pieces. First, the branches were broken off with a crackling noise; then went the upper part of the massy trunks; and in many places whole trees of gigantic size were falling entire to the ground. So rapid was the progress of the storm, that before I could think of taking measures to insure my safety, the hurricane was passing opposite the place where I stood. Never can I forget the scene which at that moment presented itself. The tops of the trees were seen moving in the strangest manner, in the central current of the tempest, which carried along with it a mingled mass of twigs and foliage, that completely obscured the view. Some of the largest trees were seen bending and writhing under the gale; others suddenly snapped across; and many, after a momentary resistance, fell uprooted to the earth. The mass of branches, twigs, foliage and dust that moved through the air, was whirled onwards like a cloud of feathers, and on passing, disclosed a wide space filled with fallen trees, naked stumps, and heaps of shapeless ruins, which marked the path of the tempest. This space was about a fourth of a mile in breadth, and to my imagination resembled the dried-up bed of the Mississippi, with its thousands of planters and sawyers, strewed in the sand, and inclined in various degrees. The horrible noise resembled that of the great cataracts of Niagara, and as it howled along in the track of the desolating tempest, produced a feeling in my mind which it were impossible to describe.

The principal force of the hurricane was now over, although millions of twigs and small branches, that had been brought from a great distance, were seen following the blast, as if drawn onwards by some mysterious power. They even floated in the air for some hours after, as if supported by the thick mass of dust that rose high above the ground. The sky had now a greenish lurid hue, and an extremely disagreeable sulphurous odour was diffused in the atmosphere. I waited in amazement, having sustained no material injury, until nature at length resumed her wonted aspect. For some moments, I felt undetermined whether I should return to Morgantown, or attempt to force my way through the wrecks of the tempest. My business, however, being of an urgent nature, I ventured into the path of the storm, and after encountering innumerable difficulties, succeeded in crossing it. I was obliged to lead my horse by the bridle, to enable him to leap over the fallen trees, whilst I scrambled over or under them in the best way I could, at times so hemmed in by the broken tops and tangled branches, as almost to become desperate. On arriving at my house, I gave an account of what I had seen, when, to my surprise, I was told that there had been very little wind in the neighbourhood, although in the streets and gardens many branches and twigs had fallen in a manner which excited great surprise.

Many wondrous accounts of the devastating effects of this hurricane were circulated in the country, after its occurrence. Some log houses, we were told, had been overturned, and their inmates destroyed. One person informed me that a wire-sifter had been conveyed by the gust to a distance of many miles. Another had found a cow lodged in the fork of a large half-broken tree. But, as I am disposed to relate only what I have myself seen, I shall not lead you into the region of romance, but shall content myself with saying that much damage was done by this awful visitation. The valley is yet a desolate place, overgrown with briars and bushes, thickly entangled amidst the tops and trunks of the fallen trees, and is the resort of ravenous animals, to which they betake themselves when pursued by man, or after they have committed their depredations on the forms of the surrounding district. I have crossed the path of the storm, at a distance of a hundred miles from the spot where I witnessed its fury, and, again, four hundred miles farther off, in the State of Ohio. Lastly, I observed traces of its ravages on the summits of the mountains connected with the Great Pine Forest of Pennsylvania, three hundred miles beyond the place last mentioned. In all these different parts, it appeared to me not to have exceeded a quarter of a mile in breadth.

HOYLE'S MOUTH

PHILIP HENRY GOSSE

The people talk a good deal of a curious cavern called Hoyle's Mouth, about which they have some strange notions. It opens at the end of a long limestone hill or range of hills, about a mile inland; and the popular legend is, that it is the termination of a natural subterranean which communicates with the great cave called the Hogan, under Pembroke Castle, some eight miles distant. It was once traversed, they say, by a dog, which, entering at one end, emerged from the other, with all his hair rubbed off! A gentleman is said to have penetrated to a considerable distance, and found "fine rooms." But the vulgar are very averse to exploring even its mouth, on the ostensible ground that a Boar, "a wild pig," dwells there; I fear, however, that there are more unsubstantial terrors in the case.

I walked out to look at it; and if I found no dragons, nor giants, nor "pigs," I enjoyed a most delightful rural walk. There was not much to be noticed till I had passed Holloway Marsh, where the wind, whistling and whispering among the acres of bending reeds, recalled the asinine fate of the royal fiddler of Phrygia. I say there was not *much*; but the splendid blue of the Borage which grows in large beds by the way-side is always something to be admired, and its rigid transparent hairs and some other peculiarities in its structure make it interesting to a naturalist.

But a little beyond the bridge, we leave the Pembroke Road, and suddenly plunge down into a narrow lane with tall, almost meeting hedges, a perfect wilderness of flowers. There was the crimson Campion, so variable in the size and hue of its blossoms; the coarse blue spikes of Bugle; the Meadow Vetchling trailing about and throwing its racemes of yellow over the brambles; and the Mountain Willow-herb, with its white flowers tipped with pink; and the modest laughing little Forget-me-not, and blushing Dog-roses, and sugary Honeysuckles in profuse luxuriance. There, too, was plenty of Toadflax, but in leaf only, or only just showing the budding spike—a beautiful plant even so; perhaps those that I saw in flower the other day at St. Issel's were prematurely early; and indeed I hope so, for though I think the flower beautiful, I never see it without a painful reminder that "the glorious summer time" is already waning.

Spruce Chaffinches, birds that understand the difficult art of dressing well, are flitting hither and thither; the sweet Skylark is singing all about the sky; and numbers of warblers, more easily heard than seen, are chirping in the thick hedges,—young birds of the year, I presume, from their pertinacity. Yet theirs is nothing to the pertinacity of the flies, that keep pitching on my face every moment, and when driven from one cheek immediately alight on the other. Pshaw! how annoying they are! Next to poultry, I do think flies are the most impudent of all creatures.

I pass through a gate whose posts are of massive masonry, out of the chinks of which spring many graceful plants,—the Strawberry, the rich and glossy Ivy, the Hart's-tongue, and the Wall and the Black-stalked Spleenworts, festooning the grey and lichened stone; while the Roses trail and hang over all. How much of our sense of beauty is derived from the free and wayward negligence of such plants! The light and feathery sprays of herbage are tossed here and there, or dance up and down in the breeze; while the great variety in the form and tint of the leaves, no less than of the flowers, constantly charms the mind and pleases the taste. How different are the large, glossy, empurpled, heart-shaped leaves of the Black Bryony, from the many-paired, tendriled leaves of the Vetches; and these from the stiff, tall, and narrow blades of the Yellow Iris, the oval spotted leaves of the Orchis, or the much divided irregular ones of the fragrant Meadow-sweet! But all these are charming; perhaps most of all the Vetches, whether the handsome peak-like blossom of the Common Vetch, almost worthy of garden culture, or the beautiful crowded racemes of blue and purple flowers of the Tufted Vetch, that are thrown so wildly and profusely over the hedge, and that, I fear, would flourish nowhere else.

"All these are very common flowers." Yes, such as one may see in almost any rural walk. I do not mention them because I think them extraordinary, but because it is these, and such as these, that make up the beauty of nature. My own eye continually rests on them with delight, and my mind lingers on the contemplation of them; and that not at all the less, because I am familiar with them, and have admired them a hundred times before. I can appreciate the technical joy of finding a rarity; but this is a very different thing from the full enjoyment which one receives from the profuse loveliness of nature in the height of summer,—an enjoyment sometimes so overpowering that we feel we must have sympathy with another mind, or we can scarcely bear it.

If I felt that I needed to "cite precedent" for the love of common flowers, I would refer to our Father of Poets, Chaucer, whose love for the Daisy was more like devotion than an ordinary admiration for the beautiful in nature. You remember how simply, yet how touchingly, he describes his early risings to see his favourite flower expand its petals; how he was wont to go "doune on knees" to observe it more closely; with what affection he speaks of the "smale, softe, swete gras;" and how, after lingering there the long summer's day, he reluctantly retired, looking for a renewal of the same delight to-morrow. I must quote the passage in its antique garb.

> "As soon as ever the Sunne ginneth west
> To seen this floure, hot is will goe to rest
> For feare of night, so hateth she darknesse.
> Her chere is playnly spred in the brightnesse
> Of the Sunne, for there it will unclose.

> "And doune on knees anon right I me sette,
> And as I could this freshe floure I grette,
> Kneelynge alway till it unclosed was,
> Upon the smale, softe, swete gras,
> That was with floures swete embrouded all,
> Of soch swetenesse, and soch odour over all,
> That for to speak of gomme, herbe, or tree,
> Comparison may not ymaked be;
> For it surmounteth plainly all odours,
> And of riche beaute of floures.

> And leaning on my elbow and my side,
> The long day I shope me for to abyde,
> For nothing els, and I shal not lie
> But for to look upon the daisie,
> That well by reason men it calle may
> The daisie, or els the eye of the day,
> The Emprisse and floure of floures all.
> I pray to God that faire mote she fall,
> And all that loven floures for her sake.

When that the Sunne out of the south gan west,
And that this floure gan close, and gan to rest,
For darknes of the night, the which she dred,
Home to mine house full swiftly I me sped,
To gone to rest, and earely for to rise
To seene this floure to sprede, as I device."

By the aid of the guide-book, and a little verbal direction, I find a certain gate, beyond which is the slope of a hill covered with shrubs and underwood. A tangled grassy path, barely recognisable, winds up, and in a few moments there yawns the Cavern. It is a low vault of somewhat gothic form, dividing within into two gothic arches, much like an old time-worn church. The left arch soon ends; but the right narrows gradually to a hole, through which one might creep; but dark as pitch, of course. The groins and sides of the cave are fresh and green with the close-adhering drapery of *Marchantia*; and the Hart's-tongue Fern throws out its arching fronds in profusion from the angles of the ground all along the sides as far as the direct light of the sky falls; but ceases at that point. The boundary of the *Marchantia* is perhaps even more distinctly marked. So much is vegetation, and especially its beautiful green hue, dependent on light! The face of the rock around the mouth is festooned luxuriantly with ivy.

In the afternoon Arthur and I determined to explore it, taking with us candles, lucifers, and a ball of twine. The entrance-hall we found seven yards long; then a narrow passage for five yards, at which point the roof closed to a narrow fissure, so that we had to stoop and creep under it. Thence for five yards more we walked upright, crawled a few feet, and opened into an oval chamber three yards long and two wide. At the end of this a hole led off in a direction considerably to the right of the line hitherto followed: it was not more than as high above the floor as our knees, and just wide enough to wriggle through lying along; we did not, however, attempt this. On the right side of the first passage there was a niche or shelf, where Arthur prudently deposited his hat. The roof all along, and the sides partially, were coated with a rough stalactite; the floor was strewn with broken bits of stone, dirty with clay, certainly brought from without, and doubtless by animals running in.

We returned, satisfied at having penetrated about sixty feet by the line, without disproving the alleged permeability.

PROPHETIC AUTUMN

GRANT ALLEN

The year used once to begin in March. That was simple and natural—to let it start on its course with the first warmer breath of returning spring. It begins now in January—which has nothing to recommend it. I am not sure that Nature does not show us it really begins on the first of October.

"October!" you cry, "when all is changing and dying! when trees shed their leaves, when creepers crimson, when summer singers desert our woods, when flowers grow scanty in field or hedgerow! What promise then of spring? What glad signs of a beginning?"

Even so things look at a superficial glance. Autumn, you would think, is the season of decay, of death, of dissolution, the end of all things, without hope or symbol of rejuvenescence. Yet look a little closer as you walk along the lanes, between the golden bracken, more glorious as it fades, and you will soon see that the cycle of the year's life begins much more truly in October than at any other date in the shifting twelvemonth you can easily fix for it. Then the round of one year's history draws to a beautiful close, while the round of another's is well on the way to its newest avatar.

Gaze hard at the alders by the side of this little brook in the valley, for example, or at the silvery-barked birches here on the wind-swept moor-land. They have dropped their shivering leaves, all wan yellow on the ground, and the naked twigs now stand silhouetted delicately in Nature's etching against the pale grey-blue background. But what are those dainty little pendulous cylinders, brown and beaded with the mist, that hang in tiny clusters half-unnoticed on the branches? Those? Why, can't you

8 1

guess? They are next April's catkins. Pick them off, and open one, and you will find inside it the wee yellowish-green stamens, already distinctly formed, and rich with the raw material of future golden pollen. The birch and the alder toiled, like La Fontaine's ant, through all the sunny summer, and laid by in their tissues the living stuff from which to produce next spring's fluffy catkins. But that they may lose no time when April comes round again, and may take advantage of the first sunshiny day with a fine breeze blowing for the dispersal of their pollen, they just form the hanging masses of tiny flowers beforehand, in the previous autumn, keep them waiting in stock, so to speak, through the depth of winter, and unfold them at once with the earliest hint of genial April weather. Observe, though, how tightly the flowerets are wrapped in the close-fitting scales, overlapping like Italian tiles, to protect their tender tissues from the frost and snow; and how cleverly they are rolled up in their snug small cradles. As soon as spring breathes warm on them, however, the close valves will unfold, the short stamens will lengthen into hanging tassels, and the pollen will shake itself free on the friendly breezes, to be wafted on their wings to the sensitive surface of the female flowers.

Look, again, at the knobs which line the wand-like stems and boughs of the willows. Do you know what they are? Buds, you say. Yes, leaves for next spring, ready-made in advance, and curled up in embryo, awaiting the summer. If you unfold them carefully with a needle and pocket-lens, you will find each miniature leaf is fully formed beforehand: the spring has even now begun by anticipation; it only waits for the sun to unfold and realize itself. Or see, once more, the big sticky buds on the twigs of the horse-chestnut, how tightly and well they protect the new leaves; and notice at the same time the quaint horseshoe scar, with marks as of nails, left where the old leaves have just now fallen off, the nails being, in point of fact, the relics of the vascular bundles. Death, says the old proverb, is the gate of life. "Le roi est mort; vive le roi!" No sooner is one summer fairly over than another summer begins to be, under the eyes of the observer.

To those among us who shrink with dread from the Stygian gloom of English winter, there is something most consoling in this cheerful idea of Prophetic Autumn—this sense that winter is but a temporary sleep, during which the life already formed and well on its way to flower and foliage just holds its breath awhile in expectation of warmer weather. Nay, more, the fresh young life of the new year has even begun in part to show itself already. Autumn, not spring, is the real season of seedlings. Cast your eyes on the bank by the roadside yonder, and what do you see? The ground is green with tiny baby plants of prickly cleavers and ivy-leaved veronica. The seeds fall from the mother-plant on the soil in August, sprout and germinate with the September rains, and have formed a thick carpet of spring-like verdure by the middle of October. That is the common way with most of our wild animals. Unlike so many pampered garden flowers, but like "fall" wheat in cold climates, they sow themselves in autumn, come up boldly at once, straggle somehow through the winter, of course with enormous losses, and are ready by spring to welcome the first rays of returning sunshine.

Even the animals in like manner are busy with their domestic preparations for next summer. The foundress wasps, already fertilized by the autumn brood of drones, are retiring with their internal store of eggs to warm winter quarters, ready to lay and rear them in the earliest May weather. The dormouse is on the look-out for a snug hiding-place in the hazels. The caterpillars are spinning cocoons or encasing themselves in iridescent chrysalis shells, from which to emerge in April as full-fledged moths or gay cabbage butterflies. Everything is preparing for next summer's idyll. Winter is but a sleep, if even that; thank Heaven, I see in autumn the "promise and potency" of all that makes June sweet or April vocal.

❋ ❋ ❋

We have been sitting this afternoon in the Big Drawing-room, enjoying the view from its extensive windows. It is a spacious apartment for so small a house—about three acres large, with windows that open all round over miles of moorland. The carpet has a groundwork of fallen pine-needles and green grass and bracken, irregularly threaded with a tiny pattern of brocaded flowers—yellow tormentil, white bedstraw, golden stonecrop, red sheep-sorrel; while by way of roof the room is covered by a fretted ceiling of interlocking fir-branches, through which one can catch at frequent intervals deep glimpses of a high and bright blue dome that overarches with its vast curve the entire Big Drawing-room. No finger throne-hall has any earthly king; it is quite good enough for ourselves and our visitors.

But as we leaned back in our easy-chairs—spring seats of brake, backed with a bole of red pine-bark—we gazed upward overhead through the gaps in the boughs, and saw our winged house-fellows, the black-and-white martins, sweeping round in long curves after flies in the sunshine.

It was immensely picturesque for the martins and ourselves; how the flies regard the question I forbear to inquire at the present juncture. We had lamb chops for lunch; let him that is without sin amongst us—for example, the editor of the *Vegetarian Times*—cast the first stone at the house-martins. For myself, I am too conscious of carnivorous and other sinful tastes to cast stones at anybody. We are all human, say I, or at any rate vertebrate; let us agree to take things with vertebrate toleration.

The house-martins abide under the same roof with ourselves; literally under the same roof, for their tiny mud nests cling close beneath the eaves of our two spare bedrooms, familiarly known as the Maiden's Bower and the Prophet's Chamber—the last because it is most often inhabited by our friend the curate, and furnished, after the scriptural precedent, with "a bed, and a table, and a stool, and a candlestick"—"Every luxury that wealth can afford," said the Shunammite lady. "Under *our* roof," we say, when we speak of it; but the house-martins think otherwise. "Goodness gracious," I heard one of them twitter amazed to his wife the day we moved in for the first time to our newly-built cottage, "how terribly inconvenient! Here are some of those great nasty creatures, that walk so awkwardly erect, come to live in *our* house without so much as asking us. How they'll frighten the children!" For to tell you the truth, they were here before us. They came while the builders were still occupied in giving those "finishing touches" which are never finished; and they regarded our arrival as an unwarrantable intrusion. I could tell it from the aggrieved tone in which they chirped and chattered: "Gross infringement of the liberty of the subject;" "In England, every martin's nest is called his castle;" "Was it for this our fathers fought and bled at Agincourt against the intrusive sparrows?"—and so forth *ad infinitum*. But after a day or two, they cooled down and established a *modus vivendi*, the terms of the concordat being that we mutually agreed to live and let live, they under the eaves, and we in the interior. Since then, this arrangement has been so honourably carried out on both sides by the high contracting parties, that the martins allow us to stand close under them on the garden terrace, and watch while they bring flies in their mouths to their callow young, which poke out their gaping mouths at the nest door to receive them. They know us individually, and return with punctuality and despatch to their accustomed home each summer. But when strangers stand by, I notice that, though the parent birds dart back to the nest with a mouthful of flies, they do not dare to enter it or to feed their young; they turn hurriedly on the wing, three inches from the door, with a disappointed twitter, a sharp cheep of disgust, and won't return to their crying chicks, which strain their wide mouths and crane their necks to be fed, till the foreign element has been eliminated from the party.

For myself, I will admit, I just love the house-martins. They may be given to eating flies; but what of that? The skylark himself—Shelley's skylark, Meredith's skylark—affects a diet of worms, and nobody thinks one penny the worse of him. Even Juliet, I don't doubt, ate lamb chops like the rest of us. Indeed, it happened to me a few mornings since, during some very hot weather, to be positively grateful for these insectivorous tastes on the part of our feathered fellow-citizens. We were sitting on the verandah, much tried by a plague of flies; it was clear that "the blood of an Englishman" attracted whole swarms of midges and other unwelcome visitors. As soon as the house-martins became aware of this fact, they drew nearer and nearer to us in their long curves of flight, swooping down upon the insects attracted by our presence before they had time to arrive at the verandah. We sat quite still, taking no notice of the friendly birds' maneuvres; till after a while they mustered up courage to come close to our faces, flying so low and approaching us so boldly, that we might almost have put out our hands and caught them. I am aware, of course, that the martins merely regarded us from the selfish point of view, as fine bait for midges; while we in return were glad to accept their services as vicarious fly-catchers. But on what else are most human societies founded save such mutual advantage? And do we not often feel real friendship for those who serve us for hire well and faithfully? In the midst of so much general distrust of man, I accept with gratitude the confidence of the house-martins.

All members of the British swallow-kind are amply represented in and about our three acres. The common swallows breed under the thatched eaves of the ruined shed in the Frying Pan, and hawk all day over the shallow trout-stream that bickers down its middle. You can tell them on the wing by their very forked tail. It is, I think, in part a distinguishing mark by which they recognize their own kind, and discriminate it from the martins; for the outer-tail feathers are particularly long and noticeable in the male birds, whence I take them to be of the nature of attractive ornaments. At the beginning of the breeding season, too, the males assume a beautiful pinky blush on the lighter parts of the plumage, which may specially be observed as they turn flashing for a moment in bright April sunshine. The sand-martins, again, the engineers of their race, have excavated their long tunnelled nests in the crumbling yellow cliff that flanks the cutting on the high road opposite; I love to see them fly in with unerring aim at the narrow mouth as they return all agog from their aërial hunting expeditions on cool summer evenings. They are the smallest and dingiest of our swallows; they have no sheeny blue-black plumage like their handsome cousins, but are pale brown above, and dirty white below. The house-martins, last of all, can be recognized at once upon the wing by his conspicuous belt of pure white plumage, almost dazzling in its brilliancy, which stretches in a band across the lower half of his back; as he pirouettes on the wing, this badge of his kind gleams for a moment against the sky, and then fades as if by magic. His shorter tail scarcely shows forked at a distance, but when you watch him at close quarters, it is delightful to observe how he broadens or narrows it as he flies, to steady and steer himself. In order fully to appreciate this point, however, you must have the quick keen eye of the born observer. As for the pure black swifts—those canonical birds that haunt the village steeple—they are not swallows at all, but dark and long-winged northern representatives of the humming-birds and trogons. All these alike are summer migrants in England, for they can but come to us when insects on the wing are cheap and plentiful.

A Ramble in May

Charles A. Hall

We will take our lunch on that dry bank, from which we can get a view of the woods and the streamlet that skirts the meadow. This is a good position to take up, and I have no doubt we shall see plenty of things to talk about while we enjoy our sandwiches.

The water from a spring empties itself into the brook just below us, and I believe I see some Watercress (*Nasturtium officinale*) growing at the edge of the stream; a few sprigs of it would make a lovely and a healthy salad. I think you might gather some, Victor; wash it carefully in the spring-water, and bring it here as quickly as you can.

You call that Watercress? What a mistake! That stuff is Brooklime (*Veronica beccabunga*), a member of the Speedwell family which haunts brooks and ditches. It has opposite, elliptical leaves quite different from those of the Watercress, which are pinnate and alternate. Watercress belongs to the Cruciferae, and bears white flowers, whereas the Brooklime is one of the Scrophulariaceae. Neither plant flowers until June, when you will be able to see that Watercress bears white flowers, and the Brooklime lovely little blue flowers in axillary racemes.

Profit by your mistakes. After this little lesson I don't think you will make a similar error again. Go back to the brook, and bring us Watercress this time, please.

The other day a naturalist friend told me a remarkable story about an incident in bird-life which happened in the quarry we have just visited. He was rambling quietly in the quarry, when he saw three Pied Wagtails (*Motacilla lugubris*)—two males and a female. It was the mating season, and both males were anxious to mate with the lady, who, however, seemed "coy and hard to please." She seemed to think, "How happy could I be with either were the other dear charmer away!" The males got angry, and began to fight, the lady looking on. One of the males settled on a stone and displayed his charms, dipping his graceful tail and swaying his lovely body in proper Wagtail fashion. He was not allowed to enjoy his advantage long, for the other male swooped down on him, and literally knocked him off his perch. The love-lorn swain picked himself up, and flew to a jutting crag on the quarry face, followed by his angry antagonist, who dashed at him, and fastened his beak into his neck. Both fell to the ground, turning repeated somersaults in their descent. Alas! the first male could display his charms no longer; he was picked up panting by my friend, and died from a broken neck in a second or so. The victorious male made up to the lady, and the two flitted about in lover-like manner, just as if no tragedy had happened. In the animal world it is a common thing for the females to select mates who have displayed superior strength, and many a love-affair is settled through "trial by combat."

You think there is a terrible amount of bloodshed in Nature? As the poet said, "Nature is red in tooth and claw." Even plants fight. But there is a good amount of co-operation in Nature too. A few miles from here there is a colony of Black-headed Gulls (*Larus ridibundus*). Thousands of them make their nests and rear their families on a little island in the middle of a good-sized lake. They are massed together in a perfect crowd, and when an enemy approaches he is completely outnumbered, and easily driven off by a large company of the Gulls. They say that "Birds of a feather flock together," and this is extensively true; the flock may quarrel among themselves, but they are as one man when attacked by a common enemy. At any rate, human beings, with their intelligence, should not take example from the savagery of the lover animals; on the other hand, they should learn the good lesson of co-operation which Nature teaches, and live together in brotherliness and good-will.

Listen to the Skylarks (*Alauda arvensis*)! I hear several singing within a short distance of one another. Like us, they are enjoying the good weather and taking advantage of the sunshine. It is remarkable how sunshine and blue skies draw the songs out of our hearts; and, on the other hand, how storms appeal to our strength, and give us a stern determination to overcome difficulties. The folk of the "Sunny South" are a tuneful people; but the men of the Highlands, who see Nature in her frowning moods and content with torrents and tempests, are a hardy and determined folk; they may sing less, but they accomplish more.

But the Skylarks. I suppose you will have learned Shelley's famous ode to this soaring, songful bird. It commences:

"Hail to thee, blithe spirit—
Bird thou never wert—
That from heaven or near it
Pourest thy full heart
In profuse strains of unpremeditated art.

Higher still and higher
From the earth thou springest:
Like a cloud of fire,
The blue deep thou wingest,
And singing still dost soar, and soaring ever singest."

Several poets have attempted to immortalize the Skylark in their verses, but I think Shelley has succeeded beyond them all. I like the concluding lines of the ode:

"Teach me half the gladness
That thy brain must know;
Such harmonious madness
From my lips would flow,
The world should listen then as I am listening now."

It always seems significant to me that this bird, which sings so gloriously and soars so high, makes its simple nest and rears its family on the ground. There seems to be a suggestion of poetry in the facts. Does it not often happen that the sweetest music, the most moving poetry, and the noblest lives emanate from the humblest and most lowly hearts?

While we are thinking about birds, just take the field-glass and watch the common Sandpiper (*Tringoïdes hypoleucus*) that is slowly and jerkily making its way along the brook, heading up the stream. Notice that it has a habit of dipping its tail after the manner of the Wagtails, but not nearly so gracefully. It seems to be always trying to balance itself. You will see it is bigger and, to my mind, more awkward than the Wagtails, and it is not nearly so gaily clad. I am told that the Sandpiper spends its winters in Africa, and visits us about the end of April. Just think of the miles that bird has flown, and what a traveller it is! Common Sandpipers do not nest in this district, but their nests are commonly found farther north and in Scotland. Don't you remember the great numbers of this bird that we saw on the west coast of Scotland in June, 1910? I wished to photograph one of their nests, but had great difficulty in finding one, although I knew there were plenty about. These birds are very cunning about their nests. If disturbed while sitting, they fly away very silently and with a peculiar kind of flight. When they get some distance away they utter weird sort of cries, which are intended to mislead a hunter for their eggs or young. They seem to say, "Here's the nest! Here's the nest!" and an unskilled searcher is often led to look for an hour where the nest is not. You may depend upon it that the nest is always some distance from the "weet-weeting" Sandpipers; they are deceivers ever. Someone said, "All men are liars." Such a statement would be highly true of these birds. I did not, with all my searching, have the honour of finding a Sandpiper's nest, but two were pointed out to me by a girl who had blundered across them; so I got my photograph, and a good one, too. The nests are poor affairs; usually a little dried grass in a hollow in a bank near water.

I suppose you know the Yellow Iris (*Iris pseudacorus*), the flowers of which are sometimes called "Flags." I see a clump growing down there on the moist ground by the brook. The leaves of this plant are like swords. There are plenty of buds, but no flowers yet; some buds are beginning to burst, and a few flowers will be open in less than a week if the weather continues favourable. The Iris is a true Monocotyledon; it could not be mistaken for anything else. Its beautiful showy yellow flowers glorify damp and muddy places, which, without them, would be thought uninteresting, and far from wholesome. The styles of the pistil of the Iris are very like petals, so much so that the unskilled observer might declare they were petals. I have known two or three persons who used to collect Iris seeds and roast them; they said they made a good substitute for coffee.

The Water Avens (*Geum rivale*) grows abundantly at the side of the brook. This is a member of the Rose tribe, Natural Order Rosaceae. The flowers, which have a drooping habit, have a dull appearance, the calyx being tinged with a dull purple, while the petals are a blend of purple, pink, and orange. The name of the plant is a clear indication of its love of damp places, particularly by the sides of streams. Our friend "Johns" gives the months of June and July as the flowering time of the Water Avens, but I have seen it in splendid bloom as early as April 30, and it has flowered by this brook during the whole of the present month (May).

There is another species of Avens, called the Herb Bennet (*Geum urbanum*), which frequents thickets and hedges. It is more erect than *G. rivale*, and its small yellow flowers do not droop. I have never seen this in flower about here until the middle of June. By the end of July you will be able to see lots of this plant in seed, and if you push by them they will hook themselves on to your clothes. Each carpel is crowned with a hardened style, terminating with a hook. The hook clings to the fur of rabbits and other animals, as well as the clothes of man, and thus the seed is carried long distances from the parent plants. In this remarkable way the seeds of the Wood Avens, or Herb Bennet, are dispersed and new ground is insured for future plants.

I have often remarked that it is wise for a naturalist on the prowl to sit down on some mossy bank or other inviting ground for an hour or so. I heard of some friends who were out hunting for what they might see the other day. They climbed a steep hill, and thought it would be good to sit down and rest after their exertions; as a consequence, they spied what they might never have seen had they continued to walk—the Moonwort Fern (*Batrychium lunaria*), which, indeed, is a most interesting plant. Most ferns bear spores on the backs of the fronds, but this one has a split frond, one half of which bears semicircular or moon-shaped frondlets, while the other bears only spore cases, which are held upright and appear like clusters of small berries. As we sit quietly we may see many interesting things—beetles, grasshoppers, spiders, ants, bees, wasps, flies, and innumerable other creatures, as well as plants. If we are very still, birds will approach us, and even rabbits will gambol not far away. That is one thing the young naturalist has to learn—to be quiet and patient. Use your eyes as much as you can; open your ears to every sound, but make no movement and no noise. I was once sitting quietly on a hedge-bank, seeing many things to interest me, when a Hare came leisurely along a track, and actually jumped over my outstretched legs. I had never had so good a look at a Hare in a state of nature before. On another occasion I was resting on a boulder in the bed of a Scottish burn, when I noticed a big Rat gliding noiselessly about here and there without being at all distressed by my presence; perhaps he thought I was part of the scenery. I have even had butterflies settle on my coat and sun themselves there. Study to be quiet.

Had we not been sitting here, we might have overlooked the Moss which grows all about us. It is bigger and coarser than those Mosses which grow on the rockeries and walls at home. Here is some over six inches in height, green in the upper parts but looking withered at the base. What is particularly interesting is the stalked capsule which each plant seems to bear. See, each capsule is covered by a little brownish hood, which I can remove, just as if it were a candle-extinguisher! Now the hood is removed, you see the naked capsule, which is closed at the top by a kind of beaked lid. There is a little ring which marks the junction of the lid and the main body of the capsule. Very soon that ring will break, the lid will fall off, and the spores which are ripening in the capsule will escape. From the spores new Moss-plants will develop. This is the Common Hair-Moss; its scientific name is *Polytrichum commune*. Mosses are such lowly plants that they seem to have been ignored by all but a few botanists. Yet they have a most interesting life-story, which I had better not trouble you with now; but I am sure, if you keep up your Nature interest, you will some day want to know something about it. There are about six hundred kinds of Mosses in Great Britain, some of them exceedingly small. One cannot study them without the aid of a microscope, but I can tell you from experience that, once you get on to their study, you are not likely to give it up in a hurry. I could not imagine a more fascinating group of plants.

What is that red mossy growth on the Wild Rose (*Rosa canina*)? Oh, that is called a Rose Bedeguar. Is it not curious? and how lovely is the rich red colour! "Robin's Pincushion" is another name which has been given to the growth. It is caused by the larvae of the Gall Gnat (*Rhodites rosae*); if you open the growth, you will find some inside. The eggs or larvae cause a kind of irritation to the plant, and the growth is the consequence. This reminds me of the bird's-nest-like growth which is commonly seen on Birch-trees. Many a time when I was a boy did I mistake these growths for bird's-nests. They are popularly called "Witches' Brooms"; some of them are caused by a fungus, which, of course, is a lowly plant, and others by a Gall Mite (*Phytoptus rudis*). So, you see, these growths are the homes of curious creatures or other plants. Oak-apples are not the fruit of the Oak, but growths due to another gall-fly. There are numerous kinds of galls, each one having its own particular cause, and being a peculiarity of the plant on which it grows. There is no end to Nature: galls alone provide study for a lifetime.

In coming along the lane this morning I noticed the strong growth of the Brambles. They should be in bloom fairly soon. The Bramble gets on well in a hedge, because it can hook itself on to the Hawthorn by its prickles, and pull itself up to the light. It seems to have equipped itself for such a situation; it does not thrive so well where it is left to itself, and has no other plant to climb by. By the time the Bramble is in full bloom the summer is well advanced, and, as you know, its luscious fruit is not usually ripe until September, when we all go blackberrying, and enjoy the good jam and jelly. One might say the Bramble is exceedingly cunning. It wraps its hard seeds in delicious pulp, which the birds eat; but the seeds themselves are indigestible; they pass through the body, or are scattered by the birds as they eat the fruit. In this way the parent plant attempts to avoid overcrowding. It does not want its youngsters to take away its supplies, so by a strange device it sends them abroad. The same trick is adopted by the Rose and Hawthorn: the red "hips and haws" attract the birds, who feed on the fleshy parts, and scatter the seeds so neatly packed inside.

Are there any snakes about here? I have occasionally seen Adders (*Vipera berus*) among the Heather on the hill yonder; that specimen I have in the museum at home was caught there; it was a big one, no less than two feet long, which is about as big as Adders grow. It was easily caught. The friend who gave it me saw it sunning itself after a good meal; it seemed too well filled and lazy to care about moving. My friend approached it with ease, held it down to the ground by pressing the point of his walking-stick on its neck, and then prevented it from doing any damage by removing its poison fang with a knife. The bite of an Adder is not fatal, but it might cause a serious illness. No one need have any difficulty in knowing an Adder when he sees one; none but an ignoramus would mistake it for the common Ring Snake. The Adder is more serpent-like than the Ring Snake, thick in the middle of the body, and tapering quickly to both neck and tail. The Ring Snake is a more slender reptile. The Adder is a dull yellow, with black spots linked into each other along its back, while its sides have triangular black markings. It is black underneath. The Ring Snake is greenish-yellow in colour; it grows to a greater length than the Adder, and its tail is drawn out to a fine point.

I saw a paragraph in the newspaper the other day about our famous politician, Mr. Lloyd George, having an encounter with an Adder. As the story was told, it would seem as if there had been an alarming fight, and that our Chancellor of the Exchequer was in danger of his life. I'm afraid the newspaper reporter must have drawn upon his journalistic imagination; he certainly could not have been a naturalist. Adders do not attack men unless they are cornered; and even if they did make an attack, it would be the easiest thing in the world to get out of their way. I have seen scores of Adders in the Scottish Highlands, but I have never come across one that was not eager to get out of my way.

Ring Snakes deposit eggs from which their young are hatched, whereas Adders bring forth their young alive. The former are termed *oviparous* (Latin, *ovum* = egg; *parere* = to bring forth), and the latter *viviparous* (Latin, *vivus* = alive; and *parere*). I have read many stories about Adders swallowing their young when threatened by danger; but the stories are discounted by many observers, and as I have never seen such a thing happen I don't feel in a position to give an opinion on the subject. Mr. A. Nicol Simpson F.Z.S., a good Scottish naturalist and competent observer, says such stories are the outcome of superstition.

Adders will swim when it is necessary for them to do so, but they do not seem to care for the water; Ring Snakes seem to delight in it. I have seen specimens over a yard long swimming with their heads above water along the big drains of the Fen district. I must tell you that when I was a small boy I was an enthusiastic naturalist, and spent all my holidays in prowling about the country-side. One day I had the fortune to capture a Ring Snake fully four feet long. At first I tried to kill it by hitting it on the head, but that method did not work; then I called to mind the old wives' story about killing snakes by blows on the tail; I tried that way, but without success. By this time I remembered hearing that snakes never died until sunset; even if you cut them up into small pieces, each piece would wriggle until sundown. So I determined to hold my specimen by the neck, coiling its body round my arm, and to carry it home that way. I intended to produce it at supper-time, when I hoped to put my sisters into a state of consternation. However, I had not walked very far when the beastly reptile exuded a stench on to my coat sleeve that made me drop him in an instant. Such an indescribable stench it was; I had to wash my sleeve as well as I could in a stream, but I was not able to get entirely rid of the smell until I could get the use of soap and soda. Ring Snakes have some glands in their bodies from which they can exude a stinking fluid when roughly handled. Perhaps that power is a protection to their kind. I cannot imagine any animal or man desiring to retain hold of a Ring Snake in spite of the smell.

As I have said, I have seen Adders on the hill, but I have not found any Ring Snakes in this district. What are known as "Slow" or "Blind Worms" are common. They, however, are not snakes; indeed, to be correct, they are legless lizards, which do not as a rule grow more than twelve inches long. Why this reptile should have been called "slow" or "blind" I cannot understand. It can move quickly enough when it wants to get out of danger; it will sometimes even leave its tail in your hand if you happen to have caught it by that appendage! Surely a convenient way of escape, but an example we could not easily follow! We are reminded of the Brittle-stars, which will leave parts of themselves in their enemies hands, arms, or mouths, and make good their escape. And the reptile is not blind, although its bright eyes are very small. When very young, the Slow Worm has a whitish appearance, but as it grows it becomes copper-coloured. It haunts manure-heaps, where it often brings forth its young, always in a living condition (viviparous), and it may also be found in thickets and heaps of rubbish.

Before we leave this delightful resting-place, I want to tell you something about the meanings of some Latin words that are often used as specific names of plants. When you know those words and their meanings you will the more easily understand the habits of the plants to which they are attached, or the uses to which they have been put.

The Watercress, as I told you, is named *Nasturtium officinale*. The word *officinale* comes from the Latin *officina* = a workshop, or laboratory. The term is applied to plants that are, or have been, used medicinally. Watercress is supposed to have valuable medical properties; hence its specific name *officinale*. The same term is applied to the Great Wild Valerian (*Valeriana officinalis*), of which I see some specimens about ready to flower by the side of the brook; and to a number of other plants. *Vulgaris* is another commonly used word; it means "common," and is applied frequently to common species of genera; take, for example, the Yellow Rocket (*Barbarea vulgaris*), which grows in the quarry, as well as by the side of the stream. The word *perennis* is from *per* = through; *annus* = a year; and it indicates that the plant to which it is attached is a perennial, living for several years. The Daisy is named *Bellis perennis*. *Paluster* is from *palus* = a swamp or marsh; the word occurs in *Caltha palustris*, the Marsh Marigold. Where you find the word *palustris* or *palustre* in the name of a plant, you may be sure that it grows specially well in marshes. *Pratensis* is from *pratum* = a meadow; the word is used in the names of plants that are generally found in meadows, such as the Meadow Crane's-bill (*Geranium pratense*), which you will see in flower hereabouts in the course of two or three weeks. It belongs to the Geranium family, and is a very handsome plant, its big blue flowers being singularly beautiful. *Sylvaticus* and *sylvestris* (*silva* = a wood) are words indicating that the plants to which they are applied are occupants of the woodlands. *Hirsutum* means rough or bristly; *arvensis*, from *arvum* = a ploughed field, describes plants that grow in fields that have been cultivated; *procumbens*, from *procumbo* = I fall forward, describes trailing plants. *Repens* and *reptans* mean "creeping"; *maritimus* (*mare* = the sea) means growing by the sea, and the same meaning is attached to *litoralis* (*litus* = the seashore).

You will find an occasional hour spent in looking up the Latin names of plants in the pages of your Latin dictionary will provide you with a lot of useful information, and I am sure you will have great enjoyment in the process. Next to being useful to your fellows, the greatest delight is discovered in the acquisition of knowledge; and the more knowledge you possess, the more useful you can be.

We have had a long rest and a long talk; now we will have a rinse in the brook and a good walk.

AN OCTOBER DIARY

CHARLES C. ABBOT

OCTOBER 21   I found a pair of magnificent emeralds this evening—small, it is true, but they made up in brilliancy all they lacked in size. Dark though it happened to be, they glistened as I had never seen gems glisten before. They seemed almost to be sources of light and to illuminate their immediate surroundings. When within reach I stopped—and they were not there. The weasel that owned them was not green, whatever the tint of those wonderful gems. This was the weasel, I suppose, that has been running at large in the cellar, and daring among the apple-barrels, when not wishing to be seen. I speak advisedly, for at times he is bold as a hawk, and ready to fight if molested. Better a weasel than the rats he preys upon, so long may he flourish!

❋   ❋   ❋

I took my fence-rail spider a handful of flies this morning, but she was out of humor and returned me no thanks. Indeed, she did not feign to notice in any way my contribution to her larder. So far as I could discover, nothing had gone wrong with the elaborate web; and the cause of the sulkiness could only be attributed to over-feeding or injury. She sat, or, more properly, stood, in the door of her den and looked at me, but did not stir a hair's-breadth, although fly after fly, of the score I had brought, were escaping from the web. I sat down as near the place as practicable, determined to see when the spider would condescend to step out or back into the recesses of her quarters. Perhaps I saw five minutes—it seemed an hour—but nothing like voluntary movement on the spider's part occurred. Finally, just as I was about to change my position, to get a closer view, I felt a slight stinging sensation on the end of my nose, and waving my hand involuntarily before my face, I found myself cabled, in a flimsy way, to the fence and the branches of the tree nearest me. A spider, nesting in the tree, had selected my hat as the support of some new webbing, and had fastened a hundred cables to it, selecting my nose as an additional support. Regretting I had so rudely disturbed the plans of the new-comer, I rose to go; but not before I had solved the mystery of the motionless spider before me. Placing my forefinger upon it, to my disgust I found that I had been staring at the mere ghost of my friend. Something had attacked her, and sucked out all her juices; not a trace of moisture remained; she was hollow as a "locust-shell."

If the spider that had utilized my hat and nose, in spreading additional webs, had done this murder, did it also set my defunct friend in this life-like position, as a trick on me? There was every appearance of this; but not until after many similar results will I admit even any degree of probability in the matter.

There is, without doubt, no class of animals that offer a more fruitful field for study than do spiders. Their habits show a marked degree of cunning, and I have no hesitation in placing them on a level with ants in the scale of intelligence.

The evening was very warm, and the full tide of insect-life common to August appears to have wholly revived. The flies and the frost play such remarkable tricks with our theories that, before a new idea can be formulated, the frost or the flies upsets our preconception.

OCTOBER 22   No fog, save scattered remnants of the veil of mist that yesterday draped the meadows. Every indication is that of a warm south rain; and this usually does not introduce a cold wave, such as is still reported to be coming. The crows fly low, and this is a sign of rain. How strange it is, that men otherwise intelligent should believe such nonsensical sayings. Certainly more than half the time crows fly very near the ground, a few feet above the level of the fields, and just skimming the tree-tops. All through a drought of five weeks they flew as low to the ground as I ever knew them to; and so it is all winter, stormy or clear, moderate or cold, quiet or windy; but the facts have no value in the sight of my neighbors. What they have always heard they always believe; and one

proclaimed to the audience, at the close of a lecture, as a settler to my
"newfangled notions," that "as these sayings originated in the *good* old
times, none of 'em could be *bad*." I was about to reply, when he closed the
discussion prematurely by adding that "these science men can get up new
things as much as they please; but they needn't try to push the old ways to
the wall; there's room enough for both." He is right, there is room enough
for both, and ignorance will survive for years to come. Teach the young the
fallacy of weather lore, but let the older generations believe in it all, in
peace. My lecture on "Weather Lore" fell flat on that audience. Every
blessed one of the old folks voted me a crank, and the very few young
people did not hear it, or failed to catch my meaning.

For hours the crows have been flying low, and when the day was done
a rolling black cloud and a puff of wind ushered in a rain-storm from the
south; and soon began the steady pour which means an inky-black night
and scarcely any creature astir. It is useless to go abroad at such a time. You
can see nothing and hear nothing, and what you chance to touch may
mislead you; for dripping feathers and soaked fur, handled in the dark,
are a trial to the flesh and vexation to the spirit.

It seems never to have occurred to Wilson, Audubon, or Nuttall that
birds are gifted with intelligence like our own, differing only in degree—as
a rule, having less, except in some one or two directions—while their
capabilities are greater. Probably in no one way is the identity of human
and bird intelligence shown more clearly than in the marked variation in
individual dispositions. This has been entirely overlooked in the works of
the authors mentioned, and in a vast number of instances what is recorded
of a single pair of birds that chanced to come under observation is assumed to be an exhaustive life-history of the species.

What is needed is to write the lives of our birds so that the creatures
may be recognized without the aid of an illustration. It can be done.

This thought occurred to me as I saw the first linnets of the season, an
hour before the rain began. I thought of it again as a little saw-whet owl
crossed my path, skimming the ground like a whip-poor-will. The linnets
were in a flock of fully one hundred, and, as usual, they dropped from the
clouds. I happened to be near the tree upon which they all alighted, and
just as I saw another flock, months ago, come to the big elm in the yard,
so these came directly from overhead, to the tall sassafras "on the line." For
years past I have noticed this peculiarity.

Wilson, in 1808–10, and George Ord, a few years later, refer to the
rarity of this bird in the neighborhood of Philadelphia, considering its
appearance as only an exceptional occurrence in severe winters.

This is wholly a mistake. Linnets are as sure to put in an appearance as snow-birds or pine finches. They are not often seen as early as October, in this latitude, it is true, but why should it excite surprise, when it is the rule for them to remain until late in April? Their apparent rarity, in winter, is really due to the abruptness of arrival and departure, and unless there is much snow, they remain closely among the tall forest tree; if systematic search is made, linnets will be found in Central New Jersey from November to March, both inclusive, year in and year out. I base this statement on notes of their presence jotted down during the past twenty years.

October 23   At sunrise there came a shower of liquid bird-notes trickling through the pines—songs that resembled the lower tones of the musical water-jars of the ancient Peruvians. They were uttered by a flock of fifty or more cowpen-birds, singing in concert. The birds sat in short rows on the branches of the pines, and did not move the while, except to slightly raise their wings and spread their tails, as the soft sounds came bubbling up to their beaks and trickled over. They are curious birds. Cuckoo-like, they build no nests, but drop their eggs, here and there, in the nests of much smaller birds. Thus much all the world knows, or ought to know; but how little besides has been recorded of them! In Central New Jersey they are not migratory. They come and go, erratically, like the robin. A week or perhaps a month may pass without one being seen, and then, some bright morning, they may be the first birds to attract our attention as we venture out of doors.

It is commonly stated that these birds are gregarious the year through; but this is, at least, open to discussion; and depends very much upon the number of birds needed to make a "flock." From March to September they are most frequently seen in pairs or trios, and quite often singly. They associate with the robins, and are constant companions of meadow-larks, whose flight, even, they sometimes purposely imitate. When the female is ready to lay her eggs, she skulks through the bushes to find a suitable nest; and sometimes does not wait until the nest is finished. During the past summer, watching a pair of white-eyed greenlets while building, I, one afternoon, saw a cowpen-bird fly to the half-finished nest, and in less than two minutes fly away. In that brief space of time she deposited an egg. Meanwhile, the rightful owners of the nest were much exercised, and held a long discussion over the occurrence. This resulted in a remodelling of the bottom of the structure, the egg being neatly floored over.

Young cowpen-birds, for a short time after leaving the nest, associate with their foster-parents; but, as the season wears away, the birds that were

hatched in one neighborhood finally meet, and a flock is eventually organized, retaining its numbers until the breaking-up of winter. During the
spring and early summer of 1884 I found eleven nests containing eggs of
the cowpen-bird, the nests being in one limited area of a hundred or more
acres. In a very short time after they were able to fly these young cowpen-
birds would find the company of their own kind preferable to that of the
warblers and fly-catchers that had nursed them. I have never seen them
with their foster-parents after the nesting season of the latter was practically over.

Another peculiarity of the bird has been wholly overlooked. During
July, August, and even September, the female cowpen-birds continue to
drop single eggs at irregular intervals, and, when so doing, they do not
look up some deserted nest, but drop the eggs upon the ground, and then
descend from their perches to eat them. This I have witnessed on several
occasions. But, to further determine the facts concerning this extraordinary
habit, I have killed numbers of female cowpen-birds even as late as September, and in several found eggs nearly ready for extrusion. They were,
to all appearances, fertile.

❋ ❋ ❋

Last night's steady rain cleared the air and earth of dust. The gorgeous
tints of the autumn foliage now show to perfection. Now is the one favor-
able time to realize how grand a color is a bright green. Some of the
trees still retain it in various shades, and it shows forth in all its beauty in
the setting of contrasting tints wrought by the frost.

❋ ❋ ❋

The promised cold wave has come. Even in the full glare of the noon-
day sun it is cold, and the fitful west wind shakes the trees with sudden
shivering, and millions of bright leaves flutter through the air, and star the
grass with flakes of red and yellow.

For exercise I climbed a chinkapin-tree after the few nuts remaining
on it, and brought down upon my head the fury of indignant blue-jays.
One slapped my hand with its wing as I was reaching upward to a cluster
of burrs. These jays were as bold as though I was after their nest. Had I,
in their fearlessness, as shown this morning, an evidence of quick-
wittedness on their part; did they realize my comparative helplessness
while in the tree? Probably so. No bird, I think, fears man when in a tree as

it does when he is standing on the ground. They seem to know that, with his hands grasping the branches, it is highly improbable that he has a gun with him, and so approach on the part of a bird is comparatively safe. A crow would reason in this manner, I know, and the evidence favors a like intelligence on the part of other birds.

*   *   *

Shortly after sunset a cat-owl screamed from some distant shelter in the meadows, and the pleasant sound, borne by the wind and toned with the sighs of the tall pines, added a charm to the evening. To me it has ever been a matter of wonder that the cries of owls should be thought mournful. In a little poem by Alexander Wilson, called "The Foresters," the author speaks of

> "The hollow, quivering, loud-repeated howl,
> Full overhead, betrays the haggard owl."

To what haggard owl he refers I am uncertain, but probably this long-eared one, that, from the varied notes of its cry, is locally known as "cat-owl." Formerly it was more abundant than now, and its place in the meadows is taken by the short-eared or marsh owls. The voices of the two are quite different, and by this means the birds are as readily distinguished as when seen. The marsh-owls, as found in the meadows, offer one peculiarity not noticed by ornithologists as occurring elsewhere. They build in cavernous hollows of old trees, and not on the ground. Either this, or the young, as soon as they are hatched, leave the nest and take shelter in such hollows. I can readily understand why this should be the case. They frequent only the wet marshes, where there is an abundance of mice and of reed-birds at certain seasons. These are their sole food-supply, and the birds do not need to wander any distance from the marshes. To nest on the ground would be to expose the eggs and young to freshets, and it probably has resulted from this cause that hollow trees—the proper home of owls— have been resorted to. Either this, or the young resort, when but a few days old, to the trees. While I have never found the eggs, I have so frequently found the young that I have never doubted but that they were hatched in the hollows where they were seen.

*   *   *

"Sometimes a tame cat takes to the woods, and when it does it gets wilder than a wild cat," was the remark of Miles Overfield, who gave me a rambling account of his having seen such a cat. It was a strange coincidence, for to-night I crossed Poaetquissings above the flood-gates, and the scream of a cat was decidedly horricapillatory. I felt my hairless scalp to be unpleasantly ridged, and the same effect was produced on the night-herons near by, for they straightway ruffled their feathers and flew into the outer darkness. I listened for its repetition, yet half hopeful I should not hear it; and I was both pleased and sorry that the cat remained quiet so long as I tarried by the creek-side. This cat, which I know to be one that has "taken to the woods," uttered this evening probably the wildest cry I have ever heard in my rambles. Not so startling as that of a barn-owl, perhaps, but simply because it is uttered more deliberately. You have time to catch your breath; but when the barn-owl yells its wild kr-r-r-ick! you are apt to be bewildered by its abruptness. The sound was unlike that made by any domestic cat, varied and unmusical as their vocal efforts are, and did approximate to the cry of a cougar, as I have occasionally heard it at the Zoo.

Perhaps it may provoke a smile to refer to cats when treating of the scattered remnants of wild nature, but it can be accepted without qualification that a cat that takes to a wild life will be so essentially feral that a person, a stranger to domestic cats, would never infer the truth. Of a number of such instances I have collected careful, trustworthy data, and they all accord with what I have myself observed. Such cats become arboreal and strictly nocturnal; they haunt the remotest portions of wooded districts, and utter a cry different from any of the sounds characteristic of domestic Toms or Tabbies.

OCTOBER 24 Frost put a quietus on creation in the night. Even the crackling leaves are still this morning. Squirrels, if they move at all, step on tiptoe. A long line of voiceless crows pass over the meadows, winging their way so stilly one might think them a wind-driven thunder-cloud. The brook best shows the footsteps of the frost-king, where ranks of icy spear-points glitter in the sun. Every projecting pebble is encased in crystal, and the cheerful waters sing a rapid roundelay as they hurry by. Autumn has chosen her time and placed on view her choicest handiwork. But its beauty avails it nothing; it is fated to quickly pass and be utterly forgotten, for who that shudders in the early morning at the sight of frosted fields thinks of the matchless beauty of the ice-crystals spread so lavishly before him?

Yet I doubt if, in all nature, there are more exquisite shapes. From the clear sky the meadow-larks give promise of a splendid day, for they are silent as death if it is going to storm—so it is said; but he is not a wise traveller that has no better barometer. Grass-finches, that had shivered in their weedy caves through the long night, now rejoice at the victory of the rising sun, and sing with increasing ardor as the generous warmth stirs them to action. Bluebirds, in straggling dozens, lined the worm-fences, and a flock—perhaps a thousand—of red-wings came chattering up against the westerly breeze, and clothed the bare branches of an old apple-tree as with summer's full complement of leaves.

A half-hour in the early morning works a wonderful change in upland and meadow, and it is not well to be discouraged if, at first, either locality appears deserted.

THE ENCANTADAS

HERMAN MELVILLE

Take five-and-twenty heaps of cinders dumped here and there in an outside city lot, imagine some of them magnified into mountains, and the vacant lot the sea, and you will have a fit idea of the general aspect of the Encantadas, or Enchanted Isles. A group rather of extinct volcanoes than of isles, looking much as the world at large might after a penal conflagration.

It is to be doubted whether any spot of earth can, in desolateness, furnish a parallel to this group. Abandoned cemeteries of long ago, old cities by piecemeal tumbling to their ruin, these are melancholy enough; but, like all else which has but once been associated with humanity, they still awaken in us some thoughts of sympathy, however sad. Hence, even the Dead Sea, along with whatever other emotions it may at times inspire, does not fail to touch in the pilgrim some of his less unpleasurable feelings.

And as for solitariness, the great forests of the north, the expanses of unnavigated waters, the Greenland ice fields, are the profoundest of solitudes to a human observer; still the magic of their changeable tides and seasons mitigates their terror, because, though unvisited by men, those forests are visited by the May; the remotest seas reflect familiar stars even as Lake Erie does; and in the clear air of a fine Polar day, the irradiated, azure ice shows beautifully as malachite.

But the special curse, as one may call it, of the Encantadas, that which exalts them in desolation above Idumea and the Pole, is that to them change never comes; neither the change of seasons nor of sorrows. Cut by the Equator, they know not autumn, and they know not spring; while, already reduced to the lees of fire, rain itself can work little more upon them. The showers refresh the deserts, but in these isles rain never falls. Like split Syrian gourds left withering in the sun, they are cracked by an everlasting drought beneath a torrid sky. "Have mercy upon me," the wailing spirit of the Encantadas seems to cry, "and send Lazarus that he may dip the tip of his finger in water and cool my tongue, for I am tormented in this flame."

Another feature in these isles is their emphatic uninhabitableness. It is deemed a fit type of all-forsaken overthrow that the jackal should den in the wastes of weedy Babylon, but the Encantadas refuse to harbor even the outcasts of the beasts. Man and wolf alike disown them. Little but reptile life is here found: tortoises, lizards, immense spiders, snakes, and that strangest anomaly of outlandish nature, the *iguana*. No voice, no low, no howl is heard; the chief sound of life here is a hiss.

On most of the isles where vegetation is found at all, it is more un-grateful than the blankness of Aracama. Tangled thickets of wiry bushes, without fruit and without a name, springing up among deep fissures of calcined rock and treacherously masking them, or a parched growth of distorted cactus trees.

In many places the coast is rock-bound, or, more properly, clinker-bound; tumbled masses of blackish or greenish stuff like the dross of an iron furnace, forming dark clefts and caves here and there, into which a ceaseless sea pours a fury of foam, overhanging them with a swirl of gray, haggard mist, amidst which sail screaming flights of unearthly birds heightening the dismal din. However calm the sea without, there is no rest for these swells and those rocks; they lash and are lashed, even when the outer ocean is most at peace with itself. On the oppressive, clouded days, such as are peculiar to this part of the watery Equator, the dark, vitrified masses, many of which raise themselves among white whirlpools and breakers in detached and perilous places off the shore, present a most Plutonian sight. In no world but a fallen one could such lands exist.

Those parts of the strand free from the marks of fire stretch away in wide level beaches of multitudinous dead shells, with here and there decayed bits of sugar cane, bamboos, and coconuts, washed upon this other and darker world from the charming palm isles to the westward and southward, all the way from Paradise to Tartarus, while mixed with the relics of distant beauty you will sometimes see fragments of charred wood and moldering ribs of wrecks. Neither will anyone be surprised at meeting these last, after observing the conflicting currents which eddy throughout nearly all the wide channels of the entire group. The capriciousness of the tides of air sympathizes with those of the sea. Nowhere is the wind so light, baffling, and every way unreliable, and so given to perplexing calms, as at the Encantadas. Nigh a month has been spent by a ship going from one isle to another, though but ninety miles between; for owing to the force of the current, the boats employed to tow barely suffice to keep the craft from sweeping upon the cliffs, but do nothing towards accelerating her voyage. Sometimes it is impossible for a vessel from afar to fetch up with the group itself, unless large allowances for prospective leeway have been made ere its coming in sight. And yet, at other times, there is a mysterious indraft, which irresistibly draws a passing vessel among the isles, though not bound to them.

True, at one period, as to some extent at the present day, large fleets of whalemen cruised for spermaceti upon what some seamen call the Enchanted Ground. But this, as in due place will be described, was off the great outer isle of Albemarle, away from the intricacies of the smaller isles, where there is plenty of sea room, and hence to that vicinity the above remarks do not altogether apply, though even there the current runs at times with singular force, shifting, too, with as singular a caprice.

Indeed, there are seasons when currents quite unaccountable prevail for a great distance round about the total group, and are so strong and irregular as to change a vessel's course against the helm, though sailing at the rate of four or five miles the hour. The difference in the reckonings of navigators produced by these causes, along with the light and variable winds, long nourished a persuasion that there existed two distinct clusters of isles in the parallel of the Encantadas, about a hundred leagues apart. Such was the idea of their earlier visitors, the Buccaneers; and as late as 1750 the charts of that part of the Pacific accorded with the strange delusion. And this apparent fleetingness and unreality of the locality of the isles was most probably one reason for the Spaniards calling them the Encantadas, or Enchanted Group.

But not uninfluenced by their character, as they now confessedly exist, the modern voyager will be inclined to fancy that the bestowal of this name might have in part originated in that air of spellbound desertness which so significantly invests the isles. Nothing can better suggest the aspect of once living things malignly crumbled from ruddiness into ashes. Apples of Sodom, after touching, seem these isles.

However wavering their place may seem by reason of the currents, they themselves, at least to one upon the shore, appear invariably the same: fixed, cast, glued into the very body of cadaverous death.

Nor would the appellation "enchanted" seem misapplied in still another sense. For concerning the peculiar reptile inhabitant of these wilds— whose presence gives the group its second Spanish name, Gallipagos— concerning the tortoises found here, most mariners have long cherished a superstition not more frightful than grotesque. They earnestly believe that all wicked sea officers, more especially commodores and captains, are at death (and in some cases before death) transformed into tortoises, thenceforth dwelling upon these hot aridities, sole solitary lords of Asphaltum.

Doubtless, so quaintly dolorous a thought was originally inspired by the woebegone landscape itself; but more particularly, perhaps, by the tortoises. For, apart from their strictly physical features, there is something strangely self-condemned in the appearance of these creatures. Lasting sorrow and penal hopelessness are in no animal form so suppliantly expressed as in theirs; while the thought of their wonderful longevity does not fail to enhance the impression.

Nor even at the risk of meriting the charge of absurdly believing in enchantments can I restrain the admission that sometimes, even now, when leaving the crowded city to wander out July and August among the Adirondack Mountains, far from the influences of towns and proportionally nigh to the mysterious ones of nature; when at such times I sit me down in the mossy head of some deep-wooded gorge, surrounded by prostrate trunks of blasted pines, and recall, as in a dream, my other and far-distant rovings in the baked heart of the charmed isles, and remember the sudden glimpses of dusky shells, and long languid necks protruded from the leafless thickets; and again have beheld the vitreous inland rocks worn down and grooved into deep ruts by ages and ages of the slow draggings of tortoises in quest of pools of scanty water; I can hardly resist the feeling that in my time I have indeed slept upon evilly enchanted ground.

Nay, such is the vividness of my memory, or the magic of my fancy, that I know not whether I am not the occasional victim of optical delusion concerning the Gallipagos. For, often in scenes of social merriment, and especially at revels held by candlelight in old-fashioned mansions, so that shadows are thrown into the further recesses of an angular and spacious room, making them put on a look of haunted undergrowth of lonely woods, I have drawn the attention of my comrades by my fixed gaze and sudden change of air, as I have seemed to see, slowly emerging from those imagined solitudes, and heavily crawling along the floor, the ghost of a gigantic tortoise, with "Memento * * * * * " burning in live letters upon his back.

NIGHTWATCH

ANNIE DILLARD

I stood in the Lucas meadow in the middle of a barrage of grasshoppers. There must have been something about the rising heat, the falling night, the ripeness of grasses—something that mustered this army in the meadow where they have never been in such legions before. I must have seen a thousand grasshoppers, alarums and excursions clicking over the clover, knee-high to me.

I had stepped into the meadow to feel the heat and catch a glimpse of the sky, but these grasshoppers demanded my attention, and became an event in themselves. Every step I took detonated the grass. A blast of bodies like shrapnel exploded around me; the air burst and whirred. There were grasshoppers of all sizes, grasshoppers yellow, green and black, short-horned, long-horned, slant-faced, band-winged, spur-throated, cone-headed, pygmy, spotted, striped and barred. They sprang in salvos, dropped in the air, and clung unevenly to stems and blades with their legs spread for balance, as redwings ride cattail reeds. They clattered around my ears; they ricocheted off my calves with an instant clutch and release of tiny legs.

I was in shelter, but open to the sky. The meadow was clean, the world new, and I washed by my walk over the waters of the dam. A new, wild feeling descended upon me and caught me up. What if these grasshoppers were locusts, I thought; what if I were the first man in the world, and stood in a swarm?

* * *

I had been reading about locusts. Hordes of migrating locusts have always appeared in arid countries, and then disappeared as suddenly as they had come. You could actually watch them lay eggs all over a plain, and the next year there would be no locusts on the plain. Entomologists would label their specimens, study their structure, and never find a single one that was alive—until years later they would be overrun again. No one knew in what caves or clouds the locusts hid between plagues.

In 1921 a Russian naturalist named Ulvarov solved the mystery. Locusts are grasshoppers: they are the same animal. Swarms of locusts are ordinary grasshoppers gone berserk.

If you take ordinary grasshoppers of any of several species from any of a number of the world's dry regions—including the Rocky Mountains—and rear them in glass jars under crowded conditions, they go into the migratory phase. That is, they turn into locusts. They literally and physically changes from Jekyll to Hyde before your eyes. They will even change, all alone in their jars, if you stimulate them by a rapid succession of artificial touches. Imperceptibly at first, their wings and wing-covers elongate. Their drab color heightens, then saturates more and more, until it locks at the hysterical locust yellows and pinks. Stripes and dots appear on the wing-covers; these deepen to a glittering black. They lay more egg-pods than grasshoppers. They are restless, excitable, voracious. You now have jars full of plague.

Under ordinary conditions, inside the laboratory and out in the deserts, the eggs laid by these locusts produce ordinary solitary grasshoppers. Only under special conditions—such as droughts that herd them together in crowds near available food—do the grasshoppers change. They shun food and shelter and seek only the jostle and clack of their kind. Their ranks swell; the valleys teem. One fine day they take to the air.

In full flight their millions can blacken the sky for nine hours, and when they land, it's every man to your tents, O Israel. "A fire devoureth before them; and behind them a flame burneth: the land is as the garden of Eden before them, and behind them a desolate wilderness; yes, and nothing shall escape them." One writer says that if you feed one a blade of grass, "the eighteen components of its jaws go immediately into action, lubricated by a brown saliva which looks like motor oil." Multiply this action by millions, and you hear a new sound: "The noise their myriad jaws make when engaged in their work of destruction can be realized by any one who has fought a prairie fire or heard the flames passing along before a brisk wind, the low crackling and rasping." Every contour of the land, every twig, is inches deep in bodies, so the valleys seethe and the hills tremble. Locusts: it is an old story.

A man lay down to sleep in a horde of locusts, Will Barker says. Instantly the suffocating swarm fell on him and knit him in a clicking coat of mail. The metallic mouth parts meshed and pinched. His friends rushed in and woke him at once. But when he stood up, he was bleeding from the throat and wrists.

✳ ✳ ✳

The world has locusts, and the world has grasshoppers. I was up to my knees in the world.

Not one of these insects in this meadow could change into a locust under any circumstance. I am King of the Meadow, I thought, and raised my arms. Instantly grasshoppers burst all around me, describing in the air a blur of angular trajectories which ended in front of my path in a wag of grasses. As *if* I were king, dilly-dilly.

A large gray-green grasshopper hit with a clack on my shirt, and stood on my shoulder, panting. "Boo," I said, and it clattered off. It landed on a grass head several yards away. The grass bucked and sprang from the impact like a bronc, and the grasshopper rode it down. When the movement ceased, I couldn't see the grasshopper.

I walked on, one step at a time, both instigating and receiving this spray of small-arms fire. I had to laugh. I'd been had. I wanted to see the creatures, and they were gone. The only way I could see them in their cunning was to frighten them in their innocence. No charm or cleverness of mine could conjure or draw them; I could only flush them, triggering the grossest of their instincts, with the physical bluntness of my passage. To them I was just so much trouble, a horde of commotion, like any rolling stone. Wait! Where did you go? Does not any one of you, with your eighteen mouth-parts, wish to have a word with me here in the Lucas meadow? Again I raised my arms: there you are. And then gone. The grasses slammed. I was exhilarated, flushed. I was the serf of the meadow, exalted; I was the bride who waits with her lamp filled. A new wind was stirring; I had received the grasshoppers the way I received this wind. All around the meadow's rim the highest trees heaved soundlessly.

I walked back toward the cottage, maneuvering the whole squadron from one end of the meadow to the other. I'd been had all along by grasshoppers, muskrats, mountains–and like any sucker, I come back for more. They always get you in the end, and when you know it from the beginning, you have to laugh. You come for the assault, you come for the flight—but really you know you come for the laugh.

This is the fullness of late summer now; the green of what is growing and grown conceals. I can watch a muskrat feed on a bank for ten minutes, harvesting shocks of grass that bristle and droop from his jaws, and when he is gone I cannot see any difference in the grass. If I spread the patch with my hands and peer closely, I am hard put to locate any damage from even the most intense grazing. Nothing even looks trampled. Does everything else but me pass so lightly? When the praying mantis egg cases hatched in June, over a period of several days, I watched the tiny translucent mantises leap about leggily on the egg case, scraggle down the hedge's twigs, and disappear in the grass. In some places I could see them descend in a line like a moving bridge from stem to ground. The instant they crossed the horizon and entered the grass, they vanished as if they had jumped off the edge of the world.

Now it is early September, and the paths are clogged. I look to water to see sky. It is the time of year when a honeybee beats feebly at the inside back window of every parked car. A frog flies up for every foot of bank, bubbles tangle in a snare of blue-green algae, and Japanese beetles hunch doubled on the willow leaves. The sun thickens the air to jelly; it bleaches, flattens, dissolves. The skies are a milky haze—nowhere, do-nothing summer skies. Every kid I see has a circular grid on his forehead, a regular cross-hatching of straight lines, from spending his days leaning into screen doors.

I had come to the Lucas place to spend a night there, to let come what may. The Lucas place is paradise enow. It has everything: old woods, young woods, cliffs, meadows, slow water, fast water, caves. All it needs is a glacier extending a creaking foot behind the cottage. This magic garden is just on the other side of the oxbow in Tinker Creek; it is secluded because it is hard to approach. I could have followed the rock cliff path through the old woods, but in summer that path is wrapped past finding in saplings, bushes, kudzu, and poison oak. I could have tacked down the shorn grass terraces next to the cliff, but to get there I would have had to pass a vicious dog, who is waiting for the day I forget to carry a stick. So I planned on going the third way, over the dam.

I made a sandwich, filled a canteen, and slipped a palm-sized flashlight into my pocket. Then all I had to do was grab a thin foam pad and my sleeping bag, walk down the road, over the eroded clay hill where the mantis laid her eggs, along the creek downstream to the motorbike woods, and through the woods' bike trail to the dam.

I like crossing the dam. If I fell, I might not get up again. The dam is three or four feet high; a thick green algae, combed by the drag and sudden plunge of the creek's current, clings to its submersed, concrete brim. Below is a jumble of fast water and rocks. But I face this threat every time I cross the dam, and it is always exhilarating. The tightest part is at the very beginning. That day as always I faced the current, planted my feet firmly, stepped sideways instead of striding, and I soon emerged dripping in a new world.

✳ ✳ ✳

Now, returning from my foray into the grasshopper meadow, I was back where I started, on the bank that separates the cottage from the top of the dam, where my sleeping bag, foam pad, and sandwich lay. The sun was setting invisibly behind the cliffs' rim. I unwrapped the sandwich and looked back over the way I had come, as if I could have seen the grasshoppers spread themselves again over the wide meadow and hide enfolded in its thickets and plush.

This is what I had come for, just this, and nothing more. A fling of leafy motion on the cliffs, the assault of real things, living and still, with shapes and powers under the sky—this is my city, my culture, and all the world I need. I looked around.

What I call the Lucas place is only a part of the vast Lucas property. It is one of the earliest clearings around here, a garden in the wilderness; every time I cross the dam and dry my feet on the bank, I feel like I've just been born. Now to my right the creek's dammed waters were silent and deep, overhung by and reflecting bankside tulip and pawpaw and ash. The creek angled away out of sight upstream; this was the oxbow, and the dam spanned its sharpest arc. Downstream the creek slid over the dam and slapped along sandstone ledges and bankside boulders, exhaling a cooling breath of mist before disappearing around the bend under the steep wooded cliff.

I stood ringed and rimmed in heights, locked and limned, in a valley within a valley. Next to the cliff fell a grassy series of high terraces, suitable for planting the hanging gardens of Babylon. Beyond the terraces, forest erupted again wherever it could eke a roothold on the sheer vertical rock. In one place, three caves cut into the stone vaults, their entrances hidden by honeysuckle. One of the caves was so small only a child could enter it crawling; one was big enough to explore long after you have taken the initiatory turns that shut out the light; the third was huge and shallow, filled with cut wood and chicken wire, and into its nether wall extended another tiny cave in which a groundhog reared her litter this spring.

Ahead of me in the distance I could see where the forested cliffs mined with caves gave way to overgrown terraces that once must have been cleared. Now they were tangled in saplings swathed in honeysuckle and wild rose brambles. I always remember trying to fight my way up that steepness one winter when I first understood that even January is not muscle enough to subdue the deciduous South. There were clear trails through the undergrowth—I saw once I was in the thick of it—but they were rabbit paths, unfit for anyone over seven inches tall. I had emerged scratched, pricked, and panting in the Lucas peach orchard, which is considerably more conveniently approached by the steep gravel drive that parallels the creek.

In the flat at the center of all this rimrock was the sunlit grasshopper meadow, and facing the meadow, tucked up between the grass terrace and the creek's dam, was the heart of the city, the Lucas cottage.

I stepped to the porch. My footfall resounded; the cliffs rang back the sound, and the clover and grasses absorbed it. The Lucas cottage was in fact mostly porch, airy and winged. Gray-painted two-by-fours wobbled around three sides of the cottage, split, smashed, and warped long past plumb. Beams at the porch's four corners supported a low, peaked roof that vaulted over both the porch and the cottage impartially, lending so much importance to the already huge porch that it made the cottage proper seem an afterthought, as Adam seems sometimes an afterthought in Eden. For years an old inlaid chess table with a broken carved pedestal leaned against the cottage on one wing of the porch; the contrasting brown patches of weathered inlay curled up in curves like leaves.

The cottage was scarcely longer than the porch was deep. It was a one-room cottage; you could manage (I've thought this through again and again—building more spartan mansions, o my soul) a cot, a plank window-desk, a chair (two for company, as the man says), and some narrow shelves. The cottage is mostly windows—there are five—and the windows are entirely broken, so that my life inside the cottage is mostly Tinker Creek and mud dauber wasps.

It's a great life—luxurious, really. The cottage is wired for electricity; a bare-bulb socket hangs from the unfinished wood ceiling. There is a stovepipe connection in the roof. Beyond the porch on the side away from the creek is a big brick fireplace suitable for grilling whole steers. The steers themselves are fattening just five minutes away, up the hill and down into the pasture. The trees that shade the cottage are walnuts and pecans. In the spring the edge of the upstream creek just outside the cottage porch comes up in yellow daffodils, all the way up to the peach orchard.

That day it was dark inside the cottage, as usual; the five windows framed five films of the light and living world. I crunched to the creekside window, walking on the layer of glass shards on the floor, and stood to watch the creek lurch over the dam and round the shaded bend under the cliff, while bumblebees the size of ponies fumbled in the fragrant flowers that flecked the bank. A young cottontail rabbit bounded into view and froze. It crouched under my window with its ears flattened to its skull and its body motionless, the picture of adaptive invisibility. With one ridiculous exception. It was so very young, and its shoulder itched so maddeningly, that it whapped away at the spot noisily with a violent burst of a hind leg—and then resumed its frozen alert. Over the dam's drop of waters, two dog-faced sulphur butterflies were fighting. They touched and patted, ascending in a vertical climb, as though they were racing up an invisible spiraling vine.

All at once something wonderful happened, although at first it seemed perfectly ordinary. A female goldfinch suddenly hove into view. She lighted weightlessly on the head of a bankside purple thistle and began emptying the seedcase, sowing the air with down.

The lighted frame of my window filled. The down rose and spread in all directions, wafting over the dam's waterfall and wavering between the tulip trunks and into the meadow. It vaulted towards the orchard in a puff; it hovered over the ripening pawpaw fruit and staggered up the steep-faced terrace. It jerked, floated, rolled, veered, swayed. The thistledown faltered toward the cottage and gusted clear to the motorbike woods; it rose and entered the shaggy arms of pecans. At last it strayed like snow, blind and sweet, into the pool of the creek upstream, and into the race of the creek over rocks down. It shuddered onto the tips of growing grasses, where it poised, light, still wracked by errant quivers. I was holding my breath. Is this where we live, I thought, in this place at this moment, with the air so light and wild?

The same fixity that collapses stars and drives the mantis to devour her mate eased these creatures together before my eyes: the thick adept bill of the goldfinch, and the feathery, coded down. How could anything be amiss? If I myself were lighter and frayed, I could ride these small winds, too, taking my chances, for the pleasure of being so purely played.

The thistle is part of Adam's curse. "Cursed is the ground for thy sake; in sorrow shalt thou eat of it all the days of thy life; Thorns also and thistles shall it bring forth to thee." A terrible curse: But does the goldfinch eat thorny sorrow with the thistle, or do I? If this furling air is fallen, then the fall was happy indeed. If this creekside garden is sorrow, then I seek martyrdom. This crown of thorns sits light on my skull, like wings. The Venetian Baroque painter Tiepolo painted Christ as a red-lipped infant clutching a goldfinch; the goldfinch seems to be looking around in search of thorns. Creation itself was the fall, a burst into the thorny beauty of the real.

The goldfinch here on the fringed thistletop was burying her head with each light thrust deeper into the seedcase. Her fragile legs braced to her task on the vertical, thorny stem; the last of the thistledown sprayed and poured. Is there anything I could eat so lightly, or could I die so fair? With a ruffle of feathered wings the goldfinch fluttered away, out of range of the broken window's frame and toward the deep blue shade of the cliffs where late fireflies already were rising alight under trees. I was weightless; my bones were taut skins blown with buoyant gas; it seemed that if I inhaled too deeply, my shoulders and head would waft off. Alleluia.

✳   ✳   ✳

Later I lay half out of my sleeping bag on a narrow shelf of flat ground between the cottage porch and the bank to the dam. I lay where a flash flood would reach me, but we have had a flood; the time is late. The night was clear; when the fretwork of overhead foliage rustled and patted, I could see the pagan stars.

Sounds fell all about me; I vibrated like still water ruffed by wind. Cicadas—which Donald E. Carr calls "the guns of August"—were out in full force. Their stridulations mounted over the meadow and echoed from the rim of cliffs, filling the air with a plaintive, mysterious urgency. I had heard them begin at twilight, and was struck with the way they actually do "start up" like an out-of-practice orchestra, creaking and grinding and all out of synch. It had sounded like someone playing a cello with a wide-toothed comb. The frogs added their unlocatable notes, which always seem to me to be so arbitrary and anarchistic, and crickets piped in, calling their own tune which they have been calling since the time of Pliny, who noted bluntly of the cricket, it "never ceaseth all night long to creak very shrill."

Earlier a bobwhite had cried from the orchardside cliff, now here, now there, and his round notes swelled sorrowfully over the meadow. A bobwhite who is still calling in summer is lorn; he has never found a mate. When I first read this piece of information, every bobwhite call I heard sounded tinged with desperation, suicidally miserable. But now I am somehow cheered on my way by that solitary signal. The bobwhite's very helplessness, his obstinate Johnny-two-notedness, takes on an aura of dogged pluck. God knows what he is thinking in those pendant silences between calls. God knows what I am. But: bob*white*. (Somebody showed me once how to answer a bobwhite in the warbling, descending notes of the female. It works like a charm. But what can I do with a charmed circle of male bobwhites but weep? Still, I am brutalized enough that I give the answering call occasionally, just to get a rise out of the cliffs, and a bitter laugh.) Yes, it's tough, it's tough, that goes without saying. But isn't waiting itself and longing a wonder, being played on by wind, sun, and shade?

* * *

In his famous *Camping and Woodcraft*, Horace Kephart sounds a single ominous note. He writes in parentheses: "Some cannot sleep well in a white tent under a full moon." Every time I think of it, I laugh. I like the way that handy woodsy tip threatens us with the thrashings of the spirit.

I was in no tent under leaves, sleepless and glad. There was no moon at all; along the world's coasts the sea tides would be springing strong. The air itself also has lunar tides: I lay still. Could I feel in the air an invisible sweep and surge, and an answering knock in my lungs? Or could I feel the starlight? Every minute on a square mile of this land—on the steers and the orchard, on the quarry, the meadow, and creek—one ten thousandth of an ounce of starlight spatters to earth. What percentage of an ounce did that make on my eyes and cheeks and arms, tapping and nudging as particles, pulsing and stroking as waves? Straining after these tiny sensations, I nearly rolled off the world when I heard, and at the same time felt through my hips' and legs' bones on the ground, the bang and shudder of distant freight trains coupling.

Night risings and fallings filled my mind, free executions carried out invisibly while the air swung up and back and the starlight rained. By day I had watched water striders dimple and jerk over the deep bankside water slowed by the dam. But I knew that sometimes a breath or call stirs the colony, and new forms emerge with wings. They cluster at night on the surface of their home waters and then take to the air in a rush. Migrating they sail over meadows, under trees, cruising, veering towards a steady gleam in a flurry of glistening wings: "phantom ships in the air."

Now also in the valley night a skunk emerged from his underground burrow to hunt pale beetle grubs in the dark. A great horned owl folded his wings and dropped from the sky, and the two met on the bloodied surface of earth. Spreading over a distance, the air from the spot thinned to a frail sweetness, a tinctured wind that bespoke real creatures and real encounters at the edge ... events, events. Over my head black hunting beetles crawled up into the high limbs of trees, killing more caterpillars and pupae than they would eat.

I had read once about a mysterious event of the night that is never far from my mind. Edwin Way Teale described an occurrence so absurd that it vaults out of the world of strange facts and into that startling realm where power and beauty hold sovereign sway.

The sentence in Teale is simple: "On cool autumn nights, eels hurrying to the sea sometimes crawl for a mile or more across dewy meadows to reach streams that will carry them to salt water." These are adult eels, silver eels, and this descent that slid down my mind is the fall from a long spring ascent the eels made years ago. As one-inch elvers they wriggled and heaved their way from the salt sea up the coastal rivers of America and Europe, upstream always into "the quiet upper reaches of rivers and brooks, in lakes and ponds—sometimes as high as 8,000 feet above sea level." There they had lived without breeding "for at least eight years." In the late summer of the year they reached maturity, they stopped eating, and their dark color vanished. They turned silver; now they are heading to the sea. Down streams to rivers, down rivers to the sea, south in the North Atlantic where they meet and pass billions of northbound elvers, they are returning to the Sargasso Sea, where, in floating sargassum weed in the deepest waters of the Atlantic, they will mate, release their eggs, and die. This, the whole story of eels at which I have only just hinted, is extravagant in the extreme, and food for another kind of thought, a thought about the meaning of such wild, incomprehensible gestures. But it was feeling with which I was concerned under the walnut tree by the side of the Lucas cottage and dam. My mind was on that meadow.

Imagine a chilly night and a meadow; balls of dew droop from the curved blades of grass. All right: the grass at the edge of the meadow begins to tremble and sway. Here come the eels. The largest are five feet long. All are silver. They stream into the meadow, sift between grasses and clover, veer from your path. There are too many to count. All you see is a silver slither, like twisted ropes of water falling roughly, a one-way milling and mingling over the meadow and slide to the creek. Silver eels in the night: a barely-made-out seething as far as you can squint, a squirming, jostling torrent of silver eels in the grass. If I saw that sight, would I live? If I stumbled across it, would I ever set foot from my door again? Or would I be seized to join that compelling rush, would I cease eating, and pale, and abandon all to start walking?

✳ ✳ ✳

Had this place always been so, and had I not known it? These were blowings and flights, tossings and heaves up the air and down to grass. Why didn't God let the animals in Eden name the man; why didn't I wrestle the grasshopper on my shoulder and pin him down till he called my name? I was thistledown, and now I seemed to be grass, the receiver of grasshoppers and eels and mantises, grass the windblown and final receiver.

For the grasshoppers and thistledown and eels went up and came down. If you watch carefully the hands of a juggler, you see they are almost motionless, held at precise angles, so that the balls seem to be of their own volition describing a perfect circle in the air. The ascending arc is the hard part, but our eyes are on the smooth and curving fall. Each falling ball seems to trail beauty as its afterimage, receding faintly down the air, almost disappearing, when lo, another real ball falls, shedding its transparent beauty, and another....

And it all happens so dizzyingly fast. The goldfinch I had seen was asleep in a thicket; when she settled to sleep, the weight of her breast locked her toes around her perch. Wasps were asleep with their legs hanging loose, their jaws jammed into the soft stems of plants. Everybody grab a handle: we're spinning headlong down.

I am puffed clay, blown up and set down. That I fall like Adam is not surprising: I plunge, waft, arc, pour, and dive. The surprise is how good the wind feels on my face as I fall. And the other surprise is that I ever rise at all. I rise when I receive, like grass.

I didn't know, I never have known, what spirit it is that descends into my lungs and flaps near my heart like an eagle rising. I named it full-of-wonder, highest good, voices. I shut my eyes and saw a tree stump hurled by wind, an enormous tree stump sailing sideways across my vision, with a wide circular brim of roots and soil like a tossed top hat.

And what if those grasshoppers had been locusts descending, I thought, and what if I stood awake in a swarm? I cannot ask for more than to be so wholly acted upon, flown at, and lighted on in throngs, probed, knocked, even bitten. A little blood from the wrists and throat is the price I would willingly pay for that pressure of clacking weights on my shoulders, for the scent of deserts, groundfire in my ears—for being so in the clustering thick of things, rapt and enwrapped in the rising and falling real world.

CRUSOE'S ISLAND

DANIEL DEFOE

With these Considerations I walk'd very leisurely forward, I found that Side of the Island where I now was, much pleasanter than mine, the open or *Savanna* Fields sweet, adorn'd with Flowers and Grass, and full of very fine Woods. I saw Abundance of Parrots, and fain I would have caught one, if possible to have kept it to be tame, and taught it to speak to me. I did, after some Pains taking, catch a young Parrot, for I knock'd it down with a Stick, and having recover'd it, I brought it home; but it was some Years before I could make him speak: However, at last I taught him to call me by my Name very familiarly: But the Accident that follow'd, tho' it be a Trifle, will be very diverting in its Place.

I was exceedingly diverted with this Journey: I found in the low Grounds Hares, as I thought them to be, and Foxes, but they differ'd greatly from all the other Kinds I had met with; nor could I satisfy my self to eat them, tho' I kill'd several: But I had no Need to be ventrous; for I had no Want of Food, and of that which was very good too; especially these three Sorts, *viz.* Goats, Pidgeons, and Turtle or Tortoise; which, added to my Grapes, *Leaden-hall* Market could not have furnish'd a Table better than I, in Proportion to the Company; and tho' my Cafe was deplorable enough, yet I had great Cause for Thankfulness, that I was not driven to any Extremities for Food; but rather Plenty, even to Dainties.

I never travell'd in this Journey above two Miles outright in a Day, or thereabouts; but I took so many Turns and Returns, to see what Discoveries I could make, that I came weary enough to the Place where I resolv'd to sit down for all Night; and then I either repos'd my self in a Tree, or surrounded my self with a Row of Stakes set upright in the Ground, either from one Tree to another, or so as no wild Creature could come at me, without waking me.

As soon as I came to the Sea Shore, I was surpriz'd to see that I had taken up my Lot on the worst Side of the Island; for here indeed the Shore was cover'd with innumerable Turtles, whereas on the other Side I had found but three in a Year and half. Here was also an infinite Number of Fowls, of many Kinds, some which I had seen, and some which I had not seen of before, and many of them very good Meat; but such as I knew not the Names of, except those call'd *Penguins*.

I could have shot as many as I pleas'd, but was very sparing of my Powder and Shot; and therefore had more Mind to kill a she Goat, if I could, which I could better feed on; and though there were many Goats here more than on my Side the Island, yet it was with much more Difficulty that I could come near them, the Country being flat and even, and they saw me much sooner than when I was on the Hill.

I confess this Side of the Country was much pleasanter than mine, but yet I had not the least Inclination to remove; for as I was fix'd in my Habituation, it became natural to me, and I seem'd all the while I was here, to be as it were upon a Journey, and from Home: However, I travell'd along the Shore of the Sea, towards the *East*, I suppose about twelve Miles; and the setting up a great Pole upon the Shore for a Mark, I concluded I would go Home again; and that the next Journey I took should be on the other Side of the Island. *East* from my Dwelling, and so round till I came to my Post again: Of which in its Place.

I took another Way to come back than that I went, thinking I could easily keep all the Island so much in my View, that I could not miss finding my first Dwelling by viewing the Country; but I found my self mistaken; for being come about two or three Miles, I found my self descended into a very large Valley; but so surrounded with Hills, and those Hills cover'd with Wood, that I could not see which was my Way by any Direction but that of the Sun, nor even then, unless I knew very well the Position of the Sun at that Time of the Day.

It happen'd to my farther Misfortune, That the Weather prov'd hazey for three or four Days, while I was in this Valley; and not being able to see the Sun, I wander'd about very uncomfortably, and at last was oblig'd to find out the Sea Side, look for my Post, and come back the same Way I went; and then by easy Journies I turn'd Homeward, the Weather being exceeding hot, and my Gun, Ammunition, Hatchet, and other Things very heavy.

In this Journey my Dog surpriz'd a young Kid, and seiz'd upon it, and I running to take hold of it, caught it, and sav'd it alive from the Dog: I had a great Mind to bring it Home if I could; for I had often been musing, Whether it might not be possible to get a Kid or two, and so raise a Breed of tame Goats, which might supply me when my Powder and Shot should be all spent.

I made a Collar to this little Creature, and with a String which I made of some Rope-Yarn, which I always carry'd about me, I led him along, tho' with some Difficulty, till I came to my Bower, and there I enclos'd him and left him; for I was very impatient to be at Home, from whence I had been absent about a Month.

I cannot express what a Satisfaction it was to me, to come into my old Hutch, and lye down in my Hamock-Bed: This little wandering Journey, without settled Place of Abode, had been so unpleasant to me, that my own House, as I call'd it to my self, was a perfect Settlement to me, compar'd to that; and it rendred every Thing about me so comfortable, that I resolv'd I would never go a great Way from it again, while it should be my Lot to stay on the Island.

I repos'd my self here a Week, to rest and regale my self after my long Journey; during which, most of the Time was taken up in the weighty Affair of making a Cage for my Poll, who began now to be a meer Domestick, and to be mighty well acquainted with me. Then I began to think of the poor Kid, which I had penn'd in within my little Circle, and resolv'd to go and fetch it Home, or give it some Food; accordingly I went, and found it where I left it; for indeed it could not get out, but almost starv'd for want of Food: I went and cut Bows of Trees, and Branches of such Shrubs as I could find, and threw it over, and having fed it, I ty'd it as I did before, to lead it away; but it was so tame with being hungry, that I had no need to have ty'd it; for it follow'd me like a Dog; and as I continually fed it, the Creature became so loving, so gentle, and so fond, that it became from that Time one of my Domesticks also, and would never leave me afterwards.

The rainy Season of the *Autumnal Equinox* was now come, and I kept the 30th of *Sept.* in the same solemn Manner as before, being the Anniversary of my Landing on the Island, having now been there two Years, and no more Prospect of being deliver'd, than the first Day I came there. I spent the whole Day in humble and thankful Acknowledgments of the many wonderful Mercies which my Solitary Condition was attended with, and without which it might have been infinitely more miserable. I gave humble and hearty Thanks that God had been pleas'd to discover to me, even that it was possible I might be more happy in this Solitary Condition, than I should have been in a Liberty of Society, and in all the Pleasures of the World. That he could fully make up to me, the Deficiencies of my Solitary State, and the want of Humane Society by his Presence, and the Communications of his Grace to my Soul, supporting, comforting, and encouraging me to depend upon his Providence here, and hope for his Eternal Presence hereafter.

JOURNAL 1866

GERARD MANLEY HOPKINS

MAY 3   Cold. Morning raw and wet, afternoon fine. Walked then with Addis, crossing Bablock Hythe, round by Skinner's Weir through many fields into the Witney Road. Sky sleepy blue without liquidity. Fr. Cumnor Hill saw St. Philip's and the other spires through blue haze rising pale in a pink light. On further side of the Witney road hills, just fleeced with grain or other green growth, by their dips and waves foreshortened here and there and so differenced in brightness and opacity the green on them, with delicate effect. On left, brow of the near hill glistening with very bright newly turned sods and a scarf of vivid green slanting away beyond the skyline, agst. which the clouds shewed the slightest tinge of rose or purple. Copses in grey-red or grey-yellow—the tinges immediately forerunning the opening of full leaf. Meadows skirting Seven-bridge road voluptuous green. Some oaks are out in small leaf. Ashes not out, only tufted with their fringy blooms. Hedges springing richly. Elms in small leaf, with more or less opacity. White poplars most beautiful in small grey crisp spray-like leaf. Cowslips capriciously colouring meadows in creamy drifts. Bluebells, purple orchis. Over the green water of the river passing the slums of the town and under its bridges swallows shooting, blue and purple above and shewing their amber-tinged breasts reflected in the water, their flight unsteady with wagging wings and leaning first to one side then the other. Peewits flying. Towards sunset the sky partly swept, as often, with moist white cloud, tailing off across which are morsels of grey-black woolly clouds. Sun seemed to make a bright liquid hole in this, its texture had an upward northerly sweep or drift fr. the W. marked softly in grey. Dog violets. Eastward after sunset range of clouds rising in bulky heads moulded softly in tufts or bunches of snow—so it looks—and membered somewhat elaborately, rose-coloured. Notice often imperfect fairy rings. Apple and other fruit trees blossomed beautifully. A.* talking about the whole story of the home affairs. His idea was (when he went down three years ago and was all the Long† preparing for confession) that 7 yrs. was a moderate time during wh. to fast within the boundaries of life and abstain from communicating. Being not allowed to read he took long walks, and it must have been on one of these that he fainted as he once told me. . . .

MAY 6 Grey. A little time ago on much such another day noticed Trinity gardens. Much distinctness, charm, and suggestiveness abt. the match of white grey sky, solid smooth lawn, firs and yews, dark trees, below, and chestnuts and other brighter-lined trees above, the young green having a fresh moist opaque look and there being in the whole picture an absence of projection, and apprehension of colour. On such a day also last Friday week boated with H. Dugmore to Godstow, but the warm greyness of the day, the river, the spring green, and the cuckoo wanted a canon by wh. to harmonise and round them in—e.g. one of feeling.

JUNE 30 Thunderstorms all day, great claps and lightning running up and down. When it was bright betweentimes great towering clouds behind which the sun put out his shaded horns very clearly and a longish way. Level curds and whey sky after sunset.—Graceful growth of Etzkolt-zias‡ or however those unhappy flowers are spelt. Yews and evergreen trees now very thin and putting out their young pale shoots.

JULY 1 Sharp showers, bright between. Late in the afternoon, the light and shade being brilliant, snowy blocks of cloud were filing over the sky, and under the sun hanging above and along the earth-line were those multitudinous up-and-down crispy sparkling chains with pearly shadows up to the edges. At sunset, wh. was in a grey bank with moist gold dabs and racks, the whole round of skyline had level clouds naturally lead-

---

*W. E. Addis.
†i.e. the Long Vacation.
‡Eschscholtzias.

colour but the upper parts ruddled, some more, some less, rosy. Spits or beams braided or built in with slanting pellet flakes made their way. Through such clouds anvil-shaped pink ones and up-blown fleece-of-wool flat-topped dangerous-looking pieces.

JULY 11   Oats: hoary blue-green sheaths and stalks, prettily shadow-stroked spikes of pale green grain. Oaks: the organisation of this tree is difficult. Speaking generally no doubt the determining planes are concentric, a system of brief contiguous and continuous tangents, whereas those of the cedar wd. roughly be called horizontals and those of the beech radiating but modified by droop and by a screw-set towards jutting points. But beyond this since the normal growth of the boughs is radiating and the leaves grow some way in there is of course a system of spoke-wise clubs of green—sleeve-pieces. And since the end shoots curl and carry young and scanty leaf-stars these clubs are tapered, and I have seen also the pieces in profile with chiselled outlines, the blocks thus made detached and lessening towards the end. However the star knot is the chief thing: it is whorled, worked round, a little and this is what keeps up the illusion of the tree: the leaves are rounded inwards and figure out ball-knots. Oaks differ much, and much turns on the broadness of the leaf, the narrower giving the crisped and starry and catharine-wheel forms, the broader the flat-pieced mailed or shard-covered ones, in wh. it is possible to see composition in dips, etc., on wider bases than the single knot or cluster. But I shall study them further. See the 19th.

JULY 17   It was this night I believe but possibly the next that I saw clearly the impossibility of staying in the Church of England, but resolved to say nothing to anyone till three months are over, that is the end of the Long, and then of course to take no step till after my Degree.

JULY 18   Bright. Sunset over oaks a dapple of rosy clouds blotted with purple, sky round confused pale green and blue with faint horned rays, crimson sparkles through the leaves below. . . .

JULY 19   Alone in the woods and in Mr. Nelthorpe's park, whence one gets such a beautiful view southwards over the country. I have now found the law of the oak leaves. It is of platter-shaped stars altogether; the leaves lie close like pages, packed, and as if drawn tightly to. But these old packs, wh. lie at the end of their twigs, throw out now long shoots alternately and slimly leaved, looking like bright keys. All the sprays but markedly these ones shape out and as it were embrace greater circles and the dip and toss of these make the wider and less organic articulations of the tree.

AUGUST 23, 1867   Fine and cloudless; fiery sunset.—Some wych-elms seem to have leaves smaller, others bigger, than the common elm: . . .

AUGUST 30   Fair; in afternoon fine; the clouds had a good deal of crisping and mottling.—A round by Plumley.*—Stands of ash in a copse: they consisted of two or three rods most gracefully leaved, for each wing or comb finally curled inwards, that is upwards.—Putting my hand up against the sky whilst we lay on the grass I saw more richness and beauty in the blue than I had known of before, not brilliance but glow and colour. It was not transparent and sapphire-like, but turquoise-like, swarming and blushing round the edge of the hand and in the pieces clipped in by the fingers, the flesh being sometimes sunlit, sometimes glassy with reflected light, sometimes lightly shadowed in that violet one makes with cobalt and Indian red.

APRIL 27, 1868   Generally fine betw. hard showers; some hail, wh. made the evening very cold, a flash of lightning, a clap of thunder, and a bright rainbow; some grey cloud betw. showers ribbed and draped and some wild bright big brown flix at the border of a great rack with blue rising behind—though it was too big in character to be called flix. To Roehampton into retreat. . .

MAY 2   Fine, with some haze, and warm. This day, I think, I resolved. See *supra* last 23rd August and *infra* May 11.

MAY 3   Bright, with haze—dark-in-bright—, hot, and like summer; when cloud formed it was delicately barred.—Cuckoo singing all day. Oaks out, wych-elms not, except a few leaves.

MAY 4   Dull; then fine; cold, esp. in wind.—Note the elm here on one side of beautiful build with one great limb overhanging the sunk fence into

---

*Village in Devonshire.

the Park and headed like the one near the house at Shanklin but when seen fr. the opposite side to this limb uninteresting or clumsy.

MAY 5   Cold. Resolved to be a religious.

MAY 6   Fine but rather thick and with a very cold N.E. wind.

MAY 7   Warm; misty morning; then beautiful turquoise sky. Home, after having decided to be a priest and religious but still doubtful betw. St. Benedict and St. Ignatius. . . .

MAY 11   Dull; afternoon fine. Slaughter of the innocent.* See above, the 2nd.

JUNE 27   Silver mottled clouding, and clearer; else like yesterday. At the Nat. Gallery. That Madonna by Beltraffio. Qy. has not Giotto the in-stress of loveliness? Mantegna's draperies.

JULY 3   Started with Ed. Bond for Switzerland. We went by Dover and Ostende to Brussels....

JULY 5   To mass at the cathedral [Cologne]. Then up the Rhine to Mainz. The Rhine hills are shaped in strict planes and coigns. Where the banks are flat mossy or velvet eyots of poplar edged with osier rise plump from the river.
The day was, I think, dull.
Watching from close the motion of a flag in the wind.

JULY 6   Rainy till lately (5 o'clock), when a low rainbow backed by the Black Forest hills, which were partly dimmed out with wet mist, appeared, and—what I never saw before—rays of shadow crossed it, all its round, and where they crossed it paled the colour. It was a "blue bow." That evening saw a shepherd *leading* his flock through the town.
By railway to Basel. Beautiful view from the train of the hills near Mülheim etc. They were clothed with wood and at the openings in this and indeed all upward too they were charactered by vertical stemming, dim in the distance. Villages a little bare like Brill rise in blocks of white and deep

---

*This probably refers to the burning of his poems.

russet tiling. The nearer hills terraced with vineyards deep and vertical, the pale grey shaven poles close on the railway leaning capriciously towards one another.—Here we met the young Englishman who had been to see Charlotte Brontë's school in Brussels. . . .

But Basel at night! with a full moon waking the river and sending up straight beams from the heavy clouds that overhung it. We saw this from the bridge. The river runs so strong that it keeps the bridge shaking. Then we walked about the place and first of all had the adventure of the little Englishwoman with her hat off. We went through great spacious streets and places dead still and came to fountains of the clearest black water through which pieces of things at the bottom gleamed white. We got up to a height where a bastion-shaped vertical prominence shaded with chestnut trees looked down on the near roofs, which then in the moonlight were purple and velvety and edged along with ridges and chimneys of calk white. A woman came to a window with a candle and some mess she was making, and then that was gone and there was no light anywhere but the moon. We heard music indoors about. We saw the courtyard of a charming house with some tree pushing to the windows and a fountain. A church too of immensely high front all dead and flush to the top and next to it three most graceful flamboyant windows. Nothing cd. be more taking and fantastic than this stroll.

JULY 7   Fine morning; rain betw. Basel and Lucerne and in the evening. We saw the Münster and the Museum—where there is a noble dead Christ by the younger Holbein, but the other Holbeins were unimpressive; also a Crucifixion by a German master in which the types of the two thieves, especially the good thief—a young man with a moustache and modern air—were in the wholeness and general scape of the anatomy original and interesting. (The prominence of the peculiar square-shaped drapery etc. in Holbein and his contemporaries is remarkable—e.g. as a determination of German art.) ...

Swiss trees are, like English, well inscaped—in quains.

JULY 9   Before sunrise looking out of window saw a noble scape of stars—the Plough all golden falling, Cassiopeia* on end with her bright

---

*In July the principal stars of this constellation form a sort of flattened W on end—in two base angles ("quains") pointing to the right.

quains pointing to the right, the graceful bends of Perseus underneath her, and some great star whether Capella or not I am not sure risen over the brow of the mountain. Sunrise we saw well: the north landscape was blighty but the south, the important one, with the Alps, clear; lower down all was mist and flue of white cloud, wh. grew thicker as the day went on and like a junket lay scattered on the lakes. The sun lit up the bright acres of the snows at first with pink but afterwards clear white: the snow of the Bernese Highland remained from its distance pinkish all day.—The mountain ranges, as any series or body of inanimate like things not often seen, have the air of persons and of interrupted activity; they are multitudinous too, and also they express a second level with an upper world or shires of snow.—In going down betw. Pilatus and a long streak of cloud the blue sky was greenish. Since I have found this colour is seen in looking fr. the snow to the sky but why I do not understand: can there possibly be a rose hue suppressed in the white (—*purpurea candidior nive*)?

JULY 11   Fine. We took a guide up the Wylerhorn but the top being clouded dismissed him and stayed up the mountain, lunching by a waterfall. Presently after long climbing—for there was a good chance of a clearance—we nearly reached the top, when a cloud coming on thick frightened me back: had we gone on we shd. have had the view, for it cleared quite. Still we saw the neighbouring mountains well. The snow is often cross-harrowed and lies too in the straightest paths as though artificial, wh. again comes fr. the planing. In the sheet it glistens yellow to the sun. How fond of and warped to the mountains it wd. be easy to become! For every cliff and limb and edge and jutty has its own nobility.—Two boys came down the mountain yodelling.—We saw the snow in the hollows for the first time. In one the surface was crisped across the direction of the cleft and the other way, that is across the broader crisping and down the stream, combed: the stream ran below and smoke came fr. the hollow: the edge of the snow hewn in curves as if by moulding planes.—Crowd of mountain flowers—gentians; gentianellas; blood-red lucerne; a deep blue glossy spiked flower like plantain, flowering gradually up the spike, so that at the top it looks like clover or honeysuckle; rich big harebells glistening black like the cases of our veins when dry and heated fr. without; and others. All the herbage enthronged with every fingered or fretted leaf.—Firs very tall, with the swell of the branching on the outer side of the slope so that the peaks seem to point inwards to the mountain peak, like the lines of the

Parthenon, and the outline melodious and moving on many focuses.—I wore my pagharee and turned it with harebells below and gentians in two rows above like double pan-pipes.—In coming down we lost our way and each had a dangerous slide down the long wet grass of a steep slope.

Waterfalls not only skeined but silky too—one saw it fr. the inn across the meadows: at one quain of the rock the water glistened above and took shadow below, and the rock was reddened a little way each side with the wet, wh. sets off the silkiness. . . .

JULY 19, 1868   Sunday, but no Catholics, I found, at Meyringen. The day fine.

Walked up the valley of the Aar, sallow-coloured and torrent, to the Grimsel. The heights bounding the valley soon became a mingle of lilac and green, the first the colour of the rock, the other the grass crestings, and seemed to group above in crops and rounded buttresses, yet to be cut sharp in horizontal or leaning planes below.

We came up with a guide who reminded me of F. John. He took E. B.'s knapsack and on finding the reason why I would not let him take mine said "Le bon Dieu n'est pass comme ca." The man probably was a rational Protestant; if a Catholic at least he rationalised gracefully, as they do in Switzerland.

At a turn in the road the foam-cuffs in the river, looked down upon, were of the crispiest endive spraying.

We lunched at Guttanmen, where there was that strange party of Americans.

I was arguing about the planing of rocks and made a sketch of two in the Aar, and after that it was strange, for Nature became Nemesis, so precise they were, and E. B. himself pointed out two which looked, he said, as if they had been sawn. And of the hills themselves it could sometimes be seen, but on the other hand the sides of the valley often descended in trending sweeps of vertical section and so met at the bottom.

At times the valley opened in *cirques*, amphitheatres, enclosing levels of plain, and the river then ran between flaky flat-fish isles made of cindery lily-white stones.—In or near one of these openings the guide cries out "Voulez-vous une Alp-rose?" and up he springs the side of the hill and brings us each bunches of flowers down.

In one place over a smooth table of rock came slipping down a blade of water looking like and as evenly crisped as fruitnets let drop and falling slack.

We saw Handeck waterfall. It is in fact the meeting of two waters, the right the Aar sallow and jade-coloured, the left a smaller stream of clear lilac foam. It is the greatest fall we have seen. The lower half is hidden in spray. I watched the great bushes of foam-water, the texture of branchings and water-spandrils which makes them up. At their outsides nearest the rock they gave off showers of drops strung together into little quills which sprang out in fans.

On crossing the Aar again there was as good a fall as some we have paid to see, all in jostling foam-bags.

Across the valley too we saw the fall of the Gelmer—like milk: chasing round blocks of coal; or a girdle or long purse of white weighted with irregular black rubies, carelessly thrown aside and lying in jutty bends, with a black clasp of the same stone at the top—for those were the biggest blocks, squared, and built up, as it happened, in lessening stories, and the cascade enclosed them on the right and left hand with its foam; or once more like the skin of a white snake square-pied with black.

JULY 20   Fine.

Walked down to the Rhone glacier. It has three stages—first a smoothly-moulded bed in a pan or theatre of thorny peaks, swells of ice rising through the snow-sheet and the snow itself tossing and fretting into the sides of the rock walls in spray-like points: this is the first stage of the glaciers generally; it is like bright-plucked water swaying in a pail—; second, after a slope nearly covered with landslips of moraine, was a ruck of horned waves steep and narrow in the gut: now in the upper Grindelwald glacier between the bed or highest stage was a descending limb which was like the rude and knotty bossings of a strombus shell—; third the foot, a broad limb opening out and reaching the plain, shaped like the fan-fin of a dolphin or a great bivalve shell turned on its face, the flutings in either case being suggested by the crevasses and the ribs by the risings between them, these being swerved and inscaped strictly to the motion of the mass. Or you may compare the three stages to the heel, instep, and ball or toes of a foot.—The second stage looked at from nearer appeared like a box of plaster of Paris or starch or tooth-powder a little moist, tilted up and then struck and jarred so that the powder broke and tumbled in shapes and rifts.

We went into the grotto and also the vault from which the Rhone flows. It looked like a blue tent and as you went further in changed to lilac. As you come out the daylight glazes the groins with gleaming rosecolour. The ice inside has a branchy wire texture. The man shewed us the odd way in which a little piece of ice will stick against the walls—as if drawn by a magnet.

Standing on the glacier saw the prismatic colours in the clouds, and worth saying what sort of clouds: it was fine shapeless skins of fretted make, full of eyebrows or like linings of curled leaves which one finds in shelved corners of a wood.

I had a trudge over the glacier and a tumble over the side moraine, which was one landslip of limestone. It was neighboured however by hot sweet smells and matty flowers—small crimson pinks, the brown tulip-like flower we have seen so often, another which we first saw yesterday like Solomon's seal but rather coarser with a spike of greenish veiny-leaved blossom, etc.

FLOWERY TUSCANY

D. H. LAWRENCE

I

Each country has its own flowers, that shine out specially there. In England it is daisies and buttercups, hawthorn and cowslips. In America, it is goldenrod, stargrass, June daisies, Mayapple and asters, that we call Michaelmas daisies. In India, hibiscus and dattura and champa flowers, and in Australia mimosa, that they call wattle, and sharp-tongued strange heath-flowers. In Mexico it is cactus flowers, that they call roses of the desert, lovely and crystalline among many thorns; and also the dangling yard-long clusters of the cream bells of the yucca, like dropping froth.

But by the Mediterranean, now as in the days of the Argosy, and, we hope, for ever, it is narcissus and anemone, asphodel and myrtle, Narcissus and anemone, asphodel, crocus, myrtle, and parsley, they leave their sheer significance only by the Mediterranean. There are daisies in Italy too: at Paestum there are white little carpets of daisies, in March, and Tuscany is spangled with celandine. But for all that, the daisy and the celandine are English flowers, their best significance is for us and for the North.

The Mediterranean has narcissus and anemone, myrtle and asphodel and grape hyacinth. These are the flowers that speak and are understood in the sun round the Middle Sea.

Tuscany is especially flowery, being wetter than Sicily and more homely than the Roman hills. Tuscany manages to remain so remote, and secretly smiling to itself in its many sleeves. There are so many hills popping up, and they take no notice of one another. There are so many little deep valleys with streams that seem to go their own little way

entirely, regardless of river or sea. There are thousands, millions of utterly
secluded little nooks, though the land has been under cultivation these
thousands of years. But the intensive culture of vine and olive and wheat,
by the ceaseless industry of naked human hands and winter-shod feet,
and slow-stepping, soft-eyed oxen does not devastate a country, does not
denude it, does not lay it bare, does not uncover its nakedness, does not
drive away either Pan or his children. The streams run and rattle over wild
rocks of secret places, and murmur through blackthorn thickets where the
nightingales sing all together, unruffled and undaunted.

It is queer that a country so perfectly cultivated as Tuscany, where half
the produce of five acres of land will have to support ten human mouths,
still has so much room for the wild flowers and the nightingale. When little
hills heave themselves suddenly up, and shake themselves free of neighbours, man has to build his garden and his vineyard, and sculp his landscape. Talk of hanging gardens of Babylon, all Italy, apart from the
plains, is a hanging garden. For centuries upon centuries man has been
patiently modelling the surface of the Mediterranean countries, gently
rounding the hills, and graduating the big slopes and the little slopes into
the almost invisible levels of terraces. Thousands of square miles of Italy
have been lifted in human hands, piled and laid back in tiny little flats,
held up by the drystone walls, whose stones came from the lifted earth. It
is a work of many, many centuries. It is the gentle sensitive sculpture of all
the landscape. And it is the achieving of the peculiar Italian beauty which
is so exquisitely natural, because man, feeling his way sensitively to the
fruitfulness of the earth, has moulded the earth to his necessity without
violating it.

Which shows that it *can* be done. Man *can* live on the earth and by the
earth without disfiguring the earth. It has been done here, on all these
sculptured hills and softly, sensitively terraced slopes.

But, of course, you can't drive a steam plough on terraces four yards
wide, terraces that dwindle and broaden and sink and rise a little, all
according to the patch and the breaking outline of the mother hill. Corn
has got to grow on these little shelves of earth, where already the grey olive
stands semi-invisible, and the grapevine twists upon its own scars. If oxen
can step with that lovely pause at every little stride, they can plough the
narrow field. But they will have to leave a tiny fringe, a grassy lip over
the drystone wall below. And if the terraces are too narrow to plough, the
peasant digging them will still leave the grassy lip, because it helps to
hold the surface in the rains.

And here the flowers take refuge. Over and over and over and over has this soil been turned, twice a year, sometimes three times a year, for several thousands of years. Yet the flowers have never been driven out. There is a very rigorous digging and sifting, the little bulbs and tubers are flung away into perdition, not a weed shall remain.

Yet spring returns, and on the terrace lips, and in the stony nooks between terraces, up rise the aconites, the crocuses, the narcissus and the asphodel, the inextinguishable wild tulips. There they are, for every hanging on the precarious brink of an existence, but for ever triumphant, never quite losing their footing. In England, in America, the flowers get rooted out, driven back. They become fugitive. But in the intensive cultivation of ancient Italian terraces, they dance round and hold their own.

Spring begins with the first narcissus, rather cold and shy and wintry. They are the little bunchy, creamy narcissus with the yellow cup like the yolk of the flower. The natives call these flowers *tazzette*, little cups. They grow on the grassy banks rather sparse, or push up among thorns.

To me they are winter flowers, and their scent is winter. Spring starts in February, with the winter aconite. Some icy day, when the wind is down from the snow of the mountains, early in February, you will notice on a bit of fallow land, under the olive trees, tight, pale-gold little balls, clenched tight as nuts, and resting on round ruffs of green near the ground. It is the winter aconite suddenly come.

The winter aconite is one of the most charming flowers. Like all the early blossoms, once her little flower emerges it is quite naked. No shutting a little green sheath over herself, like the daisy or the dandelion. Her bubble of frail, pale, pure gold rests on the round frill of her green collar, with the snowy wind trying to blow it away.

But without success. The *tramontana* ceases, comes a day of wild February sunshine. The clenched little nuggets of the aconite puff out, they become light bubbles, like small balloons, on a green base. The sun blazes on, with February splendour. And by noon, all under the olives are wide-open little suns, the aconites spreading all their rays; and there is an exquisitely sweet scent, honeysweet, no narcissus-frosty; and there is a February humming of little brown bees.

Till afternoon, when the sun slopes, and the touch of snow comes back into the air.

But at evening, under the lamp on the table, the aconites are wide and excited, and there is a perfume of sweet spring that makes one almost start humming and trying to be a bee.

Aconites don't last very long. But they turn up in all odd places—on clods of dug earth, and in land where the broad-beans are thrusting up, and along the lips of terraces. But they like best land left fallow for one winter. There they throng, showing how quick they are to seize on an opportunity to live and shine forth.

In a fortnight, before February is over, the yellow bubbles of the aconite are crumpling to nothingness. But already in a cosy-nook the violets are dark purple, and there is a new little perfume in the air.

Like the debris of winter stand the hellebores, in all the wild places, and the butcher's broom is flaunting its last bright red berry. Hellebore is Christmas roses, but in Tuscany the flowers never come white. They emerge out of the grass towards the end of December, flowers wintry of winter, and they are delicately pale green, and of a lovely shape, with yellowish stamens. They have a peculiar wintry quality of invisibility, so lonely rising from the sere grass, and pallid green, held up like a little hand-mirror that reflects nothing. At first they are single upon a stem, short and lovely, and very wintry-beautiful, with a will not to be touched, not to be noticed. One instinctively leaves them alone. But as January draws towards February, these hellebores, these greenish Christmas roses become more assertive. Their pallid water-green becomes yellower, pale sulphur-yellow-green, and they rise up, they are in tufts, in throngs, in veritable bushes of greenish open flowers, assertive, bowing their faces with a hellebore assertiveness. In some places they throng among the bushes and above the water of the stream, giving the peculiar pale glimmer almost of primroses, as you walk among them. Almost of primroses, yet with a coarse hellebore leaf and an uprearing hellebore assertiveness, like snakes in winter.

And as one walks among them, one brushes the last scarlet of the butcher's broom. This low little shrub is the Christmas holly of Tuscany, only a foot or so high, with a vivid red berry stuck on in the middle of its sharp hard leaf. In February the last red ball rolls off the prickly plume, and winter rolls with it. The violets already are emerging from the moisture.

But before the violets make any show, there are the crocuses. If you walk up through the pine-wood, that lifts its umbrellas of pine so high, up till you come to the brow of the hill at the top, you can look south, due south, and see snow on the Apennines, and on a blue afternoon, seven layers of blue-hilled distance.

Then you sit down on that southern slope, out of the wind, and there it is warm, whether it be January or February, *tramontana* or not. There the earth has been baked by innumerable suns, baked and baked again; moistened by many rains, but never wetted for long. Because it is rocky, and full to the south, and sheering steep in the slope.

And there, in February, in the sunny baked desert of that crumbly slope, you will find the first crocuses. On the sheer aridity of crumbled stone you see a queer, alert little star, very sharp and quite small. It has opened out rather flat, and looks like a tiny freesia flower, creamy, with a smear of yellow yolk. It has no stem, seems to have been just lightly dropped on the crumbled, baked rock. It is the first hill-crocus.

II

North of the Alps, the everlasting winter is interrupted by summers that struggle and soon yield; south of the Alps, the everlasting summer is interrupted by spasmodic and spiteful winters that never get a real hold, but that are mean and dogged. North of the Alps, you may have a pure winter's day in June. South of the Alps, you may have a midsummer day in December or January or even February. The in-between, in either case, is just as it may be. But the lands of the sun are south of the Alps, for ever.

Yet things, the flowers especially, that belong to both sides of the Alps, are not much earlier south than north of the mountains. Through all the winter there are roses in the garden, lovely creamy roses, more pure and mysterious than those of summer, leaning perfect from the stem. And the narcissus in the garden are out by the end of January, and the little simple hyacinths early in February.

But out in the fields, the flowers are hardly any sooner than English flowers. It is mid-February before the first violets, the first crocus, the first primrose. And in mid-February one may find a violet, a primrose, a crocus in England, in the hedgerows and the garden corner.

And still there is a difference. There are several kinds of wild-crocus in this region of Tuscany: being little spiky mauve ones, and spiky little cream ones, that grow among the pine-trees of the bare slopes. But the beautiful ones are those of a meadow in the corner of the woods, the low hollow meadow below the steep, shadowy pine-slopes, the secretive grassy dip where the water seeps through the turf all winter, where the stream runs between thick bushes, where the nightingale sings his mightiest in May, and where the wild thyme is rosy and full of bees, in summer.

Here the lavender crocuses are most at home—here sticking out of the deep grass, in a hollow like a cup, a bowl of grass, come the lilac-coloured crocuses, like an innumerable encampment. You may see them at twilight, with all the buds shut, in the mysterious stillness of the grassy under-world, palely glimmering like myriad folded tents. So the apaches still camp, and close their tepees, in the hollows of the great hills of the West, at night.

But in the morning it is quite different. Then the sun shines strong on the horizontal green cloud-puffs of the pines, the sky is clear and full of life, the water runs hastily, still browned by the last juice of crushed olives. And there the earth's bowl of crocuses is amazing. You cannot believe that the flowers are really still. They are open with such delight, and their pistil-thrust is so red-orange, and they are so many, all reaching out wide and marvelous, that it suggests a perfect ecstasy of radiant, thronging movement, lit-up violet and orange, and surging in some invisible rhythm of concerted, delightful movement. You cannot believe they do not move, and make some sort of crystalline sound of delight. If you sit still and watch, you begin to move with them, like moving with the stars, and you feel the sound of their radiance. All the little cells of the flowers must be leaping with flowery life and utterance.

And the small brown honey-bees hop from flower to flower, dive down, try, and off again. The flowers have been already rifled, most of them. Only sometimes a bee stands on his head, kicking slowly inside the flower, for some time. He has found something. And all the bees have little loaves of pollen, bee-bread, in their elbow-joints.

The crocuses last in their beauty for a week or so, and as they begin to lower their tents and abandon camp, the violets begin to thicken. It is already March. The violets have been showing like tiny dark hounds for some weeks. But now the whole pack comes forth, among the grass and the tangle of wild thyme, till the air all sways subtly scented with violets, and the banks above where the crocuses had their tents are now swarming brilliant purple with violets. They are the sweet violets of early spring, but numbers have made them bold, for they flaunt and ruffle till the slopes are a bright blue-purple blaze of them, full in the sun, with an odd late crocus still standing wondering and erect amongst them.

And now that it is March, there is a rush of flowers. Down by the other stream, which turns sideways to the sun, and has tangles of brier and bramble, down where the hellebore has stood so wan and dignified all winter, there are now white tufts of primroses, suddenly come. Among the tangle and near the water-lip, tufts and bunches of primroses, in abundance. Yet they look more wan, more pallid, more flimsy than English primroses. They lack some of the full wonder of the northern flowers. One tends to overlook them, to turn to the great, solemn-faced purple violets that rear up from the bank, and above all, to the wonderful little towers of the grape-hyacinth.

I know no flower that is more fascinating, when it first appears, than the blue grape-hyacinth. And yet, because it lasts so long, and keeps on coming so repeatedly, for at least two months, one tends later on to ignore it, even to despise it a little. Yet that is very unjust.

The first grape-hyacinths are flowers of blue, thick and rich and meaningful, above the unrenewed grass. The upper buds are pure blue, shut tight; round balls of pure, perfect warm blue, blue, blue; while the lower bells are darkish blue-purple, with the spark of white at the mouth. As yet, none of the lower bells has withered, to leave the greenish, separate sparseness of fruiting that spoils the grape-hyacinth later on, and makes it seem naked and functional. All hyacinths are like that in the seeding.

But, at first, you have only a compact tower of night-blue clearing to dawn, and extremely beautiful. If we were tiny as fairies, and lived only a summer, how lovely these great trees of bells would be to us, towers of night and dawn-blue globes. They would rise above us thick and succulent, and the purple globes would push the blue ones up, with white sparks of ripples, and we should see a god in them.

As a matter of fact, someone once told me they were the flowers of the many-breasted Artemis; and it is true, the Cybele of Ephesus, with her clustered breasts was like a grape-hyacinth at the bosom.

This is the time, in March, when the sloe is white and misty in the hedge-tangle by the stream, and on the slope of land the peach tree stands pink and alone. The almond blossom, silvery pink, is passing, but the peach, deep-toned, bluey, not at all ethereal, this reveals itself like flesh, and the trees are like isolated individuals, the peach and the apricot.

A man said this spring: "Oh, I *don't* care for peach blossom! It is such a vulgar pink!" One wonders what anybody means by a "vulgar" pink. I think pink flannelette is rather vulgar. But probably it's the flannelette's fault, not the pink. And peach blossom has a beautiful sensual pink, far from vulgar, most rare and private. And pink is so beautiful in a landscape, pink houses, pink almond, pink peach and purply apricot, pink asphodels.

It is so conspicuous and so individual, that pink among the coming green of spring, because the first flowers that emerge from winter seem always white or yellow or purple. Now the celandines are out, and along the edges of the *podere*, the big, sturdy, black-purple anemones, with black hearts.

They are curious, these great, dark-violet anemones. You may pass them on a grey day, or at evening or early morning, and never see them. But as you come along in the full sunshine, they seem to be baying at you with all their throats, baying deep purple into the air. It is because they are hot and wide open now, gulping the sun. Whereas when they are shut, they have a silkiness and a curved head, like the curve of an umbrella handle, and a peculiar outward colourlessness, that makes them quite invisible. They may be under your feet, and you will not see them.

Altogether anemones are odd flowers. On these last hills above the plain, we have only the big black-purple ones, in tufts here and there, not many. But two hills away, the young green corn is blue with the lilac-blue kind, still the broad-petalled sort with the darker heart. But these flowers are smaller than our dark-purple, and frailer, more silky. Our are substantial, thickly vegetable flowers, and not abundant. The others are lovely and silky-delicate, and the whole corn is blue with them. And they have a sweet, sweet scent, when they are warm.

Then on the priest's *podere* there are the scarlet, Adonis-blood anemones: only in one place, in one long fringe under a terrace, and there by a path below. These flowers above all you will never find unless you look for them in the sun. Their silver silk outside makes them quite invisible, when they are shut up.

Yet, if you are passing in the sun, a sudden scarlet faces on to the air, one of the loveliest scarlet apparitions in the world. The inner surface of the Adonis-blood anemone is as fine as velvet, and yet there is no suggestion of pile, not as much as on a velvet rose. And from this inner smoothness issues the red colour, perfectly pure and unknown of earth, no earthiness, and yet solid, not transparent. How a colour manages to be perfectly strong and impervious, yet of a purity that suggests condensed light, yet not luminous, as least, not transparent, is a problem. The poppy in her radiance is translucent, and the tulip in her utter redness has a touch of opaque earth. But the Adonis-blood anemone is neither translucent nor opaque. It is just pure condensed red, of a velvetiness without velvet, and a scarlet without glow.

This red seems to me the perfect premonition of summer—like the red on the outside of apple blossom—and later, the red of the apple. It is the premonition in redness of summer and of autumn.

The red flowers are coming now. They wild tulips are in bud, hanging their grey leaves like flags. They come up in myriads, wherever they get a chance. But they are holding back their redness till the last days of March, the early days of April.

Still, the year is warming up. By the high ditch the common magenta anemone is hanging its silky tassels, or opening its great magenta daisy-shape to the hot sun. It is much nearer to red than the big-petalled anemones are; except the Adonis-blood. They say these anemones sprang from the tears of Venus, which fell as she went looking for Adonis. At that rate, how the poor lady must have wept, for the anemones by the Mediterranean are common as daisies in England.

The daisies are out here too, in sheets, and they too are red mouthed. The first ones are big and handsome. But as March goes on, they dwindle to bright little things, like tiny buttons, clouds of them together. That means summer is nearly here.

The red tulips open in the corn like poppies, only with a heavier red. And they pass quickly, without repeating themselves. There is little lingering in a tulip.

In some places there are odd yellow tulips, slender, spiky, and Chinese-looking. They are very lovely, pricking out their dulled yellow in slim spikes. But they too soon lean, expand beyond themselves, and are gone like an illusion.

And when the tulips are gone, there is a moment's pause, before summer. Summer is the next move.

III

In the pause towards the end of April, when the flowers seem to hesitate, the leaves make up their minds to come out. For some time, at the very ends of the bare boughs of fig tees, spurts of pure green have been burning like little cloven tongues of green fire vivid on the tips of the candelabrum. Now these spurts of green spread out, and begin to take the shape of hands, feeling for the air of summer. And tiny green figs are below them, like glands on the throat of a goat.

For some time, the long stiff whips of the vine have had knobby pink buds, like flower buds. Now these pink buds begin to unfold into greenish, half-shut fans of leaves with red in the veins, and tiny spikes of flower, like seed-pearls. Then, in all its down and pinky dawn, the vine-rosette has a frail, delicious scent of a new year.

Now the aspens on the hill are all remarkable with the translucent membranes of blood-veined leaves. They are gold-brown, but not like autumn, rather like the thin wings of bats when like birds—call them birds—they wheel in clouds against the setting sun, and the sun glows through the stretched membrane of their wings, as through thin, brown-red stained glass. This is the red sap of summer, not the red dust of autumn. And in the distance the aspens have the tender panting glow of living membrane just come awake. This is the beauty of the frailty of spring.

The cherry tree is something the same, but more sturdy. Now, in the last week of April, the cherry blossom is still white, but waning and passing away: it is late this year; and the leaves are clustering thick and softly copper in their dark, blood-filled glow. It is queer about fruit trees in this district. The pear and the peach were out together. But now the pear tree is a lovely thick softness of new and glossy green, vivid with a tender fullness of apple-green leaves, gleaming among all the other green of the landscape, the half-high wheat, emerald, and the grey olive, half-invisible, the browning green of the dark cypress, the black of the evergreen oak, the rolling, heavy green puffs of the stone-pines, the flimsy green of small peach and almond trees, the sturdy young green of horse-chestnut. So many greens, all in flakes and shelves and tilted tables and round shoulders and plumes and shaggles and uprisen bushes, of greens and greens, sometimes blindingly brilliant at evening, when the landscape looks as if it were on fire from inside, with greenness and with gold.

The pear is perhaps the greenest thing in the landscape. The wheat may shine lit-up yellow, or glow bluish, but the pear tree is green in itself. The cherry has white, half-absorbed flowers, so has the apple. But the plum is rough with her new foliage, and inconspicuous, inconspicuous as the almond, the peach, the apricot, which one can no longer find in the landscape, though twenty days ago they were the distinguished pink individuals of the whole countryside. Now they are gone. It is the time of green, pre-eminent green, in ruffles and flakes and slabs.

In the wood, the scrub-oak is only just coming uncrumpled, and the pines keep their hold on winter. They are wintry things, stone-pines. At Christmas, their heavy green clouds are richly beautiful. When the cypresses raise their tall and naked bodies of dark green, and the osiers are vivid red-orange, on the still blue air, and the land is lavender, then, in mid-winter, the landscape is most beautiful in colour, surging with colour.

But now, when the nightingale is still drawing out his long, wistful, yearning, teasing plant-note, and following it up with a rich and joyful burble, the pines and the cypresses seem hard and rusty, and the wood has lost its subtlety and its mysteriousness. It still seems wintry in spite of the yellowing young oaks, and the heath in flower. But hard, dull pines above, and hard, dull, tall heath below, all stiff and resistant, this is out of the mood of spring.

In spite of the fact that stone-white heath is in full flower, and very lovely when you look at it, it does not, casually, give the impression of blossom. More the impression of having its tips and crests all dipped in hoarfrost; or in a whitish dust. It has a peculiar ghostly colourlessness amid the darkish colourlessness of the wood altogether, which completely takes away the sense of spring.

Yet the tall white heath is very lovely, in its invisibility. It grows sometimes as tall as a man, lifting up its spires and its shadowy-white fingers with a ghostly fullness, amid the dark, rusty green of its lower bushiness; and it gives off a sweet honeyed scent in the sun, and a cloud of fine white stone-dust, if you touch it. Looked at closely, its little bells are most beautiful, delicate and white, with the brown-purple inner eye and the dainty pin-head of the pistil. And out in the sun at the edge of the wood, where the heath grows tall and thrusts up its spires of dim white next a brilliant, yellow-flowering vetch-bush, under a blue sky, the effect has a real magic.

And yet, in spite of all, the dim whiteness of all the flowering heath-fingers only adds to the hoariness and out-of-date quality of the pine-woods, now in the pause between spring and summer. It is the ghost of the interval.

Not that this week is flowerless. But the flowers are little lonely things, here and there: the early purple orchid, ruddy and very much alive, you come across occasionally, then the little groups of bee-orchid, with their ragged concerned indifference to their appearance. Also there are the huge bud-spikes of the stout, thick-flowering pink orchid, huge buds like fat ears of wheat, hard-purple and splendid. But already odd grains of the wheat-ear are open, and out of the purple hangs the delicate pink rag of a floweret. Also there are very lovely and choice cream-coloured orchids with brown spots on the long and delicate lip. These grow in the more moist places, and have exotic tender spikes, very rare-seeming. Another orchid is a little, pretty yellow one.

But orchids, somehow, do not make a summer. They are too aloof and individual. The little slate-blue scabious is out, but not enough to raise an appearance. Later on, under the real hot sun, he will bob into notice. And by the edges of the paths there are odd rosy cushions of wild thyme. Yet

these, too, are rather samples than the genuine thing. Wait another month,
for wild thyme.

The same with the irises. Here and there, in fringes along the upper
edge of terraces, and in odd bunches among the stones, the dark-purple
iris sticks up. It is beautiful, but it hardly counts. There is not enough of it,
and it is torn and buffeted by too many winds. First the wind blows with
all its might from the Mediterranean, not cold, but infinitely wearying,
with its rude and insistent pushing. Then, after a moment of calm, back
comes a hard wind from the Adriatic, cold and disheartening. Between the
two of them, the dark-purple iris flutters and tatters and curls as if it were
burnt: while the little yellow rock-rose streams at the end of its thin stalk,
and wishes it had not been in such a hurry to come out.

There is really no hurry. By May, the great winds will drop, and the
great sun will shake off his harassments. Then the nightingale will sing an
unbroken song, and the discreet, barely audible Tuscan cuckoo will be a
little more audible. Then the lovely pale-lilac irises will come out in all
their showering abundance of tender, proud, spiky bloom, till the air will
gleam with mauve, and a new crystalline lightness will be everywhere.

The iris is half-wild, half-cultivated. The peasants sometimes dig up
the roots, iris root, orris root (orris powder, the perfume that is still used).
So, in May, you will find ledges and terraces, fields just lit up with the
mauve light of irises, and so much scent in the air, you do not notice it,
you do not even know it. It is all the flowers of iris, before the olive
invisibly blooms.

There will be tufts of iris everywhere, rising up proud and tender.
When the rose-coloured wild gladiolus is mingled in the corn, and the
love-in-the-mist opens blue: in May and June, before the corn is cut.

But as yet it is neither May nor June, but end of April, the pause
between spring and summer, the nightingale singing interruptedly, the
bean-flowers dying in the bean-fields, the bean-perfume passing with
spring, the little birds hatching in the nests, the olives pruned, and the
vines, the last bit of late ploughing finished, and not much work to hand,
now, not until the peas are ready to pick, in another two weeks or so. Then
all the peasants will be crouching between the pea-rows, endlessly, endlessly gathering peas, in the long pea-harvest which lasts two months.

So the change, the endless and rapid change. In the sunny countries,
the change seems more vivid, and more complete than in the grey countries. In the grey countries, there is a grey or dark permanency, over whose
surface passes change ephemeral, leaving no real mark. In England, winters

and summers shadowily give place to one another. But underneath lies the
grey substratum, the permanency of cold, dark reality where bulbs live,
and reality is bulbous, a thing of endurance and stored-up, starchy energy.

But in the sunny countries, change is the reality and permanence is
artificial and a condition of imprisonment. In the North, man tends instinctively to imagine, to conceive that the sun is lighted like a candle, in an
everlasting darkness, and that one day the candle will go out, the sun will
be exhausted, and the everlasting dark will resume uninterrupted sway.
Hence, to the northerner, the phenomenal world is essentially tragical,
because it is temporal and must cease to exist. Its very existence implies
ceasing to exist, and this is the root of the feeling of tragedy.

But to the southerner, the sun is so dominant that, if every phenomenal body disappeared out of the universe, nothing would remain but
bright luminousness, sunniness. The absolute is sunniness; and shadow, or
dark, is only merely relative: merely the result of something getting between one and the sun.

This is the instinctive feeling of the ordinary southerner. Of course, if
you start to *reason*, you may argue that the sun is a phenomenal body.
Therefore it came into existence, therefore it will pass out of existence,
therefore the very sun is tragic in its nature.

But this is just argument. We think, because we have to light a candle
in the dark, therefore some First Cause had to kindle the sun in the infinite
darkness of the beginning.

The argument is entirely shortsighted and specious. We do not know
in the least whether the sun ever came into existence, and we have not the
slightest possible ground for conjecturing that the sun will ever pass out of
existence. All that we do know, by actual experience, is that shadow comes
into being when some material object intervenes between us and the sun,
and that shadow ceases to exist when the intervening object is removed. So
that, of all temporal or transitory or bound-to-cease things that haunt our
existence, shadow or darkness, is the one which is purely and simply
temporal. We can think of death, if we like, as of something permanently
intervening between us and the sun: and this is at the root of the southern,
under-world idea of death. But this doesn't alter the sun at all. As far as
experience goes, in the human race, the one thing that is always there is the
shining sun, and dark shadow is an accident of intervention.

Hence, strictly, there is no tragedy. The universe contains no tragedy,
and man is only tragical because he is afraid of death. For my part, if the
sun always shines, and always will shine, in spite of millions of clouds of

words, then death, somehow, does not have many terrors. In the sunshine, even death is sunny. And there is no end to the sunshine.

This is why the rapid change of the Tuscan spring is utterly free, for me, of any sense of tragedy. "Where are the snows of yesteryear?" Why, precisely where they ought to be. Where are the little yellow aconites of eight weeks ago? I neither know nor care. They were sunny and the sun shines, and sunniness means change, and petals passing and coming. The winter aconites sunnily came, and sunnily went. What more? The sun always shines. It is our fault if we don't think so.

THE MARGINAL WORLD

RACHEL CARSON

The edge of the sea is a strange and beautiful place. All through the long history of Earth it has been an area of unrest where waves have broken heavily against the land, where the tides have pressed forward over the continents, receded, and then returned. For no two successive days is the shore line precisely the same. Not only do the tides advance and retreat in their eternal rhythms, but the level of the sea itself is never at rest. It rises or falls as the glaciers melt or grow, as the floor of the deep ocean basins shifts under its increasing load of sediments, or as the earth's crust along the continental margins warps up or down in adjustment to strain and tension. Today a little more land may belong to the sea, tomorrow a little less. Always the edges of the sea remains an elusive and indefinable boundary.

The shore has a dual nature, changing with the swing of the tides, belonging now to the land, now to the sea. On the ebb tide it knows the harsh extremes of the land world, being exposed to heat and cold, to wind, to rain and drying sun. On the flood tide it is a water world, returning briefly to the relative stability of the open sea.

Only the most hardy and adaptable can survive in a region so mutable, yet the area between the tide lines is crowded with plants and animals. In this difficult world of the shore, life displays its enormous toughness and virility by occupying almost every conceivable niche. Visibly, it carpets the intertidal rocks; or half hidden, it descends into fissures and crevices, or hides under boulders, or lurks in the wet gloom of sea caves. Invisibly, where the casual observer would say there is no life, it lies deep in the sand, in burrows and tubes and passageways. It tunnels into solid rock and bores into peat and clay. It encrusts weeds or drifting spars or the hard, chitinous shelf of a lobster. It exists minutely, as the film of bacteria that spreads over a rock surface or a wharf piling; as spheres of protozoa, small as pinpricks, sparkling at the surface of the sea; and as Lilliputian beings swimming through dark pools that lie between the grains of sand.

The shore is an ancient world, for as long as there has been an earth and sea there has been this place of the meeting of land and water. Yet it is a world that keeps alive the sense of continuing creation and of the relentless drive of life. Each time that I enter it, I gain some new awareness of its beauty and its deeper meanings, sensing that intricate fabric of life by which one creature is linked with another, and each with its surroundings.

In my thoughts of the shore, one place stands apart for its revelation of exquisite beauty. It is a pool hidden within a cave that one can visit only rarely and briefly when the lowest of the year's low tides fall below it, and perhaps from that very fact it acquires some of its special beauty. Choosing such a tide, I hoped for a glimpse of the pool. The ebb was to fall early in the morning. I knew that if the wind held from the northwest and no interfering swell ran in from a distant storm the level of the sea should drop below the entrance to the pool. There had been sudden ominous showers in the night, with rain like handfuls of gravel flung on the roof. When I looked out into the early morning the sky was full of a gray dawn light but the sun had not yet risen. Water and air were pallid. Across the bay the moon was a luminous disc in the western sky, suspended above the dim line of distant shore—the full August moon, drawing the tide to the low, low levels of the threshold of the alien sea world. As I watched, a gull flew by, above the spruces. Its breast was rosy with the light of the unrisen sun. The day was, after all, to be fair.

Later, as I stood above the tide near the entrance to the pool, the promise of that rosy light was sustained. From the base of the steep wall of rock on which I stood, a moss-covered ledge jutted seaward into deep water. In the surge at the rim of the ledge the dark fronds of oarweeds swayed, smooth and gleaming as leather. The projecting ledge was the path to the small hidden cave and its pool. Occasionally, a swell, stronger than the rest, rolled smoothly over the rim and broke in foam against the cliff. But the intervals between such swells were long enough to admit me to the ledge and long enough for a glimpse of that fairy pool, so seldom and so briefly exposed.

And so I knelt on the wet carpet of sea moss and looked back into the dark cavern that held the pool in a shallow basin. The floor of the cave was only a few inches below the roof, and a mirror had been created in which all that grew on the ceiling was reflected in the still water below.

Under water that was clear as glass the pool was carpeted with green sponge. Gray patches of sea squirts glistened on the ceiling and colonies of soft coral were a pale apricot color. In the moment when I looked into the cave a little elfin starfish hung down, suspended by the merest thread, perhaps by only a single tube foot. It reached down to touch its own reflection, so perfectly delineated that there might have been, not one starfish, but two. The beauty of the reflected images and of the limpid pool itself was the poignant beauty of things that are ephemeral, existing only until the sea should return to fill the little cave.

Whenever I go down into this magical zone of the low water of the spring tides, I look for the most delicately beautiful of all the shore's inhabitants—flowers that are not plant but animal, blooming on the threshold of the deeper sea. In that fairy cave I was not disappointed. Hanging from its roof were the pendent flowers of the hydroid Tabularia, pale pink, fringed and delicate as the wind flower. Here were creatures so exquisitely fashioned that they seemed unreal, their beauty too fragile to exist in a world of crushing force. Yet every detail was functionally useful, every stalk and hydranth and petal-like tentacle fashioned for dealing with the realities of existence. I knew that they were merely waiting, in that moment of the tide's ebbing, for the return of the sea. Then in the rush of water, in the surge of surf and the pressure of the incoming tide, the delicate flower heads would stir with life. They would sway on their slender stalks, and their long tentacles would sweep the returning water, finding in it all that they needed for life.

And so in that enchanted place on the threshold of the sea the realities that possessed my mind were far from those of the land world I had left an hour before. In a different way the same sense of remoteness and of a world apart came to me in a twilight hour on a great beach on the coast of Georgia. I had come down after sunset and walked far out over sands that lay wet and gleaming, to the very edge of the retreating sea. Looking back across that immense flat, crossed by winding, water-filled gullies and here and there holding shallow pools left by the tide, I was filled with awareness that this intertidal area, although abandoned briefly and rhythmically by the sea, is always reclaimed by the rising tide. There at the edge of low water the beach with its reminders of the land seemed far away. The only sounds were those of the wind and the sea and the birds. There was one sound of wind moving over water, and another of water sliding over the sand and tumbling down the faces of its own wave forms. The flats were astir with birds, and the voice of the willet rang insistently. One of them stood at the edge of the water and gave its loud, urgent cry; an answer came from far up the beach and the two birds flew to join each other.

The flats took on a mysterious quality as dusk approached and the last evening light was reflected from the scattered pools and creeks. Then birds became only dark shadows, with no color discernible. Sanderlings scurried across the beach like little ghosts, and here and there the darker forms of the willets stood out. Often I could come very close to them before they would start up in alarm—the sanderlings running, the willets flying up, crying. Black skimmers flew along the ocean's edge silhouetted against the dull, metallic gleam, or they went flitting above the sand like large, dimly seen moths. Sometimes they "skimmed" the winding creeks of tidal water, where little spreading surface ripples marked the presence of small fish.

The shore at night is a different world, in which the very darkness that hides the distractions of daylight brings into sharper focus the elemental realities. Once, exploring the night beach, I surprised a small ghost crab in the searching beam of my torch. He was lying in a pit he had dug just above the surf, as though watching the sea and waiting. The blackness of the night possessed water, air, and beach. It was the darkness of an older world, before Man. There was no sound but the all-enveloping, primeval sounds of wind blowing over water and sand, and of waves crashing on the beach. There was no other visible life—just one small crab near the sea. I have seen hundreds of ghost crabs in other settings, but suddenly I was filled with the odd sensation that for the first time I knew the creature in its own world—that I understood, as never before, the essence of its being. In that moment time was suspended; the world to which I belonged did not exist and I might have been an onlooker from outer space. The little crab alone with the sea became a symbol that stood for life itself—for the delicate, destructible, yet incredibly vital force that somehow holds its place amid the harsh realities of the inorganic world.

The sense of creation comes with memories of a southern coast, where the sea and the mangroves, working together, are building a wilderness of thousands of small islands off the southwestern coast of Florida, separated from each other by a tortuous pattern of bays, lagoons, and narrow waterways. I remember a winter day when the sky was blue and drenched with sunlight; though there was no wind one was conscious of flowing air like cold clear crystal. I had landed on the surf-washed tip of one of those islands, and then worked my way around to the sheltered bay side. There I found the tide far out, exposing the broad mud flat of a cove bordered by the mangroves with their twisted branches, their glossy leaves, and their long prop roots reaching down, grasping and holding the mud, building the land out a little more, then again a little more.

The mud flats were strewn with the shells of that small, exquisitely colored mollusk, the rose tellin, looking like scattered petals of pink roses. There must have been a colony nearby, living buried just under the surface of the mud. At first the only creature visible was a small heron in gray and rusty plumage—a reddish egret that waded across the flat with the stealthy, hesitant movements of its kind. But other land creatures had been there, for a line of fresh tracks wound in and out among the mangrove roots, marking the path of a raccoon feeding on the oysters that gripped the supporting roots with projections from their shells. Soon I found the tracks of a shore bird, probably a sanderling, and followed them a little; then they turned toward the water and were lost, for the tide had erased them and made them as though they had never been.

Looking out over the cove I felt a strong sense of the interchangeability of land and sea in this marginal world of the shore, and of the links between the life of the two. There was also an awareness of the past and of the continuing flow of time, obliterating much that had gone before, as the sea had that morning washed away the tracks of the bird.

The sequence and meaning of the drift of time were quietly summarized in the existence of hundreds of small snails—the mangrove periwinkles—browsing on the branches and roots of the trees. Once their ancestors had been sea dwellers, bound to the salt waters by every tie of their life processes. Little by little over the thousands and millions of years the ties had been broken, the snails had adjusted themselves to life out of water, and now today they were living many feet above the tide to which they only occasionally returned. And perhaps, who could say how many ages hence, there would be in their descendants not even this gesture of remembrance for the sea.

The spiral shells of other snails—these quite minute—left winding tracks on the mud as they moved about in search of food. They were horn shells, and when I saw them I had a nostalgic moment when I wished I might see what Audubon saw, a century and more ago. For such little horn shells were the food of the flamingo, once so numerous on this coast, and when I half closed my eyes I could almost imagine a flock of these magnificent flame birds feeding in that cove, filling it with their color. It was a mere yesterday in the life of the earth that they were there; in nature, time and space are relative matters, perhaps most truly perceived subjectively in occasional flashes of insight, sparked by such a magical hour and place.

There is a common thread that links these scenes and memories—the spectacle of life in all its varied manifestations as it has appeared, evolved, and sometimes died out. Underlying the beauty of the spectacle there is meaning and significance. It is the elusiveness of that meaning that haunts us, that sends us again and again into the natural world where the key to the riddle is hidden. It sends us back to the edge of the sea, where the drama of life played its first scene on earth and perhaps even its prelude; where the forces of evolution are at work today, as they have been since the appearance of what we know as life; and where the spectacle of living creatures faced by the cosmic realities of their world is crystal clear.

BIRDS

Part loosely wing the Region, part more wise
In common, rang'd in figure wedge their way,
Intelligent of seasons, and set forth
Their Aierie Caravan high over Seas
Flying, and over Lands with mutual wing
Easing their flight. . . .
. . . The Aire
Floats, as they pass, fann'd with unnumbered plumes:
From Branch to Branch the smaller Birds with song
Solac'd the Woods, and spread their painted wings.

—JOHN MILTON
Paradise Lost, 1667

Into the Amazon

Charles Waterton

Let us now, gentle reader, retire from the busy scenes of man and journey on towards the wilds in quest of the feathered tribe.

Leave behind you your high-seasoned dishes, your wines and your delicacies: carry nothing but what is necessary for your own comfort and the object in view, and depend upon the skill of an Indian, or your own, for fish and game. A sheet about twelve feet long, ten wide, painted, and with loop-holes on each side, will be of great service: in a few minutes you can suspend it betwixt two trees in the shape of a roof. Under this, in your hammock, you may defy the pelting shower, and sleep heedless of the dews of night. A hat, a shirt and a light pair of trousers will be all the raiment you require. Custom will soon teach you to tread lightly and barefoot on the little inequalities of the ground, and show you how to pass on unwounded amid the mantling briers.

Snakes, in these wilds, are certainly an annoyance, though perhaps more in imagination than reality, for you must recollect that the serpent is never the first to offend: his poisonous fang was not given him for conquest—he never inflicts a wound with it but to defend existence. Provided you walk cautiously and do not absolutely touch him, you may pass in safety close by him. As he is often coiled up on the ground, and amongst the branches of the trees above you, a degree of circumspection is necessary lest you unwarily disturb him.

Tigers are too few, and too apt to fly before the noble face of man, to require a moment of your attention.

The bite of the most noxious of the insects, at the very worst, only causes a transient fever with a degree of pain more or less.

Birds in general, with a few exceptions, are not common in the very remote parts of the forest. The sides of rivers, lakes and creeks, the borders of savannas, the old abandoned habitations of Indians and woodcutters, seem to be their favourite haunts.

Though least in size, the glittering mantle of the humming-bird entitles it to the first place in the list of the birds of the new world. It may truly be called the bird of paradise: and had it existed in the Old World, it would have claimed the title instead of the bird which has now the honour to bear it. See it darting through the air almost as quick as thought!—now it is within a yard of your face!—in an instant gone!—now it flutters from flower to flower to sip the silver dew—it is now a ruby—now a topaz—now an emerald—now all burnished gold! It would be arrogant to pretend to describe this winged gem of Nature after Buffon's elegant description of it.

Cayenne and Demerara produce the same hummingbirds. Perhaps you would wish to know something of their haunts. Chiefly in the months of July and August, the tree called bois immortel, very common in Demerara, bears abundance of red blossom which stays on the tree for some weeks; then it is that most of the different species of humming-birds are very plentiful. The wild red sage is also their favourite shrub, and they buzz like bees round the blossom of the wallaba tree. Indeed, there is scarce a flower in the interior, or on the sea-coast, but what receives frequent visits from one or other of the species.

On entering the forests, on the rising land in the interior, the blue and green, the smallest brown, no bigger than the humble-bee, with two long feathers in the tail, and the little forked-tail purple-throated humming-birds, glitter before you in ever-changing attitudes. One species alone never shows his beauty to the sun: and were it not for his lovely shining colours, you might almost be tempted to class him with the goat-suckers, on account of his habits. He is the largest of all the humming-birds, and is all red and changing gold-green, except the head, which is black. He has two long feathers in the tail which cross each other, and these have gained him the name of karabimiti, or ara humming-bird, from the Indians. You never find him on the sea-coast, or where the river is salt, or in the heart of the forest, unless fresh water be there. He keeps close by the side of woody fresh-water rivers and dark and lonely creeks. He leaves his retreat before sunrise to feed on the insects over the water; he returns to it as soon as the sun's rays cause a glare of light, is sedentary all day long, and comes out again for a short time after sunset. He builds his nest on a twig over the water in the unfrequented creeks: it looks like tanned cow-leather.

As you advance towards the mountains of Demerara other species of humming-birds present themselves before you. It seems to be an erroneous opinion that the humming-bird lives entirely on honey-dew. Almost every flower of the tropical climates contains insects of one kind or other. Now the humming-bird is most busy about the flowers an hour or two after sunrise and after a shower of rain, and it is just at this time that the insects come out to the edge of the flower in order that the sun's rays may dry the nocturnal dew and rain which they have received. On opening the stomach of the humming-bird dead insects are almost always found there.

Next to the humming-birds, the cotingas display the gayest plumage. They are of the order of Passer, and you number five species betwixt the sea-coast and the rock Saba. Perhaps the scarlet cotinga is the richest of the five, and is one of those birds which are found in the deepest recesses of the forest. His crown is flaming red; to this abruptly succeeds a dark shining brown, reaching half-way down the back: the remainder of the back, the rump and tail, the extremity of which is edged with black, are a lively red; the belly is a somewhat lighter red; the breast reddish-black; the wings brown. He has no song, is solitary, and utters a monotonous whistle which sounds like "quet." He is fond of the seeds of the hitia-tree and those of the siloabali- and bastard siloabali-trees, which ripen in December and continue on the trees for above two months. He is found throughout the year in Demerara; still nothing is known of his incubation. The Indians all agree in telling you that they have never seen his nest.

The purple-breasted cotinga has the throat and breast of a deep purple, the wings and tail black, and all the rest of the body a most lovely shining blue.

The purple-throated cotinga has black wings and tail, and every other part a light and glossy blue, save the throat, which is purple.

The pompadour cotinga is entirely purple, except his wings, which are white, their four first feathers tipped with brown. The great coverts of the wings are stiff, narrow and pointed, being shaped quite different from those of any other bird. When you are betwixt this bird and the sun, in his flight, he appears uncommonly brilliant. He makes a hoarse noise which sounds like "wallababa." Hence his name amongst the Indians.

None of these three cotingas have a song. They feed on the hitia, siloabali- and bastard siloabali-seeds, the wild guava, the fig, and other fruit-trees of the forest. They are easily shot in these trees during the months of December, January and part of February. The greater part of them disappear after this, and probably retire far away to breed. Their nests have never been found in Demerara.

The fifth species is the celebrated campanero of the Spaniards, called dara by the Indians, and bell-bird by the English. He is about the size of the jay. His plumage is white as snow. On his forehead rises a spiral tube nearly three inches long. It is jet black, dotted all over with small white feathers. It has a communication with the palate, and when filled with air looks like a spire; when empty it becomes pendulous. His note is loud and clear, like the sound of a bell, and may be heard at the distance of three miles. In the midst of these extensive wilds, generally on the dried top of an aged mora, almost out of gun-reach, you will see the campanero. No sound or song from any of the winged inhabitants of the forest, not even the clearly pronounced "Whip-poor-will" from the goat-sucker, cause such astonishment as the toll of the campanero.

With many of the feathered race he pays the common tribute of a morning and an evening song; and even when the meridian sun has shut in silence the mouths of almost the whole of animated nature the campanero still cheers the forest. You hear his toll, and then a pause for a minute, then another toll, and then a pause again, and then a toll, and again a pause. Then he is silent for six or eight minutes, and then another toll, and so on. Acteon would stop in mid-chase, Maria would defer her evening song, and Orpheus himself would drop his lute to listen to him, so sweet, so novel and romantic is the toll of the pretty snow-white campanero. He is never seen to feed with the other cotingas, nor is it known in what part of Guiana he makes his nest.

While the cotingas attract your attention by their superior plumage, the singular form of the toucan makes a lasting impression on your memory. There are three species of toucans in Demerara, and three diminutives, which may be called toucanets. The largest of the first species frequents the mangrove trees on the sea-coast. He is never seen in the interior till you reach Macoushia, where he is found in the neighbourhood of the River Tacatou. The other two species are very common. They feed entirely on the fruits of the forest and, though of the pie kind, never kill the young of other birds or touch carrion. The larger is called bouradi by the Indians (which means nose), the other scirou. They seem partial to each other's company, and often resort to the same feeding-tree and retire together to the same shady noon-day retreat. They are very noisy in rainy weather at all hours of the day, and in fair weather at morn and eve. The sound which the bouradi makes is like the clear yelping of a puppy-dog, and you fancy he says "pia-po-o-co," and thus the South-American Spaniards call him piapoco.

All the toucanets feed on the same trees on which the toucan feeds, and every species of this family of enormous bill lays its eggs in the hollow trees. They are social, but not gregarious. You may sometimes see eight or ten in company, and from this you would suppose they are gregarious; but upon a closer examination you will find it has only been a dinner-party, which breaks up and disperses towards roosting-time.

You will be at a loss to conjecture for what ends Nature has over-loaded the head of this bird with such an enormous bill. It cannot be for the offensive, as it has no need to wage war with any of the tribes of animated nature, for its food is fruits and seeds, and those are in superabundance throughout the whole year in the regions where the toucan is found. It can hardly be for the defensive, as the toucan is preyed upon by no bird in South America and, were it obliged to be at war, the texture of the bill is ill-adapted to give or receive blows, as you will see in dissecting it. It cannot be for any particular protection to the tongue, as the tongue is a perfect feather.

The flight of the toucan is by jerks: in the action of flying it seems incommoded by this huge disproportioned feature, and the head seems as if bowed down to the earth by it against its will. If the extraordinary form and size of the bill expose the toucan to ridicule, its colours make it amends. Were a specimen of each species of the toucan presented to you, you would pronounce the bill of the bouradi the most rich and beautiful: on the ridge of the upper mandible a broad stripe of most lovely yellow extends from the head to the point; a stripe of the same breadth, though somewhat deeper yellow, falls from it at right angles next the head down to the edge of the mandible; then follows a black stripe, half as broad, falling at right angles from the ridge and running narrower along the edge to within half an inch of the point. The rest of the mandible is a deep bright red. The lower mandible has no yellow: its black and red are distributed in the same manner as on the upper one, with this difference, that there is black about an inch from the point. The stripe corresponding to the deep yellow stripe on the upper mandible is sky-blue. It is worthy of remark that all these brilliant colours of the bill are to be found in the plumage of the body and the bare skin round the eye.

All these colours, except the blue, are inherent in the horn: that part which appears blue is in reality transparent white, and receives its colour from a thin piece of blue skin inside. This superb bill fades in death, and in three or four days' time has quite lost its original colours.

Till within these few years no idea of the true colours of the bill could be formed from the stuffed toucans brought to Europe. About eight years ago, while eating a boiled toucan, the thought struck me that the colours in the bill of a preserved specimen might be kept as bright as those in life. A series of experiments proved this beyond a doubt. If you take your penknife and cut away the roof of the upper mandible, you will find that the space betwixt it and the outer shell contains a large collection of veins and small osseous fibres running in all directions through the whole extent of the bill. Clear away all these with your knife, and you will come to a substance more firm than skin, but of not so strong a texture as the horn itself. Cut this away also, and behind it is discovered a thin and tender membrane: yellow where it has touched the yellow part of the horn, blue where it has touched the red part, and black towards the edge and point; when dried this thin and tender membrane becomes nearly black; as soon as it is cut away nothing remains but the outer horn, red and yellow, and now become transparent. The under mandible must undergo the same operation. Great care must be taken and the knife used very cautiously when you are cutting through the different parts close to where the bill joins on to the head: if you cut away too much the bill drops off; if you press too hard the knife comes through the horn; if you leave too great a portion of the membrane it appears through the horn and, by becoming black when dried, makes the horn appear black also, and has a bad effect. Judgment, caution, skill and practice will ensure success.

You have now cleared the bill of all those bodies which are the cause of its apparent fading, for, as has been said before, these bodies dry in death and become quite discoloured, and appear so through the horn; and reviewing the bill in this state, you conclude that its former bright colours are lost.

Something still remains to be done. You have rendered the bill transparent by the operation, and that transparency must be done away to make it appear perfectly natural. Pound some clean chalk and give it enough water till it be of the consistency of tar, add a proportion of gum-arabic to make it adhesive, then take a camelhair brush and give the inside of both mandibles a coat; apply a second when the first is dry, then another, and a fourth to finish all. The gum-arabic will prevent the chalk from cracking and falling off. If you remember, there is a little space of transparent white in the lower mandible which originally appeared blue, but which became transparent white as soon as the thin piece of blue skin was cut away: this must be painted blue inside. When all this is completed the bill will please you: it will appear in its original colours. Probably your own abilities will suggest a cleverer mode of operating than the one here described. A small gouge would assist the penknife and render the operation less difficult.

The houtou ranks high in beauty amongst the birds of Demerara. His whole body is green, with a bluish cast in the wings and tail; his crown, which he erects at pleasure, consists of black in the centre, surrounded with lovely blue of two different shades; he has a triangular black spot, edged with blue, behind the eye extending to the ear, and on his breast a sable tuft consisting of nine feathers edged also with blue. This bird seems to suppose that its beauty can be increased by trimming the tail, which undergoes the same operation as our hair in a barber's shop, only with this difference, that it uses its own beak, which is serrated, in lieu of a pair of scissors. As soon as his tail is full grown, he begins about an inch from the extremity of the two longest feathers in it and cuts away the web on both sides of the shaft, making a gap about an inch long. Both male and female adonise their tails in this manner, which gives them a remarkable appearance amongst all other birds. While we consider the tail of the houtou blemished and defective, were he to come amongst us he would probably consider our heads, cropped and bald, in no better light. He who wishes to observe this handsome bird in his native haunts must be in the forest at the morning's dawn. The houtou shuns the society of man: the plantations and cultivated parts are too much disturbed to engage it to settle there; the thick and gloomy forests are the places preferred by the solitary houtou. In those far-extending wilds, about daybreak, you hear him articulate, in a distinct and mournful tone, "houtou, houtou." Move cautious on to where the sound proceeds from, and you will see him sitting in the underwood about a couple of yards from the ground, his tail moving up and down every time he articulates "houtou." He lives on insects and the berries amongst the underwood, and very rarely is seen in the lofty trees, except the bastard siloabali-tree, the fruit of which is grateful to him. He makes no nest, but rears his young in a hole in the sand, generally on the side of a hill.

While in quest of the houtou, you will now and then fall in with the jay of Guiana, called by the Indians ibibirou. Its forehead is black, the rest of the head white, the throat and breast like the English magpie; about an inch of the extremity of the tail is white, the other part of it, together with the back and wings, a greyish changing purple; the belly is white. There are generally six or eight of them in company: they are shy and garrulous, and tarry a very short time in one place. They are never seen in the cultivated parts.

Through the whole extent of the forest, chiefly from sunrise till nine o'clock in the morning, you hear a sound of "wow, wow, wow, wow." This is the bird called boclora by the Indians. It is smaller than the common pigeon, and seems, in some measure, to partake of its nature: its head and breast are blue; the back and rump somewhat resemble the colour on the peacock's neck; its belly is a bright yellow. The legs are so very short that it always appears as if sitting on the branch: it is as ill-adapted for walking as the swallow. Its neck, for above an inch all round, is quite bare of feathers, but this deficiency is not seen, for it always sits with its head drawn in upon its shoulders. It sometimes feeds with the cotingas on the guava- and hitia-trees, but its chief nutriment seems to be insects, and, like most birds which follow this prey, its chaps are well armed with bristles: it is found in Demerara at all times of the year, and makes a nest resembling that of the stock-dove. This bird never takes long flights, and when it crosses a river or creek it goes by long jerks.

The boclora is very unsuspicious, appearing quite heedless of danger: the report of a gun within twenty yards will not cause it to leave the branch on which it is sitting, and you may often approach it so near as almost to touch it with the end of your bow. Perhaps there is no bird known whose feathers are so slightly fixed to the skin as those of the boclora. After shooting it, if it touch a branch in its descent, or if it drop on hard ground, whole heaps of feathers fall off: on this account it is extremely hard to procure a specimen for preservation. As soon as the skin is dry in the preserved specimen the feathers become as well fixed as those in any other bird.

Another species, larger than the boclora, attracts much of your notice in these wilds; it is called cuia by the Indians, from the sound of its voice. Its habits are the same as those of the boclora, but its colours different; its head, breast, back and rump are a shining, changing green; its tail not quite so bright; a black bar runs across the tail towards the extremity, and the outside feathers are partly white, as in the boclora; its belly is entirely vermilion, a bar of white separating it from the green on the breast.

There are diminutives of both these birds: they have the same habits, with a somewhat different plumage, and about half the size. Arrayed from head to tail in a robe of richest sable hue, the bird called rice-bird loves spots cultivated by the hand of man. The woodcutter's house on the hills in the interior, and the planter's habitation on the sea-coast, equally attract this songless species of the order of pie, provided the Indian-corn be ripe there. He is nearly of the jackdaw's size and makes his nest far away from the haunts of men. He may truly be called a blackbird: independent of his plumage, his beak, inside and out, his legs, his toes and claws are jet black.

Mankind, by clearing the ground and sowing a variety of seeds, induces many kinds of birds to leave their native haunts and come and settle near him: their little depredations on his seeds and fruits prove that it is the property, and not the proprietor, which has the attractions.

One bird, however, in Demerara is not actuated by selfish motives: this is the cassique. In size he is larger than the starling: he courts the society of man, but disdains to live by his labours. When Nature calls for support he repairs to the neighbouring forest, and there partakes of the store of fruits and seeds which she has produced in abundance for her aerial tribes. When his repast is over he returns to man, and pays the little tribute which he owes him for his protection. He takes his station on a tree close to his house, and there, for hours together, pours forth a succession of imitative notes. His own song is sweet, but very short. If a toucan be yelping in the neighbourhood, he drops it, and imitates him. Then he will amuse his protector with the cries of the different species of the wood-pecker, and when the sheep bleat he will distinctly answer them. Then comes his own song again; and if a puppy-dog or a guinea-fowl interrupt him, he takes them off admirably, and by his different gestures during the time you would conclude that he enjoys the sport.

The cassique is gregarious, and imitates any sound he hears with such exactness that he goes by no other name than that of mocking bird amongst the colonists.

At breeding-time a number of these pretty choristers resort to a tree near the planter's house, and from its outside branches weave their pendulous nests. So conscious do they seem that they never give offence, and so little suspicious are they of receiving any injury from man, that they will choose a tree within forty yards from his house, and occupy the branches so low down that he may peep into the nests. A tree in Waratilla Creek affords a proof of this.

The proportions of the cassique are so fine that he may be said to be a model of symmetry in ornithology. On each wing he has a bright yellow spot, and his rump, belly and half the tail are of the same colour. All the rest of the body is black. His beak is the colour of sulphur, but it fades in death, and requires the same operation as the bill of the toucan to make it keep its colours. Up the rivers, in the interior, there is another cassique, nearly the same size and of the same habits, though not gifted with its powers of imitation. Except in breeding-time, you will see hundreds of them retiring to roost amongst the moca-moca-trees and low shrubs on the banks of the Demerara, after you pass the first island. They are not common on the sea-coast. The rump of this cassique is a flaming scarlet. All the rest of the body is a rich glossy black. His bill is sulphur-colour. You may often see numbers of this species weaving their pendulous nests on one side of a tree, while numbers of the other species are busy in forming theirs on the opposite side of the same tree. Though such near neighbours, the females are never observed to kick up a row or come to blows!

Another species of cassique, as large as a crow, is very common in the plantations. In the morning he generally repairs to a large tree, and there, with his tail spread over his back and shaking his lowered wings, he produces notes which, though they cannot be said to amount to a song, still have something very sweet and pleasing in them. He makes his nest in the same form as the other cassiques. It is above four feet long, and when you pass under the tree, which often contains fifty or sixty of them, you cannot help stopping to admire them as they wave to and fro, the sport of every storm and breeze. The rump is chestnut; ten feathers of the tail are a fine yellow, the remaining two, which are the middle ones, are black, and an inch shorter than the others. His bill is sulphur-colour; all the rest of the body black, with here and there shades of brown. He has five or six long narrow black feathers on the back of his head, which he erects at pleasure.

There is one more species of cassique in Demerara which always prefers the forests to the cultivated parts. His economy is the same as that of the other cassiques. He is rather smaller than the last described bird. His body is greenish, and his tail and rump paler than those of the former. Half of his beak is red.

You would not be long in the forests of Demerara without noticing the woodpeckers. You meet with them feeding at all hours of the day. Well may they do so. Were they to follow the example of most of the other birds, and only feed in the morning and evening, they would be often on short allowance, for they sometimes have to labour three or four hours at the tree before they get to their food. The sound which the largest kind makes in hammering against the bark of the tree is so loud that you would never suppose it to proceed from the efforts of a bird. You would take it to be the woodman, with his axe, trying by a sturdy blow, often repeated, whether the tree were sound or not. There are fourteen species here: the largest the size of a magpie, the smallest no bigger than the wren. They are all beautiful, and the greater part of them have their heads ornamented with a fine crest, movable at pleasure.

It is said, if you once give a dog a bad name, whether innocent or guilty, he never loses it. It sticks close to him wherever he goes. He has many a kick and many a blow to bear on account of it; and there is nobody to stand up for him. The woodpecker is little better off. The proprietors of woods in Europe have long accused him of injuring their timber by boring holes in it and letting in the water, which soon rots it. The colonists in America have the same complaint against him. Had he the power of speech, which Ovid's birds possessed in days of yore, he could soon make a defence: "Mighty lord of the woods," he would say to man, "why do you wrongfully accuse me? Why do you hunt me up and down to death for an imaginary offence? I have never spoiled a leaf of your property, much less your wood. Your merciless shot strikes me at the very time I am doing you a service. But your shortsightedness will not let you see it, or your pride is above examining closely the actions of so insignificant a little bird as I am. If there be that spark of feeling in your breast which they say man possesses, or ought to possess, above all other animals, do a poor injured creature a little kindness and watch me in your woods only for one day. I never wound your healthy trees. I should perish for want in the attempt. The sound bark would easily resist the force of my bill; and were I even to pierce through it, there would be nothing inside that I could fancy or my stomach digest. I often visit them it is true, but a knock or two convince me that I must go elsewhere for support; and were you to listen attentively to the sound which my bill causes, you would know whether I am upon a healthy or an unhealthy tree. Wood and bark are not my food. I live entirely upon the insects which have already formed a lodgment in the distempered tree. When the sound informs me that my prey is there, I labour for hours together till I get at it, and by consuming it for my own support, I prevent its further depredations in that part. Thus I discover for you your hidden and unsuspected foe, which has been devouring your wood in such secrecy that you had not the least suspicion it was there. The hole which I make in order to get at the pernicious vermin will be seen by you as you pass under the tree. I leave it as a signal to tell you that your tree has already stood too long. It is past its prime. Millions of insects, engendered by disease, are preying upon its vitals. Ere long it will fall a log in useless ruins. Warned by this loss, cut down the rest in time, and spare, O spare the unoffending woodpecker."

In the rivers and different creeks you number six species of the kingfisher. They make their nest in a hole in the sand on the side of the bank. As there is always plenty of foliage to protect them from the heat of the

sun, they feed at all hours of the day. Though their plumage is prettily
varied, still it falls far short of the brilliancy displayed by the English
kingfisher. This little native of Britain would outweigh them altogether in
the scale of beauty.

A bird called jacamar is often taken for a kingfisher, but it has no
relationship to that tribe. It frequently sits in the trees over the water, and
as its beak bears some resemblance to that of the kingfisher, this may
probably account for its being taken for one; it feeds entirely upon insects;
it sits on a branch in motionless expectation, and as soon as a fly, butterfly,
or moth pass by, it darts at it, and returns to the branch it had just left. It
seems an indolent, sedentary bird, shunning the society of all others in the
forest. It never visits the plantations, but is found at all times of the year in
the woods. There are four species of jacamar in Demerara. They are all
beautiful: the largest, rich and superb in the extreme. Its plumage is of so
fine a changing blue and golden-green that it may be ranked with the
choicest of the humming-birds. Nature has denied it a song, but given a
costly garment in lieu of it. The smallest species of jacamar is very common
in the dry savannas. The second size, all golden-green on the back, must be
looked for in the wallaba-forest. The third is found throughout the whole
extent of these wilds, and the fourth, which is the largest, frequents the
interior, where you begin to perceive stones in the ground.

When you have penetrated far into Macoushia, you hear the pretty
songster called troupiale pour forth a variety of sweet and plaintive notes.
This is the bird which the Portuguese call the nightingale of Guiana. Its
predominant colours are rich orange and shining black, arrayed to great
advantage. His delicate and well-shaped frame seems unable to bear
captivity. The Indians sometimes bring down troupiales to Stabroek, but in
a few months they languish and die in a cage. They soon become very
familiar, and if you allow them the liberty of the house, they live longer
than in a cage and appear in better spirits, but when you least expect it
they drop down and die in epilepsy.

Smaller in size, and of colour not so rich and somewhat differently
arranged, another species of troupiale sings melodiously in Demerara.
The woodcutter is particularly favoured by him, for while the hen is sitting
on her nest, built in the roof of the woodcutter's house, he sings for hours
together close by. He prefers the forests to the cultivated parts.

You would not grudge to stop for a few minutes, as you are walking in
the plantations, to observe a third species of troupiale: his wings, tail
and throat are black; all the rest of the body is a bright yellow. There is

something very sweet and plaintive in his song, though much shorter than that of the troupiale in the interior.

A fourth species goes in flocks from place to place, in the cultivated parts, at the time the indian-corn is ripe; he is all black, except the head and throat, which are yellow. His attempt at song is not worth attending to.

Wherever there is a wild fig-tree ripe, a numerous species of birds called tangara is sure to be on it. There are eighteen beautiful species here. Their plumage is very rich and diversified. Some of them boast six separate colours; others have the blue, purple, green and black so kindly blended into each other that it would be impossible to mark their boundaries; while others again exhibit them strong, distinct and abrupt. Many of these tangaras have a fine song. They seem to partake much of the nature of our linnets, sparrows and finches. Some of them are fond of the plantations; others are never seen there, preferring the wild seeds of the forest to the choicest fruits planted by the hand of man.

On the same fig-trees to which they repair, and often accidentally up and down the forest, you fall in with four species of manikin. The largest is white and black, with the feathers on the throat remarkably long; the next in size is half red and half black; the third black, with a white crown; the fourth black, with a golden crown, and red feathers at the knee. The half-red and half-black species is the scarcest. There is a creek in the Demerara called Camouni. About ten minutes from the mouth you see a common-sized fig-tree on your right hand, as you ascend, hanging over the water; it bears a very small fig twice a year. When its fruit is ripe this manikin is on the tree from morn till eve.

On all the ripe fig-trees in the forest you see the bird called the small tiger-bird. Like some of our belles and dandies, it has a gaudy vest to veil an ill-shaped body. The throat, and part of the head, are a bright red; the breast and belly have black spots on a yellow ground; the wings are a dark green, black, and white; and the rump and tail black and green. Like the manikin, it has no song: it depends solely upon a showy garment for admiration.

Devoid, too, of song, and in a still superber garb, the yawaraciri comes to feed on the same tree. It has a bar like black velvet from the eyes to the beak; its legs are yellow; its throat, wings and tail black; all the rest of the body a charming blue. Chiefly in the dry savannas, and here and there accidentally in the forest, you see a songless yawaraciri still lovelier than the last: his crown is whitish blue, arrayed like a coat of mail; his tail is black, his wings black and yellow; legs red; and the whole body a glossy blue. Whilst roving through the forest, ever and anon you see individuals of the wren species busy amongst the fallen leaves, or seeking insects at the roots of the trees.

Here, too, you find six or seven species of small birds whose backs appear to be overloaded with silky plumage. One of these, with a chestnut breast, smoke-coloured back, tail red, white feathers like horns on his head, and white narrow-pointed feathers under the jaw, feeds entirely upon ants. When a nest of large light-brown ants emigrates, one following the other in meandering lines above a mile long, you see this bird watching them and every now and then picking them up. When they disappear he is seen no more: perhaps this is the only kind of ant he is fond of. When these ants are stirring, you are sure to find him near them. You cannot well mistake the ant after you have once been in its company, for its sting is very severe, and you can hardly shoot the bird and pick it up without having five or six upon you.

Parrots and paroquets are very numerous here, and of many different kinds. You will know when they are near you in the forest not only by the noise they make, but also by the fruits and seeds which they let fall while they are feeding.

The hia-hia parrot, called in England the parrot of the sun, is very remarkable: he can erect at pleasure a fine radiated circle of tartan feathers quite round the back of his head from jaw to jaw. The fore-part of his head is white; his back, tail and wings green; and his breast and belly tartan.

Superior in size and beauty to every parrot of South America, the ara will force you to take your eyes from the rest of animated nature and gaze at him: his commanding strength, the framing scarlet of his body, the lovely variety of red, yellow, blue and green in his wings, the extraordinary length of his scarlet and blue tail, seem all to join and demand for him the title of emperor of all the parrots. He is scarce in Demerara till you reach the confines of the Macoushi country: there he is in vast abundance. He mostly feeds on trees of the palm species. When the coucourite-trees have ripe fruit on them they are covered with this magnificent parrot. He is not shy or wary: you may take your blow-pipe and quiver of poisoned arrows and kill more than you are able to carry back to your hut. They are very vociferous, and, like the common parrots, rise up in bodies towards sunset and fly two and two to their place of rest. It is a grand sight in ornithology to see thousands of aras flying over your head, low enough to let you have a full view of their flaming mantle. The Indians find their flesh very good, and the feathers serve for ornaments in their head-dresses. They breed in the holes of trees, are easily reared and tamed, and learn to speak pretty distinctly.

Another species frequents the low-lands of Demerara. He is nearly the size of the scarlet ara, but much inferior in plumage. Blue and yellow are his predominant colours.

Along the creeks and river-sides, and in the wet savannas, six species of the bittern will engage your attention. They are all handsome, the smallest not so large as the English water-hen.

In the savannas, too, you will sometimes surprise the snow-white egret, whose back is adorned with the plumes from which it takes its name. Here, too, the spurwinged water-hen, the blue and green water-hen and two other species of ordinary plumage are found. While in quest of these, the blue heron, the large and small brown heron, the boatbill and muscovy duck now and then rise up before you.

When the sun has sunk in the western woods, no longer agitated by the breeze; when you can only see a straggler or two of the feathered tribe hastening to join its mate, already at its roosting-place, then it is that the goat-sucker comes out of the forest, where it has sat all day long in slumbering ease, unmindful of the gay and busy scenes around it. Its eyes are too delicately formed to bear the light, and thus it is forced to shun the flaming face of day and wait in patience till night invites him to partake of the pleasures her dusky presence brings.

The harmless, unoffending goat-sucker, from the time of Aristotle down to the present day, has been in disgrace with man. Father has handed down to son, and author to author, that this nocturnal thief subsists by milking the flocks. Poor injured little bird of night, how sadly hast thou suffered, and how foul a stain has inattention to facts put upon thy character! Thou hast never robbed man of any part of his property nor deprived the kid of a drop of milk.

When the moon shines bright you may have a fair opportunity of examining the goat-sucker. You will see it close by the cows, goats and sheep, jumping up every now and then under their bellies. Approach a little nearer—he is not shy: "he fears no danger, for he knows no sin." See how the nocturnal flies are tormenting the herd, and with what dexterity he springs up and catches them as fast as they alight on the belly, legs and udder of the animals. Observe how quiet they stand, and how sensible they seem of his good offices, for they neither strike at him nor hit him with their tail, nor tread on him, nor try to drive him away as an uncivil intruder. Were you to dissect him, and inspect his stomach, you could find no milk there. It is full of the flies which have been annoying the herd.

The prettily-mottled plumage of the goat-sucker, like that of the owl, wants the lustre which is observed in the feathers of the birds of the day. This at once marks him as a lover of the pale moon's nightly beams. There are nine species here. The largest appears nearly the size of the English wood-owl. Its cry is so remarkable that, having once heard it, you will never forget it. When night reigns over these immeasurable wilds, whilst lying in your hammock you will hear this goat-sucker lamenting like one in deep distress. A stranger would never conceive it to be the cry of a bird. He would say it was the departing voice of a midnight murdered victim or the last wailing of Niobe for her poor children before she was turned into stone. Suppose yourself in hopeless sorrow, begin with a high loud note, and pronounce "ha, ha, ha, ha, ha, ha, ha," each note lower and lower, till the last is scarcely heard, pausing a moment or two betwixt every note, and you will have some idea of the moaning of the largest goat-sucker in Demerara.

Four other species of the goat-sucker articulate some words so distinctly that they have received their names from the sentences they utter, and absolutely bewilder the stranger on his arrival in these parts. The most common one sits down close by your door, and flies and alights three or four yards before you, as you walk along the road, crying, "Who-are-you, who-who-who-are-you." Another bids you "Work-away, work-work-work-away." A third cries, mournfully, "Willy-come-go, willy-willy-willy-come-go." And high up in the country a fourth tells you to "Whip-poor-will, whip-whip-whip-poor-will."

You will never persuade the negro to destroy these birds or get the Indian to let fly his arrow at them. They are birds of omen and reverential dread. Jumbo, the demon of Africa, has them under his command, and they equally obey the Yabahou, or Demerara Indian devil. They are the receptacles for departed souls, who come back again to earth, unable to rest for crimes done in their days of nature; or they are expressly sent by Jumbo, or Yabahou, to haunt cruel and hard-hearted masters and retaliate injuries received from them. If the largest goat-sucker chance to cry near the white man's door, sorrow and grief will soon be inside: and they expect to see the master waste away with a slow consuming sickness. If it be heard close to the negro's or Indian's hut, from that night misfortune sits brooding over it: and they await the event in terrible suspense.

You will forgive the poor Indian of Guiana for this. He knows no better; he has nobody to teach him. But shame it is that in our own civilised country the black cat and broomstaff should be considered as conductors to and from the regions of departed spirits.

Many years ago I knew poor harmless Mary; old age had marked her strongly, just as he will mark you and me, should we arrive at her years and carry the weight of grief which bent her double. The old men of the village said she had been very pretty in her youth, and nothing could be seen more comely than Mary when she danced on the green. He who had gained her heart left her for another, less fair, though richer, than Mary. From that time she became sad and pensive; the rose left her cheek, and she was never more seen to dance round the maypole on the green. Her expectations were blighted; she became quite indifferent to everything around her, and seemed to think of nothing but how she could best attend her mother, who was lame and not long for this life. Her mother had begged a black kitten from some boys who were going to drown it, and in her last illness she told Mary to be kind to it for her sake.

When age and want had destroyed the symmetry of Mary's fine form, the village began to consider her as one who had dealings with spirits: her cat confirmed the suspicion. If a cow died, or a villager wasted away with an unknown complaint, Mary and her cat had it to answer for. Her broom sometimes served her for a walking-stick: and if ever she supported her tottering frame with it as far as the maypole, where once, in youthful bloom and beauty, she had attracted the eyes of all, the boys would surround her and make sport of her, while her cat had neither friend nor safety beyond the cottage-wall. Nobody considered it cruel or uncharitable to torment a witch; and it is probable, long before this, that cruelty, old age and want have worn her out, and that both poor Mary and her cat have ceased to be.

Would you wish to pursue the different species of game, well-stored and boundless is your range in Demerara. Here no one dogs you, and afterwards clandestinely inquires if you have a hundred a year in land to entitle you to enjoy such patrician sport. Here no saucy intruder asks if you have taken out a licence, by virtue of which you are allowed to kill the birds which have bred upon your own property. Here

You are as free as when God first made man,
Ere the vile laws of servitude began,
And wild in woods the noble savage ran.

Before the morning's dawn you hear a noise in the forest which sounds like "duraquaura" often repeated. This is the partridge, a little smaller than and differing somewhat in colour from the English partridge: it lives entirely in the forest, and probably the young brood very soon leaves its parents, as you never flush more than two birds in the same place, and in general only one.

About the same hour, and sometimes even at midnight, you hear two species of maam, or tinamou, send forth their long and plaintive whistle from the depth of the forest. The flesh of both is delicious. The largest is plumper, and almost equals in size the blackcock of Northumberland. The quail is said to be here, though rare.

The hannaquoi, which some have compared to the pheasant, though with little reason, is very common.

Here are also two species of the powise, or hocco, and two of the small wild turkeys called maroudi: they feed on the ripe fruits of the forest and are found in all directions in these extensive wilds. You will admire the horned screamer as a stately and majestic bird: he is almost the size of the turkey-cock, on his head is a long slender horn, and each wing is armed with a strong, sharp, triangular spur an inch long.

Sometimes you will fall in with flocks of two or three hundred war-acabas, or trumpeters, called so from the singular noise they produce. Their breast is adorned with beautiful changing blue and purple feathers; their head and neck like velvet; their wings and back grey, and belly black. They run with great swiftness, and when domesticated attend their master in his walks with as much apparent affection as his dog. They have no spurs, but still, such is their high spirit and activity, they browbeat every dunghill fowl in the yard and force the guinea-birds, dogs and turkeys to own their superiority.

If, kind and gentle reader, thou shouldst ever visit these regions with an intention to examine their productions, perhaps the few observations contained in these wanderings may be of service to thee. Excuse their brevity: more could have been written, and each bird more particularly described, but it would have been pressing too hard upon thy time and patience.

Soon after arriving in these parts thou wilt find that the species here enumerated are only as a handful from a well-stored granary. Nothing has been said of the eagles, the falcons, the hawks and shrikes; nothing of the different species of vultures, the king of which is very handsome, and seems to be the only bird which claims regal honours from a surrounding tribe. It is a fact beyond all dispute that, when the scent of carrion has drawn together hundreds of the common vultures, they all retire from the carcass as soon as the king of the vultures makes his appearance. When his majesty has satisfied the cravings of his royal stomach with the choicest bits from the most stinking and corrupted parts, he generally retires to a neighbouring tree, and then the common vultures return in crowds to gobble down his leavings. The Indians, as well as the whites, have observed this, for when one of them, who has learned a little English, sees the king, and wishes you to have a proper notion of the bird, he says: "There is the governor of the carrion-crows."

Now the Indians have never heard of a personage in Demerara higher than that of governor; and the colonists, through a common mistake, call the vultures carrion-crows. Hence the Indian, in order to express the dominion of this bird over the common vultures, tells you he is governor of the carrion-crows. The Spaniards have also observed it, for through all the Spanish Main he is called Rey de Zamuros, king of the vultures. The many species of owls, too, have not been noticed; and no mention made of the columbine tribe. The prodigious variety of water-fowl on the sea-shore has been but barely hinted at.

There, and on the borders and surface of the inland waters, in the marshes and creeks, besides the flamingos, scarlet curlews and spoonbills already mentioned, will be found greenish-brown curlews, sandpipers, rails, coots, gulls, pelicans, jabirus, nandapoas, crabiers, snipes, plovers, ducks, geese, cranes and anhingas; most of them in vast abundance; some frequenting only the sea-coast, others only the interior, according to their different natures; all worthy the attention of the naturalist, all worthy of a place in the cabinet of the curious.

Should thy comprehensive genius not confine itself to birds alone, grand is the appearance of other objects all around. Thou art in a land rich in botany and mineralogy, rich in zoology and entomology. Animation will glow in thy looks and exercise will brace thy frame in vigour. The very time of thy absence from the tables of heterogeneous luxury will be profitable to thy stomach, perhaps already sorely drenched with Londo-Parisian sauces, and a new stock of health will bring thee an appetite to relish the wholesome food of the chase. Never-failing sleep will wait on thee at the time she comes to soothe the rest of animated nature, and ere the sun's rays appear in the horizon thou wilt spring from thy hammock fresh as the

April lark. Be convinced also that the dangers and difficulties which are generally supposed to accompany the traveller in his journey through distant regions are not half so numerous or dreadful as they are commonly thought to be.

The youth who incautiously reels into the lobby of Drury Lane after leaving the table sacred to the god of wine is exposed to more certain ruin, sickness and decay than he who wanders a whole year in the wilds of Demerara. But this will never be believed because the disasters arising from dissipation are so common and frequent in civilised life that man becomes quite habituated to them, and sees daily victims sink into the tomb long before their time without ever once taking alarm at the causes which precipitated them headlong into it.

But the dangers which a traveller exposes himself to in foreign parts are novel, out-of-the-way things to a man at home. The remotest apprehension of meeting a tremendous tiger, of being carried off by a flying dragon, or having his bones picked by a famished cannibal: oh, that makes him shudder. It sounds in his ears like the bursting of a bombshell. Thank Heaven he is safe by his own fireside.

Prudence and resolution ought to be the traveller's constant companions. The first will cause him to avoid a number of snares which he will find in the path as he journeys on; and the second will always lend a hand to assist him if he has unavoidably got entangled in them. The little distinctions which have been shown him at his own home ought to be forgotten when he travels over the world at large, for strangers know nothing of his former merits, and it is necessary that they should witness them before they pay him the tribute which he was wont to receive within his own doors. Thus to be kind and affable to those we meet, to mix in their amusements, to pay a compliment or two to their manners and customs, to respect their elders, to give a little to their distressed and needy, and to feel, as it were, at home amongst them, is the sure way to enable you to pass merrily on, and to find other comforts as sweet and palatable as those which you were accustomed to partake of amongst your friends and acquaintance in your own native land. We will now ascend in fancy on Icarian wing and take a view of Guiana in general. See an immense plain! betwixt two of the largest rivers in the world, level as a bowling-green, save at Cayenne, and covered with trees along the coast quite to the Atlantic wave, except where the plantations make a little vacancy amongst the foliage.

Though nearly in the centre of the Torrid Zone, the sun's rays are not so intolerable as might be imagined, on account of the perpetual verdure and refreshing north-east breeze. See what numbers of broad and rapid rivers intersect it in their journey to the ocean, and that not a stone or a pebble is to be found on their banks, or in any part of the country, till your eye catches the hills in the interior. How beautiful and magnificent are the lakes in the heart of the forests, and how charming the forests themselves, for miles after miles on each side of the rivers! How extensive appear the savannas or natural meadows, teeming with innumerable herds of cattle, where the Portuguese and Spaniards are settled, but desert as Saara where the English and Dutch claim dominion! How gradually the face of the country rises! See the sandhills all clothed in wood first emerging from the level, then hills a little higher, rugged with bold and craggy rocks, peeping out from amongst the most luxuriant timber. Then come plains and dells and far-extending valleys, arrayed in richest foliage; and beyond them mountains piled on mountains, some bearing prodigious forests, others of bleak and barren aspect. Thus your eye wanders on over scenes of varied loveliness and grandeur, till it rests on the stupendous pinnacles of the long-continued Cordilleras de los Andes, which rise in towering majesty and command all America.

How fertile must the low-lands be from the accumulation of fallen leaves and trees for centuries! How propitious the swamps and slimy beds of the rivers, heated by a downward sun, to the amazing growth of alligators, serpents and innumerable insects! How inviting the forests to the feathered tribes, where you see buds, blossoms, green and ripe fruit, full grown and fading leaves all on the same tree! How secure the wild beasts may rove in endless mazes! Perhaps those mountains, too, which appear so bleak and naked, as if quite neglected, are, like Potosi, full of precious metals.

Let us now return the pinions we borrowed from Icarus, and prepare to bid farewell to the wilds. The time allotted to these wanderings is drawing fast to a close. Every day for the last six months has been employed in paying close attention to natural history in the forests of Demerara. Above two hundred specimens of the finest birds have been collected and a pretty just knowledge formed of their haunts and economy. From the time of leaving England, in March 1816, to the present day, nothing has intervened to arrest a fine flow of health, saving a quartan ague which did not tarry, but fled as suddenly as it appeared.

And now I take leave of thee, kind and gentle reader. The new mode of preserving birds heretofore promised thee shall not be forgotten. The plan is already formed in imagination, and can be penned down during the passage across the Atlantic. If the few remarks in these wanderings shall have any weight in inciting thee to sally forth and explore the vast and well-stored regions of Demerara, I have gained my end. Adieu.

BIRDS OF SIBERIA

HENRY SEEBOHM

Alexievka is the shipping-port of the Petchora Timber-trading Company. It is a group of houses built upon an island in the delta of the great river, where the ships are laden with larch for Cronstadt. The larch is felled in the forests 500 or 600 miles up the river, and roughly squared into logs varying from two to three feet in diameter. It is floated down in enormous rafts, the logs being bound together with willows and hazel-boughs. These rafts are manned by a large crew, some of whom help to steer it down the current with oars and poles, while others are hired for the season to assist in loading the ships at Alexievka. Many of the men bring their wives with them to cook for the party; sleeping huts are erected on the raft, and it becomes to all intents and purposes a little floating village, which is frequently three months in making the voyage down the river. Marriages have been known to take place on these rafts. Occasionally a funeral has to be performed, and sometimes all hands are engaged in helping to keep the raft under the lee of an island or a promontory to avoid the danger of having it broken up by the violence of the waves. With the greatest care in the world this will sometimes happen. The Russian has a good deal of the fatal facility to blunder which characterises the Englishman, and shiploads of stranded logs of larch are strewn on the islands of the delta and on the shores of the lagoon of this great river.

When we landed on the island of Alexievka it was a rapidly drying-up willow-swamp of perhaps half a dozen square miles, some six feet above the level of the Petchora, which swept past it with a rapid current.

In some places the willow-swamp was impenetrable, in others bare grassy oases varied the flat landscape, and there were one or two largish lakes on the island. During the floods which accompanied the break-up of the ice, the whole of the island was under water, and men were busily clearing away the mud which had deposited itself on the floors of the houses. An extensive series of wooden fortifications protected the various buildings from being carried away by the ice. For four months of the year the village was a busy scene, full of life and activity, but for the remaining eight months a solitary man and a dog kept watch over the property of the Company, and even they had to desert their charge and escape to the shore during the breaking-up of the ice.

Three rooms were generously placed at our disposal, and we proceeded to make ourselves as comfortable as the circumstances would permit. Our first care was to buy a brace of willow-grouse and a bean-goose for the pot; our next to purchase eggs of the yellow-headed wagtail, bean-goose, willow-grouse, and long-tailed duck. A nest of the white wagtail which we found contained remarkably brown eggs; it was made chiefly of roots and a little stalky grass, and was lined with reindeer hair. The next day peasants brought us two nests of the yellow-headed wagtail, which were also composed of fine roots and dry leafy grass, the inside lined with reindeer hair; one had, besides, two small feathers and a piece of duck-down.

The mosquitoes, which of late had tried us severely, were now giving us a respite, driven back by the cold north wind and occasional snow-storms. All day I kept indoors, going out but for half an hour, when I bagged a Siberian chiffchaff and a red-throated pipit perched in a tree. The nests came in plentifully. The first day of our stay there were brought to us those of the blue-throat, the redpoll, the reed-bunting, the willow-warbler, two of the bean-goose, with the goose snared upon it, and one of the pintail duck. With these were brought two wigeon's eggs. The weather continued very cold; the Petchora looked sullen and tempestuous under the dark sky and bleak wind. The next day we again kept indoors, profiting by our enforced captivity in having a general overhauling of our skins. We found the Siberian chiffchaff the commonest warbler amongst the willows of Alexievka. Its note is a "ching-chevy" repeated three or four times in rapid succession with the accent laid on the "ching," and the warble generally, but not always, ending with a final "ching." Probably owing to the coldness of the weather we did not then hear it in full song, as we did at Ust-Zylma and Habariki. We found Buffon's skuas numerous in Alexievka; they were usually in flocks of five or six. There seemed to be only one common sparrow in the place, and this I shot.

The 22nd of June was inscribed in our journal as a red-letter day. We were dead tired when we turned into our hammocks at half-past ten the night before, and slept the clock round and an hour over rising at half-past eleven. When we woke we found it was a bright warm day, the wind had dropped, and the great river looked no longer like an angry sea. We decided to cross it, ordered our men to get the boat ready, made a hasty breakfast, and set sail at last for the land of promise, the mysterious tundra. We pictured this great land to ourselves as a sort of ornithological Cathay, where all sorts of rare and possibly unknown birds might be found. So far we had been just a little disappointed with the results of our trip. July would soon be upon us, and we had not yet solved one of the six problems that we had proposed to ourselves as the main objects of our journey. We had not seen the least trace of the knot, the curlew sandpiper, the sanderling, or the grey plover. Some birds that we had at first fancied might be Little stints in full breeding plumage, we were now thoroughly convinced were nothing but Temminck's stints, and as we had hitherto met with but one species of swan, we had reluctantly come to the conclusion that we had not yet seen Bewick's swan. We congratulated ourselves that our observations on the arrival of migratory birds at Ust-Zylma were not without interest. We were much pleased that we had shot one specimen of the Arctic willow-warbler. The abundance of yellow-headed wagtails, and the prospect of bringing home many of the eggs of this rare bird, was a source of considerable satisfaction to us. Our two best things were undoubtedly the new pipit and the Siberian chiffchaff. We hoped that both these birds might be new, but our acquaintance with the various Indian species that might possibly migrate into this region was not sufficient to warrant us in entertaining more than a hope. We therefore looked forward to our first day on the tundra with more than usual anxiety and interest.

The tundra forms the east bank of the Petchora, and we anchored our boat under a steep cliff, perhaps sixty feet high, a crumbling slope of clay, earth, sand, gravel, turf, but no rock. We looked over a gently rolling prairie country, stretching away to a flat plain, beyond which was a range of low rounded hills, some eight or ten miles off. It was in fact a moor, with here and there a large flat bog, and everywhere abundance of lakes. For seven or eight months in the year it is covered with from two to three feet of snow. Snow was still lying in large patches in the more sheltered recesses of the steep river-banks, and on one of the lakes a large floe of ice, six inches thick, was still unmelted. The vegetation on the dry parts of the tundra was chiefly sedges, moss, and lichen, of which the familiar reindeer-moss was especially abundant. In some places there was an abundance of cranberries, with last year's fruit still eatable, preserved by the frost and snow of winter. Here and there we met with a dwarf shrub, not unlike a rhododendron, with a white flower and aromatic-scented leaves (*Ledum palustre*), a heath-like plant with a pale red flower (*Andromeda polifolia*), and dwarf birch (*Betula nana*) running on the ground almost like ivy. The flat boggy places had evidently been shallow lakes a few weeks ago after the sudden thaw, and were now black swamps; water in the middle, grown over with yellow-green moss, and sedges towards the edge. They were separated from each other by tussocky ridges of moor, which intersected the plain like the veins on the rind of a melon. We found no difficulty in going where we liked; our indiarubber waterproofs were all-sufficient. We crossed the wettest bogs with impunity, seldom sinking more than a foot before reaching a good foundation, a solid pavement of ice. Birds were but thinly scattered over the ground, but there were sufficient to keep our curiosity on the *qui vive*. The commonest bird was the Lapland bunting, and we took two of their nests in the tussocky ridges between the little bogs. The next commonest bird was the red-throated pipit, and we found two of their nests in similar positions. As we marched across the tundra we fell in with some dunlins, and took a couple of their nests. This was encouraging. The dunlin was a bird we had not seen at Ust-Zylma, and one possibly that migrated direct across country to Ust-Ussa. We had not walked more than a couple of miles inland before we came upon a small party of plovers. They were very wild, and we found it impossible to get within shot of them; but a distant view through our binocular almost convinced us that we had met with the grey plover at last. On going a little farther other plovers rose, and we determined to commence a diligent search for the nest, and offered half a rouble to any of our men who should find one. Our interpreter laughed at us, and marched away into the tundra with a "C'est impossible, monsieur." We appealed to our Samoyede, who stroked his beardless chin and cautiously replied, "Mozhna." The other men wandered aimlessly up and down, but the Samoyede tramped the ground systematically, and after more than an hour's search found a nest on one of the dry tussocky ridges intersecting the bog, containing four eggs about the size and shape of those of the golden plover, but more like those of the lapwing in colour. The nest was a hollow, evidently scratched, perfectly round, somewhat deep, and containing a

handful of broken slender twigs and reindeer-moss. Harvie-Brown concealed himself as well as he could behind a ridge, to lie in wait for the bird
returning to the nest, and after half an hour's watching shot a veritable
grey plover. Soon afterwards another of our men found a second nest, also
containing four eggs, in an exactly similar situation. Harvie-Brown took
this nest also in hand, and in about an hour succeeded in shooting the
female. The third nest was found by the Samoyede. This time I lay down
behind a ridge some thirty yards from the nest, and after waiting a quarter
of an hour caught sight of the bird on the top of a distant tussock. Presently
she ran nearer to another ridge, looked round, and then ran on to the next,
until she finally came within fifty yards of where I was lying. I had just
made up my mind to risk a shot when she must have caught sight of me,
and flew right away. In a quarter of an hour I caught sight of her again,
approaching by short stages as before, but from an opposite direction. I
must have been in full sight of her. When she had approached within fifty
yards of me, as near as I could guess, I fired at her with No. 4 shot and
missed. I remained reclining where I was, with little hope that she would
try a third time to approach the nest, and whiled away the time with
watching a Buffon's skua through my glass as it cautiously approached in
my direction. Turning my head round suddenly I caught sight of the grey
plover running towards the nest within fifty yards of me. I lifted my gun
and fired again, but was so nervous that I missed her a second time. I was
so vexed that I got up and walked towards the skua, which still remained
in statu quo. I missed a shot at it too, spent some time in a vain search for its
nest, and returned to my old quarters. In ten minutes I saw the grey plover
flying up. It took a wheel in my direction, coming almost within shot, and
evidently took stock of me, and satisfied itself that I was a harmless animal
practising with blank cartridge, and having no evil design upon its eggs. It
alighted about fifty yards beyond the nest, and approached less timidly
than before. When it came within fifty yards of me I fired, this time with
No. 6 shot, and laid the poor bird upon its back. As we returned to our boat
Harvie-Brown found a fourth nest, and, after watching as before, secured
the bird. We accidentally broke two of the eggs belonging to the third nest,
but reached Alexievka at midnight with fourteen identified grey plover's
eggs. Two sittings were quite fresh, and made us an excellent omelette for
breakfast the next morning. The other two were very slightly incubated.

On the tundra we saw several Buffon's skuas, and shot two. I also
shot a willow-grouse on a piece of swampy ground near a lake, where a
few dwarf willows were growing. On the lakes we saw many pairs of long-

tailed ducks. A few pairs of yellow-headed wagtails, which evidently had nests, a redwing, a Temminck's stint, a few pairs of bean-geese, a redpoll, and a hawk, which, as far as I could make out with my glass, was a male peregrine—this completed the list of birds we saw on the tundra.

On our return to headquarters we found that the price we had paid for the eggs to the workmen had induced many of them to go out bird-nesting, and at night our bag for the day stood as under, as far as eggs were concerned:

Grey plover	14
Dunlin	7
Great snipe	4
Lapland bunting	25
Red-throated pipit	39
Yellow-headed wagtail	10
Mealy redpoll	16
Reed-bunting	12
Redwing	3
Bean-goose	11
Wigeon (with down)	17
Temminck's stint	4
	162

This was a grand haul. Any little lingering feeling of disappointment which we had experienced was now completely gone. The grey plover eggs alone would have made our trip a success. They were unquestionably the first that had ever been taken in Europe. We spent the next two days in blowing our eggs and writing up our journals, occasionally strolling out among the willows on the island to bag a few yellow-headed wagtails and other birds to keep Piottuch employed. We found that the swans' eggs that we had brought from Kuya were perfectly fresh. The eggs of the bean-goose, on the contrary, some of them more than a week old, were mostly considerably incubated. The ducks' eggs were all fresh, or nearly so. Most of these were wigeon's, pale cream-coloured eggs; the down large, dark brown, very distinctly tipped with white and with pale whitish centres. The red-throated pipits and Lapland buntings' eggs were, many of them, too much sat upon to be easily blown, as were also the dunlins' eggs. The eggs of Temminck's stint, red-necked phalarope, yellow-headed wagtail, and most of the redpolls were all fresh or very slightly sat upon. The eggs of the gulls, both those of the common species and of the Arctic herring-gull, were quite fresh, whilst some of those of the Arctic tern were fresh, and some considerably incubated. During these two days we found several nests of the fieldfare on the island, a nest of the willow-warbler, and one of the yellow-headed wagtail. The latter was on the ground, concealed amongst the old tangled grass which the floods had twisted round a stake. It was principally composed of dry herbage, with one or two feathers in the lining. Our two *raræ aves*, which we christened the Petchora pipit, and the Siberian chiffchaff, were by no means uncommon, but we failed to find either of their nests. Amongst the nests, however, which our excellent coadjutors the Zyriani brought us was one which we at once concluded could belong only to the Petchora pipit (*Anthus gustavi*). It contained five perfectly fresh eggs, larger than those of the red-throated pipit, and similar in colour to those of the meadow-pipit. The nest was somewhat larger than that of the red-throated pipit, composed of more aquatic-looking flat-leaved grass, and containing fragments of *Equisetum* in the lining. Our collection of eggs increased rapidly. We had now 145 sittings, numbering 681 eggs.

THE WILD GEESE
OF WYNDYGOUL

ERNEST THOMPSON SETON

THE BUGLING ON THE LAKE

Who that knows the Wild Northland of Canada can picture that blue and green wilderness without hearing in his heart the trumpet "honk" of the Wild Geese? Who that has ever known it there can fail to get again, each time he hears, the thrill it gave when first for him it sounded on the blue lake in the frame of green? Older than ourselves is the thrill of the gander-clang. For without a doubt that trumpet note in springtime was the inspiring notice to our far-back forebears in the days that were that the winter famine was at end—the Wild Geese come, the snow will melt, and the game again be back on the browning hills. The ice-hell of the winter time is gone; the warm bright heaven of the green and perfect land is here. This is the tidings it tells, and when I hear the honker-clang from the flying wedge in the sky, that is the message it brings me with a sudden mist in the eyes and a choking in the throat, so I turn away, if another be there, unless that other chance to be one like myself, a primitive, a "hark back" who, too, remembers and who understands.

So when I built my home in the woods and glorified a marshy swamp into a deep blue brimming lake, with Muskrats in the water and intertwining boughs above, my memory, older than my brain, harked hungry for a sound that should have been. I knew not what; I tried to find by subtle searching, but it was chance in a place far off that gave the clue. I want to hear the honkers call, I long for the clang of the flying wedge, the trumpet note of the long-gone days.

So I brought a pair of the Blacknecks from another lake, pinioned to curb the wild roving that the seasons bring, and they nested on a little island, not hidden, but open to the world about. There in that exquisite bed of soft gray down were laid the six great ivory eggs. On them the patient mother sat four weeks unceasingly, except each afternoon she left them half an hour. And round and round that island, night and day, the gander floated, cruised, and tacked about, like a war ship on patrol. Never once did the gander cover the eggs, never once did the mother mount on guard. I tried to land and learn about the nest one day. The brooding goose it was that gave the danger call. A short quack, a long, sharp hiss, and before my boat could touch the shore the gander splashed between and faced me. Only over his dead body might my foot defile their isle—so he was left in peace.

The young ones came at length. The six shells broke and the six sweet golden downlings "peeped" inspiringly. Next day they quit the nest in orderly array. The mother first, the downlings closely bunched behind, and last the warrior sire. And this order they always kept, then and all other times that I have knowledge of. It gave me food for thought. The mother always leads, the father, born a fighter, follows—yes, obeys. And what a valiant guard he was; the Snapping Turtle, the Henhawk, the Blacksnake, the Coon, and the vagrant dog might take their toll of duckling brood or chicken yard, but there is no thing alive the gander will not face for his little ones, and there are few things near his bulk can face him.

The flock grew big and strong. Before three months they were big almost as the old ones, and fairly fledged; at four their wings were grown; their voices still were small and thin, they had not got the trumpet note, but seemed the mother's counterparts in all things else. Then they began to feel their wings, and take short flights across the lake. As their wings grew strong their voices deepened, till the trumpet note was theirs, and the thing I had dreamed of came about; a wild goose band that flew and bugled in the air, and yet came back to their home water that was also mine. Stronger they grow, and long and high their flights. Then came the moon of falling leaves, and with its waning flocks of small birds flew, and in the higher sky the old loud clang was heard. Down from the north they came, the arrow-heads of geese. All kinsmen these, and that ahead without a doubt the mother of the rest.

THE FIFTH COMMANDMENT

The Wild Geese on my lake turned up their eyes and answered back, and lined up on the lake. Their mother led the way and they whispered all along the line. Their mother gave the word, swimming fast and faster, then quacked, then called, and then their voices rose to give the "honk"; the broad wings spread a little, while they spattered on the glassy lake, then rose to the measured "Honk, honk"; soaring away in a flock, they drifted into line, to join those other honkers in the Southern sky.

"Honk, honk, honk!" they shouted as they sped. "Come on! Come on!" they inspired each other with the marching song; it set their wings aquiver. The wild blood rushed still faster in their wilding breasts. It was like a glorious trumpet. But—what! Mother is not in the line. Still splashed she on the surface of the lake, and father, too—and now her strident trumpet overbore their clamorous "On, on! Come on!" with a strong "Come back! Come back!" And father, too, was bugling there. "Come back! Come back!"

So the downlings wheeled, and circling high above the woods came sailing, skirting, kiting, splashing down at the matriarchal call.

"What's up? What's up?" they called lowly all together, swimming nervously. "Why don't we go?" "What is it, mother?"

And mother could not tell. Only this she knew, that when she gave the bugle note for all to fly, she spattered with the rest, and flapped, but it seemed she could not get the needed send-off. Somehow she failed to get well under way; the youngsters rose, but the old ones, their strong leaders, had strangely failed. Such things will come to all. Not quite run enough no doubt. So mother led them to the northmost arm of the lake, an open stretch of water now, and long. They here lined up again, mother giving a low, short double "honk" ahead, the rest aside and yet in line, for the long array was angling.

Then mother passed the word "Now, now," and nodding just a little swam on, headed for the south, the young ones passed the word "Now, now," and nodding swam, and father at the rear gave his deep, strong, "Now, now," and swam. So swam they all, then spread their wings, and spattered with their feet, as they put on speed, and as they went they rose, and rising bugled louder till the marching song was ringing in full chorus. Up, up and away, above the treetops. *But again*, for some strange reason, mother was not there, and father, too, was left behind on the pond, and once again the bugle of retreat was heard, "Come back! Come back!"

And the brood, obedient, wheeled on swishing wings to sail and slide and settle on the pond, while mother and father both expressed in low, short notes their deep perplexity.

Again and again this scene took place. The autumn message in the air, the flying wedges of their kin, or the impulse in themselves lined up that flock on the water. All the law of ceremony was complied with, and all went well but the climax.

When the Mad Moon came the mania was at its height; not once but twenty times a day I saw them line up and rise, but ever come back to the mother's call, the bond of love and duty stronger than the annual custom of the race. It was a conflict of their laws indeed, but the strongest was, *obey*, made absolute by love.

After a while the impulse died and the flock settled down to winter on the pond. Many a long, far flight they took, but allegiance to the older folk was strong and brought them back. So the winter passed.

Again, when the springtime came, the Blacknecks flying north stirred up the young, but in a less degree.

That summer came another brood of young. The older ones were warned away whenever near. Snapper, Coon, and ranging cur were driven off, and September saw the young ones on the lake with their brothers of the older brood.

Then came October, with the southward rushing of the feathered kinds. Again and again that line upon the lake and the bugle sound to "fly," and the same old scene, though now there were a dozen flyers who rose and circled back when mother sounded the "retreat."

FATHER OR MOTHER

So through the moon it went. The leaves were fallen now, when a strange and unexpected thing occurred. Making unusual effort to meet this most unusual case, good Mother Nature had prolonged the feathers of the pinioned wing and held back those of the other side. It was slowly done, and the compensating balance not quite made till near October's end. Then on a day, the hundredth time at least that week, the bugle sang, and all the marchers rose. *Yes! mother, too*, and bugling louder till the chorus was complete, they soared above the trees, and mother marshalled all her brood in one great arrow flock, so they sailed and clamoring sailed away, to be lost in the southward blue—and all in vain on the limpid lake behind the gander trumpeted in agony of soul, "Come back! Come back!"

His wings had failed him, and in the test, the young's allegiance bound them to their mother and the seeking of the southern home.

All that winter on the ice the gander sat alone. On days a snow-time Hawk or some belated Crow would pass above, and the ever-watchful eye of Blackneck was turned a little to take him in and then go on unheeding. Once or twice there were sounds that stirred the lonely watcher to a bugle call, but short and soon suppressed. It was sad to see him then, and sadder still as we pondered, for this we knew; his family never would come back. Tamed, made trustful by life where men were kind, they had gone to the land of gunners, crafty, pitiless and numberless: they would learn too late the perils of the march. Next, he never would take another mate, for the Wild Goose mates for life, and mates but once: the one surviving has no choice—he finishes his journey alone.

Poor old Blackneck, his very faithfulness it was that made for endless loneliness.

The bright days came with melting snow. The floods cut through the ice, and again there were buglers in the sky, and the gander swam on the open part of the lake and answered back:

"Honk, Honk, come back,
Come back. Come back!"

but the flying squads passed on with a passing "honk!"

Brighter still the days, and the gander paddled with a little exultation in the opening pond. How we pitied him, self-deluded, faithful, doomed to a long, lone life.

Then balmy April swished the woods with green; the lake was brimming clear. Old Blackneck never ceased to cruise and watch, and answer back such sounds as touched him. Oh, sad it seemed that one so staunch should find his burden in his very staunchness.

But on a day, when the peeper and the woodwale sang, there came the great event! Old Blackneck, ever waiting, was astir, and more than wont. Who can tell us whence the tidings came? With head at gaze he cruised the open pond, and the short, strong honk seemed sad, till some new excitation raised the feathers on his neck. He honked and honked with a brassy ring. Then long before we heard a sound, he was bugling the marching song, and as he bugled answering sounds came—from the sky—and grew—then swooping, sailing from the blue, a glorious array of thirteen Wild Geese, to sail and skate and settle on the pond; and their loud honks gave place to softer chatter as they crowded round and bowed in grave and loving salutation.

There was no doubt of it. The young were now mature and they seemed strange, of course, but this was sure the missing mate: the mother had come back, and the faithful pair took up their life—and live it yet.

The autumn sends the ordered flock afar, the father stays perforce on guard, but the bond that binds them all and takes them off and brings them back is stronger than the fear of death. So I have learned to love and venerate the honker Wild Goose whom Mother Nature dowered with love unquenchable, constructed for her own good ends a monument of faithfulness unchanging, a creature heir of all the promises, so master of the hostile world around that he lives and spreads, defying plagues and beasts, and I wonder if this secret is not partly that the wise and patient mother leads. The long, slow test of time has given a minor place to the valiant, fearless, fighting male; his place the last of all, his mode of open fight the latest thing they try. And by a law inscrutable, inexorable, the young obey the matriarch. Wisdom their guide, not force. Their days are long on earth and the homeland of their race grows wide while others pass away.

THE CROWS

RICHARD JEFFRIES

On one side of the road immediately after quitting the suburb there is a small cover of furze. The spines are now somewhat browned by the summer heats, and the fern which grows about every bush trembles on the balance of colour between green and yellow. Soon, too, the tall wiry grass will take a warm brown tint, which gradually pales as the autumn passes into winter, and finally bleaches to greyish white.

Looking into the furze from the footpath, there are purple traces here and there at the edge of the fern where the heath-bells hang. On a furze branch, which projects above the rest, a furze chat perches, with yellow blossom above and beneath him. Rushes mark the margin of small pools and marshy spots, so overhung with brambles and birch branches, and so closely surrounded by gorse, that they would not otherwise be noticed.

But the thick growth of rushes intimates that water is near, and upon parting the bushes a little may be seen, all that has escaped evaporation in the shade. From one of these marshy spots I once—and once only—observed a snipe rise, and after wheeling round return and settle by another. As the wiry grass becomes paler with the fall of the year, the rushes, on the contrary, from green become faintly yellow, and presently brownish. Grey grass and brown rushes, dark furze, and fern almost copper in hue from frost, when lit up by a gleam of winter sunshine, form a pleasant breadth of warm colour in the midst of bare fields.

After continuous showers in spring, lizards are often found in the adjacent gardens, their dark backs as they crawl over the patches being almost exactly the tint of the moist earth. If touched, the tail is immediately coiled, the body stiffens, and the creature appears dead. They are popularly supposed to come from the furze, which is also believed to shelter adders.

There is, indeed, scarcely a cover in Surrey and Kent which is not said to have its adders; the gardeners employed at villas close to the metropolis occasionally raise an alarm, and profess to have seen a viper in the shrubberies, or the ivy, or under an old piece of bast. Since so few can distinguish at a glance between the common snake and the adder it is as well not to press too closely upon any reptile that may chance to be heard rustling in the grass, and to strike tussocks with the walking stick before sitting down to rest, for the adder is only dangerous when unexpectedly encountered.

In the roadside ditch by the furze the figwort grows, easily known by its coarse square stem; and the woody bines, if so they may be called, or stalks of bitter-sweet, remain all the winter standing in the hawthorn hedge. The first frosts, on the other hand, shrivel the bines of white bryony, which part and hang separated, and in the spring a fresh bine pushes up with greyish green leaves, and tendrils feeling for support. It is often observed that the tendrils of this bryony coil both ways, with and against the sun.

But it must be remembered in looking for this that it is the same tendril which should be examined, and not two different ones. It will then be seen that the tendril, after forming a spiral one way, lengthens out like a tiny green wax taper, and afterwards turns the other. Sometimes it resumes the original turn before reaching a branch to cling to, and may thus be said to have revolved in three directions. The dusty celandine grows under the bushes; and its light green leaves seem to retain the white dust from the road. Ground ivy creeps everywhere over the banks, and covers the barest spot. In April its flowers, though much concealed by leaves, dot the sides of the ditches with colour, like the purple tint that lurks in the amethyst.

A small black patch marks the site of one of those gorse fires which are so common in Surrey. This was extinguished before it could spread beyond a few bushes. The crooked stems remain black as charcoal, too much burnt to recover, and in the centre a young birch, scorched by the flames stands leafless. This barren birch, bare of foliage and apparently unattractive, is the favourite resort of yellow-hammers. Perching on a branch towards evening a yellow-hammer will often sit and sing by the hour together, as if preferring to be clear of leafy sprays.

The somewhat dingy hue of many trees as the summer begins to wane is caused not only by the fading of the green, but by the appearance of spots upon the leaves, as may be seen on those birches which grow among the furze. But in spring and early summer their fresh light green contrasts with masses of bright yellow gorse bloom. Just before then—just as the first leaves are opening—the chiffchaffs come.

The first spring I had any knowledge of this spot was mild, and had been preceded by mild seasons. The chiffchaffs arrived all at once, as it seemed, in a bevy, and took possession of every birch about the furze, calling incessantly with might and main. The willow-wrens were nearly as numerous. All the gorse seemed full of them for a few days. Then by degrees they gradually spread abroad, and dispersed among the hedges.

But in the following springs nothing of the kind occurred. Chiffchaff and willow-wren came as usual, but they did not arrive in a crowd at once. This may have been owing to the flight going elsewhere, or possibly the flock were diminished by failure to rear the young broods in so drenching a season as 1879, which would explain the difference observed next spring. There was no scarcity, but there was a lack of the bustle and excitement and flood of song that accompanied their advent two years before.

Upon a piece of waste land at the corner of the furze a very large cinder and dust-heap was made by carting refuse there from the neighbouring suburb. During the sharp and continued frosts of the winter this dust-heap was the resort of almost every species of bird—sparrows, starlings, greenfinches, and rooks searching for any stray morsels of food. Some birdcatchers soon noticed this concourse, and spread their nets among the adjacent rushes, but fortunately with little success.

I say fortunately, not because I fear the extinction of small birds, but because of the miserable fate that awaits the captive. Far better for the frightened little creature to have its neck at once twisted and to die than to languish in cages hardly large enough for it to turn in behind the dirty panes of the windows in the Seven Dials.

The happy greenfinch—I use the term of forethought, for the greenfinch seems one of the very happiest of birds in the hedges—accustomed during all its brief existence to wander in company with friends from bush to bush and tree to tree, must literally pine its heart out. Or it may be streaked with bright paint and passed on some unwary person for a Java sparrow or a "blood-heart."

The little boy who dares to take a bird's nest is occasionally fined and severely reproved. The ruffian-like crew who go forth into the pastures and lanes about London, snaring and netting full-grown birds by the score, are permitted to ply their trade unchecked. I mean to say that there is no comparison between the two things. An egg has not yet advanced to consciousness or feeling: the old birds, if their nest is taken, frequently build another. The lad has to hunt for the nest, to climb for it or push through thorns, and may be pricked by brambles and stung by nettles. In a degree there is something to him approaching to sport in nesting.

But these bird-catchers simply stand by the ditch with their hands in their pockets sucking a stale pipe. They would rather lounge there in the bitterest northeast wind that ever blew than do a single hour's honest work. Blackguard is written in their faces. The poacher needs some courage, at least; he knows a penalty awaits detection. These fellows have no idea of sport, no courage, and no skill, for their tricks are simplicity itself, nor have they the pretence of utility, for they do not catch birds for the good of the farmers or the market gardeners, but merely that they may booze without working for the means.

Pity it is that any one can be found to purchase the product of their brutality. No one would do so could they but realize the difference to the captive upon which they are lavishing their mistaken love, between the cage, the alternately hot and cold room (as the fire goes out at night), the close atmosphere and fumes that lurk near the ceiling, and the open air and freedom to which it was born.

The rooks only came to the dust-heap in hard weather, and ceased to visit it so soon as the ground relaxed and the ploughs began to move. But a couple of crows looked over the refuse once during the day for months till men came to sift the cinders. These crows are permanent residents. Their rendezvous is a copse, only separated from the furze by the highway.

They are always somewhere near, now in the ploughed fields, now in the furze, and during the severe frosts of last winter in the road itself, so sharply driven by hunger as to rise very unwillingly on the approach of passengers. A meadow opposite the copse is one of their favourite resorts. There are anthills, rushes, and other indications of not too rich a soil in this meadow, and in places the prickly rest-harrow grows among the grass, bearing its pink flower in summer. Perhaps the coarse grass and poor soil are productive of grubs and insects, for not only the crows, but the rooks, continually visit it.

One spring, hearing a loud chattering in the copse, and recognizing the alarm notes of the missel-thrush, I cautiously crept up the hedge, and presently found three crows up in a birch tree, just above where the thrushes were calling. The third crow—probably a descendant of the other two—had joined in a raid upon the missel-thrushes' brood. Both defenders and assailants were in a high state of excitement; the thrushes screeching, and the crows, in a row one above the other on a branch, moving up and down it in a restless manner. I fear they had succeeded in their purpose, for no trace of the young birds was visible.

The nest of the missel-thrush is so frequently singled out for attack by crows that it would seem the young birds must possess a peculiar and attractive flavour; or is it because they are large? There are more crows round London than in a whole county, where the absence of manufactures and the rural quiet would seem favourable to bird life. The reason, of course, is that in the country the crows frequenting woods are shot and kept down as much as possible by gamekeepers.

In the immediate environs of London keepers are not about, and even a little further away the land is held by many small owners, and game preservation is not thought of. The numerous pieces of waste ground, "to let on building lease," the excavated ground, where rubbish can be thrown, the refuse and ash heaps—these are the haunts of the London crow. Suburban railway stations are often haunted by crows, which perch on the telegraph wires close to the back windows of the houses that abut upon the metals. There they sit, grave and undisturbed by the noisy engines which pass beneath them.

In the shrubberies around villa gardens, or in the hedges of the small paddocks attached, thrushes and other birds sometimes build their nests. The children of the household watch the progress of the nest, and note the appearance of the eggs with delight. Their friends of larger growth visit the spot occasionally, and orders are given that the birds shall be protected, the gardeners become gamekeepers, and the lawn or shrubbery is guarded like a preserve. Everything goes well till the young birds are almost ready to quit the nest, when one morning they are missing.

The theft is, perhaps, attributed to the boys of the neighbourhood, but unjustly, unless plain traces of entry are visible. It is either cats or crows. The cats cannot be kept out, not even by a dog, for they watch till his attention is otherwise engaged. Food is not so much the object as the pleasure of destruction, for cats will kill and yet not eat their victim. The crow may not have been seen in the garden, and it may be said that he could not have known of the nest without looking round the place. But the crow is a keen observer, and has not the least necessity to search for the nest.

He merely keeps a watch on the motions of the old birds of the place, and knows at once by their flight being so continually directed to one spot that there their treasure lies. He and his companion may come very early in the morning—summer mornings are bright as noonday long before the earliest gardener is abroad—or they may come in the dusk of the evening. Crows are not so particular in retiring regularly to roost as the rook.

The furze and copse frequented by the pair which I found attacking the missel-thrushes are situate in the edge of extensive arable fields. In these, though not overlooked by gamekeepers, there is a good deal of game which is preserved by the tenants of the farms. After the bitter winter and wet summer of 1879, there was a complaint, too well founded, that the partridges were diminished in numbers. But the crows were not. There were as many of them as ever. When there were many partridges the loss of a few eggs or chicks was not so important. But when there are but few, every egg or chick destroyed retards the re-stocking of the fields.

The existence of so many crows all round London is, in short, a constant check upon the game. The belt of land immediately outside the houses, and lying between them and the plantations which are preserved, is the crow's reserve, where he hunts in security. He is so safe that he has almost lost all dread of man, and his motions can be observed without trouble. The ash-heap at the corner of the furze, besides the crows, became the resort of rats, whose holes were so thick in the bank as to form quite a bury. After the rats came the weasels.

When the rats were most numerous, before the ash-heap was sifted, there was a weasel there nearly every day, slipping in and out of their holes. In the depth of the country an observer might walk some considerable distance and wait about for hours without seeing a weasel; but here by the side of a busy suburban road there were plenty. Professional rat-catchers ferreted the bank once or twice, and filled their iron cages. With these the dogs kept by dog-fanciers in the adjacent suburb were practised in destroying vermin at so much a rat. Though ferreted and hunted down by the weasels the rats were not rooted out, but remained till the ash-heap was sifted and no fresh refuse deposited.

In one place among the gorse, the willows, birches, and thorn bushes make a thick covert, which is adjacent to several of the hidden pools previously mentioned. Here a brook-sparrow or sedge-reedling takes up his quarters in the spring, and chatters on, day and night, through the summer. Visitors to the opera and playgoers returning in the first hours of the morning from Covent-garden or Drury-lane can scarcely fail to hear him if they pause but one moment to listen to the nightingale.

The latter sings in one bush and the sedge-reedling in another close together. The moment the nightingale ceases the sedge-reedling lifts his voice, which is a very penetrating one, and in the silence of the night may be heard some distance. This bird is credited with imitating the notes of several others, and has been called the English mocking-bird, but I strongly doubt the imitation. Nor, indeed, could I ever trace the supposed resemblance of its song to that of other birds.

It is a song of a particularly monotonous character. It is distinguishable immediately, and if the bird happens to nest near a house, is often disliked on account of the loud iteration. Perhaps those who first gave it the name of the mocking-bird were not well acquainted with the notes of the birds which they fancied it to mock. To mistake it for the nightingale, some of whose tones it is said to imitate, would be like confounding the clash of cymbals with the soft sound of a flute.

Linnets come to the furze, and occasionally magpies, but these latter only in winter. Then, too, golden-crested wrens may be seen searching in the furze bushes, and creeping round and about the thorns and brambles. There is a road side pond close to the furze, the delight of horses and cattle driven along the dusty way in summer. Along the shelving sandy shore the wagtails run, both the pied and the yellow, but few birds come here to wash; for that purpose they prefer a running stream if it be accessible.

Upon the willow trees which border it, a reed sparrow or blackheaded bunting may often be observed. One bright March morning, as I came up the road, just as the surface of the pond became visible it presented a scene of dazzling beauty. At that distance only the tops of the ripples were seen, reflecting the light at a very low angle. The result was that the eye saw nothing of the water or the wavelet, but caught only the brilliant glow. Instead of a succession of sparkles there seemed to be a golden liquid floating on the surface as oil floats—a golden liquid two or three inches thick, which flowed before the wind.

Besides this surface of molten gold there was a sheen and flicker above it, as if a spray or vapour, carried along, or the crests of the wavelets blown over, was also of gold. But the metal conveys no idea of the glowing, lustrous light which filled the hollow by the dusty road. It was visible from one spot only, a few steps altering the angle lessened the glory, and as the pond itself came into view there was nothing but a ripple on water somewhat thick with suspended sand. Thus things change their appearance as they are looked at in different ways.

A patch of water crowsfoot grows on the farthest side of the pond, and in early summer sends up lovely white flowers.

WHY BIRDS SING

JACQUES DELAMAIN

November morning. The bird choruses begin with a soft whispering. On the edge of the wood, in the peat-bog, where trails of mist still linger above over-flowing ditches, a flock of green Siskins arrived a few days ago from the forests of the north, burst forth from the alders with a crackling of metallic notes. More distant, in the sheltered valley, a band of Starlings fills the top of a poplar with a gossiping sung, spoken, and whistled, all at once, composed of all the sounds of nature, which these mimics in black coats dotted with white have picked up in their comings and goings between the plain and the forest. A dozen little Serins, green like the Siskins, but tinier and with shorter bills, send filtering through the needles of the sea-pines a thread of thin strident sound like the rustling noise of grasshoppers. On the sunny slope of the limestone hillock a ringing like the knocking together of glass beads identifies in the walnut tree a flock of Corn Buntings motionless as the brown leaves that winter has probably forgotten on their branches. A little later, with the last burnished rays of light, another chorus, clearest and freshest of all perhaps, the Linnets, will cheer up the dying day.

A bird is never quite silent. Sociable creature, high-strung, perpetually on the alert, a flap of the wing carrying him off into space, he must communicate constantly with his fellow creatures across the sky. His signal must go far, penetrate the thick wood, pierce the wind. From his throat with its multiple membranes, commanded by powerful muscles, sounds issue forth, different for each species, each sound having a particular meaning. The callnote rallies the band dispersed in the stubbles, vibrates through the squall on the sea-coast, convening the Gulls and Terns to the common feast; or resounds, sharp and mysterious, assuring contact among nocturnal wayfarers. The signal of alarm bursts forth sonorously under the stroke of surprise, or arises muted and as if whispered from one to another, at the threat of the Sparrow Hawk's flight. The notes of astonishment and anger, thrust by the anxious mother at the intruder, make the brood crouch low in the hollow of the nest. Or else, in a tumult of challenging rally-calls to the combat, the Little Owl, discovered in broad daylight on the fork of the elm tree branch, is abused by the Titmice and the Chaffinches. And again, when the Harrier rises into view, far off in the sky, his mate, protecting her little ones clothed in white down, flies away toward him. She has perceived, much sooner than the human ear, the sharp vibration announcing that he holds in one of his claws a field mouse for the brood's dinner.

Like all these cries, the winter voices are not yet true song, but are the expression of simple emotions, the emanation of the flock spirit. The solidarity of hard times has united the birds, by species. Together they have flown to the feeding-territory, slept in the low brush-wood, or in the thick pine tree tops. The first ray of sunshine in the cold morning brings forth joyous notes from their throats: the sensation of well-being, of wings still moist from the bath spread out to the light; the joy of being together, of having the same plumage, the same life and the same soul.

In this state of community there is no individual virtuosity. The permanent colonies do not produce great singers in any season, any more than do the ephemeral winter flocks. The silvery Herring-Gulls, on the rock by the sea, where each cavity holds a trio of brown eggs, and the Black-headed Gulls and Terns, grouping their nests close together on the slope of the dunes, utter only clamorous noises. From the old church walls, where the Sparrows nest in flocks, only cheeping issues forth. The House Martin, who hangs up his closed nests in dozens on the eaves of our houses, and his brown cousin, the Sand-Martin, who riddles the river banks with little black holes digging his galleries, have only a clear chirp. For the flock spirit kills the artist. The Chaffinch, in order to resume his outburst of song in February, will have to break with his band of winter companions. The Lark will rise singing into the air only when he shall have separated himself from his migratory brothers.

During the most beautiful noontides of February the Redwings, those little red flanked Thrushes, arriving for the grape harvest from northern Europe and Asia to spend the winter with us, are assembled, motionless and invisible, in the pines that remind them of their native forests. There is a chorus of liquid, crystal voices. But a little later, on a day in March, when this chorus dies down, a pathetic, deep note, repeated five or six times, prolongs it, with a new accent. This is the outline of the nuptial song of the male Redwing. At eventide, in the rosy light, perched on an acacia branch, and isolated from his companions asleep in the brushwood, he will repeat it, a little raucous still.

But even in the middle of winter, indeed, for some of our sedentary species, the new promise is felt in hostile nature. From December on, on warm mornings, when the west wind blows, the large Thrush of the mistletoe, the Mistle-Thrush, throws into the storm his loud brief phrase, resounding like a challenge. Toward Christmas the whistling of the Nuthatch, now rolled out, now sharp and short, betrays the agitation of the little slate grey body, creeping up the tree trunks with the dry noise of claws gripping the bark. The three precise notes of the Great Titmouse, sonorous and as if hammered on a clear anvil, precede by a few days the cadenced stridulation of the Blue Titmouse. Hardly songs, these, but already so charged, in the heart of the cold season, with everything that the fine days are to bring, that no sound of spring will seem sweeter to us.

From the clump of blossoming, snow sprinkled furze, the Wren's precipitated trill gushes out, so strong and vibrant that it is astonishing to see a tiny brown bird rise up, fleeing at the level of the frozen soil on little round wings. The bare hedge has its winter song, sweet and a little sad, that of the Hedge-Sparrow. The Lark drops from on high onto the field still all white the joyous torrent of his song, and like an inevitable and charming accompaniment, the voice of the Robin Redbreast modulates, tireless and clear. Even the icy January night has its song: the primitive, savage refrain of the great Tawny Owl, articulated now and then like a sorrowful human cry.

Why these singers in winter, when we believe Nature to be asleep ? It is because in them, the amorous impulse, which may be slumbering but is never quite absent, awakens. Adapted to the winters of our climate, these species have escaped the necessity of distant migration which disperses the bird travelers over continents. For some, like the Titmice, the winter band breaks up very early: the male and female, until now lost in the vagabond flock, take up again their life together. With others, the couple has never been separated. Doubtless the hour of passion has not yet come, when the female, with wings a-quiver, will call her companion for the mating. But intimacy and tenderness already link the pair. Together, they roam all day in search of subsistence, and evening come, it is the same cluster of juniper, the same hollow tree trunk, or the same clod of earth that will shelter them during the night.

But here is the hour of the great life-giving force. Timid at first and hesitant, it becomes more imperious with the days' increasing light and warmth. Until now, both sexes have had the same cries of appeal and of alarm, the same note of joy. Now the contribution of the new flux, which the female is to accumulate silently in her vital reserves,—for with her everything must be consecrated to the approaching accomplishment of the task of maternity,—will blaze forth in the male in profuse activity, in strength and beauty of voice, in brilliance of plumage, in strange or frenzied dancing. He is the one to proclaim the rising of desire, the expectation of mating.

The song is not only a hymn to the beloved one. It expresses the complex, multifarious emotions that the male, under the imperious or latent influence of the passion lifting him out of himself, cannot confine in a simple cry: assertion of himself, of his vigour and beauty, of his happiness at being alive and at having his place in nature. Thus, at the slightest suspicion of an unfamiliar presence, the Cetti's Warbler fills the reeds with the uproar of his irritated and blustering song. Keeper of his canton, the Robin lets everyone know, in infinitely varied phrases, that he is in possession of the territory and that he intends to remain master there. For singing, to a bird, is throwing a challenge, too. Before the timid females, rivals affront each other with their voices. From one tree top to another the male Chaffinches ceaselessly toss each other their triumphal refrain, as if they were seeking the last breath of their adversaries. In the depths of the hawthorn bushes two Nightingales, face to face, listen to each other sing in turn as if each were trying to carry off the secret that makes singing more beautiful. Over the fields and woods the males' boasting rises thus, loud or discreet, sweet or harsh, repeated from place to place. At the limits of the species' habitat where the struggle of voices becomes attenuated between isolated rivals, the singing loses its strength and beauty.

Indeed, this beauty is not primitive. Descendants of the Saurians by the winged and lizard-tailed fossil, Archaeopteryx, the birds, having gained dry land after the miry marshes of the secondary epoch, and then having raised themselves into the air, preserve in their voices the traces of the croaking of their ancestors. Even in the finest artists themselves the atavistic taint reappears at times. The Nightingale interrupts his most beautiful stanzas with a "carr" that one might say had come from the flabby throat of a Batrachian. In the Blackbird, the flaw in the precious metal, a guttural note, is found at the end of his whistled phrase. In the Thrush it slips in among the purest cadences in hard, sharp sounds. The Melodious Warbler starts his song on three raucous notes. The sonorous cascade of the Lark, the intimate sweet song of the Bullfinch, the clear, silvery one of the Linnet, all bear, at moments, the mark of the original tare.

Each year, in the springtime, the bird works to strip his song of the primitive stain. The finer the artist, the harder the labour. For weeks his throat must be made more supple, and each day the sounds issue forth a little purer. In January, on mild evenings, the Blackbird practices before sunset. About the same time the Lark, on short flights, drops a few bits of song. On their return to the nesting country in March and April the Black-cap and the Nightingale are apprentices seeking the accents of the year before. The young male, singing for the first time, must recall the paternal voice to which he listened last summer when he was still crouched in the bottom of the nest. Here individual temperament and virtuosity assert themselves in the effort toward perfection. Under the apparent uniformity of phrases, cadences, and tone of the same species, nothing is more plastic than the singing of a bird. Beside mediocre singers fine soloists reveal themselves. The setting often has a degrading influence. The Blackbird and the Blackcap, when bred in marshy regions, mingle with their habitual notes the raucous and jerky ones of the Great Reed Warblers. Elsewhere, homes of fine and pure tradition are established.

Innumerable species scarcely rise above a cry in their singing. Indeed, love softens, from January on, the Carrion-Crow's cawing, and gives a tone of confidence to the rough chatter of the Magpie. Under its influence, the sharp notes of the bird-of-prey take on a new resonance. The Kestrel, in his soaring circles of February, the Barn-Owl with his white twilight flight, will screech almost musically. But all art is absent from these voices. In order to understand the ascending evolution of their singing from a primitive cry, one must follow the successive habitats of the birds through the ages, pass from the ocean, cradle of all life, to the slime of the estuaries, to the lake of fresh water, then to the vegetation of the plains, and finally to the forest. The sea has not a single singer; its expanse, the noise of its billows, the hard existence it imposes upon living beings, stifle artistic effort, and permit only the cry of the Gulls, the raucous call of the Guillemots, Petrels, and Penguins. But already, at the time when it relents in its less harsh coves, on the mire it deposes in the bays among the grassy dunes, graceful, slender-winged creatures of powerful flight have found musical expression: the fluted call of the Sandpipers, the strange plaint of the Great Curlew, the harmonious notes of the Ringed Plover, the trill, already nearly a song, of the Redshanks. Still further away, on the sheltered expanse of the marshes, where so many species, Grallae or Palmipedes, utter only nasal or metallic sounds, the Teals whisper in soft whistling sounds and, for the first time, a real song appears, that of a great white bird, the Whooping Swan. His strong voice, master of the full octave, resounds fiercely, triumphantly, tenderly, on the lakes of Iceland, when his wide, silvery flight brings him back close to his mate who is brooding on the big nest of dried grasses. To hear this song, the peasants yonder say, is to forget everything one knows and to remember everything one has forgotten. But the Swan is an exceptional creature. He disdains the prudence of protective coloration and surpasses the winged folk of the waters by his strength and beauty. He alone among his near kindred, the Geese and Ducks, is endowed with a musical voice.

In order to find the phalanx of true singers, you must reach the bank of the stream, the field mounting in a gentle slope to the hilltop, the hedge bordering the field of grain, the forest of high trees. There the Passeres lives, love, and sing: the Fringillidae with cone-shaped seed-grinding beaks, Larks and brown Meadow-Pipits, slender Wagtails, Warblers, and Thrushes, sober of colour and rich of voice, and still others, the last tribes come of the great winged family, the most highly evolved and the most gifted, for not only have they the most beautiful songs, but the most beautiful nests, too.

Close to these, living in the same place the heavy Gallinae, Partridges, Pheasants, and Grouse, bound to the soil, have scarcely been able to modify their cry. This is because the artist needs to be free from too great servitude to the ground. He needs the easy soaring, the light ascension toward the high point whence his notes may fall more clearly and may carry farther. It is in full flight, sustained only by the air, that the Larks and the Meadow-Pipits sing. As for the other Passeres, the branch of a tree, the twig of a bush, or the fragile stem of an herbaceous plant bears the singer. For all of them, whether they live on seeds or on small living prey, the forest or the field, supplying abundant and easy nourishment, assures the leisure indispensable to the development of their voices.

Musical art is born of the satisfaction which a being experiences in expressing his life by a sound. The golden fly, buzzing, loves the noise of his wings; the cicada, in the ecstasy of his vibration, forgets the enemy watching for him. A bird enjoys the note modulated by his own throat. But if he attains art it is because, endowed with a sense of the beautiful, he is able to choose among his notes the clearest, the purest, and the fullest, to link one to another, to find the rhythm, compose the phrase, transpose the tones, thus achieve pure music, and make a song gush out from a cry. And it is in his search for beauty that the art of the bird touches us. We comprehend and interpret his Esthetic effort. The Lark's song becomes for us the expression of courageous and serene cheer; in the stanzas of the Nightingale we find an accent of fervour.

In the most gifted, even the Passeres, the song hesitates and gropes its way before attaining beauty. Many species have only a single note, hardly distinguishable from a cry. The Cirl-Bunting, perched on a hawthorn bush, indefatigably lisps his single syllable. His cousins, the Yellowhammer and the Ortolan, have found a simple phrase, monotonous at the start but expanding at the end on a clear, held note. The Chaffinch amplifies it in his precise refrain with a loud crescendo. The Linnet and the Goldfinch prolong it and break it into a musical recitative, rather confused but spontaneous, ingenuous, and punctuated by fresh exclamations. The Sky-lark varies his combinations, composes, improvises, and on the simplest musical thread achieves great art. With a fuller tone, the Warblers assemble their notes, in joyous, limpid, rather facile songs. One of them, the Black-cap, in his beautiful, sonorous, full-rhythmed phrase, thrown out full-throatedly, makes us anticipate already the family of masters, the Turdi-dae, or Thrushes, who give in our climate four great artists: the Blackbird, the Song Thrush, the Nightingale, and the Robin Redbreast.

The first, a yellow-beaked black bird, king of the hedgerows, enlivens our countrysides as soon as winter begins to grow mild, with his strophe of full, fluted tones. The phrase is a little short, but rich and well-linked, the cadence is beautiful, the delivery easy, liquid, and serene. In the rhythmic chime of his clear, rapid, unexpected notes, the Song Thrush incloses all the joy of living, his gay, capricious vehemence; and his is the freshest hymn of early spring, gushing out from his russet, black-flecked breast. A little later on, in April, the Nightingale unfolds, in his nocturnal song, his passionate, ardent, sincere accents. He possesses every artistic resource. In about twenty different stanzas he accumulates his full, rich notes, links, opposes, and repeats them. Hardly has he become silent, at the first glimmer of dawn, when the voice of the Robin Redbreast with its infinite modulations is heard, a voice made up entirely of nuances, unceasingly varied in theme, successively on the pitch of every song, every cry of nature, and so elusive in his unforeseen jumps, that this little brown bird with his rust-coloured breast can sing quite close to us without our noticing him.

But here is the emotional life of the bird at its height: well-being, joy of existence, happiness at feeling in his place in a chosen corner of nature, at holding his territory in the face of rival covetousness, desire and possession of his mate. The song, liberating discharge of a vital plenitude that the bird cannot contain, is rendered by the male with attitudes which are often strange, now frenzied, now fixed, betraying the profound agitation of his being, and transfiguring him. The Buntings, perched on the extreme cluster of leaves of a shrub, throw back their heads in an ecstatic pose. The Goldfinch, wings hanging, moves his body from side to side, pivoting on his slender feet. The Hoopoe, with a grave gesture, at each "poo-poo-poo" gives his greeting, unfolding his tuft. Stone-Chat, leaving his observatory on the curving stem of the bramble, maintains himself in the air by the rapid agitation of his small wings, as if suspended by an invisible thread, while he sheds his sour little song. The Whitethroat thrusts himself above a tuft calf eglantine, pirouettes in the air, and falls back into the thicket, finishing his song there. The Serin, the Greenfinch, and the Linnet, whose flight is ordinarily short and jerky, now glide into space, wings spread out wide, with the suppleness of bats. And it is during his amorous serenade that the Capercaillie, oblivious of danger, remains deaf to the crackling of pine needles under the hunter's footstep.

In May and June the long sunny hours no longer suffice for some day singers to express the intensity of life animating them. Long after sunset the Song Thrush, the Robin Redbreast, the Stone-Chat, are still to be heard, and 'way into the night the Cuckoo calls in the woods. It is then that the Wood-Lark, the only bird to sing in full flight in the darkness, yet sister to those Larks who intoxicate themselves with sunshine, lets fall sometimes from on high, toward midnight, her exquisite song.

In July, the voices die out, one by one. The little ones demand attention; the goings and comings of the parents between the nest, where exacting mouths open unceasingly, and the tree or meadow, no longer leave any leisure for singing. And then the great annual crisis of the bird approaches, the moulting season. Each feather, worn out by the active life of the fine season, is replaced by a new one, less bright but warmer.

In August, a great silence descends upon the woods and the fields; only the cheeping of the young and furtive call notes are still to be heard in sun-burnished nature. The attraction of the south, of wintering countries, obscurely agitates our summer visitors. The first migrants, the Cuckoo, the Hoopoe, and the Oriole, are already leaving.

April and especially May, have known the apogee of songs, and yet at no moment, perhaps, is the charm of their voices more subtle than in the evenings of late June, when a little lassitude already appears in the singers. The day has been warm. Under the midday sun the monotonous, drawn-out phrase of the Ortolan has resounded alone in the vineyards full of light. With the evening breeze the sounds begin again. Then, at the decline of day, the confused gossip of little artless voices dies down. The Nightingale sings again, in fragmentary verses, without conviction. There the Oriole whistles for a last time. Voices after his, discreet, rare, and as if impregnated with the silence of the night, rise from the peace of the evening. A Blackbird holds the scene for a few moments; his low, fluted whistle comes from a shadowy corner, from a mass of foliage where the light no longer penetrates. Another, then another, answer him. The Song Thrush seems to have been waiting for them to finish in order to give in his turn his skipping song. Cuckoos in the distance repeat their familiar double note, which assumes at this hour a strange poetry. Then, with the growing darkness, the Robin at two or three intervals throws out his little note, "tictic," making us think already of autumn evenings. Finally, a strange noise, as if a spinner were turning her wheel, now nearby, now distant: the song of the dream bird, the Nightjar, whose velvety flight haunts the clearings at an indeterminate hour.

Bird Lists

John Clare

Cock   This is one of the pleasentest companions of the cottage & Farm yard there are a great variety of sorts & the Bantum is the most harmless to a garden & tho as consieted among its wives as the best game a sparrow at the barn door will almost venture to give it battle & dispute a thack right of every curnel that it finds—the crow of the cock has been long & generaly attributed as the break up warning of ghosts & Faireys & therefore is reckoned as a cheery sound in the long nights of winter—it has been considerd as a bad omen to hear the Cock crow before morning but it is generally known that game cocks crow at all hours of the night in the fighting season—Some Cocks are inveterate to chickens & others will scratch for them & brood them like the hen

Pheasant   makes its nest on the ground in bushy borders on the sides of commons & sometimes in woods side tho seldom as the Fox is its mortal enemy there & endued with ready sagasity to find the nest it lays 16, 18, & often 20 eggs of a plain green ash color like the Partridge but larger as soon as the birds are hatchd they leave the nest & follow the hen Peasant who clucks & calls them like a hen in sitting time the old ones sit so close on the nest as to be easily taken a fellow last year found a nest in a wheat close by the wood side she sat hard & he caught her on the nest the next day he went agen & the Cock had taken her place & sat on the eggs but he did not sit so close as the hen & flew off before the unfeeling fellow caught him—I was told of the nest & went twice when the Cock bird was on but the third time something had destroyed the eggs & wether the Cock followed the fate of the hen I cannot tell he appeard to sit in good earnest as if he intended to hatch them There is sometimes a Variety of these birds found I saw one last year \which I fancied a hen/ the color of the cock that wanted the red rim round the eye & had a short tail & pure White ones are somtimes found here generaly cocks one Henderson got & stuffed the other P⟨h⟩easants having fought & beaten it to death—they live on insects in summer & on acorns & hips & Awes in Autumn & winter & are very fond of a sort of little fungus that grows on the oak leaves & drop off towards autum—the young ones if hatchd under a hen are hard to tame or raise up yet it is somtimes done & I knew an old woman fond of fowl that raised a Cock bird till it was as tame as the fowl in the yard & it cohabited with the hens but its breed lost most of likness of the Peasant & took more after the hens

TURKEY   The Turkey is a proud helpless fowl & hardly capable of feeding itself a farmer at Lolham raises 3 or 4 hundred every season & a man is kept to tend them in the closes they are very fond of feeding on pismires & on Awes in Autumn they are great cowards & the Guinea bird & Cock can both drive them they have a great antipathy against anything of a red color & drop their snottles & attack every one in a red cloak or neckerchief— they are fond of laying in hedge rows away from home their eggs are of a dirty white spotted with red spots

GUINEA HEN   These are at the best but half domesticated fowl for they flye about as well as a partridge & lay about the closes like a wild bird nor will they sit on their own eggs unless they are left to sit in the hedgerows were they made their nest they are bold among fowl & often attack & beat by their excessive nimbleness a game cock their eggs are of a beautiful flesh color

THE WILL O WHISP OR JACK A LANTHORN

I have often seen these vapours or what ever philosophy may call them but I never wit nessd so remarkable an instance of them as I did last night which has robd me of the little philosophic reasoning which I had—about them I now believe them spirits but I will leave the facts to speak for themselves—There had been a great upstir in the town about the appearance of

the ghost of an old woman who had been recently drownd in a well—it
was said to appear at the bottom of neighbour Billings close in a large
white winding sheet dress & the noise excited the curosity of myself & my
neighbour to go out several nights together to see if the ghost woud be
kind enough to appear to us & mend our broken faith in its existance but
nothing came on our return we saw a light in the north east over eastwell
green & I thought at first that it was a bright meoter it presently became
larger & seemd like a light in a window it then moved & dancd up & down
& then glided onwards as if a man was riding on horsback at full speed
with a lanthorn light soon after this we discoverd another rising in the
south east on 'dead moor' they was about a furlong asunder at first & as if
the other saw it it danced away as if to join it which it soon did & after
dancing together a sort of reel as it were—it chaced away to its former
station & the other followd it like things at play & after suddenly overtak-
ing it they mingled into one in a moment or else one dissapeard & sunk in
the ground we stood wondering & gazing for a while at the odd phenomenon & then left the will o wisp dancing by itself to hunt for a fresh
companion as it chose—the night was dusky but not pitch dark & what
was rather odd for their appearnce the wind blew very briskly it was full
west—now these things are gennerally believd to be vapours rising from
the foul air from bogs & wet places were they are generaly seen & being
as is said lighter then the common air they float about at will—now this
is all very well for Mrs Philosophy who is very knowing but how is it if it is
a vapour lighter then the air that it coud face the wind which was blowing
high & always floated side ways from north to south & back—the wind
afected it nothing but I leave all as I find it I have explaind the fact as well
as I can—I heard the old alewife at the Exeters arms behind the church, M^{rs}
Nottingham, often say that she has seen from one of her chamber windows
as many as fifteen together dancing in & out in a company as if dancing
reels & dances on east well moor there is a great many there—I have seen
several there myself one night when returning home from Ashton on a
courting excursion I saw one as if meeting me I felt very terrified & on
getting to a stile I determnd to wait & see if it was a person with a lanthorn
or a will o whisp it came on steadily as if on the path way & when it got
near me within a poles reach perhaps as I thought it made a sudden stop
as if to listen me I then believed it was some one but it blazd out like a
whisp of straw & made a crackling noise like straw burning which soon
convincd me of its visit the luminous haloo that spread from it was of a
mysterious terrific hue & the enlargd size & whiteness of my own hands

frit me the rushes appeard to have grown up as large & tall as walebone whips & the bushes seemd to be climbing the sky every thing was extorted out of its own figure & magnified the darkness all round seemd to form a circalar black wall & I fancied that if I took a step forward I shoud fall into a bottomless gulph which seemd yawing all round me so I held fast by the stile post till it darted away when I took to my heels & got home as fast as I coud so much for will o whisps.

BIRD WATCHING

EDMUND SELOUS

WATCHING GREAT PLOVERS, ETC.

If life is, as some hold it to be, a vast melancholy ocean over which ships more or less sorrow-laden continually pass and ply, yet there lie here and there upon it isles of consolation on to which we may step out and for a time forget the winds and waves. One of these we may call Bird-isle—the island of watching and being entertained by the habits and humours of birds—and upon this one, for with the others I have here nothing to do, I will straightway land, inviting such as may care to, to follow me. I will speak of birds only, or almost only, as I have seen them, and I must hope that this plan, which is the only one I have found myself able to follow, will be accepted as an apology for the absence of much which, not having seen but only read of, I therefore say nothing about. Also, if I sometimes here record what has long been known and noted as though I were making a discovery, I trust that this, too, will be forgiven me, for in fact, whenever I have watched a bird and seen it do anything at all—anything, that is, at all salient—that is just how I have felt. Perhaps, indeed, the best way to make discoveries of this sort is to have the idea that one is doing so. One looks with the soul in the eyes then, and so may sometimes pick up some trifle or other that has not been noted before.

However this may be, one of the most delightful birds (for one must begin somewhere) to find, or to think one is finding things out about, is the great or Norfolk plover, or, as it is locally and more rightly called—for it is a curlew and not a plover*—the stone-curlew. These birds haunt open,

---

*I understand Professor Newton to say this.

sandy wastes to which but the scantiest of vegetation clings, and here, during the day, they assemble in some chosen spot, often in considerable numbers—fifty or more I have sometimes seen together. If it is early in the day, and especially if the weather be warm and sunny, most of them will be sitting, either crouched down on their long yellow shanks, or more upright with these extended in front of them, looking in this latter attitude as if they were standing on their stumps, their legs having been "smitten off" and lying before them on the ground. Towards evening, however— which is the best time to watch these birds—they stand attending to their plumage, or walk with picked steps in a leisurely fashion, which, with their lean gaunt figure, sad and rusty coloured, and a certain sedateness, almost punctiliousness, of manner, fancifully suggests to one the figure of Don Quixote de la Mancha, the Knight of the rueful countenance, with a touch or two, perhaps, thrown in of the old Baron of Bradwardine of Tullyveolan. One can lie on the ground and watch them from far off through the glasses, or, should a belt of bracken fringe the barren area, one has then an excellent opportunity of creeping up to within a short or, at least, a reasonable distance. To do this one must make a wide circuit and enter the bracken a long way off. Then having walked, or rather waded for some way towards them, at a certain point—experience will teach the safety-line—one must sink on one's hands and knees, and the rest is all creeping and wriggling, till at length, lying flat, one's face just pierces the edge of the cover and the harmless glasses are levelled at the quarry one does not wish to kill. The birds are standing in a long, straggling line, ganglion-like in form, swelling out into knots where they are grouped more thickly with thinner spaces between. As they preen themselves— twisting the neck to one or the other side so as to pass the primary quill feathers of the wings through the beak—one may be seen to stoop and lay one side of the head on the ground, the great yellow eye of the other side staring up into the sky in an uncanny sort of way. The meaning of this action I do not know. It is not to scratch the head, for the head is held quite still; and, moreover, as, like most birds, they can do this very neatly and effectively with the foot, other methods would seem to be superfluous. Again, and this is a more characteristic action, one having stood for some time upright and perfectly still, makes a sudden and very swingy bob forward with the head, the tail at the same time swinging up, just in the way that a wooden bird performs these actions upon one's pulling a string. This again seems to have no special reference to anything, unless it be deportment.

All at once a bird makes a swift run forward, not one of those short little dainty runs—one and then another and another, with little start-stops between—that one knows so well, but a long, steady run down upon something, and at the same moment the glasses—if one is lucky and the distance not too great—reveal the object which has occasioned this, a delicate white thing floating in the air which one takes to be a thistle-down. This is secured and eaten, and we may imagine that the bird's peckings at it after it is in his possession are to disengage the seed from the down. But all at once—before you have had time to set down the glasses and make the note that the great plover (*Œdicnemus Crepitans*) will snap at a wandering thistle-down, and having separated the delicate little seed-sails from the seed, eat the latter, etc., etc.—a small brown moth comes into view flying low over a belt of dry bushy grass that helps, with the bracken, to edge the sandy warren, for these wastes are given over to rabbits and large landowners, and are marked "warrens" on the map. Instantly the same bird (who seems to catch sight of the moth just as you do) starts in pursuit with the same rapid run and head stretched eagerly out. He gets up to the moth and essays to catch it, pecking at it in a very peculiar way, not excitedly or wildly, but with little precise pecks, the head closely and guardedly following the moth's motions, the whole strongly suggestive of professional skill. The moth eludes him, however, and the bird stops rigidly, having apparently lost sight of it. Shortly afterwards, after it has flown some way, he sees it again and makes another swift run in pursuit, catching it up again and making his quick little pecks, but unsuccessfully, as before. Then there is the same pause, followed by the same run, then a close, near chase, and finally the moth is caught and eaten. Other moths, or other insects, now appear upon the scene, or if they do not appear—for even with the best of glasses such pin-points are mostly invisible—it is evident from the actions of the birds that they are there. Chase after chase is witnessed, all made in the same manner, with sometimes a straight-up jump into the air at the end and a snap that one seems almost to hear—a last effort, but which, judging by the bird's demeanour afterwards, fails, as last efforts usually do.

A social feeling seems to pervade these hunting-scenes, a sort of "Have *you* got one? *I* have. That bird over there's caught two" idea. This may be imaginary, still the whole scene with its various little incidents suggests it to one. The stone-curlew, therefore, besides his more ordinary food of worms, slugs, and the like—I have seen him in company with peewits, searching for worms, much as do thrushes on the lawn—is likewise a runner down and "snapper up of" such "unconsidered trifles" as moths and other insects on the wing. I had seen him chasing them, indeed, long before I knew what he was doing, for I had connected those sudden, racing runs—seen before from a long distance—with something or other on the ground, imagining a fresh object for each run. Often had I wondered, first at the eyesight of the bird, which seemed to pierce the mystery of a worm or beetle at fifty or sixty yards distance, and then at its apparent want of interest each time it got to the place where it seemed to have located it. Really it had but just lost sight of what it was pursuing, but aerial game had not occurred to me, and the tell-tale spring into the air, which would have explained all, had been absent on these occasions. I have called such leaps "last efforts," but I am not quite sure if they are always the last. More than once I have thought I have seen a stone-curlew rise into the air from running after an insect, and continue the pursuit on the wing. This is a point which I would not press, yet birds often act out of their usual habits and assume those proper to other species. I remember once towards the close of a fine afternoon, when the air was peopled by a number of minute insects, and the stone-curlews had been more than usually active in their chasings, a large flock of starlings came down upon the warrens and began to behave much as they were doing, running excitedly about in the same manner and evidently with the same object. But what interested me especially was that they frequently rose into the air, pursuing and, as I feel sure, often catching the game there, turning and twisting about like fly-catchers, though with less graceful movements. Often, too, whilst flying—fairly high—from one part of the warrens to another, they would deflect their course in order to catch an insect or two *en passant*. I observed this latter action first, and doubted the motive, though it was strongly suggested. After seeing the quite unmistakable fly-catcher actions I felt more assured as to the other. Yet one may watch starlings for weeks without seeing them pursue an insect in the air. Their usual manner of feeding is widely different—viz. by repeatedly probing and searching the ground with their sharp spear-like bills, as does a snipe (with which bird they will sometimes feed side by side) with his longer and more delicate one. This is well seen whilst watching them on a lawn. They do not study to find worms lying in the holes and then seize them suddenly as do thrushes and blackbirds. With them it is "blind hookey"; each time the beak is thrust down into the grass it may find something or it may not. The mandibles are all the time working against each other, evidently searching and biting at the roots of the grass, and at intervals, but generally somewhat long ones, they will be withdrawn, holding within their grasp a large, greyish grub.

Returning to the stone-curlews. During the day, as I have said, these birds are idle and lethargic—sitting about, dozing, often, or sleeping—but as the air cools and the shadows fall, they rouse into a glad activity, and coming down and spreading themselves over the wide space of the warrens, they begin to run excitedly about, raising and waving their wings, leaping into the air, and often making little flights, or rather flittings, over the ground as a part of the disport. As a part of it I say advisedly, for they do not stop and then fly, and on alighting recommence, but the flight arises out of the wild waving and running, and this is resumed, without a pause, as the bird again touches the ground. All about now over the warrens their plaintive, wailing notes are heard, notes that seem a part of the deepening gloom and sad sky; for nature's own sadness seems to speak in the voice of these birds. They swell and subside and swell again as they are caught up and repeated in different places from one bird to another, and often swell into a full chorus of several together. Deeper now fall the shadows, "light thickens," till one catches, at last, only "dreary gleams about the moorland," as now here, now there, the wings are flung up—showing the lighter coloured inner surface—till gradually, first one and then another, or by twos or threes or fours, the birds fly off into the night, wailing as they go. But this note on the wing is not the same as that uttered whilst running over the ground. The ground-note is much more drawn out, and a sort of long, wailing twitter—called the "clamour"—often precedes and leads up to the final wail. In the air it comes just as a wail without this preliminary. But it must not be supposed that all the birds perform these antics simultaneously. If they did the effect would be more striking, but it is generally only a few at a time over a wide space, or, at most, some two or three together—as by sympathy—that act so. The eye does not catch more than a few gleams—some three or four or five—of the flung-up wings at one time over the whole space. It is a gleam here and a gleam there in the deepening gloom. "Dreary gleams about the moorland"—for warren, here, purples into moor and moor saddens into warren—is, indeed, a line that exactly describes the effect.

These birds, then, stand or sit about during the day in their chosen places of assemblage, and, if not occupied in catching insects or preening themselves, they are dull and listless. But as the evening falls and the air cools, they cast off their lassitude, think of the joys of the night, there is dance and song for a little, and then forth they fly. Sad and wailing as are their notes to our ears, they are no doubt anything but so to the birds themselves, and as the accompaniment of what seems best described by the word "dance" may, perhaps, fairly be called "song." The chants of some savages whilst dancing, might sound almost as sadly to us, pitched, as they would be, in a minor key, and with little which we would call an air. Again, if one goes by the bird's probable feelings, which may not be so dissimilar to the savage's—or indeed to our own—on similar occasions "song" and "dance" seems to be a legitimate use of words.

But whatever anyone may feel inclined to call this performance— "dance" or "antics" or "display"—it varies very much in quality, being sometimes so poor that it is difficult to use words about it without seeming to exaggerate, and at other times so fine and animated, that were the birds as large as ostriches, or even as the great bustard, much would be said and written on the subject. Moreover, so many variations and novelties and little personal incidents are to be noticed on the different occasions, that any general description must want something. I will therefore give a particular one of what I witnessed one afternoon when the dancing was especially good. It was about 5.30 when I got to the edge of the bracken, which to some extent rings round the birds' place of assembly.

"A drizzling rain soon began, and this increased gradually, but not beyond a smart drizzle. The birds, as though stimulated by the drops, now began to come down from where they had been standing on the edge of the amphitheatre, and to spread all over it till there were numbers of them, and dancing of a more pronounced, or, at least, of a more violent kind than I had yet seen, commenced. Otherwise it was quite the same, but the extra degree of excitement made it much more interesting. It was, in fact, remarkable and extraordinary. Running forward with wings extended and slightly raised, a bird would suddenly fling them high up, and then, as it were, *pitch* about over the ground, waving and tossing them, stopping short, turning, pitching forward again, leaping into the air, descending and continuing, till, with another leap, it would make a short eccentric flight low over the ground, coming down in a sharp curve and then, at once, *même jeu*. I talk of their 'pitching' about, because their movements seemed at times hardly under control, and, each violent run or plunge ending, in fact, with a sudden pitch forward of the body, the wings straggling about (often pointed forward over the head) in an uncouth dislocated sort of way, the effect was as if the birds were being blown about over the ground in a violent wind. They seemed, in fact, to be crazy, and their sudden and abrupt return, after a few mad moments, to propriety and decorum, had a curious, a bizarre effect. Though having just seen them behave so, one seemed almost to doubt that they had. One bird that had come to within a moderate distance of me, made three little runs—advancing, retiring, and again advancing—all the time with wings upraised and waving, then took a short flight over the ground, describing the segment of a circle, and, on alighting, continued as before. Half-a-dozen others were gathered together under a solitary crab-apple tree—a rose in the desert—less than 100 yards off, and both with the naked eye and the glasses I observed them all thoroughly well. One of them would often run at or pursue another with these antics. I saw one that was standing quietly, caught and, as it were, covered up in a little storm of wings before it could run away and begin waving its own.

"This and the general behaviour of the group makes it evident that the birds are stimulated in their dance-antics by each other's presence. For these little chases were in sport, clearly, not anger. Very different is the action and demeanour of two birds about to fight. This is by far the finest display of the sort that I have yet seen, and must be due, I think, to the rain, which the birds obviously enjoyed. They had been quite dull and listless before, but as soon as it fell they spread themselves over the plateau, and the dancing began. It was not only when the birds threw up their wings and, as one may say, let themselves go, that they seemed excited. The constant quick running and stopping whilst the wings were folded appeared to me to be a part—the less excited part—of the general emotion out of which the sudden frenzies arose. There was also the usual vocal accompaniment. The wailing note went up, and was caught and repeated from one part to another at greater or lesser intervals, the whole ending in flight as before."

When I first saw these dances I thought that they arose out of the excitement of the chase—that chase of moths or other insects flying low over the ground which I have noticed—that they were hunting-dances, in fact. I thought the motions of the wings were to beat down the escaping quarry, and I confounded the little springs and leaps into the air, arising out of the dance and being a part of it, with those other ones made with a snap and an object not to be mistaken; but I soon discovered my error. Insect-hunting is only indulged in occasionally, when a wandering moth or so happens to fly by. The general hunt which I have described was incident, I think, to an unusually large number of insects in the air over the warrens, by which not only a band of starlings—as before mentioned—was attracted, but, afterwards, swallows and martins. On such occasions, dancing might conceivably grow out of the excitement of the chase, so as to appear a part of it, but though the two forms of excitement may sometimes intermingle, the tendency would probably be for the one to diminish and interfere with the other. At any rate, almost every dance which I have witnessed has been a dance pure and simple.

What, then, is the meaning of this dancing, of these strange little sudden gusts of excitement arising each day at about the same time and lasting till the birds fly away? We have here a social display as distinct from a nuptial or sexual one, for it is in the autumn that these assemblages of the great plovers take place, after the breeding is all over; the deportment of the courting or paired birds towards each other—their nuptial antics—is of a different character. With birds, as with men, all outward action must be the outcome of some mental state. What kind of mental excitement is it which causes the stone-curlews to behave every evening in this mad, frantic way? I believe that it is one of expectancy and making ready, that these odd antics—the mad running and leaping and waving of the wings—give expression to the anticipation of going and desire to be gone which begins to possess the birds as evening falls. They are the prelude to, and they end in, flight. The two, in fact, merge into each other, for short flights grow out of the tumblings over the ground, and it is impossible to say when one of these may not be continued into the full flight of departure. They are a part of the dance, and, as such, the birds may almost be said to dance off. Surely in actions which lead directly up to any event there must be an idea, an anticipation of it, nor can the idea of departure exist in a bird's mind (hardly, perhaps, in a man's) except in connection with what it is departing for—food, namely, in this case, a banquet. So when I say that these birds "think of the joys of the night" need this be merely a figure? May it not be true that they do so and dance forth each night, to their joy?

I have said that the social or autumn antics of the stone-curlews— their dances, as I have called them, using the usual phraseology—are distinct from the nuptial or courting ones which they indulge in in the spring. These latter are of a different character altogether, but much more interesting to see than they are easy to describe. The birds are now paired, or in process of becoming so, and it is fashionable for two of them to walk side by side, and very close together, with little gingerly steps, as though "keeping company." They seem very much *en rapport* with each other— *sehr einig* as the Germans would say—also to have a mutual sense of their own and each other's importance, of the seemly and becoming nature of what they are doing, and (this above all) of the great value of deportment. Something there is about them—now even more than at other times— very odd, quaint, old-world, old-fashioned. The last best describes it; they are old-fashioned birds. Were the world occupied in watching them, and were they occasionally to overhear themselves being talked about, they would catch that word as often as did little Paul Dombey.

Whilst watching a couple walking side by side in this way that I have described, one of them may be seen to bend stiffly forward till the beak just touches the ground, the tail and after part of the body being elevated in the air. The other stands by, and appears both interested in and edified by the performance, and when it is over both walk on as before. Or a bird may be seen to act thus whilst walking alone, upon which another will come running from some distance towards it, as though answering to a summons or to some quite irresistible form of appeal. Upon coming close up to the rigid bird this other one stops, and turning suddenly, but also setly and rigidly, round, makes a curious little run away from it with lowered head and precise formal steps, full of a peculiar gravity and importance. Having thus played his part he again stops, and, standing idly about, seems lapsed into indifference. Meanwhile, the rigid one having remained in its set attitude for some little time longer at length comes out of it, and advancing with the same little picked, careful, gingerly steps that I have noticed, before long assumes it again, and then, relaxing, crouches low on the ground as though incubating. Having remained thus for a minute or two it rises and stands at ease. "A third bird now appears upon the scene (for this, I must say, was a little witnessed drama), advancing towards the two. As he approaches, one of them—the one which has run up in response to the appeal, and which I take to be the male—becomes uneasy as recognising a rival. He first either runs or walks (the pace, though it may be quick, is solemn) to the female, and makes her some kind of bow or obeisance of a very formal nature. Then, straightening and turning, he instantly becomes a different bird, so changed is his appearance. He is now drawn up to his full height, with the head thrown a little back, the tail is fanned out into the shape of a scallop-shell (looking very pretty), the broad, rounded end of which just touches the ground at the centre, and thus 'set,' as it were, for action, he advances upon the intruding bird with quick little stilty steps, prepared, evidently, to do battle. The would-be rival, however, retreats before this display, and the accepted suitor, having followed him thus for some little way—not rushing upon him or forcing a combat, but more as gravely and seriously-prepared for one—turns and with his former formal pace goes back to his hen." Or shall we not, rather, say to his Dulcinea del Toboso? for never does this strange, gaunt, solemn, punctilious-looking bird, with the tall figure and the strain of madness in the great glaring eyes, more remind one—fancifully—of Cervante's creation than now. Surely in that formal approach and deep reverence to his mistress, before entering upon this, perhaps, his first "emprise," we have the very figure and high courteous action of the knight, and seem almost to hear those words of his spoken on a similar occasion. "Accoredme, señora mia, en esta primera afrenta que a este vuestro avasallado pecho se le ofrece; no me desfallezca en este primera trance vuestro favor y amparo." ("Sustain me, lady mine, in this first insult offered to your captive knight. Fail me not with your favour and countenance in this my first emprise.")

In the above case it was, presumably, the female bird who assumed the curious rigid attitude, with the tail raised and head stooped forward to the ground. The attitude, however, assumed by the male, which I have described as a bow or obeisance—and, indeed, it has this appearance—was much of the same nature, if it was not precisely the same, and as far as I have been able to observe, none of the many and very singular attitudes and posturings in which these birds indulge are peculiar to either sex. At any rate, that one which would seem *par excellence* to appertain to courtship or matrimony, and which is often (as it was in the instance I am about to give) immediately followed by the actual pairing of the birds, is common to both the male and the female. The following will show this:—"A bird which has for some time been sitting now rises and shakes itself a little, presenting, as it does so, a very 'mimsy' and 'borogovy' appearance (for which adjectives, with descriptive plate, see 'Through the Looking-Glass'). It then begins uttering that long, thin, 'shrilling' sound, which goes so far and pierces the ear so pleasantly. This is answered by a similar cry, quite near, and I now see, for the first time, another bird advancing quickly to the calling one, who also advances to meet it. They approach each other, and standing side by side, with, perhaps, a foot between them, but looking different ways, each in the direction in which it has been advancing, both of them assume, at the same time, a particular and very curious posture, worth waiting days to see. First they draw themselves tall-ly up on their long, yellow, stilt-like legs, then curving the neck with a slow and formal motion, they bend the head downwards—yet still holding it at a height—and stop thus, set and rigid, the beak pointing to the ground. Having stood like this for some seconds, they assume the normal attitude. This wonderful pose, conceived and made in a vein of stiff formality, but to which the great, glaring, yellow eye gives a look of wildness, almost of insanity, has in it, both during its development and when its acme has been reached, something quite *per se*, and in vain to describe. But again one is reminded of what is past and old-fashioned, of chivalry and knight-errantry, of scutcheons and heraldic devices, of Don Quixote and the Baron of Bradwardine."

It is not only when two birds are by themselves that these or other attitudes are assumed. They will often break out, so to speak, amongst three or four birds running or chasing each other about. All at once one will stop, stiffen into one of them—that especially where the head is lowered till the beak touches, or nearly touches, the ground—and remain so for a formal period. But all such runnings and chasings are, at this time, but a part of the business of pairing, and one divines at once that such attitudes are of a sexual character. The above are a few of the gestures or antics of the great plover or stone-curlew during the spring. I have seen others, but either they were less salient, or, owing to the great distance, I was not able to taste them properly, for which reason, and on account of space, I will not further dwell upon them. What I would again draw attention to, as being, perhaps, of interest, is that here we have a bird with distinct nuptial (sexual) and social (non-sexual) forms of display or antics, and that the former as well as the latter are equally indulged in by both sexes.

THE TEMPLES OF THE HILLS

W. H. HUDSON

"The groves were God's first temples," says the poet; and viewed from the outside no groves are so like the temples made with hands, Christian or pagan, as the "clumps," as they are commonly called, growing on the chalk hills in Sussex, Hampshire, Wilts, and Dorset. Nature's way is to grow her larger trees on the lower levels, and it is doubtful that the downs have ever had a forest growth other than the kind which we find on them now, composed mainly of the lesser native trees—hawthorn, blackthorn, holly, juniper, and yews of no great size, mixed with furze, bramble, and wild clematis. All these plants are perpetually springing into existence everywhere on the downs, and are persistently fed down and killed by the sheep; take the sheep away from any down, and in a few years, as I have seen, it becomes an almost continuous thicket, and that, one imagines, must have been its original condition. We must suppose that man in early times, or during the Neolithic period when he had domestic animals and agriculture, found the chalk hills a better place than the lowlands, covered as they must then have been with a dense forest growth, the habitation of wolves and other rapacious beasts. On the hills where the thin soil produced only a dwarfish tree vegetation, it was easier to make a clearing and pasture for his cattle. No doubt it was also easier for him to defend himself and his possessions against wild beasts and savage human enemies in such situations. The hills were without water, but the discovery and invention of the dewpond, probably by some genius of the later Stone Age, made the hill-people independent of natural springs and rivers. In later times, when the country was everywhere colonised and more settled,

the hill-people probably emigrated to the lower lands, where the ground
was better suited for cattle-grazing and for growing crops. The hills were
abandoned to the shepherd and the hunter; and doubtless as the ages went
on they became more and more a sheep-walk; for it must have been observed
from early times that the effect of the sheep on the land was to change its
character and to make it more and more suited to the animal's require-
ments. Thus, the very aspect of the downs, as we know them, was first
imparted and is maintained in them by the sheep—the thousands on thousands of busy close-nibbling mouths keeping the grass and herbage close
down to the ground, and killing year by year every forest seedling. And
how wonderful they are—that great sea of vast pale green billowy hills,
extending bare against the wide sky to the horizon, clothed with that elastic
fragrant turf which it is a joy to walk on, and has nothing like it in the world!

It must have been in quite recent times, probably during the last half
of the eighteenth century, that the idea first came into the mind of a landowner here and there that a grove on the top of a high bare chalk down
would have a noble appearance, and form a striking landmark for all the
country round. The result is our hill-top clumps: and one would have
imagined that the effect would be altogether bad; for how could a tall dark
grove on a hill in a country of such an aspect, of smooth rounded pale-
green downs, be anything but inharmonious? Either it is not so, or long
custom has reconciled us to this ornament invented by man, and has even
made it pleasing to the eye. Association comes in, too: I notice that the
clumps which please me best are those which are most temple-like in their
forms. Thus, a grove of trees of various kinds growing in a dense mass, as
in the case of the famous Chanctonbury Ring on the South Downs, gives
me no pleasure at all: while a grove of Scotch firs, the trunks sufficiently
far apart as to appear like pillars upholding the dark dense foliage, has a
singular attraction. In some instances the effect on the hill itself of its crown
of trees is to give it the appearance of a vast mount artificially raised by
man on which to build or plant his temple. This is most striking when, as
at Badbury Rings, in Dorset, the hill is round and low, with a grove of old,
very large trees. In this case the effect is heightened by the huge prehistoric
earthworks, ring within ring, enclosing the grove on the space inside. Indeed, the sublimest of these temple-groves are not those which stand on
the highest hills; in many cases they stand but a little above the surrounding level, as in the case of Badbury Rings and of Hollywater Clump in
Wolmer Forest, where the soil is sand.

To my mind the best appearance presented by the higher hill-top groves is on a hot, windless summer day, during the phenomenon of "visible air," or "heat," when the atmosphere near the surface appears as a silvery mist, or as thinnest white and crystalline flames, ascending, wavering, dancing, and producing an illusion of motion in all distant solid objects, such as houses, fences, trees, and cattle. If the sun had greater power, this silvery flame-like appearance would become more visible still and take the appearance of water of a marvellous brilliancy, as of molten silver, flowing over the earth, with cattle standing knee-deep in it, and distant buildings and groves rising like islands out of it. This effect of mirage is occasionally visible in England in hot, dry summers, but is very rare. It is on these burning silvery days, when air and sunlight have a new magic, that I like best to see the hill-top grove; when at a distance of a mile or two the tall columnar trunks of the pines, showing the light between, seem to have a wavering motion, and, with the high dense roof of branches, look absolutely black against the brilliant whiteness of the air and the pale hot sky beyond.

The downland groves are, however, less to me in their æsthetic aspect, and as features in the landscape, than as haunts of wild life. It is indeed as small islands of animal life that I view them, scattered over the sea-like smooth green waste, vacant as the sea. To others it may not be so— to the artist, for example, in search of something to draw. We have each our distinct interests, aims, trades, or what you like: that which I seek adds nothing, and takes nothing from his picture, and is consequently negligible. We cannot escape the reflex effect of our own little vocations—our preoccupations with one side of things, one aspect of nature. Their life is to me their beauty, or the chief element in it, without which they would indeed be melancholy places. It refreshes me more than the shade of the great leafy roof on a burning day. On this account, because of the life in them, I prefer the clumps on the lower hills. They grow more luxuriantly, often with much undergrowth, sometimes surrounded with dense thickets of thorn, furze, and bramble. These are attractive spots to wild birds, and when not guarded by a gamekeeper form little refuges where even the shy persecuted species may breed in comparative security. It is with a sense of positive relief that I often turn my back on some great wood or forest where one naturally goes in quest of woodland species, even after many disappointments, to spend a day, or many days, with the feathered inhabitants of one of these isolated groves.

The birds, too, may be better observed in these places; they are less terrified at the appearance of the human form than in woods and forests where the pheasant is preserved, and man means (to the bird's mind) a gamekeeper with a gun in his hand. For, in many cases, especially in Wiltshire, the hill-groves are on land owned by the farmers themselves, who keep their own shootings, and do not employ a gamekeeper.

One day I was standing under a low oak-tree at the highest point in an immense wood, where the sight could range for a long distance over the tree-tops, when I was astonished at the sight of a carrion-crow flying low over the trees, and coming straight towards me. It was a wonderful thing to see in that place where I had spent several days, and had seen no crow and no bird of any kind banned by the keepers. Yet this was one of the largest woods in Wiltshire, in appearance an absolutely wild forest, covering many miles without a village or house within a mile of its borders on any side, and with no human occupants except the four or five keepers who ranged it to look after its millionaire owner's pheasants. The crow did not catch sight of me until within about forty yards from the tree under which I stood, whereupon, with a loud croak of terror, he turned instantly, and dashed away at right-angles to his original course at his utmost speed.

Leaving the great wood, I went a few miles away to visit one of the large unprotected clumps, and found there a family of four carrion-crows—two adults and two young; at my approach they flapped heavily from the tree in which they were resting, and flew slowly to another about fifty yards away, and sat there peering at me and uttering loud caws as if protesting against the intrusion.

At another unprotected clump on a low down I discovered a varied colony of birds—some breeding, others with young out of the nest. It was a large grove of old pine-trees, almost shut in with a thick growth of thorn and holly, mixed with bramble and masses of wild clematis. It was full of the crooning sound of turtle-doves, and in the high firs several wood-pigeons had their nests. There were several magpies and invariably on my coming to the spot they would put in an appearance—quaint black-and-white birds, sitting on the top boughs of the thorns always with their decorative tails behind them. A pair of carrion-crows were there too, but appeared to have no nest or young. Better still it was to find a family of long-eared owls—two adults and three young, beginning to fend for themselves. Best of all was a pair of sparrow-hawks with young in their nest; for the sparrow-hawk is one of my prime favourites, and the presence of these birds delighted me even more than that of the owls.

It was evident that these hawks did not associate my appearance with the quick sharp report of a gun and the rattle of shot about them, with perhaps the fiery sting of a pellet of lead in their flesh, for they were exceedingly bold and vociferous whenever I approached the nesting-tree. I visited them on several days for the pleasure of seeing and hearing them. The female was very bold and handsome to look at. Sometimes she would perch above me in such a position as to appear silhouetted against the blue, intensely bright sky, looking inky-black on her black branch. Then, flying to another branch where the light would be on her and a mass of dark pine-needles for a background, one could see the colouring of her plumage. Seen through a powerful binocular, she would appear as big as a goshawk, and as beautiful as that noblest of our lost hawks in her pigeon-blue wings and upper plumage, the white breast barred with brown, thin yellow shanks and long black claws, and the shining yellow eyes, exceedingly wild and fierce. Presently her little mate would appear, carrying a small bird in his claws, and begin darting wildly about among the trees, screaming his loudest, but would refuse to visit the nest. In the end my persistence would tire them out; gradually the piercing reiterated cries would grow less and less frequent, and finally cease altogether. The female would fly from tree to tree, coming nearer and still nearer to the nest, until at last she would perch directly over it and look down upon her young, and finally drop upon them and disappear from sight. And by-and-by the male, approaching in the same cautious way, would at length fly to the nest and, without alighting, just hovering a moment, drop his bird upon it, then dash away and quit the grove. She would then refuse to come off, even when I would strike loudly on the tree with a stick; yet on my return on the following day the whole performance would be gone through again.

Watching these birds from day to day with an endless delight in their beauty and vigour, their dashing flight, and shrill passionate cries of anger and apprehension, I could not help thinking of all the pleasure that hawks in general are to the lover of wild life in countries where these birds are permitted to exist, and, in a minor degree, even in this tame England—this land of glorified poultry-farms. There is no more fascinating spectacle in wild life than the chase of its quarry by a swift-winged hawk; and on this account I should be inclined to put hawking above all other sports but for the feeling which some of us can never wholly get away from, that it is unworthy of us as rational and humane beings possessing unlimited power over all other animals, to take and train any wild rapacious creature to hunt others to the death solely for the pleasure of witnessing its prowess. No such disturbing feeling can affect us in witnessing the contests of bird with bird in a state of nature. Here pursuer and pursued are but following their instincts and fulfilling their lives, and we as neutrals are but spectators of their magnificent aërial displays. Such sights are now unhappily rare with us. At one period of my life in a distant country they were common enough, and sometimes witnessed every day for weeks at a stretch. Here the noblest of our hawks are all but gone. The peregrine, the most perfect of the falcons—perhaps, as some naturalists think, the most perfect of the entire feathered race—maintains a precarious existence on the boldest sea-cliffs, and as to the hobby, it is now nearly extinct. The courageous little merlin does not range in southern England, and is very rare even in its northernmost counties. The kestrel is with us still, and it is beautiful to see him suspended motionless in mid-air with swiftly vibrating wings like a gigantic hover-fly; but he is nothing more than a mouser and an insect-eater, a falcon that has lost the noble courage of his tribe. The splendid powerful goshawk, a veritable king among hawks, has long been extinct; only his little cousin, the sparrow-hawk, lives on in ever-diminishing numbers. But although small and, as his name implies, a preyer chiefly on little birds, he has the qualities of his noble relation. In wooded places I am always on the look-out for him in hopes of witnessing one of his dashing raids on the feathered population. As a rule there is little to see, for the sparrow-hawk usually takes his quarry by surprise, rushing along the hedgerow, or masked by trees, then bounding like a small hunting leopard of the air on his victim and, if the stroke has been missed, speeding on his way. Even if I do not see this much—if I just catch a glimpse of the blue figure speeding by, seen for a moment, then vanishing among the trees—it is a pleasure to me, a satisfaction to know that he still exists, this little living link with the better vanished past, and my day has not been wasted.

Here, on the open downs where the small birds when feeding have no close refuge into which they can quickly vanish at the sight of danger, he may occasionally be watched chasing them as a dog on the ground chases a rabbit; but the best display is when he goes after a flock of starlings. At no other time does a company of these birds appear so like a single organism composed of many separate bodies governed by one will. Only when he is in the midst of the crowd, if, in spite of their quick doublings, he succeeds in getting there, do they instantly all fly apart and are like the flying fragments of a violently shattered mass; then, if he has not already made his capture, he singles out one bird to pursue.

A still better spectacle is afforded by the fiery-hearted little bird-hunter when, after the harvest, he ranges over the fields; when the village sparrows, mixed with finches of several species, are out on the stubble, often in immense congregations covering half a large field from end to end. On such occasions they like to feed near a hedge and are thickest on the ground at a distance of three or four seconds' flight from the thorny shelter. Suddenly the dreaded enemy appears, topping the hedges at its far end, and at the same instant, the whole vast gathering, extending the entire length of the field, is up in the air, their innumerable, swiftly fluttering, translucent wings, which produce a loud humming sound, giving them the appearance of a dense silvery brown mist springing up from the earth. In another instant they are safe in the hedge and not a bird is visible. In some instances the hawk is too intent on his prey to hurry on to other fields hoping for better luck next time. No, there are thousands here; he will drive them out and have one! Then, heedless of your presence, he ranges up and down the hedge, rising at intervals to a height of thirty or forty feet and, pausing to hover a few moments like a kestrel, dashes down as if to descend into the hedge to wrest a sparrow from its perch, and when just touching the surface of the thorny tangle the flight is arrested and he skims on a few yards, to mount again and repeat his feint. And at every down-ward dash a simultaneous cry of terror is uttered by the small birds—a strange sound, that cry of thousands extending the whole length of the hedge, yet like one cry! If you then walk by the hedge-side and peer into it, you will see the small birds crowded together on branchlets and twigs as near the middle of the hedge as they can get, each particular bird perched erect, stiff and motionless, like a little wooden dummy bird refusing to stir even when you stand within arm's reach of him. For though they fear and fly from the human form, the feeling is overmastered and almost vanishes in their extreme terror of the sharp-winged figure of the little feathered tyrant hovering above them.

Undoubtedly it is a fine spectacle—one that lives in the memory though less beautiful than that of the peregrine or other high-flying hawk in its chase and conquest of its quarry at a great height in the air; but in this matter of hawks and their fascinating exhibitions we have long come to the day of small things.

Something remains to be said of the owls—or rather of the long-eared owl, this being the only species I have met with in the temples of the hills. Strange as it may seem to readers who are not intimately acquainted with this bird, I was able to see it even more clearly than the sparrow-hawk in the full blaze of noonday. The binocular was not required. There were five of them—two old and three young birds—and it was their habit to spend the daylight hours sitting in a bush just outside the grove. After discovering their haunt I was able to find them on most days, and one day had a rare spectacle when I came upon the whole family, two in one bush and three sitting close together in another. I stood for some time, less than a dozen yards from these three, as they sat side by side on a dead branch in the hollow of a furze-bush, its spiny roof above them, but the cavity on my side. I gazed at them, three feathered wild cats, very richly coloured with the sun shining full on them, their long black narrow ears erect in astonishment, while they stared back at me out of three pairs of round luminous orange-yellow eyes. By-and-by, getting nervous at my presence, they flung themselves out, and, flying to a distance of twenty or thirty yards, settled down in another bush.

I had another delightful experience with long-eared owls at another of the downland groves about fifteen miles distant from the last. Here, too, it was a family—the parents and two young birds. I could not find them in the day-time; but they were always out at sunset, the young crying to be fed, the parents gliding to and fro, but not yet leaving the shadow of the trees. I went at the same hour on several evenings to watch them and experience pleasing little thrills. I would station myself in the middle of the grove and stand motionless against one of the tall pines, while the two young birds would fly backwards and forwards from end to end of the grove perching at intervals to call in their catty voices, and then resume their exercises. By-and-by a sudden puff of air would fan my cheek or it would be slightly brushed with feather-ends, and an owl would sweep by. This trick they would repeat again and again, always flying at my head from behind; and so noiseless was the flight that I could never tell that the bird was coming until it actually touched or almost touched me in passing. These were indeed the most ghostlike owls I had ever encountered; and they had no fear of the human form, though it evidently excited their curiosity and suspicion, and no knowledge of man's deadly power: for this grove, too, stood on land owned by the person who farmed it, and he was his own gamekeeper.

Thinking on my experience with these owls in an unprotected clump in Wiltshire, it occurred to me that owls of different species, where these birds are not persecuted, are apt to indulge in this same habit or trick, almost of the nature of a practical joke, of flying at you from behind and dashing close to your face to startle you. I remembered that in my early years, in a distant land where that world-ranging species, the short-eared owl, was common, I had often been made to jump by this bird.

It is sad to reflect that the few clumps which form bird refuges such as the one described—small oases of wild life in the midst of a district where all the most interesting species are ruthlessly extirpated—are never safe from the destroyer. A few years of indifference or kindly toleration or love of birds on the owner's or tenant's part may serve to people the grove, but the shooting may be let any day to the landlord or shooting-tenant of the adjoining property, whereupon his gamekeeper will step in to make a clean sweep of what he calls vermin.

Last summer I visited a hill-grove which was new to me, about thirteen miles distant from the one where I met with owls and sparrow-hawks and other persecuted species; and as it was an exceptionally large grove, surrounded by a growth of furze and black and white thorn, and at a good distance from any house, I hoped to find it a habitation of interesting bird life. But there was nothing to see or hear excepting a pair of yellow-hammers, a few greenfinches and tits, with two or three other feathered mites. It was a strictly protected grove, as I eventually discovered when I came on a keeper's gibbet where the pines were thickest. Here were many stoats, weasels, and moles suspended to a low branch: crows and rooks, a magpie, and two jays and eleven small hawks; three of these were sparrow-hawks—one in full, the others in immature plumage—and eight kestrels.

This, judging from the condition of the corpses—one or two newly killed, while the oldest were dried up to bones and feathers—was probably the harvest of a year or more. The zealous keeper had no doubt exhibited these trophies to the noble sportsman, his master, who probably rejoiced at the sight, though knowing that the kestrel is a protected species. This grove, its central tree decorated after the manner of a modern woman with wings and carcasses of birds and heads and tails of little beasts was like a small transcript of any one of those vast woods and forests in which I had spent so many days in this same downland district. The curse and degradation were on it, and from that time the sight of it was unpleasant, even when so far removed as to appear nothing but a blue cloud-like mound, no bigger than a man's hand, on the horizon.

There is something wanting in all these same great woods I have spoken of which spoils them for me and in some measure, perhaps, for those who have any feeling for Nature's wildness in them. It has been to me like an oppression during my rambles, year after year, in such woods as Savernake, Collingbourne, Longleat, Cranbourne Chase, Fonthill, Great Ridge Wood, Bentley and Groveley Woods—all within or on the borders of the Wiltshire down country. This feeling or sense of something wanting is stronger still in districts where there are higher and rougher hills, a larger landscape, and a wilder nature, as in the Quantocks—in the great wooded slopes and summits above Over Stowey, for example; the loss, in fact, is everywhere in all woodland and incult places, but I need not go away from these Wiltshire woods already named. They are great enough, one would imagine, to satisfy any person's love of wildness and solitude. Here you will find places in appearance like a primitive forest, where the trees have grown as they would for generations untouched by man's hand, and are interspersed with thorny thickets and wide sunny spaces, stony and barren or bright with flowers. Here, too, are groves of the most ancient oaks in the land, grey giants that might have been growing in the time of the Conquest, their immense horizontal branches rough with growth of fern and lichen; in the religious twilight of their shade you might spend a long summer day without meeting a human being or hearing any faintest sound of human life. A boundless contiguity of shade such as the sensitive poet desired, where he might spend his solitary life and never more have his ears pained, his soul made sick, with daily reports of oppression and deceit and wrong and outrage.

To the natural man they have another call. Like the ocean and the desert they revive a sense and feeling of which we had been unconscious, but which is always in us, in our very marrow; the sense which, as Herbert Spencer has said, comes down to us from our remote progenitors at a time when the principal activities of the race were in woods and deserts. Given the right conditions and it springs to renewed life; and we know it is this which gives to life its best savour, and not the thousand pleasures, or distractions which civilised dwellers in towns have invented as substitutes. Here we are away from them—out of doors, and able to shake the dust of such artificialities from our souls. In such moods, in these green shades, we are ready to echo every grateful word ever spoken of those who for a thousand years in a populous and industrial country, the workshop of the world, have preserved for us so much of Nature's freshness. Doubtless they did it for their own advantage and pleasure, but incidentally the good was for all.

A young American naturalist, writing to me some time ago, contrasted the state of things with regard to the preservation of wild life in his and this country. There, he said, the universal rage for destroying all the noblest and most interesting species, and the liberty possessed by every man and boy to go where he likes and do what he likes in utter disregard of penal laws, was everywhere producing a most deplorable effect. Whereas in this happier land, the great entailed estates of our old county families and aristocracy were like bulwarks to arrest the devastating and vulgarising forces, and had served to preserve our native fauna.

He spoke without sufficient knowledge, describing a condition of things which existed formerly, even down to about the thirties or forties of the nineteenth century. Then a change came over the spirit of the landowner's dreams; a new fashion in sport had arisen, and from that time onwards those who had been, indirectly, the preservers of our country's wild life became its systematic destroyers. For the sake of a big head of game, a big shoot in November, the birds being mainly hand-reared semidomestic pheasants driven to the guns, they decreed the complete extirpation of our noblest native species:

> The birds, great Nature's happy commoners,
> That haunt in woods:

Raven and buzzard, goshawk, kite, harrier-hawks, and peregrine. Besides these, a score of species of less size were also considered detrimental to the interests of the noble poultry-killer. Nor is this all. Incidentally the keepers, the men with guns in their hands who patrol the woods, have become the suppliers to the dealer and private collectors of every rare and beautiful bird they can find and kill.

But I wish now to write only of the large species named above. They are not very large—they might almost be described as small compared with many species in other lands—but they were the largest known throughout the greatest portion of England; they were birds that haunt in woods, and, above all, they were soaring birds. Seen on high in placid flight, circling and ascending, with the sunlight falling through the translucent feathers of their broad wings and tail, they looked large indeed—large as eagles and cranes. They were a feature in the landscape which made it seem vaster and the clouds higher and the sky immeasurably farther away. They were something more: the sight of them and the sound of their shrill reiterated cries completed and intensified the effect of Nature's wildness and majesty.

It is the loss of these soaring species which spoils these great woods for me, for I am always sadly conscious of it: miles on miles of wood, millions of ancient noble trees, a haunt of little dicky birds and tame pheasants bred and fed for the autumn shoot. Also the keeper laying his traps for little mousing weasels, or patiently waiting in hiding among the undergrowth to send a charge of shot through a rare kestrel's nest when the mother-bird comes back to feed and warm her young.

KING PENGUINS

DIANE ACKERMAN

Nowhere, yet, had we seen king penguins, the species I helped raise at Sea World, the most gaudily colored of all. To find them, we had to sail again across galloping seas, and when at last we dropped anchor at Cooper Island, at the tip of South Georgia, and climbed into our Zodiacs, we realized that we had arrived at one of the most astonishing places on earth.

Our first sight of land was from the rafts, on seas that smacked them hard against each swell. The mountains of Cooper Island stretch high and green to ice-capped peaks. When American ornithologist Robert Cushman Murphy visited it in 1912, he called it "a stretch of the Alps in mid-ocean." Macaroni penguins, named after the Yankee Doodle dandies because they have orange spaghetti bangs hanging from their heads, clotted the hillsides, and their collective clamor—part bray, part clack—resounded louder than the surf. Albatrosses, terns, petrels, and other birds swirled in relentless squadrons overhead, planed low over the water, squealing and chirping, or clustered on the hillside. Schools of macaroni penguins porpoised through the water all around our Zodiacs, which quickly seemed to be boiling in a cauldron of penguins. Fur seals clambered onto the many rock outcroppings near shore, and gave gargling barks. The whole scene shimmered, fluorescent with life. So many animals moved in the foreground, and in the background, that your eyes strained to focus on both at once. It was like traveling through the middle of a pop-up storybook. Magic realism had sprung to life. In each cove, penguins leapt out of the water like solid balls of rubber to land safely on the rocks, as we staggered toward one shore after another, looking for a safe place to land. Finally, we headed for a small, wave-tossed beach, hit hard, climbed out fast, and let the Zodiac return to deeper waters. Fur seals basked on the shore, some hidden behind large boulders, some sitting on top of the thronelike tussocks. Those steeply tussocked cliffs gave way to a high field above us, and beyond that stood a scree-torn mountain capped with snow.

Brittmarie, a Swedish-born climber from California, whose candor and zest I liked, looked at me, then at the craggy bluffs overhead.

"Let's do it," I said, and we exchanged grins.

Sneaking away far left, around the sleeping fur seals, we started to climb up a steep, rocky creekbed.

"Three points!" she yelled down to me as I scrambled up behind on the slippery rocks. "Always be secure at three points!"

"Words to live by!" I called back. Soon we found ourselves walled in by thick cliffs with dense tussocks hanging from them.

"It's straight up," Brittmarie said, smiling. "What do you think?"

There is an art to climbing tussock-grass mountains, I'm sure. An amateur like me could only improvise. Because the grass clumped tightly at the base, I held on securely there as I pulled myself up, stepping in the mud between the tussock clumps. Petrels had made burrows among the tussocks, which I used as footholds whenever possible. If you have the upper-body strength, you can hold on with both hands, as if climbing a rope ladder, and find safe footing. Halfway up the hill, panting hard, we paused to rest. If anything, the hill above looked even steeper, the tussocks bulging overhead. Suppose the edge tussocks weren't firmly rooted and broke off? We decided to angle up, and finally we reached the top, where a field of tussocks led across promontories to a distant group of nesting albatrosses with their chicks. Half an hour later, we managed to steal up on them in the grass. Fluffy gray chicks swiveled around to face us, each with a black bridle-shaped stripe across its mouth. One or two began clacking to warn us away. Their parents flew overhead or at eye level or soared along the cliffs below us. Perched on that height, in the windy mist, while albatrosses maneuvered, we saw the ship rolling on the freshening sea, where Captain Lampe, whose skills we had learned to respect in the iceberg-clotted channels, was holding steady against wind and current. We saw Zodiacs plunging through the water to unload. We saw lens-shaped clouds prowling the mountains, and knew they signaled stronger winds. But our goal was higher still. Hand over hand, leaping small pits and bogs, we climbed toward an unmistakable sound—a chattery braying. There, hundreds of feet above the sea, sprawled a rookery of macaroni penguins. Plump, slightly farouche-looking, with orange hair parted in the middle, they ran around like miniature Zero Mostels. How on earth they managed the climb we did not know. But climb it they often did, with their stomachs full of food, to feed their waiting young. We knew that it would be almost impossible for a creature that can't fly to get up the mountain. Fortunately, the penguins didn't know it, and here they were.

"Think of the energy it must take for a little, short-legged bird to walk up over all those sharp, rocky slopes to get to the top to breed," Brittmarie said, pulling a camera from her blue knapsack. "It's beyond comprehension."

"Tenacity," I said, thinking out loud—and not meaning the macaroni penguin's tenacity, exactly, but life's. Life hangs on in such out-of-the-way places, pushes on with such ingenuity and bravado. Turning over a mother-of-pearl-lined limpet shell on Elephant Island a few days earlier, I had seen a hundred squirming wingless flies. Life just seemed to keep reinventing itself—inside a limpet shell, or hundreds of feet up a rocky cliff above a roaring ocean.

When the seas started to grow dangerously rough, we were summoned back to the boat, and set sail at long last for the king penguin rookeries at Gold Harbor and Salisbury Plain, on the island of South Georgia. At Salisbury Plain, our Zodiacs cut through thick curling waves onto a steep beach. For some reason there was the sound of harmonicas and, occasionally, distant oncoming trains. Turning, I saw a nearby hill seemingly squirming in the sunlight and automatically walked toward it. All at once it reeled into focus as a bustling, fidgeting, buzzing, clamorous, colossal king-penguin metropolis that sprawled for miles, pouring along the scimitar-shaped beach, through interfolding valleys, spilling down the hillsides. It was penguin heaven. The adults stood tall, with those splendid pairs of orange commas on their cheeks, a radiant sun-yellow blooming at their throats, and an apricot or lavender comet along each side of their bills. Stately, curious, they allowed me to sit down right among them. One slightly potbellied king, carrying an egg on its feet, "head-flagged" with its mate, bobbing and sweeping heads like signalmen with flags, or shadow boxers. Then the female touched her bill to her brood patch—a vertical opening where she held the egg—tossed her head up, and rubbed her bill back and forth across her mate's neck, as if to sharpen it on the whetstone of his desire. A neighbor bashed them both with its flippers and they screeched a rude reply.

Kings don't like being crowded. Thousands of birds stood close together in the rookery. Like soldiers in line, replying to the command of "Dress left!" or "Dress right!" they occasionally put out a flipper to keep their neighbor at a comfortable distance. Any attacking skua would face an impenetrable sea of sharp upturned bills. It would be like flying into a bed of nails. King penguins know exactly how much space they need to feel secure but not hemmed in, and they are rarely more than a flipper smack or a bill lunge away from one another. Four bachelors strutted by smartly in a line, looking gallant and available. One paused in front of a female, pointed its apricot-striped bill skyward, thrust out its chest, cranked its flippers back, and flapped rhythmically as if he were trying to lift off. A hoarse drumbeat throbbed in his throat, then changed to a climactic braying of two tones at once—the harmonica I had heard. His ecstatic display was all aces, and the female responded. They head-flagged together for a while, then, for a long time, stared at each other and chattered. The male suddenly threw his shoulders back and strolled forward, in what scientists call the advertisement walk. Looking as swell as possible in penguin terms, he turned his head from side to side so that she could see what beautiful orange ear-patches he had. If she followed him, it was a marriage. Then, several other bachelors waddled up and tried to muscle in, gently chasing the female toward the shore. Demure, she held her flippers to her side while the bachelors crowed and raved. Ultimately, her original swain won out, and bumped her repeatedly, though gently, with his chest, herding her to the outskirts of the rookery, where they had a little more room. In time, he would stand right on top of her back, mate in as little as forty seconds with a cloacal kiss, and then climb down, leaving his muddy footprints behind.

To pledge their devotion, a nearby couple plunged into a suite of "mutual displays," which looked like ecstatic displays except that both male and female took part. Facing each other, they were soon weaving their heads from side to side and crying out in joy, finally pointing their bills up to the sky. Doing this every few minutes keeps their bond strong. Most penguins return to the same nest the following year, and the same mate, whose voice they recognize. Birds whose mates have died, or with whom they weren't able to nest successfully the previous year, must find new mates. If the rookery is disturbed for any reason, couples often engage in mutual displays, which they also do when an egg is laid or when they change shifts in incubating an egg—in fact, whenever it seems wise to restate their vows. Insinuating themselves through the rookery, at speed, two penguins did the "slender walk." All they wanted was to get from their nests to the sea without stopping to fight or give anybody grief, so they held their flippers tightly against their sides, slicked down their feathers, and slid through as inoffensively as possible. In a major rookery, everything is happening at once and you can see just about all the phases of the king's life cycle going on simultaneously. A fluffy baby peered out from under a parent's soft white belly, leaving its oversized rump outside. A small gaggle of "mohawks," molting babies that have a stripe of down on top of their heads, chased an adult and screamed to be fed. In their fury, they raced right over the remains of disemboweled chicks.

A king stood on his heels and dusted the snow behind him with his tail. By then, I had removed my parka to reveal a bright-yellow sweatsuit. Although I'm shaped wrong and don't have cheek commas, my black hair and screaming-yellow body were the right colors to interest a king penguin, which shuffled up close, cocked a head to one side, then to the other, and carefully checked me over. There is, ordinarily, a no-man's-land between us and wild animals. They fear us and shy away. But penguins are among the very few animals on earth that cross that divide. They seem to regard us as penguins, too, perhaps of a freakish species. After all, we stand upright, travel in groups, talk all the time, sort of waddle. Still, though I was black and yellow and in a submissive posture, I was not the penguin he hankered for, he decided at long last, not one of *his* kind, and he shuffled away slowly, keeping an eye on me until he disappeared into the gyrating sea of black and white.

A low, smothery cloud bank drifted overhead. It was going to be a rainy night in South Georgia. Surrounded by penguin society, which began to close its ranks behind me, I thought of brown-white-left, the fluffy chick I helped raise at Sea World in San Diego. Moved to Orlando, his final home, he would already be fledging. Even if he could understand me, how could I begin to describe his homeland and the rigors of penguin life in the Antarctic? How poor his odds would be of survival? I was probably with his parents, perhaps his brothers and sisters, certainly cousins, right here in this rookery. When I thought of the horror of a penguin being flayed alive by a leopard seal, my skin crawled. Nature neither gives nor expects mercy. I gently touched the sleek oiled back of a lovely nesting penguin, with a fine set of commas, whose feathers were tipped in a bluish gleam. For brown-white-left, life would be more artificial, of course, but also much safer, and it was good to know that he was alive a world away. Safe from hunger, leopard seal, and skua, he was probably sitting like a pensioner on a park bench as he watched the silent pageant passing on the moving sidewalk beyond the glass, where ghostly humans floated in a darkness deep as the Antarctic night.

BEASTS

I think I could turn and live with animals, they are so placid and
    self-contained;
I stand and look at them long and long,
They do not sweat and whine about their condition;
They do not lie awake in the dark and weep for their sins;
They do not make me sick discussing their duty to God;
No one is dissatisfied—not one is demented with the mania of
    owning things;
No one kneels to another, nor to his kind that lived thousands of
    years ago;
No one is respectable or industrious over the whole earth.

—WALT WHITMAN,
Song of Myself, 1881

THE CAT

EDWARD TOPSELL

Once cattes were all wilde, but afterward they retyred to houses, wherefore there are plenty of them in all countries. A cat is in all partes like a Lyonesse, (except in her sharpe eares) wherefore the Poets faine, that when *Venus* had turned a cat into a beautifull woman (calling her *Aeluros*) who forgetting her good turne, contended with the goddesse for beauty: in indignation wherof, she returned her to her first nature, onely making her outward shape to resemble a lyon, which is not altogither idle, but may admonish the wisest, that faire & foule, men and beasts, hold nothing by their owne worth and benefit, but by the vertue of their creator.

Cats are of divers colours, but for the most part gryseld, like to congealed yse, which commeth from the condition of her meate: her head is like unto the head of a Lyon, except in her sharpe eares: her flesh is soft and smooth: her eies glister above measure especialy when a man commeth to see a cat on the sudden, and in the night, they can hardly be endured, for their flaming aspect. Wherfor *Democritus* describing the *persian smaradge* saith that it is not transparent, but filleth the eie with pleasant brightnes, such as is in the eies of Panthers and cats, for they cast forth beames in the shaddow and darkenes, but in the sunshine they have no such clearnes, and thereof *Alexander Aphrodise* giveth this reason, both for the sight of Cattes and of Battes, that they have by nature a most sharpe spirit of seeing.

Albertus compareth their eye-sight to carbuncles in darke places, because in the night, they can see perfectly to kill Rattes and Myce: the root of the herbe *Valerian* (commonly called *Phu*) is very like to the eye of a

Cat, and wheresover it groweth, if cats come therunto, they instantly dig it up, for the love thereof, as I my selfe have seene in mine owne Garden, and not once onely, but often, even then when as I had caused it to bee hedged or compassed round about with thornes, for it smelleth marveilous like to a cat.

The Egyptians have observed in the eies of a cat, the encrease of the Moone-light, for with the Moone they shine more fully at the ful, and more dimly in the change and wain, and the male cat doth also vary his eyes with the Sunne; for when the sunne ariseth, the apple of his eie is long; toward noone is round, and at the evening it cannot be seene at all, but the whole eie sheweth alike.

The tongue of a cat is very attractive, and forcible like a file, attenuating by licking the flesh of a man, for which cause, when she is come neere to the blood, so that her own spittle be mingled therewith, she falleth mad. Her teeth are like a saw, and if the long haires growing about her mouth (which some call *Granons*) be cut away, she looseth hir corage. Her nailes sheathed like the nailes of a Lyon, striking with her forefeete, both Dogs and other things, as a man doth with his hand.

This beast is woonderfull nimble, setting upon her prey like a Lyon, by leaping: and therefore she hunteth both rats, all kind of Myce, & Birds, eating not onely them, but also fish, wherewithall she is best pleased. Having taken a Mouse, she first playeth with it, and then devoreth it, but her watchfull eye is most strange, to see with what pace and soft steps, she taketh birds and flies; and her nature is to hide her own dung or excrements, for she knoweth that the savour and presence thereof, will drive away her sport, the little Mouse being able by that stoole, to smell the presence of hir mortall foe.

To keepe Cats from hunting of Hens, they use to tie a little wild rew under their wings, and so likewise from Dove-coates, if they set it in the windowes, they dare not approach unto it for some secret in nature. Some have said that cats will fight with Serpentes, and Toads, and kill them, and perceiving that she is hurt by them; she presently drinketh water and is cured: but I cannot consent unto this opinion: it being rather true of the Weasell. *Ponzettus* sheweth by experience that cats and Serpents love one another, for there was (sayth he) in a certain Monastery, a Cat norished by the Monkes, and suddenly the most parts of the Monkes which used to play with the Cat fell sicke: whereof the Physitians could find no cause, but some secret poyson, and al of them were assured that they never tasted any: at the last a poore laboring man came unto them, affirming that he saw the Abbey-cat playing with a Serpent, which the Physitians under-standing, presently conceived that the Serpent had emptied some of her poyson uppon the cat, which brought the same to the Monkes, and they by stroking and handeling the cat, were infected therewith; and whereas there remained one difficulty, namely, how it came to passe, the cat her selfe was not poisoned thereby, it was resolved, that forasmuch as the Serpentes poison came from him but in playe and sporte, and not in malice and wrath, that therefore the venom thereof being lost in play, neither harmed the Cat at al, nor much endaungered the Monkes: and the very like is observed of myce that will play with Serpents.

Cats will also hunt Apes, and follow them to the woods, for in Egypt certaine Cattes set upon an Ape, who presently tooke himselfe to his heeles and climed up into a tree, after when the cattes followed with the same celerity and agility: (for they can fasten their clawes to the barke, and runne up very speedily:) the Ape seeing himselfe overmatched with num-ber of his adversaries, leaped from branch to braunch, and at last tooke hold of the top of a bough, whereupon he did hang so ingeniously, that the Cats durst not approach unto him for feare of falling, and so departed.

The nature of this Beast is, to love the place of her breeding, neither will she tarry in any strange place, although carried very farre, being never willing to forsake the house, for the love of any man, and most contrary to the nature of a Dogge, who will travaile abroad with his maister; and although their maisters forsake their houses, yet will not these Beastes beare them company, and being carried forth in close baskets or sackes, they will yet return againe or loose themselves. A Cat is much delighted to play with hir image in a glasse, and if at any time she behold it in water, presently she leapeth down into the water which naturally she doth ab-horre, but if she be not quickly pulled forth and dryed she dieth thereof, because she is impatient of al wet. Those which will keepe their Cattes within doores, and from hunting Birds abroad, must cut off their eares, for they cannot endure to have drops of rain distil into them and therfore keep themselves in harbor. Nothing is more contrary to the nature of a Cat, then is wet and water, and for this cause came the Proverbe that they love not to wet their feet. It is a neate and cleanly creature, oftentimes licking hir own body to keepe it smooth and faire, having naturally a flexible backe for this purpose, and washing hir face with her fore feet: but some observe, that if she put her feete beyond the crowne of her head, that it is a presage of raine, and if the backe of a cat be thinne the beast is of no courage or value. They love fire and warme places, whereby it falleth out that they often burne their coates. They desire to lie soft, and in the time of their lust (commonly called cat-wralling) they are wilde and fierce, especially the males, whoe at that time (except they be gelded) will not keepe the house: at which time they have a peculiar direfull voyce. The maner of their copulation is this, the Female lyeth downe and the Male standeth, and their females are above measure desirous of procreation, for which cause they provoke the male, and if he yeeld not to their lust they beate and claw him, but it is onely for love of young and not for lust: the meale is most libidinous, and therefore seeing the female will never more engender with him, during the time hir young ones sucke, hee killeth and eateth them if he meet with them, (to provoke the female to copulation with him againe, for when she is deprived of her young, she seeketh out the male of her own accord,) for which the female most warily keepeth them from his sight. When they have litered or as we commonly say kittened, they rage against Dogges, and will suffer none to come neere their young ones. The best to keep are such as are littered in March, they go with young fifty daies, and the females live not above sixe or seven years, the males live longer especially if they be gelt or libbed: the reason of their short life is their ravening of meate which corrupteth within them.

They cannot abide the savour of oyntments but fall madde thereby; they are sometimes infected with the falling evill, but are cured with *Gobium.* It is needelesse to spend any time about her loving nature to man, how she flattereth by rubbing her skinne against ones Legges, how she whurleth with her voyce, having as many tunes as turnes, for she hath one voice to beg and to complain, another to testifie her delight & pleasure, another among hir own kind by flattring, by hissing, by puffing, by spitting, insomuch as some have thought that they have a peculiar intelligible language among themselves. Therefore how she beggeth, playeth, leapeth, looketh, catcheth, tosseth with her foote, riseth up to strings held over her head, sometime creeping, sometimes lying on the back, playing with one foot, sometime on the bely, snatching, now with mouth, & anon with foot, aprehending greedily any thing save the hand of a man with divers such gestical actions, it is needelesse to stand upon; insomuch as *Coelius* was wont to say, that being free from his Studies and more urgent waighty affaires, he was not ashamed to play and sport himselfe with his Cat, and verily it may well be called an idle mans pastime. As this beast hath been familiarly nourished of many, so have they payed deare for their love, being requited with the losse of their health, and sometime of their life for their friendship: and worthily, because they which love any beasts in a high mesure, have so much the lesse charity unto man.

Therefore it must be considered what harmes and perils come unto men by this beast. It is most certaine that the breath and savour of cats consume the radicall humour and destroy the lungs, and therefore they which keepe their cats with them in their beds have the aire corrupted and fall into fever hecticks and consumptions. There was a certaine company of Monkes much given to nourish and play with Cattes, whereby they were so infected that within a short space none of them were able either to say, reade, pray, or sing, in all the monastery; and therefore also they are dangerous in the time of pestilence, for they are not onely apt to bring home venomous infection, but to poyson a man with very looking upon him; wherefore there is in some men a naturall dislike and abhorring of cats, their natures being so composed, that not onely when they see them, but being neere them and unseene, and hid of purpose, they fall into passions, fretting, sweating, pulling off their hats, and trembling fearefully, as I have knowne many in Germany, the reason whereof is, because the constellation which threatneth their bodies which is peculiar to every man, worketh by the presence and offence of these creatures: and therefore they have cryed out to take away the Cats.

The haire also of a cat being eaten unawares, stoppeth the artery and causeth suffocation: and I have heard that when a child hath gotten the haire of a cat into his mouth, it hath so cloven and stucke to the place that it could not be gotten off again, and hath in that place bred either the wens or the kings evill: to conclude this point it appeareth that this is a dangerous beast, & that therfore as for necessity we are constrained to nourish them for the suppressing of small vermine: so with a wary and discret eie we must avoyde their harmes, making more account of their use then of their persons.

In *Spaine* and *Gallia Narbon*, they eate cats, but first of al take away their head and taile, and hang the prepared flesh a night or two in the open cold aire, to exhale the savour and poyson from it, finding the flesh thereof to be almost as sweete as a Cony. It must needes be an uncleane and impure beast that liveth onely upon vermin and by ravening, for it is commonly said of a man when he neezeth, that he hath eaten with Cats: likewise the familiars of Witches do most ordinarily appeare in the shape of cats, which is an argument that this beast is dangerous in soule & body. It is said that if bread be made wherin the dung of cats is mixed, it wil drive away Rats and Mice. But we conclude the story of this beast with the medicinal observations, and tary no longer in the breath of such a creature compounded of good and evil. It is reported that the flesh of cats salted and sweetned hath power in it to draw wens from the body, & being warmed to cure the Hemorrhoids and pains in the raines and backe: *Aylsius* prescribeth a fat cat sod for the gout, first taking the fat, and annoynting therewith the sicke part, and then wetting Wooll or Towe in the same, and binding it to the offended place.

For the paine and blindnesse in the eye, by reason of any skinnes, Webs, or nailes, this is an approved medicine. Take the head of a blacke Cat, which hath not a spot of another colour in it, and burne it to pouder in an earthen pot leaded or glazed within, then take this poulder and through a quill blow it thrice a day into thy eie, and if in the nightime any heate do thereby annoy thee, take two leaves of an Oke wet in cold water and binde them to the eye, and so shall all paine fly away, and blindnes depart although it hath oppressed thee a whole yeare, and this medicine is approved by manye Physitians both elder and later.

REAL LIFE OF THE BEAVER

JOHN TIMBS

The old saying, "Man favours wonders," was never more completely exemplified than in the wonderful tales which have been told of the Beaver. It has been represented as an accomplished architect, gifted by Nature with a head to design, and instruments to execute well-planned houses containing chambers, each set apart for its appropriate purpose. The lovers of the marvellous, when they had once given the reins to their imagination, soon converted its tail into a sledge, or trowel, and astonished the world with an elaborate account of the mode in which the plaster was laid on with this, according to them, masonic implement: nay, they even turned it into an instrument of office. With it the overseers (such officers, according to the accounts given of their civil institutions, it was the custom of the community of Beavers to appoint,) were said to give the signal to the labourers whose employment they superintended, by slapping the tail on the surface of the water. All this, and more than this, has faded away before the light of truth. The houses of Beavers have sunk into rude huts, in the construction of which their tails are never used; their pile-driving, (for among other feats, they were said to drive stakes of the thickness of a man's leg three or four feet deep into the ground,) has turned out to be a mere fable; and their polity has proved to be nothing more than a combination of individuals, such as we see among many of the inferior animals, impelled by an instinct common to all to perform a task in the benefit of which all participate.

But, after discarding all exaggerations, there remains enough to make the works actually carried on by these animals a subject of deep interest, as we shall presently see. First, we shall describe the Beaver. It is a rodent or gnawing animal, with two incisor or cutting teeth, and eight molars in each jaw, twenty in all. It is particularly distinguished from all the rest of its order, by a broad, horizontally flattened tail, which is nearly oval, and covered with scales. There are five toes on each of the feet, but those of the hinder ones only are webbed, the webs extending beyond the roots of the nails. The second toe of these last is furnished with a double nail, or rather with two, like those of the other toes; and another beneath it is situated obliquely with a sharp edge directed downwards. There is also a less perfect double nail on the inner toe of the hind feet.

The incisor teeth of the Beaver are broad, flattened, and protected by a coat of very hard orange-coloured enamel, the rest of the tooth being of a comparatively soft substance; in the former a cutting, chisel-like edge is obtained: indeed, no edge-tool, with all its combination of hard and soft metal, could answer the purpose better. In fact, the Beaver's incisor tooth is fashioned much upon the same principle as that followed by the tool-maker, who forms a cutting instrument by a skilful adaptation of hard and soft materials till he produces a good edge. But the natural instrument has one advantage over the artificial tool; for the former is so organized that, as fast as it is worn away by use, it is reproduced from the base. So hard is the enamel, and so good a cutting instrument is the incisor tooth of the Beaver, that when fixed in a wooden handle, it was, according to Sir John Richardson, the naturalist and traveller, used by the Northern Indians to cut bone, and fashion their horn-tipped spears, till it was superseded by the introduction of iron, when the Beaver-tooth was supplanted by the English file. The power of these natural tools was witnessed by Lewis and Clarke, on the banks of the Missouri. "The ravages of the Beaver," say they, "are very apparent: in one place the timber was entirely prostrated for a space of three acres, in front of the river, and one in depth, and great part of it removed, although the trees were in large quantities, and some of them as thick as the body of a man." Sir John Richardson also says: "When the Beaver cuts down a tree, it gnaws it all round, cutting it, however, somewhat higher on the one side than on the other, by which the direction of its fall is determined. The stump is conical, and of such a height as a Beaver, sitting on its hind-quarters, could make." The largest tree this writer observed cut down by them was six or seven inches in diameter. By good authority it is also stated that a Beaver will lop off with his teeth, at a single effort a stem of the thickness of a common walking-stick, as cleanly as if done by a gardener's pruning-knife.

Hearne, the traveller, has truthfully described the habits of the American Beavers. The situation of their houses is various. They inhabit lakes, ponds, and rivers, and narrow creeks; but the two latter are generally chosen by them when the depth of water and other circumstances are suitable, so that they have then the advantage of a current to convey wood and other necessaries to their habitations; and because, in general, they are more difficult to be taken than those that are built in standing water. They always choose those parts that have such a depth of water as will resist the frost in winter, and prevent it from freezing to the bottom. The Beavers that build their houses in small rivers, or creeks, in which water is liable to be drained off when the back supplies are dried up by the frost, are wonderfully taught by instinct to provide against that evil by making a dam quite across the river, at a convenient distance from their houses. The materials made use of in the Beaver-dams are drift-wood, green willows, birch, and poplars if they can be got; also, mud and stones so intermixed as must evidently contribute to the strength of the dam; but there is no other order or method observed in the dams, except that of the work being carried on within a regular sweep, and all the parts being made of equal strength. In places which have been long frequented by Beavers undisturbed, their dams, by frequent repairing, become a solid bank, capable of resisting great force, both of water and ice; and as the willow, poplar, and birch generally take root and shoot up, they by degrees form a kind of regularly planted hedge, which Hearne had seen in some places so tall that birds had built their nests among the branches.

The Beaver-houses are built of the same materials as their dams, and are always proportioned in size to the number of inhabitants, which seldom exceeds four old and six or eight young ones; though by chance Hearne had seen double that number. Their houses are of much ruder structure than their dams; for, notwithstanding the sagacity of these animals, it has never been observed that they aim at any other convenience in their houses than to have a dry place to lie on; and there they usually eat their victuals, which they occasionally take out of the water. Some of the large houses have one or more partitions, if they deserve that appellation, but it is no more than a part of the main building left by the sagacity of the Beaver to support the roof. These different apartments, as some call them, have no communication with each other but by water, so that they may be called double or treble houses. Hearne saw a large Beaver-house in a small island that had near a dozen apartments under one roof; and two or three excepted, they only had communication with each other by water.

As there were Beavers enough to inhabit each apartment, it is more than probable that each family knew their own, and always entered at their own doors, and without any further connexion with their neighbours than a friendly intercourse, and joining their united labours in erecting their separate habitations, and building their dams where required. Travellers who assert that the Beavers have two doors to their houses, one on the land side and the other next the water, seem to be less acquainted with these animals than others who assign them an elegant suite of apartments. Such a construction would render their house of no use, either to protect them from their enemies, or guard them against the extreme cold of winter.

So far are the Beavers from driving stakes into the ground when building their houses, that they lay most of the wood crosswise, and nearly horizontal, and without any other order than that of leaving a hollow or cavity in the middle. When any unnecessary branches project inward, they cut them off with their teeth, and throw them in among the rest, to prevent the mud from falling through the roof. It is a mistaken notion that the wood-work is first completed and then plastered; for the whole of their houses, as well as their dams, are, from the foundation, one mass of mud and wood mixed with stones, if they can be procured. The mud is always taken from the edge of the bank, or the bottom of the creek or pond near the door of the house; and though the Beaver's fore-paws are so small, yet it is held up close between them under the throat: thus they carry both mud and stones, while they always drag the wood with their teeth. All their work is executed in the night, and they are so expeditious that in the course of one night Hearne knew them to have collected some thousand of their little handfuls. It is a great piece of policy in these animals to cover the outside of their houses every fall with fresh mud, and as late as possible in the autumn, even when the frost becomes pretty severe, as by this means it soon freezes as hard as a stone, and prevents their common enemy, the Wolverene, from disturbing them during the winter. As they are frequently seen to walk over their work, and sometimes to give a slap with their tails, particularly when plunging into the water, this has given rise to the vulgar opinion that they used their tails as a trowel, with which they plaster their houses; whereas that flapping of the tail is no more than a habit which they always preserve, even when they become tame and domestic, and more particularly so when they are startled.

Their food consists of a large root, a kind of water-lily which grows at the bottom of lakes and rivers. They also eat the bark of poplar, birch, willow, and other trees; but as the ice prevents their getting to the land in the winter, they rely for food in that season upon such sticks as they cut down in summer, and throw into the water opposite the doors of their houses. The roots are mostly their winter food; in summer they vary their diet by eating different kinds of herbage, and such berries as grow near their haunts. When the ice breaks up in the spring, the Beavers always leave their houses, and rove about until a little before the fall of the leaf, when they return to their old habitations, and lay in their winter stock of wood. When about to erect a new habitation, they begin felling the wood early in the summer, but seldom begin to build until the middle or latter end of August, and never complete it till the cold weather sets in.

When their houses are attacked, they retreat to holes in the river-banks, where they are generally captured. When the Beavers in a small river or creek are to be taken, the Indians sometimes stake the river across, to prevent them from passing; and then they search for their holes or places of retreat in the banks. Every man being furnished with an ice-chisel, lashes it to the end of a staff four or five feet long, and knocking it against the ice, he knows by its sound when he is opposite any of the Beavers' holes or vaults. As soon as he suspects any, he cuts a hole in the ice, big enough to admit an old Beaver. Meanwhile, others break open the Beaver's house, which, at times, is no easy task, for these houses are frequently five or six feet thick. Captain Cartwright describes in Labrador Beaver-dams one hundred feet long, over which he walked with the greatest safety. When the Beavers find that their habitations are invaded, they fly to their holes in the banks for shelter; and on being perceived by the Indians, which is easily done by attending to the motion of the water, they block up the entrance with stakes of wood, and then haul the Beaver out of its hole, either by hand, or by a large hook at the end of a long stick. In this kind of hunting, every man has the sole right to all the Beavers caught by him in the holes or vaults; and each person takes care to mark such as he discovers by sticking up the branch of a tree, by which he may know them. All that are caught in the house are the property of the person who finds it. Beavers can keep under water a long time, so that when their houses are broken open, and all their places of retreat discovered, they have but one choice left, as it may be called, either to be taken in their house, or their vaults; they generally prefer the latter, for where there is one Beaver caught in the house, many thousands are taken in the banks. Sometimes they are caught in nets, and very frequently in traps.

Hearne kept several Beavers till they became so domesticated as to answer to their name, and follow those persons to whom they were accustomed, in the same manner as a dog would do. They were much pleased at being fondled: in cold weather they were kept in Hearne's own sitting-room, where they were the constant companions of the Indian women and children, and were so fond of their company that when the Indians were absent for any considerable time, the Beavers showed great signs of uneasiness; and on their return showed equal marks of pleasure by fondling on them, crawling into their laps, lying on their backs, sitting erect like a squirrel, and behaving like children who see their parents but seldom. During the winter, the Beavers mostly lived on the same food as the women did, and were remarkably fond of rice and plum-pudding; they would eat partridges and fresh venison very freely. Hearne never tried them with fish, though it is said they will at times prey on them.

The instinctive building labours of the Beaver are only fully displayed in communities; indeed, the animal loses its distinguishing qualities, the moment it becomes isolated from its fellows, and condemned to live in solitude: brought up together, Beavers will live in perfect harmony, and labour in concert; but removed from society, each lives for himself alone. M. F. Cuvier describes Canadian Beavers shut up in menageries, to strongly illustrate this observation: being taken very young, and brought up in a solitary manner, in narrow cages, they never habituate themselves to anything but obedience to their master's will; whenever an attempt is made to unit them, it is followed by violent combats, and severe wounds. Cuvier mentions an extremely mild Beaver, which was habituated to the presence of men, and would suffer itself to be touched, and carried in the hand: at last, it was brought to live familiarly with some dogs; for, it is worthy of remark, that certain animals of different species will sooner contract an affection for each other, when united by man, than those of the same species.

Major Rodefort, of New York, had a tame Beaver, which he kept in his house for a year and a half, and allowed to run about like a dog: and was fed with bread and fish. He dragged all the rags and soft materials he could lay hold of into a corner where he was accustomed to sleep, and there made a bed of them. The cat belonging to the house, having kittens, took possession of his bed, and he gallantly allowed her to remain there. In the absence of the cat, the Beaver would take one of the kittens between his paws, fondle it, and hold it to his breast, as if to warm the little animal, which, on the cat's return, he restored to her. Sometimes he grumbled, but never attempted to bite.

In the menagerie at Exeter Change, in the Strand, there were, in 1820, two Beavers, which were so tame as to allow themselves to be handled by the visitors. These Beavers wrestled and played together; they seemed much amused in dragging about any moveable, but in no instance were they observed to drag anything on their tails. They gnawed wood so voraciously, that had they been allowed the full range of a room, they would have eaten their way out, and thus have escaped.

Sir Hans Sloane kept a female Beaver in his garden at Chelsea, for nearly three months: she was about half-grown, and except her tail, very much resembled a great, overgrown water-rat. Her food was bread and water; she scarcely tasted willow-boughs given to her; but when loose in the garden, she gnawed vines as high as she could reach, down to the root; she also gnawed jessamine and even holly trees. When she ate, she sat on her hind legs, and held the bread in her paws, like a squirrel. She swam with her hind webbed feet only, steering with her tail; she would keep under water two or three minutes, and then came up to breathe; she swam much swifter than any water-fowl, and moved under water as quickly as a carp. She was very lively, and enjoyed a spring for a bath; she had one day convulsive fits, very like epilepsy in men, from which she soon recovered; she was, at length, killed by a dog.

THE BONTE-QUAGGA

THEODORE ROOSEVELT AND EDMUND HELLER

In East Africa, north to the Northern Guaso Nyiro, the most plentiful big animal next to the hartebeest was the common zebra—not the very uncommon and narrowly limited mountain zebra of South Africa, but the bonte-quagga, which is found in a dozen different forms from the Orange River to beyond the equator.

The zebra is eminently gregarious. Of course, an occasional stallion is found by himself, usually an immature, a weak, or an aged animal. But ordinarily zebras are found in herds of from a dozen to a couple of hundred; and, moreover, half the time there are other animals mixed in with these herds—hartebeests, wildebeests, oryxes, elands, gazelles, or ostriches. Each herd is usually under the leadership of a master stallion.

Zebras are vicious fighters. Against a lion they make no fight at all, and against man they are only dangerous in the sense that a bull moose or wapiti is dangerous; that is, they will bite viciously if approached when wounded; and on rare occasions when crippled and brought to a standstill, but not wholly disabled, they will charge at the hunter from a distance of several rods. We, personally, have never known one do more than skin its teeth at us as we approached it when on the ground, or perhaps as we galloped through a herd after some more desirable game; but Mr. Stewart Edward White was regularly charged. It would be interesting to know whether zebras can stand off wild hounds—those inveterate enemies of other game. We once saw a zebra make a race at a wild hound which had trotted near by, and drive it off, although the pied hunter did not seem much frightened; and Loring saw a zebra standing with two wild hounds near by to which it paid not the slightest attention. But it is impossible to generalize from such instances; often game animals seem to recognize when beasts of prey are not after them, and then betray a curious indifference to the otherwise dreaded presence. We have seen zebras trot a few rods out of the path of a lion and then turn to gaze at him as he walked by. The chief fighting is done by the stallions among themselves. When at liberty the beaten party can generally escape; but if a herd is captured and left overnight in a corral, by morning the weaker males are sure to have been frightfully savaged, and some of them killed. The jaws are very powerful and inflict a merciless bite. In captivity the animals must be carefully handled, as they sometimes grow very vicious.

Zebras are noisy, much more so than any antelope. Their barking cry—qua-ha, or ba-ha—sounds not unlike that of a dog when heard at a distance; watching from behind a bush we have seen the stallions canter close by with ears forward and mouths open as they uttered this cry. They often utter it when leaving a pool after drinking, or when their alarm or curiosity is excited; and often for no reason as far as we could discern.

Game differ wonderfully in tameness and shyness, both individually and locally; and, moreover, individuals will be shy at one time, and, for no apparent reason, tame at another. On the whole, however, the common zebra is among the tamest of African game. It is, moreover, much influenced by curiosity. Again and again herds have stood watching us from different sides, even down wind, as we sat under a tree eating lunch or resting. Zebras are quick to catch motion, but will feed right up to a man lying motionless, especially if he is under or beside even the smallest and most scantily leaved bush. Their sense of smell is keen, as with all game.

They are grass-eaters, and are emphatically animals of the open plains, seeming to be indifferent as to whether these are entirely bare of trees or are thinly dotted with occasional thorny acacias. We never saw them in anything resembling thick cover, not even in such cover as that to which their companions, the hartebeests, sometimes penetrated; but in places they seemed to like the plains over which acacias were scattered, and would stand or rest at mid-day in their shade. As with other game, it was astonishing to see how they abounded, and how fat they became, in dry, open country, where water was scarce and the pasturage brown and withered. As long as they could reach water once in twenty-four hours, and find abundant pasturage of the kind they liked—no matter how dry— within eight or ten miles of the water, they throve. In such a district they lived throughout the year, seeming to migrate much less freely than the wildebeest and some other game—in fact, the only migrations we heard of were those occurring when they had to leave a given district because the water and herbage failed outright. On the Athi and Kapiti Plains we were informed by the settlers that the zebras stayed all the time, with very slight shifts of a few miles one way or the other, as the different series of pools dried or filled. In the Sotik we were informed that in times of drought the zebra and almost all the other game were obliged to abandon extensive regions in which they swarmed after the rains. Like so many big animals, zebras are not favored by a rank and luxurious plant growth. We never saw them in the forests or thick, wet bush. There were none on the cold, well-watered slopes of Kenia, with their thick growth of bush grass. They were not abundant in any of the regions fitted for a thick, agricultural population. The country which they most affected was like our own Western ranch country: the grass grew thick and fairly high on it for a short period after the rains, but during most of the time it was dry, and the grass withered and short; the trees were acacias or euphorbias, or on the lower grounds palms.

Few things are more interesting or puzzling to the naturalist in East Africa than the distribution of the various big animals. The limits of the range of many species seem in our eyes purely arbitrary, uninfluenced by any physical barriers; doubtless there is an explanation, but it has not yet been discovered. In most places the big and the small gazelles are found in abundance on the same plains, but, although there seems no change in the country, except that the altitude is lower, the small gazelles are not found northward along the Northern Guaso Nyiro, where one form of the big gazelle abounds. The wildebeest abounds in the Sotik and on the Athi and Kapiti Plains, but is not found along the Northern Guaso Nyiro. The hartebeests are the most abundant big mammals throughout their range; one species, the Coke, is the commonest game of the Sotik and the Athi, another, the Jackson, the commonest game in the 'Nzoia country, neither intruding on the range of the other, and both being absent from the Northern Guaso Nyiro, where the oryx is common; and in this case the explanation of altitude, which can be given as regards the small gazelle, does not apply, for hartebeests are found on the Nile where the altitude is the same as that of the Northern Guaso Nyiro. But the common zebra covers the range of all these animals in East Africa. It is abundant in the Sotik and on the Athi and Kapiti Plains, although inferior in number to the Coke hartebeest, with which it there associates together with the wildebeest and big and little gazelles; but the causes, whatever they are, which so sharply limit the range of the Coke hartebeest and wildebeest do not affect the zebra, which is also plentiful along the Northern Guaso Nyiro in company with the oryx and the big Grévy zebra. On the other hand, while the zebra's range overlaps that of the big hartebeests, the latter extend far to the westward of the regions in which the zebras are found; we found no zebras in the brush-covered and fairly well wooded and watered districts of Uganda in which hartebeests were not uncommon, and we saw none along the upper White Nile in regions in which hartebeests were plentiful and which were seemingly in their essential characteristics like the Sotik and the Athi, but they are known to occur locally in these regions. Moreover, while the hartebeests have become differentiated into sharply defined and totally distinct species, the common zebra extends over a range which includes several of these hartebeest species, without itself undergoing anything like the same differentiation; in fact, the different varieties of the common zebra grade into one another, from the southern form with white legs to the more richly colored northern form with fully striped legs.

Where water is plentiful and the pasturage good a herd of zebra will contentedly exist within an area of a dozen miles square, or less. In the absence of hunters such a herd normally leads an uneventful life, the placidity of which is disturbed only by the ravages of the lion. Most of the zebra's existence is spent in eating, and most of the remainder in sleeping or in drowsy rest. If undisturbed and unalarmed the herds, after drinking, graze off toward their favorite feeding grounds, or, if the grass is poor in the intervening country, walk or canter toward them, strung out in Indian file. After eating their temporary fill of grass they rest for three or four hours, sometimes lying down, more often standing. Most often they may be found resting right in the open plain; but if a clump of thorn-trees is handy they may stand or lie in the slight shade of their thinly leaved branches. After resting the herd rises and slowly grazes back to the waterhole or river. They may drink only once a day, but they are thirsty animals and prefer to visit the water at least twice every twenty-four hours. We have seen them drink in the morning and afternoon and late evening; they also drink at night. Noon is their favorite hour for rest, but they are by no means regular, and they sometimes rest at night, although we believe that they generally spend the night feeding, and are then more alert than in the daytime.

Night is the lion's hunting season, and the sight or smell of him or even the suspicion of him at that time throws the animals he hunts into a frenzy of terror. Under the influence of these ever-recurring panics, the

zebras stampede in a mad rush. This habit makes them obnoxious to the
settlers, for they are powerful animals with thick skins, and in such a
stampede they go right through any wire fence; while they are of no value
to the settlers except for their hides, as their flesh is not good eating from
the white man's standpoint, although most of the natives devour it greedily. During the moments of panic the zebra's terror is like the horrible fear
felt in a nightmare, and under its influence the animal will rush anywhere;
but as with other wild beasts the feeling is as short-lived as it is intense.
If one of their number has been killed the herd may wander about for a few
minutes whinnying; but after these few minutes they settle down to their
ordinary life business, and feed, or rest, or make love, or fight as before.
Night is a time of frequent panic, but during the day there is little fear of
present molestation, and nothing either of remembrance of past or anticipation of future molestation. In approaching the drinking-places there is
usually much watchfulness and suspicion, the advance being made by fits
and starts, with halts and sudden backward wheels; for, although the lion
generally kills them on the open plain, he also often lies in wait for them by
some much-frequented pool.

We have already discussed the alleged "protective coloration" of big
game. As regards the game of the open plains protective coloration plays
practically no part; and as regards the zebra it plays absolutely no part
whatever. Under the glaring African sun, and in the African landscape, any
animal, of any color or shape, is sometimes hard to see—a rhino, buffalo,
giraffe, or zebra, or even an elephant; and there are exceptional circumstances under which any conceivable color or coloration scheme will
merge the wearer with the surrounding. But the game animals of the East
African plains do not rely on their coloration for their protection; they are
colored in all kinds of ways, and they are neither helped nor hurt by their
coloration, whether it is concealing or revealing. The zebra has an advertising coloration; that is, its coloration reveals it far more often than it conceals it. It is less conspicuous than the wildebeest, sable, or topi; about as
conspicuous as the hartebeest; and much more conspicuous than the
eland, oryx, roan, Grant gazelle, or Thomson gazelle. When coming to
water it is, of course, in motion, never attempts to hide or slink, and is
always and under all circumstances conspicuous to every beast of prey in
the neighborhood. After drinking it immediately returns to the open country, where it can be seen at once even by dull eyes. When standing or lying
down under acacia-trees at noon it shows up as above indicated—more
conspicuously than an eland or oryx, less so than a wildebeest. The stripes,

when they can be seen at all, have an advertising effect; this is especially true of the broad rump stripes which advertise the animal at a distance at which the big Grévy zebra seems gray like an ass. At a distance the zebra is apt to look white or black, according as the sun strikes it, and then gray. Even while standing still under a thorn-tree, in the puzzling lights and shadows which tend to conceal any animal of any color, the zebra frequently whisks its tail, which at once attracts attention. All game animals with long tails are continually twitching or swinging them, and this motion catches the eye at once, even at a distance at which the coloration would neither conceal nor reveal the wearer. The only time we ever saw zebras helped by any concealing quality of their coloration was once when we found a few standing in partially burnt grass; the infrequent black or yellow stalks harmonized well with their coats, and made it difficult to see them.

At nightfall all animals become hard to see, of course; and in thick darkness all are alike invisible. In dusk, in moonlight, and on very clear, moonless nights, we found that grayish, countershaded animals like domestic asses, and eland and oryx, were most difficult to see. Zebras were much more clearly visible; they seemed whitish; if close up their stripes could be made out. Mr. Selous has recorded an interesting observation to this effect: he found that even the Grévy zebra, which is less conspicuously colored than the common kind, showed up at night more plainly than eland, oryx, or koodoo, and that in the moonlight the stripes were very distinct, making the animal readily visible.

On the Athi and Kapiti Plains ticks swarmed, and they clustered in masses around the eyes of the zebras and in the groin, and wherever there was bare skin. Yet, in spite of the abundance of these loathsome creatures, the zebras were fat and in high condition. Ticks were much less plentiful both in the Sotik and along the Northern Guaso Nyiro. Wherever they teemed, as they did on the Kapiti Plains, it was hard to understand how the game supported their presence. But the zebra and antelope were just as fat there as elsewhere. Evidently the ticks did not really trouble them, whereas the biting flies bothered them greatly.

All animals which live in herds tend to develop a herd leader. This herd leader sometimes may, and sometimes may not, be the master male. Thus in a herd of wapiti, containing a heavy master bull, we have seen an old cow assume complete leadership, watching while the herd was at rest and leading the others whenever the herd was in motion. We also once saw a Tommy doe, which was associating with four Grant gazelles, take complete charge of the whole party, its big associates following it submissively wherever it led. It seemed as if in the zebra herds the master stallion generally acted as leader, when there was any leader. He would round up the mares and drive them whither he wished; and he would trot a few paces toward any strange object, leaving the herd behind and watching intently, with ears pricked forward. We have never been able to watch a herd of wild game close enough to tell whether the individuals all fall into an ordered system of precedence, as ranch cattle do, where gradually each steer, bull, or cow seems to accept its exact place with reference to its fellows.

THE NARWHAL

BARRY LOPEZ

The first narwhals I ever saw lived far from here, in Bering Strait. The day I saw them I knew that no element of the earth's natural history had ever before brought me so far, so suddenly. It was as though something from a bestiary had taken shape, a creature strange as a giraffe. It was as if the testimony of someone I had no reason to doubt, yet could not quite believe, a story too farfetched, had been verified at a glance.

I was with a bowhead whale biologist named Don Ljungblad, flying search transects over Bering Sea. It was May, and the first bowheads of spring were slowly working their way north through Bering Strait toward their summer feeding grounds in the Chukchi and Beaufort seas. Each day as we flew these transects we would pass over belukha whale and walrus, ringed, spotted, and ribbon seals, bearded seals, and flocks of birds migrating to Siberia. I know of no other region in North America where animals can be met with in such numbers. Bering Sea itself is probably the richest of all the northern seas, as rich as Chesapeake Bay or the Grand Banks at the time of their discovery. Its bounty of crabs, pollock, cod, sole, herring, clams, and salmon is set down in wild numbers, the rambling digits of guesswork. The numbers of birds and marine mammals feeding here, to a person familiar with anything but the Serengeti or life at the Antarctic convergence, are magical. At the height of migration in the spring, the testament of life in Bering Sea is absolutely stilling in its dimensions.

The two weeks I spent flying with Ljungblad, with so many thousands of creatures moving through the water and the air, were a heady experience. Herds of belukha whale glided in silent shoals beneath transparent sheets of young ice. Squadrons of fast-flying sea ducks flashed beneath us as they banked away. We passed ice floes stained red in a hundred places with the afterbirths of walrus. Staring all day into the bright light reflected from the ice and water, however, and the compression in time of these extraordinary events, left me dazed some evenings.

Aspects of the arctic landscape that had become salient for me—its real and temporal borders: a rare, rich oasis of life surrounded by vast stretches of deserted land; the up-ending of conventional kinds of time; biological vulnerability made poignant by the forgiving light of summer— all of this was evoked over Bering Sea.

The day we saw the narwhals we were flying south, low over Bering Strait. The ice in Chukchi Sea behind us was so close it did not seem possible that bowheads could have penetrated this far; but it is good to check, because they can make headway in ice as heavy as this and they are able to come a long way north undetected in lighter ice on the Russian side. I was daydreaming about two bowheads we had seen that morning. They had been floating side by side in a broad lane of unusually clear water between a shelf of shorefast ice and the pack ice—the flaw lead. As we passed over, they made a single movement together, a slow, rolling turn and graceful glide, like figure skaters pushing off, these 50-ton leviathans. Ljungblad shouted in my earphones: "Waiting." They were waiting for the ice in the strait to open up. Ljungblad saw nearly 300 bowheads waiting calmly like this one year, some on their backs, some with their chins resting on the ice.

The narwhals appeared in the middle of this reverie. Two males, with ivory tusks spiraling out of their foreheads, the image of the unicorn with which history has confused them. They were close to the same size and light-colored, and were lying parallel and motionless in a long, straight lead in the ice. My eye was drawn to them before my conscious mind, let alone my voice, could catch up. I stared dumbfounded while someone else shouted. Not just to see the narwhals, but *here*, a few miles northwest of King Island in Bering Sea. In all the years scientists have kept records for these waters, no one had ever seen a narwhal alive in Bering Sea. Judging from the heaviness of the ice around them, they must have spent the winter here.* They were either residents, a wondrous thought, or they had

---

*The narwhal is not nearly as forceful in the ice as the bowhead. It can break through only about 6 inches of ice with its head. A bowhead, using its brow or on occasion its more formidable chin, can break through as much as 18 inches of sea ice.

come from the nearest population centers the previous fall, from waters north of Siberia or from northeastern Canada.

The appearance of these animals was highly provocative. We made circle after circle above them, until they swam away under the ice and were gone. Then we looked at each other. Who could say what this was, really?

Because you have seen something doesn't mean you can explain it. Differing interpretations will always abound, even when good minds come to bear. The kernel of indisputable information is a dot in space; interpretations grow out of the desire to make this point a line, to give it a direction. The directions in which it can be sent, the uses to which it can be put by a culturally, professionally, and geographically diverse society, are almost without limit. The possibilities make good scientists chary. In a region like the Arctic, tense with a hunger for wealth, with fears of plunder, interpretation can quickly get beyond a scientist's control. When asked to assess the meaning of a biological event—What were those animals doing out there? Where do they belong?—they hedge. They are sometimes reluctant to elaborate on what they saw, because they cannot say what it means, and they are suspicious of those who say they know. Some even distrust the motives behind the questions.

I think along these lines in this instance because of the animal. No large mammal in the Northern Hemisphere comes as close as the narwhal to having its very existence doubted. For some, the possibility that this creature might actually live in the threatened waters of Bering Sea is portentous, a significant apparition on the eve of an era of disruptive oil exploration there. For others, those with the leases to search for oil and gas in Navarin and Norton basins, the possibility that narwhals may live there is a complicating environmental nuisance. Hardly anyone marvels solely at the fact that on the afternoon of April 16, 1982, five people saw two narwhals in a place so unexpected that they were flabbergasted. They remained speechless, circling over the animals in a state of wonder. In those moments the animals did not have to mean anything at all.

※　※　※

We know more about the rings of Saturn than we know about the narwhal. Where do they go and what do they eat in the winter, when it is too dark and cold for us to find them? The Chilean poet and essayist Pablo Neruda wonders in his memoirs how an animal this large can have remained so obscure and uncelebrated. Its name, he thought, was "the most beautiful of undersea names, the name of a sea chalice that sings, the name of a crystal spur." Why, he wondered, had no one taken Narwhal for a last name, or built "a beautiful Narwhal Building?"

Part of the answer lies with a regrettable connotation of death in the animal's name. The pallid color of the narwhal's skin has been likened to that of a drowned human corpse, and it is widely thought that its name came from the Old Norse for "corpse" and "whale," *nár* + *hvalr*. A medieval belief that the narwhal's flesh was poisonous has been offered in support of this interpretation, as well as the belief that its "horn" was proof at that time against being poisoned. The eighteenth-century naturalist Buffon characterized the animal for all the generations that would read him as one that "revels in carnage, attacks without provocation, and kills without need." Among its associations with human enterprise in the inhospitable north is the following grim incident. In 1126, Arnhald, first bishop of Iceland, was shipwrecked off the Icelandic coast. Drowned men and part of the contents of the ship's hold washed up in a marsh, a place afterward called the Pool of Corpses. Conspicuous among the items of salvage were a number of narwhal tusks, "with runic letters upon them in an indelible red gum so that each sailor might know his own at the end of the voyage."

W. P. Lehmann, a professor of Germanic languages, believes the association with death is a linguistic accident. The Old Norse *nárhvalr* (whence the English *narwhal*, the French *narval*, the German *Narwal*, etc.), he says, was a vernacular play on the word *nahvalr*—the way *high-bred corn* is used in place of *hybrid corn*, or *sparrowgrass* is used for *asparagus*. According to Lehmann, *nahvalr* is an earlier, West Norse term meaning a "whale distinguished by a long, narrow projection" (the tusk).

Some, nevertheless, still call the narwhal "the corpse whale," and the unfounded belief that it is a cause of human death, or an omen or symbol to be associated with human death, remains intact to this day in some quarters. Animals are often fixed like this in history, bearing an unwarranted association derived from notions or surmise having no connection at all with their real life. The fuller explanations of modern field biology are an antidote, in part, to this tendency to name an animal carelessly. But it is also, as Neruda suggests, a task of literature to take animals regularly from the shelves where we have stored them, like charms or the most intricate of watches, and to bring them to life.

The obscurity of narwhals is not easily breeched by science. To begin with, they live underwater. And they live year-round in the polar ice, where the logistics and expense involved in approaching them are formidable barriers to field research, even in summer. Scientists have largely been limited to watching what takes place at the surface of the water in the open sea adjacent to observation points high on coastal bluffs. And to putting hydrophones in the water with them, and to making comparisons with the belukha whale, a close and better-known relative. About the regular periodic events of their lives, such as migration, breeding, and calving, in relation to climatic changes and fluctuations in the size of the population, we know next to nothing.*

Scientists can speak with precision only about the physical animal, not the ecology or behavior of this social and gregarious small whale. (It is the latter, not the former, unfortunately, that is most crucial to an understanding of how industrial development might affect narwhals.) Adult males, 16 feet long and weighing upwards of 3300 pounds, are about a quarter again as large as adult females. Males are also distinguished by an ivory tusk that pierces the upper lip on the lift side and extends forward as much as 10 feet. Rarely, a female is found with a tusk, and, more rarely still, males and females with tusks on both sides of the upper jaw.

From the side, compared with the rest of its body, the narwhal's head seems small and blunt. It is dominated by a high, rounded forehead filled with bioacoustical lipids—special fats that allow the narwhal to use sound waves to communicate with other whales and to locate itself and other objects in its three-dimensional world. Its short front flippers function as little more than diving planes. The cone-shaped body tapers from just behind these flippers—where its girth is greatest, as much as eight feet—to a vertical ellipse at the tail. In place of a dorsal fin, a low dorsal ridge about five feet long extends in an irregular crenulation down the back. The tail flukes are unique. Seen from above, they appear heartshaped, like a ginkgo leaf, with a deep-notched center and trailing edges that curve far forward.

Viewed from the front, the head seems somewhat squarish and asymmetrical, and oddly small against the deep chest. The mouth, too, seems small for such a large animal, with the upper lip just covering the edge of a short, wedge-shaped jaw. The eyes are located just above and behind the upturned corners of the mouth, which gives the animal a bemused

---

*The knowledge and insight of Eskimos on these points, unfortunately, are of little help. Of all the areas of natural history in which they show expertise, native hunters are weakest in their understanding of the population dynamics of migratory animals. The reason is straightforward. Too much of the animal's life is lived "outside the community," beyond the geographic and phenomenological landscape the Eskimos share with them.

expression. (The evolutionary loss of facial muscles, naturalist Peter War-shall has noted, means no quizzical wrinkling of the forehead, no raised eyebrow of disbelief, no pursed lip of determination.) A single, crescent-shaped blowhole on top of the head is in a transverse line with the eyes.

Narwhal calves are almost uniformly gray. Young adults show spread-ing patches and streaks of white on the belly and marbling on the flanks. Adults are dark gray across the top of the head and down the back. Lighter grays predominate on top of the flippers and flukes, whites and light yellow-whites underneath. The back and flanks are marbled with blackish grays. Older animals, especially males, may be almost entirely white. Females, say some, are always lighter-colored on their flanks.

The marbled quality of the skin, which feels like smooth, oiled stone, is mesmerizing. On the flukes especially, where curvilinear streaks of dark gray overlap whitish-gray tones, the effect could not be more painterly. Elsewhere on the body, spots dominate. "These spots," writes William Scoresby, "are of a roundish or oblong form: on the back, where they seldom exceed two inches in diameter, they are the darkest and most crowded together, yet with intervals of pure white among them. On the side the spots are fainter, smaller, and more open. On the belly, they become extremely faint and few, and in considerable surfaces are not to be seen." These patterns completely penetrate the skin, which is a half-inch thick.

In the water, depending on sunlight and the color of the water itself, narwhals, according to British whaling historian Basil Lubbock, take on "many hues, from deep sea green to even an intense lake [blue] colour."

Narwhals are strong swimmers, with the ability to alter the contours of their body very slightly to reduce turbulence. Their speed and maneu-verability are sufficient to hunt down swift prey—arctic cod, Greenland halibut, redfish—and to avoid their enemies, the orca and the Greenland shark.

Narwhals live in close association with ice margins and are sometimes found far inside heavy pack ice, miles from open water. (How they deter-mine whether the lead systems they follow into the ice will stay open behind them, ensuring their safe return, is not known.) They manage to survive in areas of strong currents and wind where the movement of ice on the surface is violent and where leads open and close, or freeze over, very quickly. (Like seabirds, they seem to have an uncanny sense of when a particular lead is going to close in on them, and they leave.) That they are not infallible in anticipating the movement and formation of ice, which seals them off from the open air and oxygen, is attested to by a relatively unusual and often fatal event called a savssat.

Savssats are most commonly observed on the west coast of Greenland. Late in the fall, while narwhals are still feeding deep in a coastal fiord, a band of ice may form in calm water across the fiord's mouth. The ice sheet may then expand toward the head of the fiord. At some point the distance from its landward to its seaward edge exceeds the distance a narwhal can travel on a single breath. By this time, too, shorefast ice may have formed at the head of the fiord, and it may grow out to meet the sea ice. The narwhals are thus crowded into a smaller and smaller patch of open water. Their bellowing and gurgling, their bovinelike moans and the plosive screech of their breathing, can sometimes be heard at a great distance.

The Danish scientist Christian Vibe visited a savssat on March 16, 1943, on the west coast of central Greenland. Hundreds of narwhals and belukhas were trapped in an opening less than 20 feet square. The black surface of the water was utterly "calm and still," writes Vibe. "Then the smooth surface was suddenly broken by black shadows and white animals which in elegant curves came up and disappeared—narwhals and white whales by the score. Side by side they emerged so close to each other that some of them would be lifted on the backs of the others and turn a somersault with the handsome tail waving in the air. First rows of narwhal, then white whales and then again narwhals—each species separately. It seethed, bobbed, and splashed in the opening. With a hollow, whistling sound they inhaled the air as if sucking it in through long iron tubes. The water was greatly disturbed ... and the waves washed far in over the ice." The splashed water froze to the rim of the breathing hole, as did the moisture from their exhalations, further reducing the size of the savssat. In spite of the frenzy, not a single animal that Vibe saw was wounded by the huge tusks of the narwhal.*

The narwhal is classed in the suborder Odontoceti, with toothed whales such as the sperm whale, in the superfamily Delphinoidea, along with porpoises and dolphins, and in the family Monodontidae with a single companion, the belukha. In contrast to the apparently coastally-

---

*Eskimo hunters killed 340 narwhals and belukhas at this savssat in a week, before the ice fractured and the rest escaped. In the spring of 1915, Eskimos at Disko Bay took more than a thousand narwhals and belukhas at two savssats over a period of several months. Inattentive birds, especially thick-billed murres and dovekies which require a lot of open water to take off, may also suddenly find themselves with insufficient room and may be trapped.

adapted belukha, biologists believe the narwhal is a pelagic or open-ocean species, that it winters farther to the north. Extrapolating on the basis of what is known of the belukha, it is thought that narwhal breed in April and give birth to a single, five-foot, 170-pound calf about fourteen months later, in June or July. Calves carry an inch-thick layer of blubber at birth to protect them against the cold water. They appear to nurse for about two years and may stay with their mothers for three years, or more. Extrapolating once again from the belukha, it is thought that females reach sexual maturity between four and seven years of age, males between eight and nine years.

Narwhals are usually seen in small groups of two to eight animals, frequently of the same sex and age. In the summer, female groups, which include calves, are sometimes smaller or more loosely knit than male groups. During spring migration, herds may consist of 300 or more animals.

Narwhals feed largely on arctic and polar cod, Greenland halibut, redfish, sculpins, and other fish, on squid and to some extent on shrimps of several kinds, and on octopus and crustaceans. They have a complex, five-chambered stomach that processes food quickly, leaving undigested the chitinous beaks of squid and octopus, the carapaces of crustaceans, and the ear bones and eye lenses of fish, from which biologists can piece together knowledge of their diets.

Two types of "whale lice" (actually minute crustaceans) cling to their skin, in the cavity where the tusk passes through the lip, in the tail notch in the flukes, and in wounds (all places where they are least likely to be swept off by the flow of water past the narwhal's body). The tracks of the sharp, hooked legs of these tiny creatures are sometimes very clear on a narwhal's skin. Older animals may carry such infestations of these parasites as to cause an observer to wince.

❋   ❋   ❋

If you were to stand at the edge of a sea cliff on the north coast of Borden Peninsula, Baffin Island, you could watch narwhals migrating past more or less continuously for several weeks in the twenty-four-hour light of June. You would be struck by their agility and swiftness, by the synchronicity of their movements as they swam and dived in unison, and by the quality of alert composure in them, of capability in the face of whatever might happen. Their attractiveness lies partly with their strong, graceful movements in three dimensions, like gliding birds on an airless day. An impressive form of their synchronous behavior is their ability to deep-dive in groups. They disappear as a single diminishing shape, gray fading to darkness. They reach depths of 1000 feet or more, and their intent, often, is then to drive schools of polar cod toward the surface at such a rate that the fish lose consciousness from the too-rapid expansion of their swim bladders. At the surface, thousands of these stunned fish feed narwhals and harp seals, and rafts of excited northern fulmars and kittiwakes.

Watching from high above, one is also struck by the social interactions of narwhals, which are extensive and appear to be well organized according to hierarchies of age and sex. The socializing of males frequently involves the use of their tusks. They cross them like swords above the water, or one forces another down by pressing his tusk across the other's back, or they face each other head-on, their tusks side by side.

Helen Silverman, whose graduate work included a study of the social organization and behavior of narwhals, describes as typical the following scene, from her observations in Lancaster Sound. "On one occasion a group of five narwhals consisting of two adult males, one adult female, one [calf] and one juvenile were moving west with the males in the lead. The group stopped and remained on the surface for about 30 [seconds]. One male turned, moved under the [calf], and lifted it out of the water twice. There was no apparent reaction from the mother. The male then touched the side of the female with the tip of its tusk and the group continued westward."

Sitting high on a sea cliff in sunny, blustery weather in late June—the familiar sense of expansiveness, of deep exhilaration such weather brings over one, combined with the opportunity to watch animals, is summed up in a single Eskimo word: *quviannikumut*, "to feel deeply happy"—sitting here like this, it is easy to fall into speculation about the obscure narwhal. From the time I first looked into a narwhal's mouth, past the accordian pleats of its tongue, at the soft white interior splashed with Tyrian purple, I have thought of their affinity with sperm whales, whose mouths are similarly colored. Like the sperm whale, the narwhal is a deep diver. No other whales but the narwhal and the sperm whale are known to sleep on the surface for hours at a time. And when the narwhal lies at the surface, it lies like a sperm whale, with the section of its back from blowhole to dorsal ridge exposed, and the rest of its back and tail hanging down in the water. Like the sperm whale, it is renowned for its teeth; and it has been pursued, though briefly, for the fine oils in its forehead.

Like all whales, the narwhal's evolutionary roots are in the Cretaceous, with insect-eating carnivores that we, too, are descended from. Its line of development through the Cretaceous and into the Paleocene follows that of artiodactyls like the hippopotamus and the antelope—and then it takes a radical turn. After some 330 million years on dry land, since it emerged from the sea during the Devonian period 380 million years ago, the line of genetic development that will produce whales returns to the world's oceans. The first proto-whales turn up in the Eocene, 45 million years ago, the first toothed whales 18 million years later, in the Oligocene. By then, the extraordinary adjustments that had to take place to permit air-breathing mammals to live in the sea were largely complete.

Looking down from the sea cliffs at a lone whale floating peacefully in the blue-green water, it is possible to meditate on these evolutionary changes in the mammalian line, to imagine this creature brought forward in time to this moment. What were once its rear legs have disappeared, though the skeleton still shows the trace of a pelvis. Sea water gave it such buoyancy that it required little in the way of a skeletal structure; it therefore has achieved a large size without loss of agility. It left behind it a world of oscillating temperatures (temperatures on the arctic headland from which I gaze may span a range of 120°F over twelve months) for a world where the temperature barely fluctuates. It did not relinquish its warm-blooded way of life, however; it is insulated against the cold with a layer of blubber two to four inches thick.

The two greatest changes in its body have been in the way it now stores and uses oxygen, and in a rearrangement of its senses to suit a world that is largely acoustical, not visual or olfactory, in its stimulations.

When I breathe this arctic air, 34 percent of the oxygen is briefly stored in my lungs, 41 percent in my blood, 13 percent in my muscles, and 12 percent in the tissues of other of my organs. I take a deep breath only when I am winded or in a state of emotion; the narwhal always takes a deep breath—its draft of this same air fills its small lungs completely. And it stores the oxygen differently, so it can draw on it steadily during a fifteen-minute dive. Only about 9 percent stays in its lungs, while 41 percent goes into the blood, another 41 percent into the muscles, and about 9 percent into other tissues. The oxygen is bound to hemoglobin molecules in its blood (no different from my own), and to myoglobin molecules in its muscles. (The high proportion of myoglobin in its muscles makes the narwhal's muscle meat dark maroon, like the flesh of all marine mammals.)

Changes in the narwhal's circulatory system—the evolution of *rete mirabile*, "wonder nets" of blood vessels; an enlargement of its hepatic veins; a reversible flow of blood at certain places—have allowed it to adapt comfortably to the great pressures it experiences during deep dives.

There is too little nitrogen in its blood for "the bends" to occur when it surfaces. Carbon dioxide, the by-product of respiration, is effectively stored until it can be explosively expelled with a rapid flushing of the lungs.

It is only with an elaborate apparatus of scuba gear, decompression tanks, wet suits, weight belts, and swim fins that we can explore these changes. Even then it is hard to appreciate the radical alteration of mammalian development that the narwhal represents. First, ours is largely a two-dimensional world. We are not creatures who look up often. We are used to exploring "the length and breadth" of issues, not their "height." For the narwhal there are very few two-dimensional experiences—the sense of the water it feels at the surface of its skin, and that plane it must break in order to breathe.

The second constraint on our appreciation of the narwhal's world is that it "knows" according to a different hierarchy of senses than the one we are accustomed to. Its chemical senses of taste and smell are all but gone, as far as we know, though narwhals probably retain an ability to determine salinity. Its tactile sense remains acute. Its sensitivity to pressure is elevated—it has a highly discriminating feeling for depth and a hunter's sensitivity to the slight turbulence created by a school of cod cruising ahead of it in its dimly lit world. The sense of sight is atrophied, because of a lack of light. The eye, in fact, has changed in order to accommodate itself to high pressures, the chemical irritation of salt, a constant rush of water past it, and the different angle of refraction of light underwater. (The narwhal sees the world above water with an eye that does not move in its socket, with astigmatic vision and a limited ability to change the distance at which it can focus.)

How different must be "the world" for such a creature, for whom sight is but a peripheral sense, who occupies, instead, a three-dimensional acoustical space. Perhaps only musicians have some inkling of the formal shape of emotions and motivation that might define such a sensibility.

The Arctic Ocean can seem utterly silent on a summer day to an observer standing far above. If you lowered a hydrophone, however, you would discover a sphere of "noise" that only spectrum analyzers and tape recorders could unravel. The tremolo moans of bearded seals. The electric crackling of shrimp. The baritone boom of walrus. The high-pitched bark and yelp of ringed seals. The clicks, pure tones, birdlike trills, and harmonics of belukhas and narwhals. The elephantine trumpeting of bowhead whales. Added to these animal noises would be the sounds of shifting sediments on the sea floor, the whine and fracture of sea ice, and the sound of deep-keeled ice grounding in shallow water.

The narwhal is not only at home in this "cacophony," as possessed of the sense of a neighborhood as we might conceivably be on an evening stroll, but it manages to appear "asleep," oblivious at the surface of the water on a summer day in Lancaster Sound.

The single most important change that took place in the whale's acoustical system to permit it to live in this world was the isolation of its auditory canals from each other. It could then receive waterborne sound independently on each side of its head and so determine the direction from which a sound was coming. (We can do this only in the open air; underwater, sound vibrates evenly through the bones of our head.) The narwhal, of course, receives many sounds; we can only speculate about what it pays attention to, or what information it may obtain from all that it hears. Conversely, narwhals also emit many sounds important, presumably, to narwhals and to other animals too.

Acoustical scientists divide narwhal sound into two categories. Respiratory sounds are audible to us as wheezes, moans, whistles, and gurgles of various sorts. The second group of sounds, those associated with, presumably, echo-location and communication, scientists divide into three categories: clicking, generated at rates as high as 500 clicks per second; pulsed tones; and pure tones. (Certain of these sounds are audible to someone in a boat in the open air, like an effervescence rising from the surface of the water.)

Narwhals, it is believed, use clicking sounds to locate themselves, their companions, their prey, and such things as floe edges and the trend of leads. Pulsed tones are thought to be social in nature and susceptible to individual modification, so each narwhal has a "signature" tone or call of its own. Pure-tone signals, too, are thought to be social or communicative in function. According to several scientists writing in the *Journal of the Acoustical Society of America*, the narwhal "seems much less noisy [than the belukha], appears to have a smaller variety of sounds, and produces many that are outside the limits of human hearing." A later study, however, found narwhals "extremely loquacious underwater," and noted that tape recordings were "almost saturated with acoustic signals of highly variable duration and frequency composition." The same study concluded, too, that much of the narwhal's acoustically related behavior "remains a matter of conjecture."

I dwell on all this because of a routine presumption—that the whale's ability to receive and generate sound indicates it is an "intelligent" creature—and an opposite presumption, evident in a Canadian government report, that the continuous racket of a subsea drilling operation, with the attendant din of ship and air traffic operations, "would not be expected to be a hazard [to narwhals] because of ... the assumed high levels of ambient underwater noise in Lancaster Sound."

It is hard to believe in an imagination so narrow in its scope, so calloused toward life, that it could write these last words. Cetaceans may well be less "intelligent," less defined by will, imagination, and forms of logic, than we are. But the *idea* that they are intelligent, and that they would be affected by such man-made noise, is not so much presumption as an expression of a possibility, the taking of a respectful attitude toward a mystery we can do no better than name "narwhal." Standing at the edge of a cliff, studying the sea-washed back of such a creature far below, as still as a cenobite in prayer, the urge to communicate, the upwelling desire, is momentarily sublime.

I stare out into Lancaster Sound. Four or five narwhals sleep on a flat calm sea, as faint on the surface as the first stars emerging in an evening sky. Birds in the middle and far distance slide through the air, bits of life that dwindle and vanish. Below, underneath the sleeping narwhal, fish surge and glide in the currents, and the light dwindles and is quenched.

* * *

The first description of a unicorn, according to British scholar Odell Shepard, appears in the writings of Ctesias, a Greek physician living in Persia in the fifth century B.C., who had heard reports of its existence from India. The existence of such an animal, a fierce, horselike creature of courageous temperament, with a single horn on its forehead, gained credibility later through the writings of Aristotle and Pliny and, later still, in the work of Isidore of Seville, an encyclopedist. The Bible became an unwitting and ironic authority for the unicorn's existence when Greek translators of the Septuagint rendered the Hebraic term *re'em* (meaning, probably, the now extinct aurochs, *Bos primigenius*) as "the unicorn."

The legend of the unicorn, and the subsequent involvement of the narwhal, is a story intriguing at many levels. Until well into the Middle Ages the legend passed only from one book to another, from one learned individual to another; it was not a part of the folk culture of Europe. During the Renaissance, scientists, scholars, and theologians put forth various learned "explanations" for the unicorn's existence. However far-fetched these explanations might have seemed to skeptics, the concrete evidence of a narwhal's tusk to hand seemed irrefutable. Furthermore, no Christian could deny the unicorn's existence without contradicting the Bible.

Scholars argue that the animal in Ctesias' original report from Persia represents the transposed idea of an oryx or a rhinoceros. It went unquestioned, they speculate, because Greeks such as Ctesias took "the grotesque monstrosities of Indian religious art" rendered in the Persian tapestries they saw for real animals. In medieval Europe, trade in rare narwhal and walrus tusks, confusion with the mythical animals of Zoroastrian as well as Christian tradition, and the bucolic practice of making bizarre alterations in the horns of domestic animals, all lent credence to the legend. The interest of the wealthy and learned in this regal animal, moreover, went beyond mere fascination; it was also practical. European royalty was besieged with politically motivated poisonings in the fourteenth and fifteenth centuries, and the unicorn's horn was reputedly the greatest proof against them.

In *The Lore of the Unicorn*, Odell Shepard writes of the great range of appreciation of Renaissance people for the unicorn's horn; it was "their companion on dark nights and in perilous places, and they held it near their hearts, handling it tenderly, as they would a treasure. For indeed it was exactly that. It preserved a man from the arrow that flieth by day and the pestilence that walketh in darkness, from the craft of the poisoner, from epilepsy, and from several less dignified ills of the flesh not to be named in so distinguished a connection. In short it was an amulet, a talisman, a weapon, and a medicine chest all in one."

The narwhal's tusk, traded in bits and pieces as the unicorn's horn, sold for a fortune in the Middle Ages, for twenty times its weight in gold. Shepard estimates that in mid-sixteenth-century Europe there were no more than fifty whole tusks to be seen, each with a detailed provenance. They were gifted upon royalty and the church and sought as booty by expeditionary forces who knew of their existence. Two tusks stolen from Constantinople in 1204 were delivered by Crusaders to the Cathedral of Saint Mark in Venice, where they may be seen to this day.

The presence of these tusks in Europe depended upon Greenlandic and Icelandic trade. The oddity was that they were delivered to Europe by men like those who drowned with the Bishop of Iceland, sailors with no notion of unicorns and no knowledge of the value of the tusk to those who did know. On the other hand, the tusk was frequently bought by people who had not the remotest notion of the existence of such an animal as the narwhal.

The first European to bring these disparate perceptions together, it seems, was the cartographer Gerhard Mercator, who clearly identified the narwhal as the source of the unicorn's horn in 1621. In 1638, Ole Wurm, a Danish professor and a "zoologist and antiquarian of high attainment," delivered a speech in Copenhagen in which he made the same connection. But by then the story of the unicorn was simply too firmly entrenched at too many levels of European society to be easily dispelled, and the horn itself was too dear an item of commerce to be declared suddenly worthless. Besides, it was argued, was not the tusk simply the horn of the unicorn of the sea? Why shouldn't it have the same power as the horn of the land unicorn?

Over time the narwhal's tusk lost its influence in medical circles, trade dwindled, and the legend itself passed out of the hands of ecclesiastics and scholars to the general populace, where it became dear to the hearts of romantics, artists, and poets. It was passed on, however, in a form quite different from the secular tradition in Ctesias. In its secular rendering the unicorn was a creature of nobility and awesome though benign power. It was a creature of compassion, though solitary, and indomitably fierce. It became, as such, the heraldic symbol of knights errant and of kings. It was incorporated into the British coat of arms by James I in 1603, and in 1671 Christian V became the first Danish king to be crowned in a coronation chair made entirely of narwhal tusks.

Under Christian influence, the story of the unicorn became the story of a captured and tamed beast. The animal lost its robust, independent qualities, that aloofness of the wild horse, and was presented as a small, goatlike animal subdued by a maiden in a pastoral garden. The central episode of its fabulous life, its power to turn a poisonous river into pure water so that other creatures might drink, as Moses had done with his staff at the waters of Marah, passed into oblivion. The creature of whom it was once written in Solinus' *Polyhistoria*, "It is an animal never to be taken alive—killed possibly, but not captured," became a symbol of domestic virginity and obeisance.

One winter afternoon in Vancouver, British Columbia, I spoke with the only person ever to have succeeded in putting an adult narwhal, briefly, on display. (The six animals, brought back from northern Canada in 1970, all died of pneumonia within a few months.) Murray Newman, director of the British Columbia Aquarium, explained the great difficulties inherent in capturing such animals and later of maintaining them in captivity, especially the male, with its huge tusk. He doubted any aquarium would ever manage it successfully. The destription from Solinus' *Polyhistoria* seemed at that moment, as we gazed across the aquarium's trimmed lawns toward Vancouver's harbor, oddly apt and prophetic.

※ ※ ※

A narwhal's tusk, hefted in the hands, feels stout but resilient. It is a round, evenly tapered shaft of ivory, hollow for most of its length. (The cavity is filled with dental pulp in the living animal.) A large tusk might weigh 20 pounds, be eight or nine feet long, and taper from a diameter of four inches at the socket down to a half-inch at the tip. The smooth, polished tip, two to three inches long, is roundly blunt or sometimes wedge-shaped. The rest of the tusk is striated in a regular pattern that spirals from right to left and may make five or six turns around the shaft before fading out. Often a single groove parallel to the spiraling strications is apparent. The tusk also shows a slight, very shallow ripple from end to end in many specimens.

The striated portion is rough to the touch, and its shallow grooves are frequently encrusted with algae. These microorganisms give the tusk a brindled greenish or maroon cast, contrasting with the white tip and with the 10 to 12 inches of yellower ivory normally embedded in the upper left side of the animal's skull.

Well into the nineteenth century there was a question about which of the sexes carried the tusk (or whether it might be both). Although many thought it was only the males, a clear understanding was confounded by authenticated reports of females with tusks (a female skull with *two* large tusks, in fact, was given to a Hamburg museum in 1684 by a German sea captain), and an announcement in 1700 by a German scientist, Solomon Reisel, that some narwhals carried "milk tusks." It did not help matters, either, that there was much conjecture but no agreement on the function of the tusk. (A more prosaic error further confused things—printers sometimes inadvertently reversed drawings, making it seem that the tusk came out of the right side of the head instead of the left, and that it spiraled from left to right.)

Several certainties eventually emerged. The tusk spirals from right to left. In normal development, two incipient tusks form as "teeth" in the upper jaw of both sexes, one on each side. In the female, both teeth usually harden into solid ivory rods with a protuberance at one end, like a meer-schaum pipe (these were Reisel's "*milk tusks*"). In males, the tusk on the right remains undeveloped, "a miniature piece of pig iron," while the one on the left almost always develops into a living organ, a continually growing, fully vascularized tooth. On very rare occasions, both tusks develop like this, in both sexes. And both tusks spiral from right to left (i.e., they are not symmetrical like the tusks of an elephant or a walrus). Viewed from above, twin tusks diverge slightly from each other. In some males the left tusk never develops (nor does the right in these instances). In perhaps 3 percent of females a single tusk develops on the left.

Solving this problem in sexual systematics and physiology proved simpler than determining the tusk's purpose. It was proposed as a rake, to stir up fish on the seabed floor; as a spear to impale prey; and as a defensive weapon. All three speculations ignored the needs of narwhals without tusks. In addition, Robin Best, a Canadian biologist with a long-standing interest in the question, has argued that the tusk is too brittle to stand repeated use as a rake or probe; that attacking the sorts of fish narwhals habitually eat with the tusk would be difficult and unnecessary and getting large fish off the tusk problematic; and that there are no records of narwhals attacking other animals or defending themselves with their tusks.

The fact that narwhals frequently cross their tusks out of water and that the base of the tusk is located in the sound-producing region of the narwhal's skull led to speculation that it might serve some role in sound reception or propagation (again ignoring the female component of the population). Oral surgeons determined that the tooth's pulp does not contain the bioacoustical lipads necessary for echolocation, but this does not mean that the narwhal can't in some way direct sound with it and, as some have suggested, "sound-joust" with other males. (On their own, the oral surgeons speculated that because the tooth was so highly vas-cularized, the narwhal could get rid of a significant amount of body heat this way, which would presumably allow males to hunt more energetically. The biologists said no.)

William Scoresby, as bright and keen-eyed an observer as ever went to sea, speculated in 1820 that the tusk was only a secondary sexual charac-teristic, like a beard in humans, and was perhaps used to fracture light ice when narwhals of both sexes needed to breathe. Scientists say narwhals are too careful with their tusks to subject them to such impact, but on the first point Scoresby was correct.

Male narwhals engage in comparative displays of their tusks, like the males of other species, but they also appear to make some kind of violent physical contact with each other occasionally. The heads of many sexually mature males are variously scarred, and scientists have even found the broken tips of tusks in wounded narwhals. (A scientist who made a detailed examination of the narwhal's musculature said the muscles are not there in the neck to allow the animals to parry and thrust with rapierlike movements. Indeed, males appear always to move their tusks with deliberation, and dexterously, as at savssats.) The circumstances under which head scarring might occur—the establishment and continual testing of a male social hierarchy, especially during the breeding season—are known; but how these wounds are suffered or how frequently they are inflicted is still widely debated. One plausible thought is that males align their tusks head-on and that the animal with the shorter tusk is grazed or sometimes severely poked in the process.

A significant number of narwhals, 20 to 30 percent, have broken tusks. Some broken tusks have a curious filling that effectively seals off the exposed pulp cavity. Oral surgeons say this rod-shaped plug is simply a normal deposition of "reparative dentine," but others have long insisted it is actually the tip of another narwhal's tusk, to which it bears an undeniable resemblance. (The broken tips of other narwhals' tusks are filled with stones and sediment.)

Exposed tooth pulp creates a site for infection, not to mention pain. That animals would try to fill the cavity (if "reparative dentine" didn't) makes sense. That one narwhal entices another into this ministration is as intriguing a notion as the thought that males put the tips of their tusks on the opposite male's sound-sensitive melon and generate a "message" in sound-jousting. It would be rash to insist categorically that narwhals don't do *something* odd with the tusk on occasion, like prodding a flatfish off the sea bottom. (Herman Melville drolly suggested they used it as a letter opener.) But it seems clear that its principal, and perhaps only, use is social. Robin Best argues, further, that because of its brittleness, its length, and the high proportion of broken tusks, the organ may have reached an evolutionary end point.

A remaining question is, Why is the tusk twisted? D'Arcy Wentworth Thompson, a renowned English biologist who died in 1948, offered a brilliant and cogent answer. He argued that the thrust of a narwhal's tail applied a very slight torque to its body. The tusk, suspended tightly but not rigidly in its socket in the upper jaw, resisted this force with a very slight degree of success. In effect, throughout its life, the narwhal revolved slowly around its own tusk, and over the years irregularities of the socket gouged the characteristic striations on the surface of the tooth.

Thompson pointed out that the tooth itself is not twisted—it is straight-grained ivory, engraved with a series of low-pitched threads. No one has disproved, proved, or improved upon Thompson's argument since he set it forth in 1942.

Because the ivory itself dried out and became brittle and hard to work, the greatest virtue of a narwhal tusk to the Eskimos who traditionally hunted the animal was its likeness to a wood timber. Some of the regions where narwhals were most intensively hunted were without either trees or supplies of driftwood. The tusk served in those places as a spear shaft, a tent pole, a sledge thwart, a cross brace—wherever something straight and long was required.

Narwhals were most often hunted by Eskimos during their near-shore migration in spring, and in bays and fiords during the summer. To my knowledge, Eskimos attach no great spiritual importance to the narwhal. Like the caribou, it is a migratory food animal whose spirit (*kirnniq*) is easily propitiated. The narwhal does not have the intercessionary powers or innate authority of the polar bear, the wolf, the walrus, or the raven.

Beyond its tusk, Greenlanders valued the narwhal's skin above all other leathers for dog harnesses, because it remained supple in very cold weather and did not stretch when it became wet. The sinews of the back were prized as thread not only for their durability but also for their great length. The outside layer of the skin was an important source of vitamin C, as rich in this essential vitamin as raw seal liver. The blubber, which burned with a bright, clean yellow flame, gave light and warmth that were utilized to carve a fishhook or sew a mitten inside the iglu in winter. A single narwhal, too, might feed a dog team for a month.

It is different now. The hunter's utilitarian appreciation of this animal is an attitude some now find offensive; and his considerable skills, based on an accurate and detailed understanding of the animal and its environment, no longer arouse the sympathetic admiration of very many people.

In the time I spent watching narwhals along the floe edge at Lancaster Sound in 1982 no whale was butchered for dog food. The dogs have been replaced by snow machines. No sinews were removed for sewing. Only the tusk was taken, to be traded in the village for cash. And muktuk, the skin with a thin layer of blubber attached, which was brought back to the hunting camp at Nuvua. (This delicacy is keenly anticipated each spring and eaten with pleasure. It tastes like hazelnuts.)

The narwhal's fate in Lancaster Sound is clearly linked with plans to develop oil and gas wells there, but current hunting pressure against them is proving to be as important a factor. In recent years Eskimo hunters on northern Baffin Island have exhibited some lack of discipline during the spring narwhal hunt. They have made hasty, long-range, or otherwise poorly considered shots and used calibers of gun and types of bullets that were inadequate to kill, all of which left animals wounded. And they have sometimes exceeded the quotas set by Department of Fisheries and Oceans Canada and monitored by the International Whaling Commission.* On the other side, Eskimos have routinely been excluded from the upper levels of decision-making by the Canadian government in these matters and have been offered no help in devising a kind of hunting behavior more consistent with the power and reach of modern weapons. For the Eskimos, there is relentless, sometimes condescending scrutiny of every attempt they make to adjust their culture, to "catch up" with the other culture brought up from the south. It is easy to understand why the men sometimes lose their accustomed composure.

In the view of Kerry Finley, a marine mammal biologist closely associated with the Baffin Island narwhal hunts, "It is critical [to the survival of the narwhals] that Inuit become involved in meaningful positions on the management of marine resources." The other problems, he believes, cannot be solved until this obligation is met.

✳ ✳ ✳

I would walk along the floe edge, then, in those days, hoping to hear narwhals, for the wonder of their company; and hoping, too, that they

*These charges are detailed in K. J. Finley, R. A. Davis, and H. B. Silverman, "Aspects of the Narwhal Hunt in the Eastern Canadian Arctic," *Report of the International Whaling Commission* 30 (1980): 459–464; and K. J. Finley and G. W. Miller, "The 1979 Hunt for Narwhals (*Monodon monoceros*) and an Examination of Harpoon Gun Technology Near Pond Inlet, Northern Baffin Island," *Report of the International Whaling Commission* 32 (1982): 449–460.

would not come. The narwhal is a great fighter for its life, and it is painful to watch its struggle. When they were killed, I ate their flesh as a guest of the people I was among, out of respect for distant ancestors, and something older than myself.

I watched closely the ivory gull, a small bird with a high, whistly voice. It has a remarkable ability to appear suddenly in the landscape, seemingly from nowhere. I have scanned tens of square miles of open blue sky, determined it was empty of birds, and then thrown a strap of seal meat into a lead, where it would float. In a few minutes an ivory gull would be overhead. It is hard to say even from what direction it has come. It is just suddenly there.

So I would watch them in ones and twos. Like any animal seen undisturbed in its own environment, the ivory gull seems wondrously adapted. To conserve heat, its black legs are shorter in proportion to its body than the legs of other gulls, its feet less webbed. Its claws are longer and sharper, to give it a better grip of frozen carrion and on the ice. It uses seaweed in its nest to trap the sun's energy, to help with the incubation of its eggs. To avoid water in winter, which might freeze to its legs, it has become deft at picking things up without landing. In winter it follows the polar bear. When no carrion turns up in the polar bear's wake, it eats the polar bear's droppings. It winters on the pack ice. Of the genus *Pagophila*. Ice lover.

And I would think as I walked of what I had read of a creature of legend in China, an animal similar in its habits to the unicorn but abstemious, like the ivory gull. It is called the *ki-lin*. The *ki-lin* has the compassion of the unicorn but also the air of a spiritual warrior, or monk. Odell Shepard has written that "[u]nlike the western unicorn, the *ki-lin* has never had commercial value; no drug is made of any part of his body; he exists for his own sake and not for the medication, enrichment, entertainment, or even edification of mankind." He embodied all that was admirable and ideal.

With our own Aristotelian and Cartesian sense of animals as objects, our religious sense of them as mere receptacles for human symbology, our single-mindedness in unraveling their workings, we are not the kind of culture to take the *ki-lin* very seriously. We are another culture, and these other times. The *ki-lin*, too, is no longer as highly regarded among modern Chinese as it was in the days of the Sung dynasty. But the idea of the *ki-lin*, the mere fact of its having taken shape, is, well, gratifying. It appeared after men had triumphed over both their fear and distrust of nature and their desire to control it completely for their own ends.

The history of the intermingling of human cultures is a history of trade—in objects like the narwhal's tusk, in ideas, and in great narratives. We appropriate when possible the best we can find in all of this. The *ki-lin*, I think, embodies a fine and pertinent idea—an unpossessible being who serves humans when they have need of its wisdom, a creature who abets dignity and respect in human dealings, who underlines the fundamental mystery with which all life meets analysis.

I do not mean to suggest that the narwhal should be made into some sort of symbolic *ki-lin*. Or that buried in the more primitive appreciation of life that some Eskimos retain is an "answer" to our endless misgivings about the propriety of our invasions of landscapes where we have no history, of our impositions on other cultures. But that in the simple appreciation of a world not our own to define, that poised arctic landscape, we might find some solace by discovering the *ki-lin* hidden within ourselves, like a shaft of light.

MONKEYS

G. D. HALE CARPENTER

One species of monkey, a *Ceropithecus*, lives on the islands, but only on the largest: they were found on Kome, Damba, Wema and Yempata out of those that were visited in the group lying off the north shore of the lake, and on Bugalla and the larger isles of the Sesse group. A very curious fact is their presence on the Isle of Nkosi, which is the southernmost of all the Sesse isles, quite small and in a very isolated and exposed position; when I visited this islet in 1913 I distinctly heard a monkey's voice, though he was not visible (see p. 92). The species is of a common type: greenish grey in colour, with black face and a white band across the forehead. It has been of very great service in the investigation of Sleeping Sickness, since the Trypanosomes which cause that disease are also pathogenic to the monkey, which can thus be used as a test for infected flies. Hence I had one with me on the islands for this purpose, and also two others as pets. The "official" one was dubbed Tommy, and, of course, had to be kept tied up, as also was the older of the two pets, named Wee Man. The third, Puffin, was a mere baby, and had not yet become sufficiently mischievous for it to be necessary to tie him up. When I first had Wee Man he was also allowed to run loose, but became so mischievous that when I moved to Bugalla he was tied up.

Being in very constant association with them, one soon became thoroughly familiar with their behaviour, their moods, facial expressions and language, and soon found oneself able to distinguish the meanings of their various utterances.

No less than fourteen sounds are used, although some of them would not be recognized as distinct by any one who had not carefully observed the monkeys, for they are often of the nature of an alteration in inflection, or accent, rather than a different word.

1. May be called a *"General remark,"* and is the commonest expression; used, seemingly, when a monkey is at a loss what to do, or when his attention is attracted by something, or when another monkey comes to him, etc., etc.

2. *Recognition.* A slight modification of No. 1 was used by Wee Man whenever he caught sight of my servant, of whom he seemed particularly fond. Often I would hear this expression and, looking out, would see the man walking about a little way away, and so in time came to know what this sound meant, for it was never used on any other occasion. It may be expressed by "Wok."

3. *Eagerness.* Another modification of No. 1 indicated eagerness; as, for example, when the monkey saw some one bringing a grasshopper which he particularly desired.

4. *Alarm* was expressed by still another modification of No. 1, and had two forms:

   a. For a bird of prey overhead, very unmistakable and emphatic.

   b. For a thunderstorm, or a bush fire, which they dread very much.

5. *Excitement*, as when a monkey sees a boy chasing a fowl, or two boys in play chasing one another. This is also derived from No. 1. I have heard one of the monkeys repeatedly make this noise when he saw a fish eagle chasing another away from its private fishing ground. He took the greatest interest in the occurrence, watching the eagles as they soared around, and being unable to restrain his excitement when one swooped down on the other.

6. *Rage.* A quite unmistakable sound, possibly connected with 5.

7. *Pain.* A kind of squeak.

8. *Cry for help.* A high-pitched squeak. Wee Man used to make this as a youngster when he became inextricably entangled in his rope.

9. *Melancholy.* A very distinct, long-drawn wail, sometimes heard in the forest, presumably indicating that the monkey had become separated from the troop. A monkey seen in the act of crying thus has a most lugubrious appearance; the mouth is held in a peculiar fashion and one quite expects to see tears rolling down the cheeks.

10. *Hunting Call.* One of the most distinct sounds in the monkey tongue. When a troop is searching the trees for food in the forest an old male sits in a very conspicuous tree top and utters a series of barking noises which can be most nearly imitated by repeating very rapidly "Kubba-kubba-kubba." To this the junior members reply by high-pitched squeaks, and the whole troop is thus enabled to keep together, as the total amount of noise produced is considerable.

11. *Dislike.* A short, expressive word, which may be represented by saying beneath one's breath the first two letters of the word "come."

12. *Intense dislike and fear.* The last mentioned sound is repeated very rapidly and with great energy when a monkey sees a snake, or anything that seems to savour of a reptile.

13. A *"baby"* noise, only made by young monkeys when they have been frightened or hurt and run for comfort to be cuddled by their mothers or friends. It can be represented by the noise "Qurra-qurra-qurra-qurra" repeated beneath one's breath.

Having been for months in close association with the pet monkeys, I found their different natures extremely interesting, and they were most charming companions, but it was necessary to keep them tied up owing to their mischievous dispositions.

At one time, when very young, Wee Man had been allowed to run loose, and whenever I left the house he would be unable to resist the temptation of working havoc among papers or anything else that took his fancy which he could destroy, although he knew quite well he would be punished, and showed it by his guilty demeanour when I returned. At this time he would frolic around the huts of the canoe-men when they were away, and make little holes through the grass walls, so that he could, if chased when the time came to tie him up for the night, dodge in and out of the huts. It was a great game every evening to try and find him, and if he managed to hide himself away and go to sleep before he was found, it was considered that he had won the game; and he did, quite often! Mischief was a very marked feature of the monkeys' games with each other, which were delightful to watch. One would be sitting on the bar, a couple of feet above the ground, his tail hanging down, and another, with a broad grin on his face, would steal up and, seizing the tail with both hands, tug furiously in the endeavour to bring down the other, who, quite appreciating the joke and also grinning, would cling on with all his might.

They were of a very affectionate disposition, and if one was beaten or threatened the other would do its utmost to bite the enemy, shrieking with rage the while. The baby Puffin, on Bugalla, was not tied up, and occasionally got into mischief in the house, when I chased him out with threatening gestures. He would at once run to the others, who would receive him anxiously and carefully examine him to see what damage had been sustained, while he made the baby noise to which they responded.

When the three settled down to sleep for the night, all cuddled together, they would give each other a long kiss, lip to lip!

But their affection for each other never went to the lengths of un-selfishness as regards food; if choice were given, a monkey would of course take the largest piece, but very often afterwards would drop that and endeavour to take from the other the piece which he had himself passed over. In fact, their maxim seems to be "the other's piece is always better than mine"!

Wee Man was the most intelligent of the three, and had a more capable-looking head. When his rope became very much entangled with that of Tommy, he would look at the tangle for a while and then deliber-ately try to disentangle it by picking up a loop and, as it were, unthreading himself by walking through it. Often, if the tangle was a simple one, he would succeed, but if the first method was not successful he would try walking through the loop in a reverse direction. Tommy, however, though he might make futile attempts, never succeeded, and seemed to do it mechanically because he had seen Wee Man do it. This is the only instance I ever saw of the reputed imitativeness of a monkey. A certain intelligence was also shown in the recognition of zoological affinity. The noise made for a snake has already been described, and the same was also made for a fish; and, one day, having found a tortoise, I brought it back to see what Wee Man would say to it.

At first the tortoise withdrew itself within the shell: Wee Man came down to look very cautiously at it, intensely curious and interested, but when it put its head out he hastily retreated to his perch with loud utter-ance of the snake noise. When it began to walk he could not restrain his excitement, and danced round and round it, chattering, though keeping at a safe distance. I am quite sure that this was the first tortoise he had ever met, for he had been a captive ever since, as a baby, he was clinging to his mother.

On Bugalla Island, where there was much open grass land as well as clumps of bush and continuous forest, when walking in the evening I often came across a troop of monkeys among the long grass hunting for grasshoppers, which are a great delicacy. A monkey would walk slowly and intently through the grass until a grasshopper took to flight just in front of him, when with a quick snatch he would catch it in his hands. The monkeys always bit off the head first, and then the powerful hind legs, if the grasshopper kicked much, and the rest was eaten at leisure. Even the largest *Acrididae*, three or four inches long, with formidable spines on the hind legs, were eaten with gusto. It always made me think of a man eating a live lobster, shell, legs and all, and not one only, but half a dozen in succession.

I once saw a small young monkey in a patch of papyrus reed, apparently hunting for insects. He climbed up one of the tall stems, but just as he reached the top it slowly bent over with his weight and he disappeared from view. Fortunately for him the papyrus was not growing in water.

In Damba forest I came across a troop, on the ground, very busily engaged in turning over dead leaves, looking for insects. So pre-occupied were they that I was enabled to creep up quite close and watch them before one looked up and gave the alarm.

The captive monkeys were always ready to eat insects, and if a species was offered of which they were afraid, such as a large bee or powerful ground beetle, they would paw it on the ground with rapid strokes of one hand after another until it was disabled, when it would be quickly picked up and nipped between the teeth, to be subsequently eaten at leisure, if desirable.

One evening on Bugalla I surprised a troop hunting in the long grass some little distance away from the nearest trees, to which they hastily retreated. A tiny youngster who had been put down by his mother was unable to escape and took refuge in a small bush, where I easily caught him—a dear little fluffy beast, all head and tail, that sat easily on the palm of my hand. Unfortunately for him the bush was occupied by a species of very powerfully biting ant, and when I got him the poor little monkey was being severely bitten by the ants deeply embedded in his fur. So I took him on my knee and soothed him while I picked out the ants with forceps, the youngster sitting quietly as if my attempts at the "cuddling noise" were quite intelligible. His parents and friends on the neighbouring trees were naturally much alarmed for his safety, and danced up and down in impotent rage, with shrieks of defiance that could plainly be interpreted as "Hurt him if you dare!" When I had freed him from the ants and smoothed him down, I showed him his friends on the trees and put him down in the grass; he ran off more or less in the right direction, and I could see him thoroughly overhauled by his parents, anxious to see what damage had been inflicted, and then conveyed by the whole party into the forest. These very young monkeys are carried about beneath the belly of the mother, their limbs embracing her body, and hands and feet firmly grasping the hair on her back.

INSECTS
AND FISH

And the insects in their hierarchies:
A queen ant, a king ant, a queen wasp, a king wasp,
A queen bee, a king bee,
And all the beetles, bugs, and mosquitoes,
Cascaded in like glittering, murmurous jewels.

But the fish had their wish,
For the rain came down.

—JOHN HEATH-STUBBS
The History of the Flood, 1965

THREE STROKES
OF A DAGGER

J. H. FABRE

There can be no doubt that the Sphex uses her greatest skill when immolating a cricket; it is therefore very important to explain the method by which the victim is sacrificed. Taught by my numerous attempts to observe the war tactics of the Cerceris, I immediately used on the Sphex the plan already successful with the former, *i.e.* taking away the prey and replacing it by a living specimen. This exchange is all the easier because, as we have seen, the Sphex leaves her victim while she goes down her burrow, and the audacious tameness, which actually allows her to take from your fingertips, or even off your hand, the cricket stolen from her and now offered, conduces most happily to a successful result of the experiment by allowing the details of the drama to be closely observed.

It is easy enough to find living crickets; one has only to lift the first stone, and you find them, crouched and sheltering from the sun. These are the young ones of the current year, with only rudimentary wings, and which, not having the industry of the perfect insect, do not yet know how to dig deep retreats where they would be beyond the investigations of the Sphex. In a few moments I find as many crickets as I could wish, and all my preparations are made. I ascend to the top of my observatory, establish myself on the flat ground in the midst of the Sphex colony and wait.

A huntress comes, conveys her cricket to the mouth of her hole and goes down alone. The cricket is speedily replaced by one of mine, but placed at some distance from the hole. The Sphex returns, looks round,

301

and hurries to seize her too distant prey. I am all attention. Nothing on earth would induce me to give up my part in the drama which I am about to witness. The frightened cricket springs away. The Sphex follows closely, reaches it, darts upon it. Then there is a struggle in the dust when sometimes conqueror, sometimes conquered is uppermost or undermost. Success, equal for a moment, finally crowns the aggressor. In spite of vigorous kicks, in spite of bites from its pincer-like jaws, the cricket is felled and stretched on its back.

The murderess soon makes her arrangements. She places herself body to body with her adversary, but in a reverse position, seizes one of the bands at the end of the cricket's abdomen and masters with her forefeet the convulsive efforts of its great hind-thighs. At the same moment her intermediate feet squeeze the panting sides of the vanquished cricket, and her hind ones press like two levers on its face, causing the articulation of the neck to gape open. The Sphex then curves her abdomen vertically, so as to offer a convex surface impossible for the mandibles of the cricket to seize, and one beholds, not without emotion, the poisoned lancet plunge once into the victim's neck, next into the jointing of the two front segments of the thorax, and then again towards the abdomen. In less time than it takes to tell, the murder is committed, and the Sphex, after setting her disordered toilette to rights, prepares to carry off her victim, its limbs still quivering in the death-throes. Let us reflect a moment on the admirable tactics of which I have given a faint sketch. The Cerceris attacks a passive adversary, incapable of flight, whose sole chance of safety is found in a solid cuirass whose weak points the murderers know. But here what a difference! The prey is armed with redoubtable mandibles, capable of disembowelling the aggressor if they can seize her, and a pair of strong feet, actual clubs, furnished with a double row of sharp spines, which can be used alternatively to enable the cricket to bound far away from an enemy or to overturn one by brutal kicks. Accordingly, note what precautions on the part of the Sphex before using her dart. The victim, lying on its back, cannot escape by using its hind levers, for want of anything to spring from, as of course it would were it attacked in its normal position, as are the big Weevils by Cerceris tuberculata. Its spiny legs, mastered by the fore-feet of the Sphex, cannot be used as offensive weapons, and its mandibles, held at a distance by the hind-feet of the Hymenopteron, open threateningly but can seize nothing. But it is not enough for the Sphex to render it impossible for her victim to hurt her: she must hold it so firmly garrotted that no movement can turn the sting from the points where the drop of poison must be instilled, and probably it is in order to hinder any motion of the abdomen that one of the end segments is grasped. If a fertile imagination had had free play to invent a plan of attack it could not have devised anything better, and it is questionable whether the athletes of the classic palestra when grappling an adversary would have assumed attitudes more scientifically calculated.

I have just said that the dart is plunged several times into the victim's body, once under the neck, then behind the prothorax, lastly near the top of the abdomen. It is in this triple blow that the infallibility, the infused science of instinct, appear in all their magnificence. First let us recall the chief conclusions to which the preceding study of the Cerceris have led us. The victims of Hymenoptera whose larva live on prey are not corpses, in spite of entire immobility. There is merely total or partial paralysis, and more or less annihilation of animal life, but vegetative life—that of the nutritive organs—lasts a long while yet, and preserves from decomposition the prey which the larvæ are not to devour for a considerable time. To produce this paralysis the predatory Hymenoptera use just those methods which the advanced science of our day might suggest to the experimental physiologist—namely, wounding, by means of a poisoned dart, those nervous centres which animate the organs of locomotion. We know too that the various centres or ganglia of the nervous chain in articulate animals act to a certain degree independently, so that injury to one only causes, at all events immediately, paralysis of the corresponding segment, and this in proportion as the ganglia are more widely separated and distant from each other. If, on the contrary, they are soldered together, injury to the common centre causes paralysis of all the segments where its ramifications spread. This is the case with Buprestids and Weevils, which the Cerceris paralyses by a single sting, directed at the common mass of the nerve centres in the thorax. But open a cricket, and what do we find to animate the three pairs of feet? We find what the Sphex knew long before the anatomist, three nerve centres far apart. Thence the fine logic of the three stabs. Proud science! humble thyself.

Crickets sacrificed by Sphex flavipennis are no more dead, in spite of all appearances, than are Weevils struck by a Cerceris. The flexibility of the integuments displays the slightest internal movement, and thus makes useless the artificial means used by me to show some remains of life in the Cleonus of Cerceris tuberculata. If one closely observes a cricket stretched on its back a week or even a fortnight or more after the murder, one sees the abdomen heave strongly at long intervals. Very often one can notice a quiver of the palpi and marked movements in the antennæ and the bands of the abdomen, which separate and then come suddenly together. By putting such crickets into glass tubes I have kept them perfectly fresh for six weeks. Consequently, the Sphex larvæ, which live less than a fortnight before enclosing themselves in their cocoons, are sure of fresh food as long as they care to feast.

The chase is over; the three or four crickets needed to store a cell are heaped methodically on their backs, their heads at the far end, their feet toward the entrance. An egg is laid on each. Then the burrow has to be closed. The sand from the excavation lying heaped before the cell door is promptly swept out backward into the passage. From time to time fair-sized bits of gravel are chosen singly, the Sphex scratching in the fragments with her forefeet, and carrying them in her jaws to consolidate the pulverised mass. If none suitable are at hand, she goes to look for them in the neighbourhood, apparently choosing with such scrupulous care as a mason would show in selecting the best stones for a building. Vegetable remains and tiny bits of dead leaf are also employed. In a moment every outward sign of the subterranean dwelling is gone, and if one has not been careful to mark its position, it is impossible for the most attentive eye to find it again. This done, a new burrow is made, provisioned and walled up as soon as the Sphex has eggs to house. Having finished laying, she returns to a careless and vagabond life until the first cold weather ends her well-filled existence.

The Sphex's task is accomplished. I will finish mine by an examination of her weapon. The organ destined for the elaboration of her poison is composed of two elegantly branched tubes communicating separately with a common reservoir or pear-shaped vial, whence proceeds a slender channel leading to the axis of the sting and conducting to its end the little poisoned drop. The dart is extremely small, and not such as one would expect from the size of the Sphex, especially from the effect which her sting produces on crickets. The point is quite smooth, without the barbs found in the sting of the hive bee. The reason of this is evident. The bee uses her sting to avenge an injury only at the cost of life, the barbs preventing its withdrawal from the wound, and thus causing mortal ruptures in the viscera at the end of the abdomen. What could the Sphex have done with a weapon which would have been fatal the first time it was used? Even supposing that the barbed dart could have been withdrawn, I doubt if any Hymenopteron using its weapon, especially to wound game destined for its progeny, would be provided with one. For here the dart is not a fine gentleman's weapon, unsheathed for vengeance, which is said to be the pleasure of the gods, but a very costly one, since the vindictive bee sometimes pays for it with life. It is a worker's tool, on which depends the future of the larvæ, thus it should be one easily used in a struggle with captured prey, plunging into and coming out of the flesh without any delay—a condition much better fulfilled by a smooth blade than by a barbed one.

I wished to ascertain at my own expense if the Sphex's sting be very painful—that sting which knocks over robust victims with frightful rapidity. Well, I own with great admiration that it is slight and cannot be at all compared as to pain with those of the bee and the irascible wasp. It hurts so little that, instead of using pincers, I never hesitated to catch with my fingers any Sphegidæ which I wanted for my researches. I may say the same of the various Cerceris, Philanthides, Palares, and even of the huge Scoliides, whose very look is terrifying, and in general of all predatory Hymenoptera which I have been able to observe. I except, however, those that hunt spiders, the Pompili, and even their sting is far less severe than that of a bee.

One last remark. We know how furiously Hymenoptera armed with a sting used only for defence rush at the bold man who disturbs their nest, and punish his temerity. Those on the contrary whose sting is used only for hunting are very pacific, as if they guessed how important for their family is the little poison drop in their vase. That droplet is the safeguard of their race—I might really say their means of subsistence; therefore they use it economically, in the serious business of the chase, with no parade of vengeful courage. I was not once punished by a sting when I established myself amid colonies of our various predatory Hymenoptera, whose nests I overturned, carrying off larvæ and provisions. To induce the creature to use its weapon, one must lay hold of it, and even then the skin is not always pierced, unless one puts within reach a part more delicate than the fingers, such as the wrist.

The Secret
of the Formicary

Maurice Maeterlinck

1

From the days of Æsop, whose sources were prehistoric, to those of La Fontaine, the ant was the most calumniated of insects. Contrasted with the cigale or cicada, which was, for some reason, endowed with all the facile and decorative virtues, she became the crabbed symbol of suspicious parsimony, of envious meanness, of narrow, malevolent, petty churlishness. As compared with the great and misunderstood artist, she represented the petty bourgeois, the small investor, the subordinate official, the small tradesman of the back streets of a little town without proper sanitation; and the very people who resembled her most closely despised her most profoundly. To rehabilitate her and to do her justice the labours of the great myrmecologists were necessary; and of these the earliest, as we have seen, was Jean-Pierre Huber.

To-day it is accepted as proven that the ant is incontestably one of the noblest, most courageous, most charitable, most devoted, most generous, and most altruistic creatures on earth. As far as that goes, she can take no credit for this, any more than we can take credit for the fact that we are the most intelligent of the creatures inhabiting our planet. We owe this advantage merely to a monstrously developed organ with which Nature has endowed us, just as the ant owes the virtues which have been enumerated to an organ of another kind with which she has been endowed in an exceptional degree, as the result of a caprice, an experiment, or a fantastic idea of the same Nature.

The ant, in fact, possesses at the entrance of the abdomen an extraordinary pouch, which might be called the social pouch or crop. This pouch explains her entire psychology and morality, and the greater part of her life's career; and for this reason we must examine it carefully before proceeding farther. This pouch is not a stomach; it contains no digestive glands, and the food which is accumulated therein is preserved intact. Since the aliment of the ant, who possesses powerful mandibles for seizing her prey or her enemy, for piercing, cutting, dividing, decapitating, and tearing, but has no teeth which can masticate, is almost entirely liquid—a sort of saccharine dew—the sac in question is a collective flagon, reserved exclusively for the community. This flagon or leather bottle is ingeniously and completely separated from the individual stomach, which the aliments contained in it do not reach until several days have elapsed, and after the common hunger has been satisfied. It is enormously elastic, occupying four-fifths of the abdomen, and thrusting aside all the other organs; and it can be dilated to such an extent that in certain American species—notably in *Myrmecocystus Hortus-Deorum* of the United States and Mexico—it assumes the form of a demijohn, a jar, or rather a bonbon, eight or ten times as voluminous as the normal stomach. These insect bonbons have one sole function: they are the living reservoirs of the community. Voluntary prisoners, who never again see the light of day, they grip the ceiling of the nest with their forefeet, hanging from it in serried ranks, giving it the appearance of a well-ordered cellar, into which the honey-dew gathered outside is disgorged, and to which the inhabitants resort in order to demand its regurgitation.

Pardon the word: it is inevitable. It reminds one of indigestion and its unpleasant concomitants; but, like the rumination of cattle, it has nothing in common with these. It is the technical term, beloved of the myrmecologists, who are forced to abuse it a little; but it must be admitted, for regurgitation, or disgorgement, is the essential and fundamental act whence the social life, the virtues, the morality, and the politics of the formicary are derived; just as that which distinguishes us from all the other inhabitants of this earth is derived from our brain.

2

"The ant," says the fable, "does not lend." That is true; she does not lend, for to lend is but the gesture of the miser; she gives without reckoning, and she never asks for repayment. She possesses nothing, not even the contents of her own body. She hardly thinks of eating. What does she live on? It is difficult to say: on the atmosphere, on diffused electricity, on vapours or effluvia. Starve her for weeks on the plaster of an artificial ants' nest, and so long as you provide a little moisture she will not suffer in any way; she will busy herself about her petty affairs, as alert and active as if her cellars were full to overflowing. A drop of dew will fill her individual stomach. All that she is constantly seeking and amassing is intended only for the collective crop, the insatiable communal sac; for the eggs, the larvæ, the nymphs, her comrades and even her enemies. She is nothing but an organ of charity. An indefatigable worker, ascetic, chaste, virgin, neuter—that is to say, sexless—her sole pleasure is to offer, to whomsoever will partake of it, the whole fruit of her labours. For her regurgitation must be an act as delightful as is for us the degustation of the choicest meats and wines. It seems evident that in this act Nature has incorporated pleasures analogous to those of the love of which she is deprived. The ant, regurgitating with reverted antennæ, has an ecstatic appearance (as Auguste Forel has remarked), and evidently experiences a greater pleasure than the comrade who is gorging herself with honey. And in most formicaries regurgitation is, so to speak, incessant, and is interrupted only by labour, the care of offspring, rest, and war.

It may even be questioned whether the ant whose social crop is dilated to bursting is able to pass a single drop into her individual stomach. We know that certain warlike races, and notably *Polyergus rufescens*, which Huber calls "the Amazon," are unable to feed without the help of regurgitating slaves, and would die of hunger in a pool of syrup. This species of perpetual communion of mouth to mouth is thus the normal and almost general form of alimentation.

To convince oneself of the fact, it is enough to tinge a few drops of honey with some blue dye, and offer them to one of our little yellow ants, whose bodies are almost transparent. We shall soon see her stomach dilating and assuming an azure tinge. Burdened with honey, she returns to her nest. Half a dozen mendicant comrades, attracted by the odour of honey, feverishly stroke her antennæ. She satisfies them immediately, and the stomachs of all those about her become blue. They have hardly finished feasting when they are solicited by other comrades, coming up from their underground galleries, who in turn partake of the revealing drop, and so on, until all is consumed. After this the first benefactress, who has given all that she possessed, trots cheerfully away, evidently happier than if she had just enjoyed three or four sumptuous meals.

3

The mendicant need not even be a fellow-citizen; any stranger, provided she is more or less impregnated with the odour of the nest, any daughter of a race which is not too obviously fundamentally hostile, if the doorkeepers have permitted her to enter the nest, or a parasite even, which may be harmful, but is for some inexplicable reason tolerated by the general benevolence, provided the suppliant understands how to set about the business, how to caress the benefactor, may obtain all the food desired. Nothing is more easily deceived than the ant's imprudent charity. We shall even see ants who in the thick of the mêlée cannot resist the solicitations of a hungry enemy; they will give her alms, and chivalrously revictual her before resuming the struggle.

Sometimes their charity goes too far, and leads to the ruin of the colony. For example, a Tunisian ant, the *Wheeleriella*, which has been studied by Dr. Santschi, introduces herself into the nest of another species, the *Monomorium Salomonis*. She is at first rather coldly received, but presently, by means of skilful caresses, she gains the favour of the workers, who end by preferring her to their own queens, whom they abandon and ill-treat for the benefit of the astute adventuress, whose charms appear to be irresistible. Shortly after this the usurper begins to lay her eggs. Her species, which is essentially parasitic, and never works, is the only one to proliferate, and substitutes itself for the too hospitable and too confident workers, whose race dies out. Misery, famine, and death follow; and the parasites disappear in their turn, the victims of a victory too complete. Have we here simply an action, purely and inexplicably imbecile, peculiar to the world of insects? Have we not in our world analogous and equally inexplicable aberrations? Is it not rather a curious and significant example of instinct, infallible in principle, which in over-civilized races, as in man, makes fatal mistakes, because intelligence, sentiment, or intrigue intervene?—We shall return to this problem later.

4

But is not our interpretation of all the foregoing actions too human? Is it not possible that the caress of the antennæ provokes a mere reflex, analogous to the erotic reflex, involuntary and irresistible? It may be so; but if we were to interpret the majority of our own actions in the same fashion we should come to the same conclusions. Do not let us go too far in our dread of anthropomorphism; for if we do, all will become purely mechanical and chemical, and there will be no room for life properly so called; and life is always unexpectedly giving the lie to the most confident determinism. Notably, in more than one instance the ant solicited repulses the caress, deliberately and obviously, expelling and maltreating the intrusive suppliant. Do not let us too hastily declare that there is nothing here but incoherence, stupidity, and automatism. If we were to argue on these lines, what would remain of the majority of our own actions, and of our virtues? Whatever their interpretation, the facts recorded are exact, and are confirmed by all those myrmecologists who have studied them; and for that matter, anyone who desires to do so may verify them, since the study of the ants, which are abundant everywhere, on the surface of the soil and even in our houses, is very much easier than that of the termites.

5

For the moment, it is interesting to note that the three insects whose civilization is vastly superior to that of all others possess a social or collective organ, which, if not identical, performs analogous functions. Thus, it is by regurgitation—stomachal in this case—that the bees nourish their nymphs and their queens. For that matter, all the honey of the hive is merely a regurgitated nectar. In the termites the altruistic organ is sometimes the stomach, and more often the abdomen. Is there some relation between the more or less complete altruism of this organ and the degree of civilization attained by the three insects? I do not know, but if I had to compare them I should place the ant in the first rank, and then the termite, and lastly, despite the prestige of its vivid life, its marvellous skill, its wax, and its honey, our domestic bee.

Let us suppose for a moment that we possessed a more or less analogous organ. What would humanity be had it no other care, no other ideal, no other aim in life than selfless giving and the happiness of others; if to work solely for one's neighbour, to sacrifice oneself permanently and wholly, were the only possible joy, the essential felicity, in a word, the supreme bliss, of which we perceive only a fugitive gleam in the arms of love?

Unhappily we are so made that the very contrary of this is true. Man is the only social animal to possess no social organ. Is this the reason why his socialism and communism are precarious and artificial? It is impossible for us to live otherwise than centripetally, whereas the ants are naturally centrifugal. The pivots of our lives turn in contrary directions. With us all is necessarily, organically, inevitably egoistic. By giving we exceed the law of our being; we betray ourselves, by an effort which makes us emerge from our proper state, and which we call an act of virtue. In the ant all is otherwise: it is in sacrificing herself, in lavishing herself that she follows her natural bent; it is in refusal that she conquers herself and transgresses her instinctive altruism. The poles of the two moralities are inverted.

We too possess an altruistic organ; but on a different plane. This organ is in our mind, and sometimes in our heart; but since it is not physical it is without efficacy. Will the function, will the moral spiritual urge end, as the transformists believe, by creating the material organ? It is not impossible. Nature, with the complicity of the centuries or the millennia, may be capable of miracles for which we dare hardly hope. Nevertheless, it must be confessed that to-day the miracle seems less imminent than of old; that many periods have been more generous than our own. The religions were, so to speak, the rough sketch, the rudiments of an altruistic and collective organ, which promised, in another world, the joys which the ant experiences by giving herself in this world. We are now in the act of extirpating them, and nothing is left us but the egoistic and individual organ of the mind, which may one day surpass itself and shatter the circle that confines it; but God alone knows when.

We must not, however, forget that even in the ants this universal charity, this perpetual communion, does not prevent wars: though the wars of the ants are less frequent and less cruel than is generally believed.

BUTTERFLIES

VLADIMIR NABOKOV

I

On a summer morning, in the legendary Russia of my boyhood, my first glance upon awakening was for the chink between the white inner shutters. If it disclosed a watery pallor, one had better not open them at all, and so be spared the sight of a sullen day sitting for its picture in a puddle. How resentfully one would deduce, from a line of dull light, the leaden sky, the sodden sand, the gruel-like mess of broken brown blossoms under the lilacs—and that flat, fallow leaf (the first casualty of the season) pasted upon a wet garden bench!

But if the chink was a long glint of dewy brilliancy, then I made haste to have the window yield its treasure. With one blow, the room would be cleft into light and shade. The foliage of birches moving in the sun had the translucent green tone of grapes, and in contrast to this there was the dark velvet of fir trees against a blue of extraordinary intensity, the like of which I rediscovered only many years later, in the montane zone of Colorado.

From the age of seven, everything I felt in connexion with a rectangle of framed sunlight was dominated by a single passion. If my first glance of the morning was for the sun, my first thought was for the butterflies it would engender. The original event had been banal enough. On the honeysuckle, overhanging the carved back of a bench just opposite the main entrance, my guiding angel (whose wings, except for the absence of a

Florentine limbus, resemble those of Fra Angelico's Gabriel) pointed out to me a rare visitor, a splendid, pale-yellow creature with black blotches, blue crenels, and a cinnabar eyespot above each chrome-rimmed black tail. As it probed the inclined flower from which it hung, its powdery body slightly bent, it kept restlessly jerking its great wings, and my desire for it was one of the most intense I have ever experienced. Agile Ustin, our town-house janitor, who for a comic reason (explained elsewhere) happened to be that summer in the country with us, somehow managed to catch it in my cap, after which it was transferred, cap and all, to a wardrobe, where domestic naphthalene was fondly expected by Mademoiselle to kill it overnight. On the following morning, however, when she unlocked the wardrobe to take something out, my Swallowtail, with a mighty rustle, flew into her face, then made for the open window, and presently was but a golden fleck dipping and dodging and soaring eastward, over timber and tundra, to Vologda, Viatka and Perm, and beyond the gaunt Ural range to Yakutsk and Verkhne Kolymsk, and from Verkhne Kolymsk, where it lost a tail, to the fair Island of St Lawrence, and across Alaska to Dawson, and southward along the Rocky Mountains—to be finally overtaken and captured, after a forty-year race, on an immigrant dandelion under an endemic aspen near Boulder. In a letter from Mr Brune to Mr Rawlins, 14 June 1735, in the Bodleian collection, he states that one Mr Vernon followed a butterfly nine miles before he could catch him (*The Recreative Review or Eccentricities of Literature and Life*, Vol. I, p. 144, London, 1821).

Soon after the wardrobe affair I found a spectacular moth, marooned in a corner of a vestibule window, and my mother dispatched it with ether. In later years, I used many killing agents, but the least contact with the initial stuff would always cause the porch of the past to light up and attract that blundering beauty. Once, as a grown man, I was under ether during appendectomy, and with the vividness of a decalcomania picture I saw my own self in a sailor suit mounting a freshly emerged Emperor moth under the guidance of a Chinese lady who I knew was my mother. It was all there, brilliantly reproduced in my dream, while my own vitals were being exposed: the soaking, ice-cold absorbent cotton pressed to the insect's lemurian head; the subsiding spasms of its body; the satisfying crackle produced by the pin penetrating the hard crust of its thorax; the careful insertion of the point of the pin in the cork-bottomed groove of the spreading board; the symmetrical adjustment of the thick, strong-veined wings under neatly affixed strips of semitransparent paper.

2

I must have been eight when, in a storeroom of our country house, among all kinds of dusty objects, I discovered some wonderful books acquired in the days when my mother's mother had been interested in natural science and had had a famous university professor of zoology (Shimkevich) give private lessons to her daughter. Some of these books were mere curios, such as the four huge brown folios of Albertus Seba's work (*Locupletissimi Rerum Naturalium Thesauri Accurata Descriptio...*), printed in Amsterdam around 1750. On their coarse-grained pages I found woodcuts of serpents and butterflies and embryos. The fetus of an Ethiopian female child hanging by the neck in a glass jar used to give me a nasty shock every time I came across it; nor did I much care for the stuffed hydra on plate CII, with its seven lion-toothed turtleheads on seven serpentine necks and its strange, bloated body which bore buttonlike tubercules along the sides and ended in a knotted tail.

Other books I found in that attic, among herbariums full of alpine columbines, and blue palemoniums, and Jove's campions, and orange-red lilies, and other Davos flowers, came closer to my subject. I took in my arms and carried downstairs glorious loads of fantastically attractive volumes: Maria Sibylla Merian's (1647–1717) lovely plates of Surinam insects, and Esper's noble *Die Schmetterlinge* (Erlangen, 1777), and Boisduval's *Icones Historiques de Lépidoptères Nouveaux ou Peu Connus* (Paris, begun in 1832). Still more exciting were the products of the latter half of the century—Newman's *Natural History of British Butterflies and Moths*, Hofmann's *Die Gross-Schmetterlinge Europas*, the Grand Duke Nikolay Mihailovich's *Mémoires* on Asiatic lepidoptera (with incomparably beautiful figures painted by Kavrigin, Rybakov, Lang), Scudder's stupendous work on the *Butterflies of New England*.

Retrospectively, the summer of 1905, though quite vivid in many ways, is not animated yet by a single bit of quick flutter or colored fluff around or across the walks with the village schoolmaster: the Swallowtail of June 1906 was still in the larval stage on a roadside umbellifer; but in the course of that month I became acquainted with a score or so of common things, and Mademoiselle was already referring to a certain forest road that culminated in a marshy meadow full of Small Pearl-bordered Fritillaries (thus called in my first unforgettable and unfadingly magical little manual, Richard South's *The Butterflies of the British Isles*, which had just come out at that time) as *le chemin des papillons bruns*. The following year I became aware that many of our butterflies and moths did not occur in England or Central Europe, and more complete atlases helped me to determine them. A severe illness (pneumonia, with fever up to 41° centigrade), in the beginning of 1907, mysteriously abolished the rather monstrous gift of numbers that had made of me a child prodigy during a few months (today I cannot multiply 13 by 17 without pencil and paper; I can add them up, though, in a trice, the teeth of the three fitting in neatly); but the butterflies survived. My mother accumulated a library and a museum around my bed, and the longing to describe a new species completely replaced that of discovering a new prime number. A trip to Biarritz, in August 1907, added new wonders (though not as lucid and numerous as they were to be in 1909). By 1908, I had gained absolute control over the European lepidoptera as known to Hofmann. By 1910, I had dreamed my way through the first volumes of Seitz's prodigious picture book *Die Gross-Schmetterlinge der Erde*, had purchased a number of rarities recently described, and was voraciously reading entomological periodicals, especially English and Russian ones. Great upheavals were taking place in the development of systematics. Since the middle of the century, Continental lepidopterology had been, on the whole, a simple and stable affair, smoothly run by the Germans. Its high priest, Dr Staudinger, was also the head of the largest firm of insect dealers. Even now, half a century after his death, German lepidopterists have not quite managed to shake off the hypnotic spell occasioned by his authority. He was still alive when his school began to lose ground as a scientific force in the world. While he and his followers stuck to specific and generic names sanctioned by long usage and were content to classify butterflies by characters visible to the naked eye, English-speaking authors were introducing nomenclatorial changes as a result of a strict application of the law of priority and taxonomic changes based on the microscopic study of organs. The Germans did their best to ignore the new trends and continued to cherish the philately-like side of entomology. Their solicitude for the 'average collector who should not be made to dissect' is comparable to the way nervous publishers of popular novels pamper the 'average reader'—who should not be made to think.

There was another more general change, which coincided with my ardent adolescent interest in butterflies and moths. The Victorian and Staudingerian kind of species, hermetic and homogeneous, with sundry (alpine, polar, insular, etc.) 'varieties' affixed to it from the outside, as it were, like incidental appendages, was replaced by a new, multiform and

fluid kind of species, organically *consisting* of geographical races or subspecies. The evolutional aspects of the case were thus brought out more
clearly, by means of more flexible methods of classification, and further
links between butterflies and the central problems of nature were provided by biological investigations.

The mysteries of mimicry had a special attraction for me. Its phenomena showed an artistic perfection usually associated with man-wrought
things. Consider the imitation of oozing poison by bubblelike macules on a
wing (complete with pseudorefraction) or by glossy yellow knobs on a
chrysalis ('Don't eat me—I have already been squashed, sampled and
rejected'). Consider the tricks of an acrobatic caterpillar (of the Lobster
Moth) which in infancy looks like bird's dung, but after molting develops
scrabbly hymenopteroid appendages and baroque characteristics, allowing the extraordinary fellow to play two parts at once (like the actor in
Oriental shows who *becomes* a pair of intertwisted wrestlers): that of a
writhing larva and that of a big ant seemingly harrowing it. When a certain
moth resembles a certain wasp in shape and color, it also walks and moves
its antennae in a waspish, unmothlike manner. When a butterfly has to
look like a leaf, not only are all the details of a leaf beautifully rendered but
markings mimicking grub-bored holes are generously thrown in. 'Natural
selection,' in the Darwinian sense, could not explain the miraculous coincidence of imitative aspect and imitative behavior, nor could one appeal to
the theory of 'the struggle for life' when a protective device was carried
to a point of mimetic subtlety, exuberance, and luxury far in excess of a
predator's power of appreciation. I discovered in nature the nonutilitarian
delights that I sought in art. Both were a form of magic, both were a
game of intricate enchantment and deception.

3

I have hunted butterflies in various climes and disguises: as a pretty
boy in knickerbockers and sailor cap; as a lanky cosmopolitan expatriate
in flannel bags and beret; as a fat hatless old man in shorts. Most of my
cabinets have shared the fate of our Vyra house. Those in our town house
and the small addendum I left in the Yalta Museum have been destroyed,
no doubt, by carpet beetles and other pests. A collection of South European
stuff that I started in exile vanished in Paris during World War Two. All my
American captures from 1940 to 1960 (several thousands of specimens
including great rarities and types) are in the Mus. of Comp. Zoology, the

Am. Nat. Hist. Mus., and the Cornell Univ. Mus. of Entomology, where they are safer than they would be in Tomsk or Atomsk. Incredibly happy memories, quite comparable, in fact, to those of my Russian boyhood, are associated with my research work at the MCZ, Cambridge, Mass. (1941–8). No less happy have been the many collecting trips taken almost every summer, during twenty years, through most of the states of my adopted country.

In Jackson Hole and in the Grand Canyon, on the mountain slopes above Telluride, Colo., and on a celebrated pine barren near Albany, N.Y., dwell, and will dwell, in generations more numerous than editions, the butterflies I have described as new. Several of my finds have been dealt with by other workers; some have been named after me. One of these, Nabokov's Pug (*Eupithecia nabokovi* McDunnough), which I boxed one night in 1943 on a picture window of James Laughlin's Alta Lodge in Utah, fits most philosophically into the thematic spiral that began in a wood in the Oredezh around 1910—or perhaps even earlier, on that Nova Zemblan river a century and a half ago.

Few things indeed have I known in the way of emotion or appetite, ambition or achievement, that could surpass in richness and strength the excitement of entomological exploration. From the very first it had a great many interwinkling facets. One of them was the acute desire to be alone, since any companion, no matter how quiet, interfered with the concentrated enjoyment of my mania. Its gratification admitted of no compromise or exception. Already when I was ten, tutors and governesses knew that the morning was mine and cautiously kept away.

In this connexion, I remember the visit of a schoolmate, a boy of whom I was very fond and with whom I had excellent fun. He arrived one summer night—in 1913, I think—from a town some twenty-five miles away. His father had recently perished in an accident, the family was ruined and the stout-hearted lad, not being able to afford the price of a railway ticket, had bicycled all those miles to spend a few days with me.

On the morning following his arrival, I did everything I could to get out of the house for my morning hike without his knowing where I had gone. Breakfastless, with hysterical haste, I gathered my net, pill boxes, killing jar, and escaped through the window. Once in the forest, I was safe; but still I walked on, my calves quaking, my eyes full of scalding tears, the whole of me twitching with shame and self-disgust, as I visualized my poor friend, with his long pale face and black tie, moping in the hot garden—patting the panting dogs for want of something better to do, and trying hard to justify my absence to himself.

Let me look at my demon objectively. With the exception of my parents, no one really understood my obsession, and it was many years before I met a fellow sufferer. One of the first things I learned was not to depend on others for the growth of my collection. One summer afternoon, in 1911, Mademoiselle came into my room, book in hand, started to say she wanted to show me how wittily Rousseau denounced zoology (in favour of botany), and by then was too far gone in the gravitational process of lowering her bulk into an armchair to be stopped by my howl of anguish: on that seat I had happened to leave a glass-lidded cabinet tray with long, lovely series of the Large White. Her first reaction was one of stung vanity: her weight, surely, would not be accused of damaging what in fact it had demolished; her second was to console me: *Allons donc, ce ne sont que des papillons de potager!*—which only made matters worse. A Sicilian pair recently purchased from Staudinger had been crushed and bruised. A huge Biarritz example was utterly mangled. Smashed, too, were some of my choicest local captures. Of these, an aberration resembling the Canarian race of the species might have been mended with a few drops of glue; but a precious gynandromorph, left side male, right side female, whose abdomen could not be traced and whose wings had come off, was lost forever: one might reattach the wings but one could not prove that all four belonged to that headless thorax on its bent pin. Next morning, with an air of great mystery, poor Mademoiselle set off for St Petersburg and came back in the evening bringing me ('something better than your cabbage butterflies') a banal Urania moth mounted on plaster. 'How you hugged me, how you danced with joy!' she exclaimed ten years later in the course of inventing a brand-new past.

Our country doctor, with whom I had left the pupae of a rare moth when I went on a journey abroad, wrote me that everything had hatched finely; but in reality a mouse had got at the precious pupae, and upon my return the deceitful old man produced some common Tortoiseshell butterflies, which, I presume, he had hurriedly caught in his garden and popped into the breeding cage as plausible substitutes (so *he* thought). Better than he, was an enthusiastic kitchen boy who would sometimes borrow my equipment and come back two hours later in triumph with a bagful of seething invertebrate life and several additional items. Loosening the mouth of the net which he had tied up with a string, he would pour out his cornucopian spoil—a mass of grasshoppers, some sand, the two parts of a mushroom he had thriftily plucked on the way home, more grasshoppers, more sand, and one battered Small White.

In the works of major Russian poets I can discover only two lepidopteral images of genuinely sensuous quality: Bunin's impeccable evocation of what is certainly a Tortoiseshell:

> *And there will fly into the room*
> *A colored butterfly in silk*
> *To flutter, rustle and pit-pat*
> *On the blue ceiling ...*

and Fet's 'Butterfly' soliloquizing;

> *Whence have I come and whither am I hasting*
> *Do not inquire;*
> *Now on a graceful flower I have settled*
> *And now respire.*

In French poetry one is struck by Musset's well-known lines (in *Le Saule*):

> *Le phalène doré dans sa course légère*
> *Traverse les prés embaumés*

which is an absolutely exact description of the crepuscular flight of the male of the geometric called in England the Orange moth; and there is Fargue's fascinatingly apt phrase (in *Les Quatres Journées*) about a garden which, at nightfall, *se glace de bleu comme l'aile du grand Sylvain* (the Poplar Admirable). And among the very few genuine lepidopterological images in English poetry, my favorite is Browning's

> *On our other side is the straight-up rock;*
> *And a path is kept 'twixt the gorge and it*
> *By boulder-stones where lichens mock*
> *The marks on a moth, and small ferns fit*
> *Their teeth to the polished block.*

> *'By the Fire-side'*

It is astounding how little the ordinary person notices butterflies. 'None,' calmly replied that sturdy Swiss hiker with Camus in his rucksack when purposely asked by me for the benefit of my incredulous companion if he had seen any butterflies while descending the trail where, a moment before, you and I had been delighting in swarms of them. It is also true that when I call up the image of a particular path remembered in minute detail but pertaining to a summer before that of 1906, preceding, that is, the date of my first locality label, and never revisited, I fail to make out one wing, one wingbeat, one azure flash, one moth-gemmed flower, as if an evil spell had been cast on the Adriatic coast making all its 'leps' (as the slangier among us say) invisible. Exactly thus an entomologist may feel some day when plodding beside a jubilant, and already helmetless botanist amid the hideous flora of a parallel planet, with not a single insect in sight; and thus (in odd proof of the odd fact that whenever possible the scenery of our infancy is used by an economically minded producer as a ready-made setting for our adult dreams) the seaside hilltop of a certain recurrent nightmare of mine, whereinto I smuggle a collapsible net from my waking state, is gay with thyme and melilot, but incomprehensibly devoid of all the butterflies that should be there.

I also found out very soon that a 'lepist' indulging in his quiet quest was apt to provoke strange reactions in other creatures. How often, when a picnic had been arranged, and I would be self-consciously trying to get my humble implements unnoticed into the tar-smelling charabanc (a tar preparation was used to keep flies away from the horses) or the tea-smelling Opel convertible (benzine forty years ago smelled that way), some cousin or aunt of mine would remark: 'Must you *really* take that net with you? Can't you enjoy yourself like a normal boy? Don't you think you are spoiling everybody's pleasure?' Near a sign NACH BODENLAUBE, at Bad Kissingen, Bavaria, just as I was about to join for a long walk my father and majestic old Muromtsev (who, four years before, in 1906, had been President of the first Russian Parliament), the latter turned his marble head toward me, a vulnerable boy of eleven, and said with his famous solemnity: 'Come with us by all means, but do not chase butterflies, child. It spoils the rhythm of the walk.' On a path above the Black Sea, in the Crimea, among shrubs in waxy bloom, in March 1918, a bow-legged Bolshevik sentry attempted to arrest me for signaling (with my net, he said) to a British warship. In the summer of 1929, every time I walked through a village in the Eastern Pyrenees, and happened to look back, I would see in my wake the villagers frozen in the various attitudes my passage had caught them in, as if I were Sodom and they Lot's wife. A decade later, in the Maritime Alps, I once noticed the grass undulate in a serpentine way behind me because a fat rural policeman was wriggling after me on his belly to find out if I were not trapping songbirds. America has shown even more of this morbid interest in my retiary activities than other countries have—perhaps because I was in my forties when I came there to live, and the older the man, the queerer he looks with a butterfly net in his hand. Stern farmers have drawn my attention to NO FISHING signs; from cars passing me on the highway have come wild howls of derision; sleepy dogs, though unmindful of the worst bum, have perked up and come at me, snarling; tiny tots have pointed me out to their puzzled mamas; broad-minded vacationists have asked me whether I was catching bugs for bait; and one morning on a wasteland, lit by tall yuccas in bloom, near Santa Fe, a big black mare followed me for more than a mile.

4

When, having shaken off all pursuers, I took the rough, red road that ran from our Vyra house toward field and forest, the animation and luster of the day seemed like a tremor of sympathy around me.

Very fresh, very dark Arran Browns, which emerged only every second year (conveniently, retrospection has fallen here into line), flitted among the firs or revealed their red markings and checkered fringes as they sunned themselves on the roadside bracken. Hopping above the grass, a diminutive Ringlet called Hero dodged my net. Several moths, too, were flying—gaudy sun lovers that sail from flower to flower like painted flies, or male insomniacs in search of hidden females, such as that rust-colored Oak Eggar hurtling across the shrubbery. I noticed (one of the major mysteries of my childhood) a soft pale green wing caught in a spider's web (by then I knew what it was: part of a Large Emerald). The tremendous larva of the Goat Moth, ostentatiously segmented, flat-headed, flesh-colored and glossily flushed, a strange creature 'as naked as a worm' to use a French comparison, crossed my path in frantic search for a place to pupate (the awful pressure of metamorphosis, the aura of a disgraceful fit in a public place). On the bark of that birch tree, the stout one near the park wicket, I had found last spring a dark aberration of Sievers' Carmelite (just another gray moth to the reader). In the ditch, under the bridgelet, a bright-yellow Silvius Skipper hobnobbed with a dragonfly (just a blue libellula to me). From a flower head two male Coppers rose to a tremendous height, fighting all the way up—and then, after a while, came the downward flash of one of them returning to his thistle. These were familiar insects, but at any moment something better might cause me to stop with a quick intake of breath. I remember one day when I warily brought my net closer and closer to an uncommon Hairstreak that had daintily settled on a sprig. I could clearly see the white W on its chocolate-brown underside. Its wings were closed and the inferior ones were rubbing against each other in a curious circular motion—possibly producing some small, blithe crepitation pitched too high for a human ear to catch. I had long wanted that particular species, and, when near enough, I struck. You have heard champion tennis players moan after muffing an easy shot. You may have seen the face of the world-famous grandmaster Wilhelm Edmundson when, during a simultaneous display in a Minsk café, he lost his rook, by an absurd oversight, to the local amateur and pediatrician, Dr Schach, who eventually won. But that day nobody (except my older self) could see me shake out a piece of twig from an otherwise empty net and stare at a hole in the tarlatan.

5

Near the intersection of two carriage roads (one, well-kept, running north-south in between our 'old' and 'new' parks, and the other, muddy and rutty, leading, if you turned west, to Batovo) at a spot where aspens crowded on both sides of a dip, I would be sure to find in the third week of June great blue-black nymphalids striped with pure white, gliding and wheeling low above the rich clay which matched the tint of their undersides when they settled and closed their wings. Those were the dung-loving males of what the old Aurelians used to call the Poplar Admirable, or, more exactly, they belonged to its Bucovinan subspecies. As a boy of nine, not knowing that race, I noticed how much our North Russian specimens differed from the Central European form figured in Hofmann, and rashly wrote to Kuznetsov, one of the greatest Russian, or indeed world, lepidopterists of all time, naming my new subspecies 'Limenitis populi rossica.' A long month later he returned my description and aquarelle of 'rossica Nabokov' with only two words scribbled on the back of my letter: 'bucovinensis Hormuzaki.' How I hated Hormuzaki! And how hurt I was when in one of Kuznetsov's later papers I found a gruff reference to 'schoolboys who keep naming minute varieties of the Poplar Nymph!'

Undaunted, however, by the *populi* flop, I 'discovered' the following year a 'new' moth. That summer I had been collecting assiduously on moonless nights, in a glade of the park, by spreading a bedsheet over the grass and its annoyed glow-worms, and casting upon it the light of an acetylene lamp (which, six years later, was to shine on Tamara). Into that arena of radiance, moths would come drifting out of the solid blackness around me, and it was in that manner, upon that magic sheet, that I took a beautiful *Plusia* (now *Phytometra*) which, as I saw at once, differed from its closest ally by its mauve-and-maroon (instead of golden-brown) forewings, and narrower bractea mark and was not recognizably figured in any of my books. I sent its description and picture to Richard South, for publication in *The Entomologist*. He did not know it either, but with the utmost kindness checked it in the British Museum collection—and found it had been described long ago as *Plusia excelsa* by Kretschmar. I received the sad news, which was most sympathetically worded ('... should be congratulated for obtaining ... very rare Volgan thing ... admirable figure ...') with the utmost stoicism; but many years later, by a pretty fluke (I know I should not point out these plums to people), I got even with the first discoverer of *my* moth by giving his own name to a blind man in a novel.

Let me also evoke the hawkmoths, the jets of my boyhood! Colors would die a long death on June evenings. The lilac shrubs in full bloom before which I stood, net in hand, displayed clusters of a fluffy gray in the dusk—the ghost of purple. A moist young moon hung above the mist of a neighboring meadow. In many a garden have I stood thus in later years—in Athens, Antibes, Atlanta—but never have I waited with such a keen desire as before those darkening lilacs. And suddenly it would come, the low buzz passing from flower to flower, the vibrational halo around the streamlined body of an olive and pink Hummingbird moth poised in the air above the corolla into which it had dipped its long tongue. Its handsome black larva (resembling a diminutive cobra when it puffed out its ocellated front segments) could be found on dank willow herb two months later. Thus every hour and season had its delights. And, finally, on cold, or even frosty, autumn nights, one could sugar for moths by painting tree trunks with a mixture of molasses, beer, and rum. Through the gusty blackness, one's lantern would illumine the stickily glistening furrows of the bark and two or three large moths upon it imbibing the sweets, their nervous wings half open butterfly fashion, the lower ones exhibiting their incredible crimson silk from beneath the lichen-gray primaries. '*Catocala adultera!*' I would triumphantly shriek in the direction of the lighted windows of the house as I stumbled home to show my captures to my father.

<h1 style="text-align:center">6</h1>

The 'English' park that separated our house from the hayfields was an extensive and elaborate affair with labyrinthine paths, Turgenevian benches, and imported oaks among the endemic firs and birches. The struggle that had gone on since my grandfather's time to keep the park from reverting to the wild state always fell short of complete success. No gardener could cope with the hillocks of frizzly black earth that the pink hands of moles kept heaping on the tidy sand of the main walk. Weeds and fungi, and ridgelike tree roots crossed and recrossed the sun-flecked trials. Bears had been eliminated in the eighties, but an occasional moose still visited the grounds. On a picturesque boulder, a little mountain ash and a still smaller aspen had climbed, holding hands, like two clumsy, shy children. Other, more elusive trespassers—lost picnickers or merry villagers—would drive our hoary gamekeeper Ivan crazy by scrawling ribald words on the benches and gates. The disintegrating process continues still, in a different sense, for when, nowadays, I attempt to follow in memory the winding paths from one given point to another, I notice with alarm that there are many gaps, due to oblivion or ignorance, akin to the terra-incognita blanks map makers of old used to call 'sleeping beauties.'

Beyond the park, there were fields, with a continuous shimmer of butterfly wings over a shimmer of flowers—daisies, bluebells, scabious, and others—which now rapidly pass by me in a kind of colored haze like those lovely, lush meadows, never to be explored, that one sees from the diner on a transcontinental journey. At the end of this grassy wonderland, the forest rose like a wall. There I roamed, scanning the tree trunks (the enchanted, the silent part of a tree) for certain tiny moths, called Pugs in England—delicate little creatures that cling in the daytime to speckled surfaces, with which their flat wings and turned-up abdomens blend. There, at the bottom of that sea of sunshot greenery, I slowly spun round the great boles. Nothing in the world would have seemed sweeter to me than to be able to add, by a stroke of luck, some remarkable new species to the long list of Pugs already named by others. And my pied imagination, ostensibly, and almost grotesquely, groveling to my desire (but all the time, in ghostly conspiracies behind the scenes, coolly planning the most distant events of my destiny), kept providing me with hallucinatory samples of small print: '... the only specimen so far known ...' '... the only specimen known of *Eupithecia petropolitanata* was taken by a Russian schoolboy ...' '... by a young Russian collector ...' '... by myself in the Government of St Petersburg, Tsarskoe Selo District, in 1910 ... 1911 ... 1912 ... 1913 ...' And then, thirty years later, that blessed black night in the Wasatch Range.

At first—when I was, say, eight or nine—I seldom roamed farther than the fields and woods between Vyra and Batovo. Later, when aiming at a particular spot half-a-dozen miles or more distant, I would use a bicycle to get there with my net strapped to the frame; but not many forest paths were passable on wheels; it was possible to ride there on horseback, of course, but, because of our ferocious Russian tabanids, one could not leave a horse haltered in a wood for any length of time: my spirited bay almost climbed up the tree it was tied to one day trying to elude them: big fellows with watered-silk eyes and tiger bodies, and gray little runts with an even more painful proboscis, but much more sluggish: to dispatch two or three of these dingy tipplers with one crush of the gloved hand as they glued themselves to the neck of my mount afforded me a wonderful empathic relief (which a dipterist might not appreciate). Anyway, on my butterfly hunts I always preferred hiking to any other form of locomotion (except, naturally, a flying seat gliding leisurely over the plant mats and rocks of an unexplored mountain, or hovering just above the flowery roof of a rain forest); for when you walk, especially in a region you have studied well, there is an exquisite pleasure in departing from one's itinerary to visit, here and there by the wayside, this glade, that glen, this or that combination of soil and flora—to drop in, as it were, on a familiar butterfly in his particular habitat, in order to see if he has emerged, and if so, how he is doing.

There came a July day—around 1910, I suppose—when I felt the urge to explore the vast marshland beyond the Oredezh. After skirting the river for three or four miles, I found a rickety footbridge. While crossing over, I could see the huts of a hamlet on my left, apple trees, rows of tawny pine logs lying on a green bank, and the bright patches made on the turf by the scattered clothes of peasant girls, who, stark naked in shallow water, romped and yelled, heeding me as little as if I were the discarnate carrier of my present reminiscences.

On the other side of the river, a dense crowd of small, bright blue male butterflies that had been tippling on the rich, trampled mud and cow dung through which I trudged rose all together into the spangled air and settled again as soon as I had passed.

After making my way through some pine groves and alder scrub I came to the bog. No sooner had my ear caught the hum of diptera around me, the guttural cry of a snipe overhead, the gulping sound of the morass under my foot, than I knew I would find here quite special arctic butterflies, whose pictures, or, still better, nonillustrated descriptions I had worshiped for several seasons. And the next moment I was among them. Over the small shrubs of bog bilberry with fruit of a dim, dreamy blue, over the brown eye of stagnant water, over moss and mire, over the flower spikes of the fragrant bog orchid (the *nochnaya fialka* of Russian poets), a dusky little Fritillary bearing the name of a Norse goddess passed in low, skimming flight. Pretty Cordigera, a gemlike moth, buzzed all over its uliginose food plant. I pursued rose-margined Sulphurs, gray-marbled Satyrs. Unmindful of the mosquitoes that furred my forearms, I stooped with a grunt of delight to snuff out the life of some silver-studded lepidopteron throbbing in the folds of my net. Through the smells of the bog, I caught the subtle perfume of butterfly wings on my fingers, a perfume which varies with the species—vanilla, or lemon, or musk, or a musty, sweetish odor difficult to define. Still unsated, I pressed forward. At last I saw I had come to the end of the marsh. The rising ground beyond was a paradise of lupines, columbines, and pentstemons. Mariposa lilies bloomed under Ponderosa pines. In the distance, fleeting cloud shadows dappled the dull green of slopes above timber line, and the gray and white of Longs Peak.

I confess I do not believe in time. I like to fold my magic carpet, after use, in such a way as to superimpose one part of the pattern upon another. Let visitors trip. And the highest enjoyment of timelessness—in a landscape selected at random—is when I stand among rare butterflies and their food plants. This is ecstasy, and behind the ecstasy is something else, which is hard to explain. It is like a momentary vacuum into which rushes all that I love. A sense of oneness with sun and stone. A thrill of gratitude to whom it may concern—to the contrapuntal genius of human fate or to tender ghosts humoring a lucky mortal.

12,000,000 COD

GUSTAV ECKSTEIN

SMELL

When in the course of ages the animal finally lifted its nose up off the ground, it began slowly to lose its sense of smell. Freud suggested that this may have been the point where the nervous disorders began. Smell and sex being so intimate in the animal, neglect of the one may well have started suppression of the other. However, the influence of smell in man's mental life is not merely Freudian. A gentleman recently related that he and some others, all boys at the time, were present when a woman burned to death, and that to each of them for years and on many occasions the smell of burned flesh would come back. The gentleman believed that that experience had changed the course of all their lives.

* * *

The animal in this that follows is man. The logbook of a nose. The nose of a man. The record begins at age seven. The place is three miles from the college, at the bottom of the valley, in the West End, a smelly part of the world. The old Cincinnati General Hospital lies in that same direction but a mile farther on. It will be abandoned shortly. Linn Street is the street.

At one corner of Linn Street is a barrel house, a drug store at the other, and two doors from the drug store—three doors from Wade Street—is another barrel house. Diagonally across from the first barrel house are the city stables—mules, horses, axle grease, tar. When the wind is from the north there are the smells from the slaughter house on Oliver Street, and when the wind is from the south there are the smells from the tannery—a hearty tannery. As for the people on Linn Street, it will be possible years later for the nose to recollect several—Mrs. Stern, Min Huber, Miss Pilsner, Mrs. Kaufman. Especially Mrs. Kaufman. Often the nose is undecided: Should it do an errand for Mrs. Kaufman and earn a penny, or not earn the penny and not have to enter Mrs. Kaufman's house. Years later, also, when an old lady of a certain style approaches, there will approach with her a whiff of Mrs. Kaufman's house.

In summer the nose vacations in Wisconsin, the edge of Lake Michigan, a town dropped into the middle of the countryside. Fogs come up from the lake—moisture to carry the smell substances. After ten months in the West End the new smells are a great relief. Fresh water, docks, upturned earth, cut grass, mown hay, pine woods. The milk inspector lifts the lid off the milk can, smells, and if there is a taint of onion or garlic or manure, pours out the milk, otherwise lets the can pass. Five miles away is the cheese center, not of the state, not of the country, of the world! The cheese inspector breaks off a piece of cheese, crumbles it in his fingers, smells his fingers, chalks down the grade. There is a grandmother. She is rich—she has a pantry. Smells—cherry pie, apple pie, currant pie, lemon pie, tables full of them, dill pickles in a barrel, whole hams hung up.

There is an aunt, too. She is just as real as any of that row of relatives that comes to Sunday dinner, though she died fifteen years before the nose was born. Not one picture of her anywhere in the house. But the nose has reconstructed her from the smell she left behind her, as the anthropologist reconstructs the total dinosaur from a footprint left in stone. The soft lines of her skin. Her floating walk. She had been a maiden lady, used powders, lotions, patent medicines. She lived in the middle room on the second floor to the left of the long hall. Then she died, and they did everything, papered the walls, plastered them, painted them, but nothing could keep Aunt Clara in.

Taste is very much smell, as anyone with a cold-in-the-head knows. Taste, strictly, is only for sour, sweet, salt, bitter. Everything else, the flavors, the seasoning, the spices—except any burning, which is temperature sense—is smell. Anatomists have done experiments on cadavers, forced air up the dead man's nose, and so proved that in quiet breathing the air passes through the lower and the middle nasal regions, but it is the high region that is the region of regions. It follows that in quiet breathing we may not be aware of a smell. As soon as a certain minimum concentration makes us aware, we dilate the nostrils, at the same time take a stronger breath, hence get the full blast. The smell nerves lead through holes in the skull straight into the smell brain. In the fish the smell brain is most of the brain. In the dog it is comparatively large. In man comparatively small.

※　※　※

The nose now is eighteen. Love. The smells of love. Every candid man knows them. Suddenly golden locks have an odor. Suddenly a hand-kerchief may be employed for something other than blowing the nose—a small handkerchief, neatly folded, that one drops between the papers in one's billfold, and in a little while brings out again and passes back and forth under the nose, as one will later a cigar. (One of the saddest phrases ever typed.) A freshly laundered stocking has a smell—when she kicks her shoe off her heel and swings it on her toes. The skin has a smell, as has a pretty dress worn long enough. She comes in, and he recognizes where she has been, and is pleased, or suspicious, and thinks with satisfaction that he never had any talent like this before. Sweat has a whole scale of smells.

In the spring of that year the Odyssey continues to France. There the nose learns how the French keep the principles and practices of love, learns how immature Americans are, how expert they. And the explana-tion is—the lilac. Every hedge, every garden, every back yard, every road, everywhere the lilac, and every day it rains. What that does to the smell brain! What the smell brain does to the romantic heart!

But a nose must take the bad with the good, and it has to be admitted that no country in the world smells as France of urine. Especially the south of France. The place is the old Roman town of Arles, at noon, the sun hot and the air dry of all moisture. Who has not pictured that famous town at some time in his previous life? Adored the houses. Adored the cobbles. And then he arrives and is so pleased that there still should remain some of the ancient Roman wall. Evening comes, and the mists slide in from the Mediterranean, and the remains of Roman wall seem now to shut him in from the world entirely—and shut in with him are the currents and the crosscurrents of every concentration, of every grade, of every age of urine. Each time the nose does the physiological act of adaptation for one aromatic chemical, another is upon it—ammonia, urea, ethereal sulphates, and all their known and unknown relatives.

✳ ✳ ✳

Five years later the nose crosses the Pacific, to the southernmost tip of a small triangular island, Kyushu, due east of Shanghai, northeast of Formosa, the bloody island of Okinawa just to the south. The nose arrives in a Kyushuan village at eleven at night. All day the skies have been emptying and everywhere the creeks are rising. The weary body falls asleep on a straw-matted floor and at two in the morning is rudely roused. Voices are calling, "*O-miya, o-miya!*" The water is in the street. By ten o'clock it is just under the second story where one Occidental and fourteen Orientals squat huddled together. A priest on a boat that is heaped with balls of rice pokes in his head: "How many needed here?" A doctor pokes in his head: "Any sick here?" Everything is floating by. Wooden walls of houses. Wooden screens. Wooden frames of floors. Wooden rice pails. Wooden kitchen utensils. The smell of wet wood. Of wet straw. But that all is trifling. These villages have open sewers, centuries old, and the contents of these are rushing, flowing, eddying, finally loitering, the filth, the feces, the offal, the excrement—phenol, skatole, indole, and all their known and unknown relatives.

But the flood subsides, and on that same triangular island the nose learns how many and how delicate are the aromas of tea. A tea tester goes to work. His bags are scattered on the straw-matted floor, fifty bags. He takes a handful of leaves, puts his Oriental face down in, breathes into the leaves his warm breath, lets the vapors rise. Rolls a leaf between his fingers. Macerates a leaf between his teeth. Sets ten teapots in front of him, cups in front of the pots, the same amount of tea in each pot. Briskly he fills the pots with boiling water. He times the steeping with an hourglass. Fills the cups. Lets himself be blindfolded. Smells the cups, somewhat rearranges their order. Pushes off the blindfold, makes notes. Then invites the guest to drink one of the teas. It is the powdered tea, *yencha*. He places a cup for the guest and for himself. The guest starts to drink. He stops him. He gives him a porcelain pestle. The guest starts to stir. He stops him. The guest is stirring too fast! At length he lifts his cup. The tea tester sniffs. The guest sniffs. The tea tester sips. The guest sips. And that, ladies and gentlemen, is the way tea should be drunk.

Age thirty. God is good. Someone dies, and there is money for a trip up the Norwegian coast. The ship goes round North Cape. Presently the nose is aware of a smell. The smell expands. Gulls are concentrating toward a point, as if the smell particles had become visible and had wings.

The ship puts in at the port of the small island of Vardö. Not a street on that island, not a path, not a space in which children play Ring-around-a-Rosey, but over their heads are racks, and on every inch of every rack, the dead headless bodies of the cod. It follows that there are also hills of cod heads, every head with two fisheyes. In Norway one hears the expression, "the good old smell of fish." Well, there it is. The rotting oil of the rotting livers runs in the street, at the edge of the sea makes patterns with the salt water—oil of the livers of twelve million cod, substitute for sunshine, health for mankind.

Later the nose is in Cairo, in the bazaar, in the shop of Ahmed Ahmed the perfumer. That shop is not bigger than the drawing room of a Pullman, and above it lives the whole of Ahmed Ahmed's family. Ahmed sits with his broad back to a wall, an Arab in a dawn-colored robe, part artist, part wizard, part scoundrel. Everything of his trade is in that shop. There is ambergris, waxy concretion formed in the intestine of the whale. There is civet, acrid glandular juice of the cat. There is musk from the musk deer and castor from the beaver. There are the aforementioned indole and skatole, in bottles, for these enter into perfumes, too. Finally, there are the essential oils. The place sways.

Ahmed Ahmed is extolling the excellences of a blend. When he thinks his customer hesitates he dips a glass rod into a greasy bottle left standing dramatically among all the pretty ones, and drops two drops into the blend. "That will be with you all your life." It is attar of rose of Bulgaria. And when the customer still hesitates Ahmed Ahmed passes the rod across the back of the customer's hand—instantly has his money and, as the saying goes, the two part friends.

Ahmed Ahmed has spoken of the relation of music and perfume, of the tones and the overtones—a well-worn speech. He has spoken of a blend that has in it three hundred factors, and if one were left out he would know. He lied, no doubt. Yet it would have its interest to run on a fellow like him, some perfumer of a caliph, some embalmer of an ancient Egyptian king, stinking unspeakably of myrrh, and 2 per cent honest, to discourse to one on perfumes.

✳   ✳   ✳

As to the pleasant and unpleasant in odors—what is good for the animal is apt to be pleasant, what bad, unpleasant. What leads to healthy food, what excites sex or gives one information about it is pleasant. What is suggestive of decomposition, of infection, of poisoning is unpleasant. In short, good smells are the conditioned stimuli to advantage, bad smells the conditioned stimuli to disadvantage.

✳ ✳ ✳

Who does not remember the last time he smelled a dead rat? He was walking past the pantry. What was that? No. He was not exactly confident in that negative. He went on into his study, Resolutely sat down to his work. But his mind wandered. The humidity must be increasing. If only it would rain. Angrily he strode back to the pantry. He looked irritably under something. Yes. No. Yes! *Yes!* He had his head right down in the cupboard now, the lowest shelf. He would just take those few things out of there. No. It must be the shelf above. An energy meanwhile was growing in him. This was a crusade. He would find this thing tonight! The sickening smell was creeping up into his sinuses. Once he stuck his head out the window for a breath of fresh air. At last he knew—it was *under the cupboard!* He moved the cupboard. Ah! Dark down there, but his mind by now had made his eyes exceeding sensitive to the shape of a certain shape of shadow. He took it by the tail and flung it into the alley.

What struck him next was how quickly the smell was gone. Once the source was gone the smell was gone. He realized how little, after all, of that smell substance must have been in the air, how little the source at any one moment was losing, how little it takes to overwhelm one. He scrubbed every cup, knife, fork, skillet, put everything back in its place. He did not leave it for the cook the next morning. He did it himself.

✳ ✳ ✳

Age forty. The nose returns to the scene of its childhood, has a permit to visit that tannery on Linn Street. As it moves across the pavement to the outer door of the place—acetic acid. As it passes through the outer door— ozone. A small ozone machine is hanging on the wall. Trim secretaries are at work, and one thinks: "Nice, the ozone oxidizes away the smell." But at that moment from some hell below the boards of the floor come wisps of death and decay.

It is but another step through an inner door into an underground light that sets the mood. A podgy workman approaches. He is asked: Does he mind the smells? He laughs. "No, Well, sometimes—when there is a shipment of hides from South America." The workman walks over to the side of the building, opens the door of a freight car, and he is right—there is something additional. He says again that he does not mind the smells. "Well, my fingers, sometimes." He smells his fingers. One thinks of his hair, the center of his pancreas, the marrow of his bones. There is a woman whose father had been a tanner, and she says that seven years after he resigned one could smell the tannery in him still. The workman talks on, explains how when the day's work is done he bathes in the tannery, puts on his street clothes, walks home, bathes again, puts on his house clothes, then in the evening maybe goes to a movie, so changes his clothes again, and after a time the lady and gentleman sitting in the seats next him get up, and look at him insultingly.

$$* \quad * \quad *$$

Did the reader ever hear a dog howl at a death? Was it before the death or after the death? That is, did the dog announce the death or mourn the death? And did the reader see the dog? Was he pointing with his nose to the house? He was smelling the death. Why not? A dog's nose is a capable organ, and doctors every day anticipate death with their eyes, with their ears, by the signs, by the symptoms. It is no longer the fashion to brag of it—and it was commoner in the old days when instruments were worse and noses had to be better—that a doctor should diagnose a disease by its smell. Measles, tuberculosis, typhoid, uremia, et cetera. Anyone's nose can diagnose an open cancer. So why not a nose smell impending death? A faint odor of partial decay, a dead spot in a life still quick. Why not? It is more difficult to understand fully the smelling of one *marked* for death, as the gypsy in Hemingway's novel, because that means preordination, God in league with the gypsy. In certain nations it is a bird that comes to announce the death. The principle there is the same, of course. In the hospital a nurse had a widespread reputation. She said things like: "No, it will not be tonight—perhaps tomorrow." *Odor mortis* is an old, old, Latin phrase.

And if the dying have an odor, perhaps the departed, too. Perhaps the ghost is an odor. There are considerations to suggest it. Those who have seen a ghost know that it is an edgeless affair. That is true also for a smell. A ghost to anyone trained in the physical sciences might well be "infinitely fine particles infinitely divided." That is a smell. One can see a log fire right through a ghost. One can through a smell. A certain ghost will settle down into a corner of the davenport and merge with it. That is a heavy ghost—a smell of high molecular weight. But most ghosts, as everyone knows, ascend—smells of low molecular weight.

Then if all this be true there are certain practical deductions. It is not the good who shall rise on Judgment Day, but the fragrant. It is not by one's deeds on earth that one shall be measured, but by whether the doorman up there has a preference for lily or for herring. And a life well spent will be that of him who has cultivated not his character—his essence!

COMMON FISH
OF AN INDIAN GARDEN

D. D. CUNNINGHAM

"Slow efts about the edges sleep;
Swift darting water-flies
Shoot on the surface; down the deep
Fast following bubbles rise.

Look down. What groves that scarcely sway!
What 'wood obscure,' profound!
What jungle! where some beast of prey
Might choose his vantage ground."

—AUSTIN DOBSON

"The pleasant'st angling is to see the fish
Cut with her golden oars the silver stream."

—*Much Ado about Nothing*

In such a swamp as that of the greater part of Lower Bengal, very few enclosures of any considerable size are devoid of ponds, or at least of waterholes of a more or less permanent nature, and hence fish of various kinds form a conspicuous feature in the garden Fauna of the region. A very attractive feature they are, as any one will allow who has ever watched the shoals of little fish that are always gliding about in the weedy shallows. Among the most alluring of them are the so-called "rainbow fish." They abound in the submerged forests of grass that fringe the water after heavy falls of rain. There they hang, hovering about, curiously investigating all the recesses of the jungle, and every now and then charging at one another in furiously hostile encounters. They are so exceedingly thin as to be almost invisible when looked at from above, but they shine out conspicuously wherever the sun's rays strike in obliquely and light up the brilliant tints of their side scales and the lateral surfaces of their fins. Then they show up, painted in a ground colour of soft greyish yellow, adorned with brown bands, and contrasting with the ruddy hue of the fins, the dorsal and ventral ones bordered behind by a line of shining blue, and the former shaded above, and capped by a sharp black spine, which is at once erected on any excitement or alarm. Swarms of other little fish accompany them, some spotted and barred with brown and red, and others shining so brightly that they look like little sudden flashes of light as they dart hither and thither through the sunlit water. Curious little creatures, too, go gliding about in troops close to the surface, so translucent and quietly coloured that they would readily escape notice were it not for the presence of a luminously white speck on the back of their heads.

Fish seem to have very little sense of proportion, as quite ludicrously little ones, hardly as large, and certainly not nearly as strong as their intended prey, may often be seen leaping out of the water and trying to lay hold of the great brown hornets, who are for ever quartering about over the surface and gleaning dragon-flies' eggs and other adherent dainties from the projecting blades of grass or leaves of floating weeds. Farther out from the banks larger fish swim slowly about, and now and then a great splash and swirl announces that a monster has come up from the depths to roll about at the surface.

As the monsoon continues many ponds are temporarily connected with the river by devious water-ways that form roads by means of which grey mullets, *Mugil corsula*, travel up in pairs and little troops to visit even very small pieces of water. Their presence in a pond is always welcome, for not only are they very good to eat, but they are very lively and amusing creatures. Whilst travelling, they swim so close to the surface that their great, goggle eyes stand out prominently above the water, and present a very curious appearance from a little distance, looking like animated bubbles coursing about in pairs or groups. Where their progress is opposed by a strong current they often prefer to travel in a series of jumps along the surface of the water, seeming to find it easier to make way in this fashion than by diving below the upper layers of the stream. It is very interesting to watch a troop of them struggling up the river at a point where a landing-stage or flight of steps projects into the stream so as to deflect the course of the current and give rise to the formation of backwaters. Their perseverance in contending with the difficulty is very striking. Everything, of course, favours their advance in the back-water beneath the projecting point, but when the latter is reached their trials set in in full force and without warning. Some fortunate individuals, and especially some of those who elect to force the passage by jumping along the surface, get through at once, but others only succeed after they have again and again been overpowered in the swirl and swept outwards to be carried down by the stream for some distance ere they manage to fight their way into the backwater and begin a fresh attempt. Their experiences are curiously reminiscent of those of country boats under like conditions. Their habit of swimming so close to the surface is a source of danger to them. They are taken in casting nets, and a fisherman may often be seen following a troop of them along the edge of the stream, guided by their projecting eyes in his endeavours to drive them into a convenient place by throwing stones into the water around them.

A particularly interesting and pretty spectacle may often be seen in clear ponds towards the end of the rainy season. On looking down through the limpid water one sees a great shoal of very small fish, each of them about an inch or somewhat less in length, of a semi-transparent brown, and decorated with three longitudinal bands of vivid yellow on the back and sides. They glide gently about close to the bank, busily feeding on invisible objects adhering to the aquatic grasses and pondweeds. The sight of such a multitude of lovely little creatures oaring themselves about in the clear water would in itself be very attractive, but what renders it specially fascinating is that the moving shoal is persistently attended by a pair, or more rarely by a single specimen, of much larger, mottled grey fish who follow it anxiously about from place to place. At first sight they might be suspected of evil intent, but a little study of their habits is enough to show that they are innocent of any desire to prey upon their little companions. The latter do not seem to be in the least alarmed by their presence, and often seem quite ready to be herded by them in their travels. Owing to their relatively large size, the chaperones are often unable to follow their charges into the recesses of the marginal fringe of weeds, and are forced to remain hovering anxiously about outside it in the open water opposite the point at which the shoal is feeding. When the fry keep together all goes well, but, if they break up into several parties, their guardians become very uneasy. So long as there are a pair of them there is not so much trouble, but, when one only is in charge, it often has very hard work before it can get its flock gathered together again. The little fish, owing to their small size, can turn round much more quickly and in much smaller spaces than their agitated attendant, whose anxiety becomes so evident as to be quite touching. The ungainly haste with which it hurries from place to place, here trying to check the progress of one part of the shoal, and there endeavouring to hurry up the loiterers, makes one quite unhappy until it has safely attained its end. The behaviour of the large fish is certainly very suggestive of parental anxiety and supervision, but it may be that its motive is of a purely selfish and commensal origin, and that the apparent affection is merely owing to a desire to keep the fry together because they are useful in disturbing and driving out prey from inconvenient shallows and tangled growths of weeds.

In gardens actually abutting on the river, the banks and gháts of the latter, and the margins of closely adjoining ponds are often haunted by throngs of common mud-skippers, *Periopthalmi*. They are most entertaining creatures, and much time may be happily spent in the study of their quaint ways. Their re-appearance on the banks of the river in autumn is one of the regular signs that the floods are abating and that cooler weather is approaching; for, during the height of the monsoon, they seem to abandon the larger streams, probably on account of the violence of the currents then prevailing in them. When they are present, the best time for studying their manners and customs is whilst the tide is ebbing. As the level of the water falls and leaves fringes of damp muddy surfaces along its margins, small grey objects may be seen coming up out of the stream to hop about over the ground or sit in strangely wide-awake fashion on any brickbats, stumps of wood, edges of steps, or other points of vantage projecting from the mud. No one would at first sight dream of regarding them as fish, for, even when closely examined, they look much more like small, slimy lizards, or gigantic tadpoles in an advanced stage of evolution. What makes them particularly unfishlike is the way in which they use their pectoral fins; for, whilst sitting still, they bring them well forward and curve the dilated ends down like little webbed feet, on which they rest with their heads and shoulders well raised, and from which they are ready to take off in a great leap on the slightest alarm. As the tide goes on falling, more and more of them emerge, until all the banks are dotted over with quaint little monsters, holding up their bull-dog muzzles and great goggle eyes with an air of grotesque defiance, while every now and then one of them will suddenly go off in a great leap in the hope of capturing an insect, or in order to assault and dislodge one of its neighbours who has secured a desirable watchtower.

The multitudes of them, who swarm over the muddy slopes of the larger tidal channels and devious water-lanes of the outer Sundarbans, must be seen to be imagined. Their habits differ markedly in different areas within the Sundarbans. A steamer in passing along a narrow channel causes a very considerable displacement of the surface of the water; an initial depression and indraught exposes great surfaces of the muddy banks, and is followed by a series of huge rushing waves that follow the vessel and wash up over the slopes with enough force to knock all the mud-skippers, who are taking an airing on them, head over heels. The fish do not at all enjoy such forced exercise, but in their endeavour to avoid it, do not act alike everywhere. In completely unreclaimed and uninhabited parts of the Sundarbans the approach of the waves is preceded by a general and precipitate flight of mud-skippers, hurrying up the slopes in order to get beyond the reach of the threatening inundation; but in channels traversing cleared and partially cultivated areas, the line of flight follows an opposite direction, and the fish hasten down in order to reach the water before it is disturbed. These differences of habit are certainly correlated with the absence or presence of a special danger. In all the inhabited parts of the Sundarbans the people live to a great extent on fish, and are consequently always on the outlook for chances of catching them. The varieties of ways of fishing that may be seen during the course of a single day's voyage are quite wonderful. One of the commonest is carried out by means of an apparatus consisting of a truncated cone of wicker-work open at either end and looking like a deep, tapering basket without a bottom. When in use, the fisherman carries it about as he wades along the muddy slopes or shallows, and, when he comes to a point at which he thinks that fish are lying, he suddenly plants the broad end of the cone down into the mud, and then passes his hand through the narrow end and gropes about for anything that may have been imprisoned within the wicker enclosure. Fishing of this kind is, of course, rendered easier by anything increasing the area of shallow water or leaving fish exposed in the mud of the banks. The passage of a steamer tends to act in this way, both by the initial indraught and by the subsequent violent inundation that it gives rise to. The fishermen fully realise this, and eagerly avail themselves of the opportunity thus afforded. This implies that, in channels where fishing is habitually carried on, the passage of a steamer exposes the mud-skippers to a twofold danger, and that they clearly adopt the best course for escaping it by immediate flight to the deeper parts of the stream. But, in places where no fishermen are present, no special danger attends farther progress up the sloping banks of mud, a course which must be most effectual as a means of avoiding all inconvenience from the temporary disturbance of the water, and here we find the fish almost all running upwards. The differences in the behaviour of the fish in connection with the differences of environment are very striking, and at first sight might be taken to imply the exercise of highly evolved intelligence. They are, however, probably merely the outcome of processes of natural selection.

It is probable that, from the outset, there was a dislike to the disturbance attending any considerable agitation of the surface of the water, and a corresponding tendency to try to avoid it, but that originally the line of flight was unspecialised and directed indifferently either upwards or downwards over the surface of the banks. But, in places where no special danger attends an upward course, those fish who naturally tended to follow it would certainly be more likely to escape injury than those who descended and thus ran a risk of being knocked about by the waves.

STARS OF THE EARTH

L. M. BUDGEN

"Among the crooked lanes, on every hedge,
The glowworm lights her gem, and through the dark
A moving radiance twinkles."

"Voir au ciel briller les étoiles,
Et sous l'herbe les vers luisans."

Besides almost every other object in the world, its various luminaries, both natural and moral, find their representatives and symbols in the insect creation. The fixed, or as it appears to our childish and, what is nearly the same thing, our unreflective view, the little twinkling star, is emulated by the modest radiance of the glowworm; the planetary bodies, for ever wheeling in their orbits, are better represented by the restless fire-fly; whilst the streaming meteor and blazing comet find their prototypes in the brilliant *Fulgoræ*, or Lantern-carriers, as described shooting in eccentric courses across the gloom of tropic skies.

Then, for the luminaries of the world considered morally, we shall be at no loss to find symbolic parallels in the varied qualities, habits, and localities of luminous insects. Our little English glowworm, as she glimmers on her mossy bank, how well, to borrow the words of a late lamented poet, does she serve to represent those quiet Christian spirits, who

"in humble trust
Shine meekly 'mid their native dust,
The glowworms of the earth!"

And if, as opposed to these modest "lights," we desire correspondents for the "stars" of the world, we may scarcely find more apt ones than in the great lantern-flies, the radiant uproarious night-singers, the *scare-sleeps* of Guiana, bearing aloft their fiery flambeaux, like torches of noisy revellers, and grating on the "ear of night" by the harsh music of their loud discordant cymbals.

The attention of philosophers was in very early ages directed to various phenomena resulting from the properties of light, and, amongst others, the remarkable phosphoric appearances of certain animal and vegetable bodies. Ancient writers allude in general terms to the existence of luminous insects, of which the species most early known is supposed to be the Linnæan *Lampyrides*, or flying glowworms, abundant in the south of Europe, as well as in Asia and some parts of Africa. The Greeks included all shining insects under the name *Lampyris*, and the Latins called them *Cicindela, Noctiluca*, and *Luciola*, under which latter designation the flying glowworms are still (as we have seen) known in Italy.

With the *Fulgoræ*, or lantern-flies, the ancients are thought to have had no acquaintance, for, though Asia produces a few species of them, the most remarkable are peculiar to the warmest parts of America. These singular insects are supposed, indeed, to have been quite unknown in Europe till the latter end of the 17th century, when Madame Merian, in her beautifully illustrated work on the Insects of Surinam, and Dr. Grew, published histories and figures of the lantern-carriers, which, by the skeptical of their time, were esteemed fictitious; and strange to say, often as they have been since described, figured, and said to have been seen by travellers, their most remarkable property, that of emitting light, would seem, even now, a matter of doubt, at all events of disputation.

This appears to have arisen from their luminosity having escaped the notice of various recent observers; but as that of the glowworm and the fire-fly is not always visible, this proves nothing. Madame Merian is not, it is true, quite so celebrated for the Dutch accuracy of her pen, as for the fidelity displayed, with few exceptions, by her pencil; but one can hardly suppose that that ingenious and indefatigable lady was deceived herself, or meant to deceive her readers, by mere *ignes fatui*, in the following often-quoted description of her first acquaintance with the light of the *Fulgoræ*:—

"Once," says she, "when the Indians brought me a number of these lantern-carriers, I put them in a wooden box without being aware of their shining at night, but being awakened by an unusual noise (probably their singing), and being much frightened, I jumped out of bed, and ordered a light, not knowing whence the sound proceeded. We soon discovered that its origin was in the box, which we opened with some degree of fear, and were still more alarmed, even to letting it fall, when there appeared to issue from it a flame which seemed to receive additional lustre as often as another insect flew out."

Donovan's minute description and figure of the Red-tipped lantern-fly* of Hindostan, would appear to leave even less room for disbelief as to the lumen of this creature's fiery proboscis, a Bardolphian nose giving it a just title to be regarded, amongst insects, as, verily, a true "Knight of the burning lamp." Our author says of a specimen in his own possession, that "its large, dark purple trunk is sprinkled with spots of white phosphores-cent powder, and the tip, which is scarlet, and somewhat pellucid, still retains a reddish glow that almost convinces us that the insect, when living, diffused light from both;"—that is, trunk and its apex. "Supposing (he adds) this conjecture right, *the illuminated apex of the trunk would resem-ble a globule of fire, and the numerous phosphoric spots on the tube form a train of glittering stars to accompany it.*" This truly would be an insect comet.

Our present rapid communication with India, and new relations with China, might soon, we should think, afford opportunities for the disper-sion of every shade of doubt, if any remains, concerning the light-giving properties of these *Fulgoræ*. Imported from the above countries in the egg, or even alive, and hatched or kept living by artificial heat, we may yet see with our own stay-at-home eyes, whether these living lanterns carry light; and if so it prove, might we not, curiously, peruse letters from China, by aid of an insect luminary which may have helped once to light a real pagoda,—have perched upon the towers of Pekin, or even have flown "betwixt the wind" and his Celestial Majesty?

Perhaps, also, amongst other benefits derived, from the ends of the world being brought so near together, may result, during the course of this economic and adaptive age, the employment of the "*Fulgora candelaria*," even to the saving of our own candle-ends, and the helping to "make both ends meet."

Yet more desirable, and more easy, doubtless, to accomplish, than the introduction, "all alive," of the lantern-carriers,† would be that of the

---

Fulgora pyrorhynchus. Donovan's 'Insects of India.'
†*Fulgoræ.*

beautiful fire-flies* so abundant in the West Indies and South America. Ocular demonstration is not indeed, in their case, wanted for the purpose of throwing light on the matter of their own effulgence, on which not a shadow of obscurity exists; but since not merely to introduce, but also to naturalize them would seem no Utopian project, it were well worth the trial, for the sake of throwing tropic radiance on our native landscapes. These brilliant foreigners being natives also of Canada and the Vaudois, where the winters are so rigorous, there seems the less reason why they should not be acclimated to Britain.

A gentleman† attempting to introduce them from the Bahamas, kept them on the voyage, from June to September, feeding them on the juice from sugar-canes, which they broke to obtain. The supplying their cages with damp moss, or their daily immersion in cold water, has been recommended for their preservation, by affording a substitute for the moisture of the damp meadows which are their favourite localities.

The great lantern-flies spoken of above, belong to that order of insects termed *Hemiptera*, being allied, unlike as they may seem, to bugs, boat-flies, and water-scorpions; but the fire-fly of the tropics, our present subject, being of the order *Coleoptera*, is a beetle. By day, as sombre and dull-looking a little animal as any to be seen; shape, longish; colour, blackish brown. When at rest, or walking, it is content with the display of only two lights, emitted from a pair of lamps, or yellow tubercles, placed on either side the chest; but when, with wings extended, it shoots across the dusky sky, another luminary, also in the thorax, but seated further back, is rendered visible.

Though we have none of these fire-flies, as yet, in England, we have certain insects of the same family, which in all, save luminosity, greatly resemble them. These are the very common longish brown beetles, known familiarly as "spring and click beetles," also "skip-jacks"—names expressive of their power, when laid upon their backs, of springing or leaping into the air, with a clicking sound.

Our readers, as we hope, all know by this time, that every beetle has been in its time a grub or larva. They have all heard, too, most likely, of that farmer's terror, the destructive wire-worm; but to some, even amongst farmers, it may possibly be a piece of information that this wire-worm is

*Elateridæ.
†Mr. Lees.

none other than a beetle grub, and the grub, moreover, of *such* a beetle as the click, or skip-jack, an *Elator*, nearly resembling the tropic fire-fly; the grub of the latter loving to feed on the roots of sugar-canes (to which, says Humboldt, it is often very injurious), in lieu of the roots of corn and other vegetables, the favourite fare of his British relative.

These foreign lights (though the last, at all events, are no *ignes fatui*) have lured us, already, somewhat wide of our self-appointed track, the haunts, namely, of our native insects; but before we return to them, we must yet wander for awhile amidst a brilliant galaxy of "winged stars," the *Lampyridæ*, or flying glowworms of the south of Europe.* These are also the Italian *Lucciole*, of the which, having, *en fabuliste*, discoursed already, we are the more beholden to give, *en naturaliste*, some brief account.

Like the tropic fire-flies, these glowworms are beetles, though of a different family, that of the *Lampyridæ*, of which the *Lucciola* is a very small species, with blackish-brown wingcases; the legs, as well as thorax, of which the shield nearly hides the head, being reddish yellow. The light of these insects, when creeping, or perching upon trees, is described as being hardly perceptible, but becoming brilliant on flight; not constant, but scintillating, as if disclosed on successive expansions of the wings. Appearing with the twilight, their full radiance shines forth in darkness; when some, shooting through the air, make luminous tracks in all directions, while others spangle the shrubs and herbage.

Their appearance and effect in the neighbourhood of Genoa has been thus described by Sir J. E. Smith;—

"On the eve of St. John the Baptist, the great festival of Genoa, the town was brilliantly illuminated, while along the purple coast to the west, the last rays of the setting sun still trembled on the hills, and the moon arose in the east. To these three contrasted lights was added the singular effect of innumerable flying glowworms darting their momentary splendour through all the streets, gardens, and rooms. We used frequently to catch these little insects, and entangle them in the ladies' hair and head-dresses, a decoration which the women of some countries adopt for themselves."

By the same writer is mentioned the superstitions of some Moorish ladies (prisoners of the Genoese), who on a sultry summer's evening shut their windows against these luminous visitants, under the idea that they were the souls of departed relatives. A similar notion is said to prevail

---

Lampyris Italica.

amongst the Italian peasantry concerning the *Lucciola*, and is entertained by the ignorant of other countries with respect to luminous insects of their own.

Some of these glowworms of southern Europe—called *flying*, because the beetles of both sexes, contrary to those of England, sport wings—have been seen, it is said, in Hertfordshire; and there is little doubt but what these, at all events, might be introduced and established in our southern counties.

Now we are at home again! From the swamps of Guiana and the jungles of India; from the savannahs and plantations of the West Indies; from the olive-groves and vineyards of southern Europe, with their noisy lantern-bearers—their effulgent fire-flies—their sparkling *lucciole*—we are returned to the quiet over-arching lanes of our own England, and the quiet radiance of our English glowworm; and, after all we have been saying about the importation of foreign stars, perhaps we should be very sorry to see the eclipse of our native gem.

As well, perhaps, might we desire to behold the modest maids and wives of England (of whom glowworms are the shining symbols) eclipsed in their quiet homes by the brilliant charmers of east, and west, and south, dazzling and restless as the luminous flutterers of their respective climes. Each, doubtless, are best in their own accordant places.

Our English glowworm* (as we presume most people are aware) is the wingless female of a winged beetle, which also carries a light, though one of much inferior lustre.† As surrounded by hedge-row flowers (symbols of home attractions), she shines from her mossy bed, supposed to guide the eye while awaiting the appearance of her active mate, truly the glowworm is a perfect image of loving maiden or anxious wife, who, at a cottage in the very lane close by, has placed a candle in the casement, or heaped wood upon the hearth, by way, at once, of pole-star and of welcome, to her hastening swain or loitering husband. Pity that an idea so pretty should have come, in these unpoetic days, to be looked on as a mere growth of fancy, nipped, though not uprooted, by the touch of cold Inquiry. But so it is; and from the winged lover being provided with a lantern of his own (albeit, a dark one), as well as from other facts, not more

---

Lampyris noctiluca.

†A solitary glowworm, resembling the English but much larger and more brilliant, was seen by Bishop Heber in Ceylon. He makes no mention of lantern-flies.

conclusive, it has been doubted whether, after all, the torches of Cupid and of Hymen have been the true illuminators of the glowworm's lamp.

Cui bono, then, the lady's taper? To answer this inquiry Conjecture has been clever, but, as usual, often at variance with herself.

While it is supposed by some, that the light of the wingless beetle is bestowed for her protection, to scare away her hungry foes, the nightingale and other birds of night; it is opined by others, that the insect's gift of brilliancy (like many of the like sort bestowed upon mankind) is the very mean of her destruction, the very lure and light by which her biped foes are assisted to discover and devour her.

Some people, again, have suggested that, whatsoever else its purpose, the glowworm's luminary may be employed as a lamp for her own supper-table, after having previously lent its aid in the finding of her evening meal. It has been observed, indeed, that, for the serving of both such uses, her light would have seemed placed more conveniently at head than tail; but its diffusion, we should think, is amply wide enough to render this objection of little import.

The *Lampyridæ*, even of our northern climate, have southern predilections, being never seen in the north of Scotland, and most universally abounding in the southern English counties.

To most of the dwellers in these her favourite resorts, the person of our insect lamp-bearer, so conspicuously displayed in her own light, must have been, we should suppose, familiar (as with ourselves) from the summer nights of childhood,—from that night, in particular, never to be forgot, which first brought one of these shining mysteries within the compass of our fingers and a box. While of other little creepers we yet scarce knew the difference betwixt head and tail, the figure of our first captive glowworm, as seen at night, and examined next morning, almost before daylight served, was stamped upon our memory; and, had we never seen another since, we should not forget her tiny head and, as we called them, horns, mocking our curious eye, as she just put forth and then withdrew them under the shielding back-plate which covered the forepart of her body; that slate-coloured, oblong, flat, wingless body, all divided into rings, and bearing at its nether extremity the *lamp*,—by night a lustrous emerald, by day a dull pale spot,—composed, as we have learnt now, of the sulphur-coloured substance which supplies its light.

Of this article, by the way, though it costs her nothing, the glowworm, it would seem, is somewhat economic; Gilbert White, at least, confirmatory of Will Shakspeare, having thought that she always puts out her light at the decent hour of eleven or twelve, or begins then, according to the poet and the poetic idea, to "pale her ineffectual fire."

Now for a word or two,—borrowed, of course, from the scientific page, but considerably at variance,—respecting the supposed nature and quality of this and other insect fires. One experimentalist, having found that the glowworm's light is neither diminished by immersion in water, nor increased by application of heat,—that it is not capable of ignition by the flame of a candle, nor possessed of any sensible heat when separate from the bearer's body, denies in this luminous matter the existence of any ordinary composition of phosphorus; suggesting, however, that the above facts are favourable to the supposition of light being a quality of matter, rather than a substance.

Another examiner, on the contrary, seems to have ascertained that the glowworm's light-diffusing substance is chiefly albumen, combined with a portion of phosphorus; and as phosphorus can only become luminous by contact with oxygen (supposing it uncombined with a fatty matter or albumen), he considers this requisite supplied by means of the male insect's respiration, which is strongest during flight; while, in the female, which flies not at all, the greater quantity of albuminous substance contained in her thick body more than compensates for the lesser respiratory action.

Enough, at all events, has been ascertained about the illuminating matter of the glowworm's lamp to prove it perfectly incapable of setting light to any tapers, save those of fairy manufacture. Who could quarrel with that pretty conceit of our immortal Bard, which converts "the glowworm's fiery eyes" into lucifers, for the use of Titania's household? Yet, in our character of entomologist, we may, perhaps, be permitted to observe, that Shakespeare has here taken more of poet's license than he is wont to do in his allusions to natural objects, which are in general so infinitely more correct than those of his modern brethren of the lyre. It is admissible enough to term "fiery" what looks luminous, but it is a long stretch, truly, even to the length of the creature's antipodes, to endow it with "fiery eyes," in lieu of a fiery-seeming tail. Though the eyes of most night-prowlers are luminous, those of the female glowworm are not, we believe, at all so, any more than those of her flying mate; but the latter are prodigiously *large*, so large as to constitute the largest portion of his head. The purpose of these disproportioned organs cannot, perhaps, be positively told; but, according to the old theory of the "light of love," we should suppose that if the lady glowworm (an insect Hero) were, on first acquaintance, to exclaim to her Leander, "Oh, my dear! what great eyes you have!" he would reply, like the wolfish granddam, though in quite another spirit, "Ah, love! they are all the better to *see* you with!"

Before having quite done with "fiery eyes," we may notice that if the "Swan of Avon" had applied this epithet to the moth instead of glowworm, his fancy would have better corresponded with fact; for a fact it is, though probably quite unknown in the days of Shakspeare, that many species of night-flying moths are endowed with luminosity in the organs of sight, the light being most visible while the insect is in motion.

"Pour l'amour de ses beaux yeux," we may perhaps, therefore, include the moth among luminous insects; but there is another, a native of England, perhaps as common as the glowworm, which, although from its habits comparatively little noticed, shares her luminous endowments to a very considerable extent. This is the electric centipede,* a black, many-legged crawler, which almost everybody must have seen and shrunk from, as it has crossed their path in the daytime. As this creature (which has been likened to a miniature model of a serpent's skeleton) moves, serpent-like, forward or backward, he leaves behind him, or before him, a tangible track of the phosphoric light, which, in darkness, strongly illuminates his unsightly form; but, as if conscious of his loathly aspect, it is mostly in daylight, when it is least conspicuous, that he issues from his lair, some abode of darkness, either in the earth, or beneath a stone.

The Mole Cricket is another insect which has been supposed to emit light; to have been, indeed, in some cases, the veritable Jack o' Lantern—the *ignis fatuus* of the benighted traveller. But of this curious insect we have already narrated facts and told a tale.

The harmless quality of all these insect lights is a kind provision of nature, no less adapted than a variety of others to attract our admiring notice.

Truly, it is a thing wonderful and beautiful, to find in animated forms a substance so nearly resembling that formidable element, fire; one possessed of its power to diffuse light, yet wholly destitute of its dangerous properties. Had it been otherwise, only imagine the direful results. Earth would have been the scene of perpetual conflagrations, and its inhabitants

---

Scolopendra electrica.

for ever on the watch to extinguish or guard against the mischief of living sparks. A few tribes of fiery insects would have sufficed to change the entire face of nature and the superstructures of man.

Where, in America, would have been the forests? Consumed, perhaps, before worthy of the name, or cleared by the fire-fly, before the settler's axe. And where the settler himself, with his log-habitation?

In Asia, wooden temples and pagodas might not have been; or scarce one would have escaped destruction, lit up almost as often by the lantern-fly without, as by the paper lanterns within; while in Europe, even in our native isle, barns would have blazed, and corn and hay-stacks have been nightly fired, and the lurking incendiaries, which no police could have detected, no jury have tried, no judge have sentenced, would have been glowworms in the grass, or centipedes in the earth, laying (Fawkes-like) their trains of combustion underground!

But have luminous insects the positive quality of *use*, as well as the negative attribute of being harmless? In common with all created things undoubtedly they have, and to themselves their luminaries serve clearly some important purpose, however we may yet be in the dark as to their exact mode of appliance. Nor, as regards mankind, are these "diamonds of the night" altogether without their value, having, as such, been made in several countries subservient both to ornament and use.

While our native glowworms have begemmed no other beauty but that of the sleeping wild-flowers, the tropic fireflies have sparkled in dark tresses, and been rivalled by flashing eyes,—have been employed by the gay in the decoration of festive garments, and by the grave in the conning of small print. The Père du Tertre, in his history of the Antilles, speaks of reading his Breviary by the light of one of these living lamps. The natives of St. Domingo, and other islands, are also said to have used them literally as "a light to their feet and a lantern to their paths," by attaching one to each foot when travelling by night, employing them also in the lighting of their habitations. Fire-flies serve, besides, the important purpose of destroying mosquitos, which are their favourite prey.

But the glimmer of our English glowworm?—*that* surely can serve no other uses save its own? *She* would be a dull diamond in the maiden's tresses—a dim sight to read by—a sorry lantern on a murky night. True; but for all that, she shines not for herself alone: for us, also, her light is not without its uses. What these are, we may best answer when returning from our summer's evening walk, as the glowworms and the stars are coming out together; for then our minds must be more creeping than the wingless light-bearers themselves, if they rise not from *them* to the glorious orbs they humbly imitate, and thence to the Great Source and Centre of Life and Light, from whom alike emanate the "stars of the earth" and the suns of the universe.

SOURCES

Charles C. Abbot, M.D., "An October Diary", from *Upland and Meadow: A Poaet-guissings Chronicle*, London, 1886.

Diane Ackerman, "King Penguins", from *The Moon by Whale Light*, New York, 1991.

Grant Allen, "Prophetic Autumn", from *Moorland Idylls*, London, 1896.

John James Audubon, "Three Natural Disasters", from *Ornithological Biography or an Account of the Habits of the Birds of the United States*, Edinburgh, 1831.

Thomas Belt, "The Atlantic Forest", from *The Naturalist in Nicaragua*, London, 1874.

Two Brothers (Anonymous), "The Falls of Niagara", from *The United States and Canada*, London, 1862.

L. M. Budgen, "Stars of the Earth", from *Episodes of Insect Life*, London, 1851.

Rachel Carson, "The Marginal World", from *The Edge of the Sea*, London, 1955.

John Clare, "Bird Lists", from *The Natural History Prose Writings by John Clare*, Oxford, 1983.

D. D. Cunningham, "Common Fish of an Indian Garden", from *Some Indian Friends and Acquaintances*, London, 1903.

R. B. Cunninghame Graham, "La Pampa", from *Thirty Stories and Sketches*, London, 1930.

Charles Darwin, "The Falkland Islands", from *Journal During the Voyages of H. M. S. 'Beagle' Round the World*, London, 1897.

Daniel Defoe, "Crusoe's Island", from *Robinson Crusoe*, London, 1719.

Jacques Delamain, "Why Birds Sing", translated by Ruth and Anna Sarason, London, 1932.

Annie Dillard, "Nightwatch", from, *Pilgrim at Tinker Creek*, New York, 1974.

Gustav Eckstein, "12,000,000 Cod", from *Everyday Miracle*, London, 1949.

J. H. Fabre, "Three Strokes of a Dagger", from *Insect Life: Souvenirs of a Naturalist*, London, 1901.

Philip Henry Gosse, "Hoyle's Mouth", from *Tenby: A Sea-Side Holiday*, London, 1856.

G. D. Hale Carpenter, "Monkeys", from *A Naturalist on Lake Victoria*, London 1920.

Charles A. Hall, "A Ramble in May", from *The Open Book of Nature*, London, 1925.

Gerard Manley Hopkins, "Journal 1866", from *Poems and Prose*, London, 1943.

W. H. Hudson, "The Temples of the Hills", from *Adventures Among Birds*, London, 1913.

Richard Jefferies, "The Crows", from *Nature Near London*, London, 1893.

D. H. Lawrence, "Flowery Tuscany", from *Phoenix: The Posthumous Papers*, New York, 1936.

Barry Lopez, "The Narwhal", from *Arctic Dreams: Imagination and Desire in a Northern Landscape*, New York, 1986.

Maurice Maeterlinck, "The Secret of the Formicary", from *The Life of the Ant*, translated by Bernard Miall, London, 1930.

Herman Melville, "The Encantadas", from *The Piazza Tales*, New York, 1928.

Vladimir Nabokov, "Butterflies", from *Speak Memory*, London, 1947.

Theodore Roosevelt and Edmund Heller, "The Bonte-Quagga", from *Life-History of African Game Animals*, London, 1915.

Henry Seebohm, "Birds of Siberia", from *The Birds of Siberia*, London, 1901.

Edmund Selous, "Bird Watching", from *Bird Watching*, London, 1901.

Ernest Thompson Seton, " The Wild Geese of Wyndygoul", from *Wild Animal Ways*, London, 1916.

Henry David Thoreau, "Shooting the Rapids in a Batteau", from *The Maine Woods*, London, 1910.

John Timbs, "Real Life of the Beaver", from *Strange Stories of the Animal World*, London, 1866.

Edward Topsell, "The Cat", from *Historie of Foure-Footed Beastes*, London, 1607.

Mark Twain, "Fauna and Flora of Nevada", from *Roughing It*, London, 1885.

Priscilla Wakefield, "Heavenly Place", from *Letters of Arthur Middleton to his Brother Edwin*, London, 1892.

Charles Waterton, "Into the Amazon", from *Wanderings in South America*, London, 1925.

AUTHOR BIOGRAPHIES

Charles C. Abbot, England (1768–1817). A Bedfordshire vicar, he was an avid botanist whose five-volume herbarium is still preserved in Turney Abbey. Other than religious works—*Parochial Divinity* (1807) and *Monody on the Death of Horatio, Lord Nelson* (1805)—he published a *Flora Bedfordiensis* (1798). His *Upland and Meadow: a Poaetquissings Chronicle* was published posthumously, in 1886.

Diane Ackerman, United States (1948–   ). A staff writer at *The New Yorker*, she taught for several years in Washington and New York State. She is the author of several books of poetry, including *Jaguar of Sweet Laughter* (1991) and four volumes of non-fiction: *Twilight of the Tenderfoot* (1980), *On Extended Wings* (1985), *A Natural History of the Senses* (1990) and *The Moon by Whale Light* (1991).

Charles Grant Blairfindie Allen, Canada (1848–1899). Professor of "mental and moral philosophy" in Jamaica for several years, he returned to England where he established himself as a popular scientist and novelist. He published *Psychological Aesthetics* (1877) and *The Colour-sense* (1879) praised by Darwin and T.H. Huxley. Among his fiction *Strange Stories* (1884) and *The Woman Who Did* (1895) are his best-known books.

John James Audubon, Haiti (1785–1851). He was educated in France and trained with the artist David, before establishing himself on his father's estate near Philadelphia. He is famous for his wonderful books of animal portraits, especially *The Birds of America* (1827–38) and *Viviparous Quadrupeds of North America* (1842–1854), the latter completed by his sons.

Thomas Belt, England (1832–1878). Traveller, geologist and gold-mining expert, the author of many scientific essays on a vast range of subjects, largely based on his experiences in the North and South America, Siberia and Australia. His most celebrated work is *The Naturalist in Nicaragua* (1874).

L. M. Budgen, England (?–?). Under the pseudonym "Acheta Domestica", she wrote several enchanting chronicles of her observations of nature, including *Episodes of Insect Life* (1849–51), *March Winds and April Showers* (1854) and *May Flowers* (1855).

G. D. Hale Carpenter, England (1882). The author of a classic study, *Mimicry* (1933), he also wrote an account of his expedition to Central Africa in the early decades of this century, *A Naturalist on Lake Victoria* (1920).

Rachel Carson, United States (1907–1964). Pioneer ecologist who achieved public recognition with her book *Silent Spring* (1963), a fierce warning against the indiscriminate use of pesticides and weed-killers. Her other books include *The Sea Around Us* (1951) and *The Edge of the Sea* (1955).

John Clare, England (1793–1864). The son of a country labourer, he learned about nature first-hand, and wrote about his observations in several books: *Poems Descriptive of Rural Life and Scenery* (1820), *The Village Minstrel* (1821), *The Shepherd's Calender* (1827) and *The Rural Muse* (1835). He died in an insane asylum.

David Douglas Cunningham, England (1843–1914). A lieutenant colonel in the British army, he studied the natural environment during his posting in India. The result was a book of memoirs, *Some Indian Friends and Acquaintances* (1903).

Robert Bontine Cunninghame Graham, Scotland (1852–1936). Traveller, rancher and anti-imperialist. He wrote about his travels in books such as *Mogreb-el-Acksa* (1898) about Morocco and *A Vanished Arcadia* (1901) about Paraguay. Other titles include *Success* (1902), *Scottish Stories* (1914) and *The Horses of the Conquest* (1930).

Charles Robert Darwin, England (1809–1882). After embarking as a naturalist on a royal expedition in 1831, he published the account of his travels in 1839 under the title *Journal of Researches into the Geology and Natural History of the various countries visited by H.M.S. Beagle.* His major works are

On the Origin of Species by means of Natural Selection (1859) and *The Descent of Man* (1871).

Daniel Defoe, England (1660–1731). Prolific writer, most famous for his *Robinson Crusoe* and *Further Adventures of Robinson Crusoe* (both 1719). Among his many books are the novels *Moll Flanders* (1722) and *Roxana* (1724) and a *Journal of the Plague Year* (1722). He is regarded as the first true English novelist.

Jacques Delamain, France (1874–1953). The author of many books on birds, his works include *Livres de nature [The Books of Nature]* (1921), *Pourquoi les oiseaux chantent [Why Birds Sing]* (1928), *Les jours et les nuits des oiseaux [Nights and Days of Birds]* (1932), *Les oiseaux s'installent et s'en vont [Birds Come and Go]* (1942) and *Portraits d'oiseaux [Bird Portraits]* (2 vols. 1942–52).

Annie Dillard, United States (1945–   ). Among her many non-fiction books are *Pilgrim at Tinker Creek* (1974) which won the Pulitzer Prize, *Holy the Firm* (1977), *Teaching a Stone to Talk* (1982), *Living by Fiction* (1982) and *An American Childhood* (1987). She is also the author of one novel, *The Living* (1992).

Gustav Eckstein, Germany (1890–1972). The author of several books on nature, among them: *Noguchi* (1931), *Canary: History of a Family* (1947), and *Everyday Miracle* (1949).

J. H. Fabre, France (1823–1915). The son of a peasant, he became a teacher and celebrated entomologist. His *Souvenirs entomologiques [Entomological Memoirs]* were published in ten volumes from 1879 to 1907. He later brought out a best-selling selection, *La vie des insectes [The Life of Insects]* (1910).

Philip Henry Gosse, England (1810–1888). He invented the institutional aquarium and compiled the first descriptive catalogue of British marine invertebrates. His books include *Manual of Marine Zoology* (2 vols. 1855–56), *Evenings at the Microscope* (1859) and *A Year at the Shore* (1865). The publication of *Omphalos* (1875), where he put forward a theory that tried to reconcile the Christian creation story with fossil finds, led him to discredit and ridicule.

Charles A. Hall, England (1872–1942). After entering the Church at an early age, he devoted much of his time to exploring the English country-side. His books include *Plant Life* (1915), *Wild Flowers and Their Wonderful Ways* (1924), *The Open Book of Nature* (1925), *Trees* (1930), and *Ponds and Fish Culture* (1949).

Gerald Manley Hopkins, England (1844–1889). One of the greatest poets of the end of the nineteenth century, he became a Jesuit in 1868 and published little during his lifetime. One volume, simply titled *Poems*, appeared post-humously in 1918, edited by his friend Robert Bridges. His letters and notebooks were published in 1935 and 1937, though there are later, more complete editions.

William Henry Hudson, Argentina (1841–1922). Born in Buenos Aires of American parents, he wrote in English both fiction and books on nature. Among the former are *The Purple Land* (1885), *The Crystal Age* (1887) and *Green Mansions* (1904); among the latter *The Naturalist in La Plata* (1892), *Idle Days in Patagonia* (1893), *Adventures Among Birds* (1913) and *Far Away and Long Ago* (1918).

Richard Jeffries, England (1848–1887). Son of a Wiltshire farmer, he began life as a reporter but soon turned to books on nature. Among the best-known are *The Gamekeeper at Home* (1878), *Wild Life in a Southern County* (1879) and *The Amateur Poacher* (1881). He also wrote a memoir of his unorthodox beliefs, *The Story of my Heart* (1883) and the futuristic fantasy *After London* (1885).

D. H. Lawrence, England (1885–1930). Novelist and traveller. His fiction includes *The White Peacock* (1911), *Sons and Lovers* (1913), *The Rainbow* (1915) *Kangaroo* (1923), *The Plumed Serpent* (1926), and *Lady Chatterley's Lover* (1928). Among his travel books are *Twilight in Italy* (1916), *Sea and Sardinia* (1921), *Mornings in Mexico* (1927) and *Etruscan Places* (1932).

Barry Lopez, United States (1945–   ). Winner of the 1986 National Book Award for *Arctic Dreams*, he has published several books of natural history and travel. Among them, *Of Wolves and Men* (1978), *The Rediscovery of North America* (1991) and *Crossing Open Ground* (1988). Among his fiction, *Desert Notes* (1976), *Giving Birth to Thunder, Sleeping with His Daughter* (1978), *River Notes* (1979), *Crow and Weasel* (1990) and *Field Notes* (1994).

Maurice Maeterlinck, Belgium (1862–1949). Poet, dramatist and essayist, he won the Nobel Prize for Literature in 1911. His literary works include *Serres Chaudes* [*Hot House Blooms*] (1889), *L'Intruse* [*The Intruder*] (1890), *Les Aveugles* [*The Blind*] (1890), *Pelléas et Mélisande* (1893), *L'oiseau bleu* [*The Blue Bird*] (1908), *Marie Magdeleine* (1910). His books on natural history are *La vie des abeilles* [*Life of the Bee*] (1901), *La vie des fourmis* [*Life of the Ant*] (1905) and *L'intelligence des fleurs* [*The Intelligence of Flowers*] (1907).

Herman Melville, United States (1819–1891). Novelist and poet, he sailed on a whaler for several years in the South Seas, recounting his experiences in the novels *Typee* (1846), *Omoo* (1847) and *Mardi* (1849). Other books include *Redburn* (1849), *White-Jacket* (1850) and his masterpiece, *Moby-Dick or, The Whale* (1851). Most of his stories were collected in *The Piazza Tales* (1856).

Vladimir Nabokov, Russia (1899–1977). He left Russia in 1919, studied in England, lived in Europe and finally moved to the United States in 1940. His novels include *King, Queen, Knave* (1928), *Laughter in the Dark* (1932), *The Gift* (1938), *The Real Life of Sebastian Knight* (1941), *Lolita* (1955), *Pale Fire* (1962), *Ada* (1969), *Transparent Things* (1972) and *Look at the Harlequins!* (1974). His autobiography, *Speak Memory*, was published in 1967.

Theodore Roosevelt, United States (1858–1919). Twenty-sixth president of the United States, from 1901 to 1909. He wrote several travel and hunting books: *The Winning of the West* (4 vols. 1889–96), *The Rough Riders* (1899), *African Game Trails* (1910), and *Through the Brazilian Wilderness* (1914). *Theodore Roosevelt: An Autobiography* appeared in 1913.

Henry Seebohm, England (1832–1895). A Quaker steel manufacturer from Sheffield, he travelled far and wide to pursue his ornithological interests. His works include *Birds of Siberia* (2 vols. 1880–1882) and *The Geographical Distribution of the Family Charadriidae* (1887).

Edmund Selous, England (1857–1934). An ardent ornithologist, his books include *Bird Watching* (1901), *The Bird Watcher in the Shetlands with Notes on Seals* (1905) and *Bird Life Glimpses* (1905), *The Romance of Insect Life: Interesting Descriptions of the Strange and Curious in the Insect World* (1906), *Realities of Bird Life, Being Extracts from a Life-Loving Naturalist* (1927).

Ernest Thompson Seton, Canada (1869–1946). When he was six years old, his family emigrated from England to Canada. His many books include *Birds of Manitoba* (1891), *Lives of the Hunted* (1901), *Monarch, the Big Bear of Tallac* (1904), *Animal Heroes* (1905), *The Life Histories of Northern Animals* (1908), *The Arctic Prairies: A Canoe Journey of 2,000 Miles in Search of the Caribou* (1911), *Wild Animals at Home* (1913), *Woodland Tales* (1921), *Great Historic Animals, Mainly About Wolves* (1937) and his autobiography, *Trail of an Artist-Naturalist* (1940).

Henry David Thoreau, United States (1817–1862). Thinker and naturalist, best known for his book *Walden* (1854), an account of his two-year stay in a hut on Walden Pond. Many of his books were posthumously published: *Excursions* (1863), *The Maine Woods* (1864), *Cape Cod* (1865) and *A Yankee in Canada* (1866). His complete *Journal*, in 14 volumes, was published in 1906.

John Timbs, England (1801–1875). The publisher of anecdotic works, he was the editor of *The Mirror of Literature* and of the *Illustrated London News* for several years. He published *Strange Stories of the Animal World* in 1866.

Edward Topsell, England (1572–1625). Elizabethan naturalist who translated and adapted earlier works of natural history, mainly those of the Swiss Conrad Gesner. His two best-known works are *Historie of Foure-Footed Beastes* (1607) and *Historie of Serpents* (1608). He also wrote *The Reward of Religion* (1596) and *The Householder, or Perfect Man* (1610).

Mark Twain, United States (1835–1910). Pseudonym of Samuel Langhorne Clements. His most famous books are *The Adventures of Tom Sawyer* (1876) and *The Adventures of Huckleberry Finn* (1884). He also wrote *The Celebrated Jumping Frog of Calaveras County and Other Sketches* (1867), *The Innocents Abroad* (1869), *Roughing It* (1872), *The Prince and the Pauper* (1882), *A Connecticut Yankee in King Arthur's Court* (1889), *The Tragedy of Pudd'nhead Wilson* (1894), *The Mysterious Stranger* (posth. 1916).

Priscilla Wakefield, England (1751–1832). Author and philantropist who published a series of educational books for young people, of which the best known are *The Juvenile Travellers* (1801) and *Excursions in North America Described in Letters from a Gentleman and his Young Companion to their Friends in England* (1819). Her other works include *Juvenile Anecdotes Founded on Facts* (1795–98) and *An Introduction to Botany* (1796).

Charles Waterton, England (1782–1865). Great traveller, naturalist, educator and eccentric. He was also an inventor and designed a method for preparing specimens which dispensed of stuffing. His collected essays appeared in three volumes in 1838, 1844 and 1857. His most celebrated book is *Wanderings in South America* (1825).

INDEX